REGIONS OF OPPORTUNITY

REGIONS OF OPPORTUNITY

A bold new strategy for real-estate investment—
with forecasts to the year 2010

BY JACK LESSINGER, Ph.D.

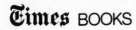 BOOKS

Library of Congress Cataloging in Publication Data
Lessinger, Jack.
  Regions of opportunity.
  Includes index.
  1. Real estate investment. 2. United States—
Economic conditions—1981– . 3. Real estate
investment—Forecasting. 4. Economic forecasting—
United States. I. Title.
HD1382.5.L46 1986 332.63'24 85-40281
ISBN 0-8129-1184-9

Designed by Betty Binns Graphics.

Manufactured in the United States of America
9 8 7 6 5 4 3 2
First Edition

Grateful acknowledgment is made to Houghton Mifflin Company for permission
to reproduce the maps, "The American Railroad System, 1870, 1900," from *A
History of American Democracy,* 3rd edition, p. 410, by John D. Hicks, George
E. Mowry, and Robert E. Burke. Copyright © 1966 by Houghton Mifflin
Company. Used by permission.

To Richard T. Ely (1854–1949), father of land economics
The principal founder of the American Economic Association in 1885 and fiery rebel against conventional economic theory, Ely fought to shift the focus of economics from a narrow concentration on self-interest to the vision of man as an emotional, historical, political, and social being.

and to David Weeks, inspiring professor of land economics

Contents

Part one: Five regions of opportunity

Part two: The theory

Part three: Forecasts: Seven classes of counties

Part four: Applications

Acknowledgments

For encouraging me to set aside the language of academia and speak plainly to friends and neighbors, I am profoundly grateful to my wife, Natalie Lessinger. She was also my ever-present editor. Without her penetrating logic, feeling for language, and love of laughter, this book would have been impossible.

I am also thankful to my former student Leonard Johnson for his sustained friendship and interest and for instigating an early version of this book; to Wilbur Thompson, who in 1961 and 1962 patiently listened and reacted to ideas now embodied here; to Dennis Strong, for his encouraging and valuable comments on early drafts; to thousands of students at the University of Washington during the last twenty years who heard my theories and contributed to their evolution; to Ann Saling, super-editor, teacher, and friend whose invaluable help extended from literary first aid to fundamental insights about the nature of great writing; to Sylvia Tacker and Michael Kane, for useful editorial suggestions; to Elisabeth Scharlatt, senior editor of Times Books, and Sherry Robb, of Andrews and Robb, literary agents, for enthusiastic encouragement; to my children, Harry and Maia Lessinger, for numerous last-minute services and joyous celebrations; and to Amar Singh, twenty-one-year-old wizard of the computer, who undertook the difficult task of wringing out the statistical potentials hidden in governmental computer tapes, and whose unflagging assistance was indispensable to this work.

Preface

PERIODICALLY, footloose and discontented Americans pack up their belongings and migrate to lands where the sky seems fairer, the people truer, and the life more bountiful. The impetus to move is always speeded by the onset of a long period of economic turbulence. We move faster and with greater conviction when pushed by a faltering economy.

Migrations are mass affairs. Like swallows flying to Capistrano, we make our way in great formations, reaping confidence from the largeness of our numbers. Unlike the swallows, we do not always return to one place. We choose new destinations. One migration sows its hopeful multitudes thinly over vast farming areas. Another deposits them in great industrial centers and still another in locations adjacent to those centers. There is always another direction, another promised land where, for a while, the future hangs more golden than anywhere else.

The places we move to become *regions of opportunity*. The elite among us come here—the rich and educated, the innovators, the avant-garde—along with the most modern and dynamic industries of our era. Property values climb in every category, from virgin forests and plains to square city blocks boasting the latest architectural designs. This is where real-estate investors will thrive.

Where we move away from, on the other hand, become dying places—*regions of obsolescence.* Spaces vacated by the fleeing elite are abandoned or filled in by the poor and disadvantaged. Opportunities decline. Real-estate values cease to rise. Investors with capital committed to the long term in regions of obsolescence will suffer heavy losses.

A new migration is unmistakably coming into view. Some areas are rapidly gaining population. Others are just as rapidly losing it. The redistribution is not simply from Frostbelt to Sunbelt, from north to south, as is commonly believed. The migration is going on within almost every state of the union. Locations where property values had been thrusting upward for decades are slipping into what threatens to be a long decline. Other locations—for decades either stable or declining—have abruptly come into sharp demand and show promise of spectacular long-run gains.

Regions of Opportunity identifies every county in the United States where major growth can be expected for the remainder of the twentieth century. It also identifies every county likely to enter a state of real-estate somnolescence, where present high prices will likely decline.

The book does much more. It analyzes the underlying reasons for migrations. By demonstrating where growth will occur in the long run—and why—it puts into the hands of the real-estate investor a trump card: the ability to forecast with greater confidence. *Regions of Opportunity* fashions that ability into a bold new strategy for real-estate investment.

Introduction

Forecasting opportunities in real estate

THE rich language and heady logic of Wall Street do not apply to real estate. Technicians, fundamentalists, chartists, and trend analysts are conspicuously missing in the real-estate profession. There are no saucer bottoms, head and shoulder tops, resistance and support levels. Nor can anyone dawdling over afternoon coffee turn to the financial section of the newspaper to find real estate's open and close, high and low, or volume of transactions. The drama of real estate plays out at a more sedate pace, in local markets far removed from the culture of Wall Street.

What are the legitimate devices of real-estate forecasting—the charts, trends, and fundamentals on which investors should fix their gaze? This is precisely the question posed to five eager, hypothetical investors. Listen in as we develop a relevant language and logic.

A Conversation with Real-Estate Investors

Author: Look at Figure 1, a graph of changing population in "County A".[1] Is this a good place to invest in land?

Investor AY: I'd say investors should be lining up the way they did in the Oklahoma land rush.

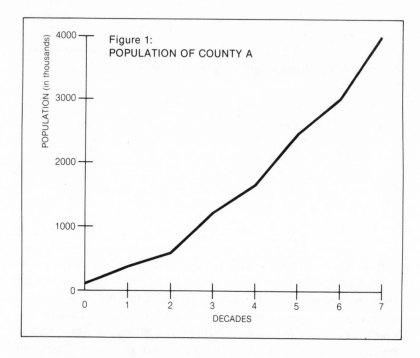

Author: Why so much enthusiasm?

Investor AY: The graph shows that people have been pouring into the county. Obviously they must be taking thousands of acres out of circulation, leaving a smaller supply for the future. The price of the remaining land must go up. Higher land values simply reflect increasing scarcity.

Investor TK: And if the price of land goes up, real-estate prices go up. Land is the major component in every kind of real estate. Every home, every store, every industrial park requires land. I can't think of a single exception.

Investor QD: No one but a hair-splitter would argue that point. But I will argue about the *causes* of higher land values. Scarcity isn't the only cause. Houses, factories, stores, streets, and schools built on new land make the remaining land more productive and therefore more valuable. A house appreciates when there are jobs nearby. An industrial site gains value if it is near a labor supply.

Investor TK: Seems to me, all we need to know is that large populations and high land values go hand in hand. Where you have one you have the other.

Author: I would rather say *rising* populations and *rising* land values go hand in hand. It may seem perfectly obvious, but it's worth emphasizing that what appeals to the real-estate investor are not *high* values, but *increasing* values.

Investor TK: Couldn't agree more. I'd be just as happy if ten thousand acres went from a hundred dollars an acre to two hundred as if a single acre went from one million to two million.

Investor EC: We're not getting down to the bedrock issue. Of course we want property values to increase. The critical question is how much of an increase in population does it take to set off a rise in values? I mean *real* values—adjusted for inflation.

Investor TK: Wish I knew. Not all population growth results in increased land values. Some increases aren't steep enough to make much difference. Is a two percent increase enough? Or ten percent? Does it have to be fifty percent? Seems to me some minimum threshold of population increase is required.

Author: I think you will find that your threshold is determined by the average growth of population in all counties. What is important is whether a county grows faster or slower than the average. When it grows faster, land prices whip upward.

Investor EC: I see what you mean—land values are pumped up by population increases. What I don't see is why those increases must be greater than the average.

Author: Look at it this way. Counties compete to attract population. A county that grows faster than average overcomes tremendous odds. It not only resists the power of other counties to raid its population, but it takes population away from other counties. People vote with their feet. Comparing different destinations for migration, they decide that one county offers more advantages. It may have special amenities—cultural, recreational, educational, or environmental. Its existing real estate may appeal to current fashions. And as new companies are drawn to this area, job opportunities multiply—not ordinary jobs, but those paying the highest salaries, in the most glamorous trades or professions.

Investor QD: Could we say that counties that grow faster than average are rich in resources prized by the national economy?

Author: That's a good way to put it.

Investor QD: And counties that grow more slowly than average?

Author: They're at a competitive disadvantage. Their industries, housing stock, and other resources do not attract migrants. Socioeconomic status falls as the brightest, most capable people move to places of greater opportunity. Modern firms tend to shun such counties.

Investor EC: I'd like to get back to the county you showed us at first. "County A," you called it. What does its comparative growth look like?

Author: Very well, let's take a look at Figure 2.

Investor EC: I suppose that whenever the graph moves upward, the

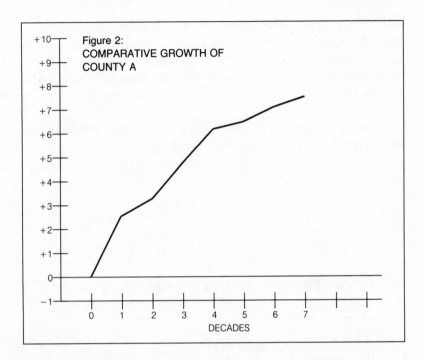

Figure 2:
COMPARATIVE GROWTH OF
COUNTY A

county is growing faster than average, and when it moves downward, it's growing slower. But by how much?

Author: The amount of rise or fall in any decade depends on two factors: the percentage change in the county's population and the percentage changes in *all* counties. And the more *unusual* the county's change (compared with all counties), the greater or lesser its comparative growth.[2]

Investor AY: I see that County A's comparative growth must have been quite high, although not as high as suggested by the population chart. I suppose we should assume, then, that it must have been heavily favored by the national economy for over half a century.

Investor QD: So we invest in County A? Does its rising comparative growth give us the green light?

Author: That's just what I wanted to ask all of you. But before you commit yourselves, I would like you to consider another county. Call it County B. *Its* comparative growth is shown in Figure 3. Now, in which county will you invest your millions? County A or County B?

Investor AY: County A, of course. That seventy-year rise makes me want to reach for my checkbook.

Investor QD: County A.

Investor TK: County A.

Investor EC: County A.

Investor ECC: County B. Just to be different.

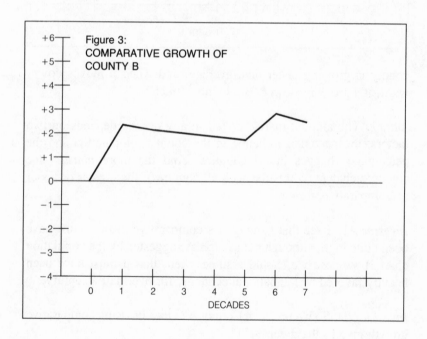

Figure 3:
COMPARATIVE GROWTH OF
COUNTY B

Author: Now I'll take off the wraps. County A is Cook County, Illinois, which includes Chicago. County B is Solano County, California, a suburb of San Francisco. The period is 1860 to 1930.

[Investors AY, QD, TK, and EC groan.]

Author: I hear your groans and sympathize with you. Had you invested in Cook County, you would have sustained some heavy losses. To show the fate of investments you might have made in 1930, let's look at graphs of a longer period—from 1840 to 1980. Figure 4 shows the comparative growth for Cook County.

Investor EC: Well, of course; 1930 was near the beginning of the Great Depression. Naturally Cook County land values fell after 1930.

Author: They did, but the Depression had little to do with it. What I'm talking about is a long-run decline. Look at the chart of Chicago land values [Figure 5].[3] We see sharp downturns in the 1870s, 1890s, and 1930s. Those were periods of severe depression. But bridging those intervals you can see a very definite long-run pattern. Both populations and land values swept upward *until* 1930. After 1930 both sloped downward. The long-run pattern is shaped like an inverted *U* with a peak around 1930. The graphs illustrate how populations and land values rise and fall together: 1930 was a year of changing trends for Cook County—in both population and land values.

Investor QD: Are we to assume that Solano County did better than Cook County after 1930?

Author: Far better. While Cook County was declining in the 1930s, Solano County was beginning a spectacular rise as Figure 6 shows.

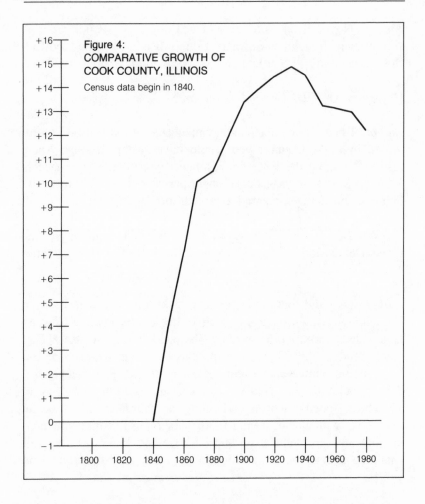

Figure 4:
COMPARATIVE GROWTH OF
COOK COUNTY, ILLINOIS

Census data begin in 1840.

Investor AY: But you didn't tell us A and B were Cook and Solano Counties.

Author: You didn't ask. You were satisfied with past performance. Trends change. Even trends lasting for half a century or more have been known to shift, often with little warning. To ensure your investment you need to forecast that shift.

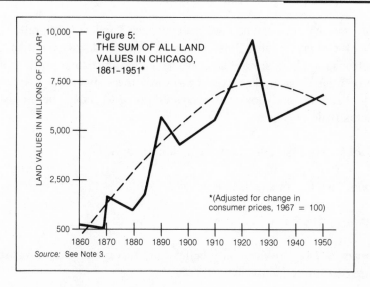

Figure 5:
THE SUM OF ALL LAND
VALUES IN CHICAGO,
1861–1951*

LAND VALUES IN MILLIONS OF DOLLAR*

*(Adjusted for change in
consumer prices, 1967 = 100)

Source: See Note 3.

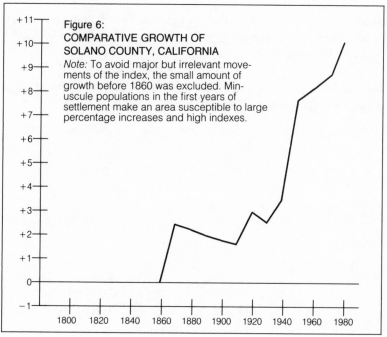

Figure 6:
COMPARATIVE GROWTH OF
SOLANO COUNTY, CALIFORNIA
Note: To avoid major but irrelevant movements of the index, the small amount of
growth before 1860 was excluded. Minuscule populations in the first years of
settlement make an area susceptible to large
percentage increases and high indexes.

Investor AY: In 1930 no one expected such a falloff in migration to Cook County, or that Solano County would suddenly rise like an astronaut. There's no blueprint to guide investors away from properties about to depreciate or toward others about to appreciate. How can anyone know that trends are going to change before they actually do change?

Author: By basing forecasts on a valid theory.

Investor TK: Is there such a theory?

Author: There is.

Investor TK: Do you really believe the theory can help investors forecast future land values?

Author: I do. Furthermore, I believe that the theory could have been invaluable to those investing in County A or County B. Or County X. In 1930, or in 1986.

Investor EC: I don't know about the others, but I'll camp on your doorstep until you tell us your theory.

Part one

Five regions of opportunity

One

Opportunity, obsolescence, and instability

IN John Steinbeck's *The Red Pony,* an old pioneer gravely explains to his small grandson that the westward migration has ended. "No place to go, Jody. Every place is taken. But that's not the worst— no, not the worst. Westering has died out of the people. Westering isn't a hunger any more. It's all done. . . . It is finished." [1]

Hungering for the pioneer frontier does seem to be "done," but the yearning to be on the move is not done, will never be done. New hungers and new migrations periodically capture the imagination of an entire nation, often engaging the passionate commitment of our brightest and most enterprising citizens. Each migration creates rewarding opportunities for investment in real estate.

There never was a true "westering," a single migration to the West, one long gulp from the shores of the Atlantic to the shores of the Pacific. Up to 1900, there were, in fact, three distinct migrations. The first (during the Colonial period) drove settlers northward and southward as much as westward. The second (early in the nineteenth century) deposited migrants in farms, plantations, and villages of the Mississippi Valley. The third (late in the nineteenth century) completed the conquest of America, created great industrial cities and, to supply them with raw materials, vast hinterlands throughout the length and breadth of the nation.

Despite many differences, one common element is inherent in every migration. It *surges*. Each migration begins, reaches a peak, and eventually ends. Each migratory surge is announced by the appearance of a new region of opportunity. This is where sweat and capital are stirred into inspiring dreams.

In a *region of opportunity* many counties, not necessarily contiguous, begin their rise, peak, and decline all more or less at the same time. What joins these counties into a single region is *timing,* the timing of their development. They all follow a similar rhythm of rise and fall. Around 1929 the rising region of opportunity included counties uniquely suited to suburban development anywhere in the country. At first it involved areas adjacent to central cities because they provided commercial and social amenities indispensable to nurturing the new development. In the earliest flush of suburban growth, the environs of New York, Chicago, New Orleans, and Los Angeles grew and flourished at the same time.

An entire region is conquered all at once, like a military objective attacked by troops sweeping into it from every side. In subsequent decades its percentage share of national population rises to a peak, then declines as a new region of opportunity emerges.[2] Eventually a county increasingly fails in its ability to maintain or attract population. When this happens it joins a *region of obsolescence*.

The appearance of each new region of opportunity is correlated with an unstable economy—declining demand, increasing unemployment, mounting bankruptcies, falling standards of living—punctuated by intermittent booms. The hardships of instability are borne primarily by those working and living in the region of obsolescence.

Since the founding of the American Republic in 1789 there have been four migratory surges, each one associated with a period of economic instability. The first migratory surge coincided with the unstable economy extending from 1760 to 1789. Migration continued afterward, until 1817. The second migratory surge coincided with the unstable period from 1817 to 1843. Migration continued to

1873. The third migratory surge coincided with the unstable period from 1873 to 1900. Migration continued to 1929. The fourth migratory surge coincided with the unstable period from 1929 through World War II and beyond. Migration continued through the 1970s. In the 1980s, a fifth migration (often mistakenly identified as a movement from Frostbelt to Sunbelt) is in an early stage of development.

Each surge overlaps the preceding surge. Each creates a new region of opportunity from a distinctive roster of counties. Each eventually tends to become part of a new region of obsolescence. Every new surge of migration creates conditions that a strategy for real-estate investment should take into account. The following fictional examination of such a strategy is a composite of numerous actual conversations.

An Interview with the Author

Investment Club: What is the relevance of changing regions of opportunity for the investor?

Author: They shape a fundamental strategy, set the scene, determine the best and worst times and places to invest in real estate.

Investment Club: Our strategy for investment is based on common sense. Buy when prices are rising; sell when they are falling. Be active on the market when the potential for profit is highest; suspend operations when that potential vanishes. We believe this is ideal.

Author: For the short term, perhaps—if the objective is to take advantage of trends lasting for weeks, months, or a few years. Under conditions of instability, however, your formula is a recipe for disaster. It's too risky to jump in and out of the real-estate market as quickly as it changes.

Investment Club: Then you're interested only in long-term investments?

Author: I am indeed. During a period of instability, long-term investments in real estate—if they are properly executed—make the most sense. My ideal game plan for the long term is the reverse of yours. Buy when the market is weak, sell when the market is strong. I can show you why this strategy is safest and most profitable.

Investment Club: Safest? You're advising us to go against the tide? To buy during a recession? I believe the word for that is *chutzpah*.

Author: Precisely.

Investment Club: When it comes to the long term we've usually preferred to stick with investments in high-tech companies. New industries, we feel, have the best chance to improve long-term equities.

Author: That's what many people think, but the risk is greater than it seems. How can the investor hope to keep abreast of the innumerable forces gnawing away at the value of his stock—changes in management, competition, technology, demand? With so much pertinent information hidden, the average investor is in no position to exercise proper discretion.

Over the long term the small, independent investor will be less vulnerable owning real estate. The forces affecting a piece of real estate are much more exposed to scrutiny. You live there. You read the local newspapers. You talk to customers, tenants, neighbors, other property holders. Information is plentiful. I would say with conviction that real estate is the more promising investment provided the investor follows my threefold strategy.

Investment Club: And that is . . . ?

Author: A moment longer, if you please. First notice that I'm talking about the period of instability. No other time. During this period there are best times and worst times to buy and sell. But don't be anxious. It is both impossible and unnecessary to forecast ideal times with absolute precision. So long as major guidelines are followed, deviations from perfect timing will not be catastrophic. Usually, they result in minor reductions of profits from maximum potentials.

Investment Club: And the threefold strategy?

Author: First, the best time to buy is near the end of a recession. (I can help you to recognize the signs.) That's a buyer's paradise, when there are low prices, few competing buyers, and many sellers. The worst time to buy is during a boom. Next worst is when a recession has just begun.

Second, the best time to sell is during a subsequent boom, when prices are rising. That's a seller's paradise: few competing sellers and many buyers. The worst time to sell is during a depression.

Third, the best places to invest are carefully selected locations within the emerging region of opportunity. The worst places to invest are in the region of obsolescence. With this strategy, an important force for profitability is the impact of increasing population in the emerging region of opportunity.

Consider Wayne County, Nebraska, during the unstable period of the late nineteenth century. Despite two serious depressions (1873–1878 and 1893–1897), percentage increases in land values steadily climbed as shown in Figure 7.[3] The long-term growth rate of Wayne County land values was unusually high. Annual appreciation varied, in the main, between 7 and 11 percent. At a time of

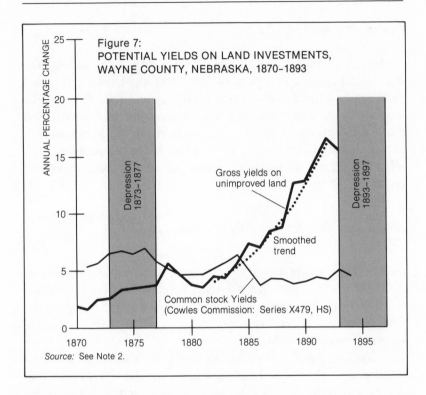

Figure 7:
POTENTIAL YIELDS ON LAND INVESTMENTS,
WAYNE COUNTY, NEBRASKA, 1870–1893

ANNUAL PERCENTAGE CHANGE

Depression 1873–1877

Depression 1893–1897

Gross yields on unimproved land

Smoothed trend

Common stock Yields
(Cowles Commission: Series X479, HS)

Source: See Note 2.

national deflation, when most prices and investment yields were falling, these were exceptional returns. As shown in the graph, stock yields fell from 7.02 in 1876 to less than 4.5 percent after 1885.

In addition to population growth, my investment strategy calls upon a second factor. Land values in the region of opportunity are also pushed upward by the rise from bust to boom, for just as pessimism unduly depresses real-estate values during a bust, optimism unduly exaggerates them during a boom. The right time to buy property in Wayne County was in the last years of the severe depression in 1873–1878. The right time to sell was during the subsequent boom of the late 1880s. That strategy would have returned at least 11 percent—a high rate in those unstable years. Those hardy souls who understood the inevitability of this county's growth during the late nineteenth century could have bought in 1880 and 1881 when prices were low and sold any time during the subsequent boom. They would have earned 15 percent on any random land investment within the county—more than three times the return received by common stockholders. Carefully chosen locations—those having unusual fertility, accessibility to railroad marshalling yards, or proximity to towns and villages—could have yielded still greater returns.

Investment Club: It looks good on paper. But we'd surely need to have a lot of faith in your system before being tempted to invest during a depression.

Author: That's natural. Read on.

Two

The first region of opportunity, 1760–1789

THE first region of opportunity and the first region of obsolescence in the history of the United States appeared during the period 1760–1789 (see Figure 8).[1]

The year 1760 was the beginning of "the morning after" for Virginia, a fact easily verified by the colony's comparative growth (see Figure 9). In preceding decades—from 1730 to 1760—the economic efforts of Virginia's tobacco planters enjoyed the world's wholehearted approval. Increasing numbers of individuals, especially people of means, had adopted the smoking, chewing, and sniffing habit. The price they paid for their addiction created unprecedented wealth for the Virginia economy. According to an authority on the period, it was then that the growers built "the handsome homes once so numerous in the older counties, many of which still remain as interesting monuments of former days; it was then that they surrounded themselves with graceful furniture and costly silverware, in large part imported from Great Britain; it was then that they collected paintings and filled their libraries with the works of standard writers; it was then that they purchased coaches and berlins."[2]

But later in the eighteenth century, those who had invested in Virginia real estate as "a sure thing"—those who had settled in to a

Figure 8:
THE FIRST REGION OF OPPORTUNITY
AND THE
FIRST REGION OF OBSOLESCENCE, 1760–1789
Locations of Counties

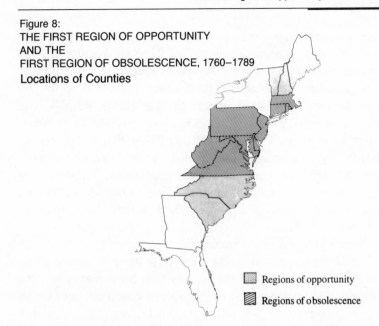

▨ Regions of opportunity

▨ Regions of obsolescence

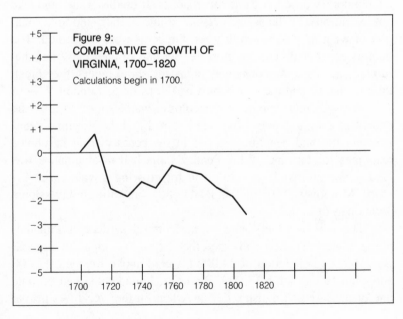

Figure 9:
COMPARATIVE GROWTH OF
VIRGINIA, 1700–1820

Calculations begin in 1700.

permanent prosperity—were in for a rude shock. After 1760 the tobacco industry, a leading industry in the New World, suffered serious reverses. Much of the commercial economy of the colonies became mired in two decades of hard times.[3]

In the case of tobacco, it was the age-old drama of supply exceeding demand. Profits, of course, attract investors to an industry, and the more prolonged and reliable the profits, the greater the attraction. By 1760, the tobacco industry's reputation as a money-maker had lured too many acres into production. Supplies hung heavy over the market. Even aristocrats were obliged to cut down on their use of what was, after all, a luxury, and therefore expendable.

Depression hit many settled areas. On February 2, 1764, the *New York Post-Boy* reported that "There are more Houses to be let in this City, than there have been at any time for 7 years past. The commerce of the continent is in a languishing condition; our Debt in Europe increases; our Power to pay it off decreases." From another contemporary observer came this report: "If creditors sue, and take out executions, the lands and personal estate . . . are sold for a small part of what they were worth when the debts were contracted. The debtors are ruined. The creditors get but part of their debts and that ruins them. Thus the consumers break the shopkeepers; they break the merchants; and the shock must be felt as far as London."

Pennsylvania, another older colony, was also affected by the depressed economy after 1760 (see Figure 10). Like Virginia, Pennsylvania too had benefitted earlier in the century from its choice resources for farming. What Pennsylvania had in abundance was land—mile after mile of fertile soil for growing a wide variety of crops. Moreover, its prevailing land policy threw the colony's doors wide open to settlers.

The whirlwind invasion by agricultural settlers of Philadelphia's hinterland soon converted that city into a giant metropolis. By 1760, its population of 24,000 towered above Boston's 16,000 and even New York's 18,000. By 1775, Philadelphia had become one of the largest English cities anywhere in the world. As people

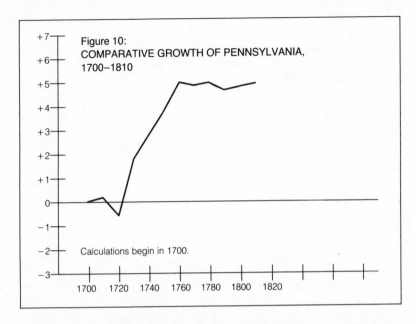

Figure 10:
COMPARATIVE GROWTH OF PENNSYLVANIA,
1700–1810

Calculations begin in 1700.

flowed in, demands for real estate escalated. Many rich financial harvests were reaped by real-estate investors. Benjamin Franklin—himself a migrant from Boston in the 1720s—was one of those investors. But the instabilities beginning in the 1760s coincided with a peak of vigorous growth for Philadelphia.

While many of the colonies in those unstable years had lost their former allure for real-estate investment, some fared surprisingly well. After 1760, five colonies—Maine, Vermont, New Hampshire, and the Carolinas—continued to attract migrants in record numbers (see Figure 11). Those with the foresight to buy real estate in the Carolinas made fortunes. They profited from the soaring value of exports as well as from increases in land values resulting from those exports. One authority has estimated a return of nearly 30 percent on capital invested in rice production and even more on indigo, another that some planters doubled their capital every three or four years and that immigrant settlers often left their children well-off. Agricultural economist George Taylor writes: "It

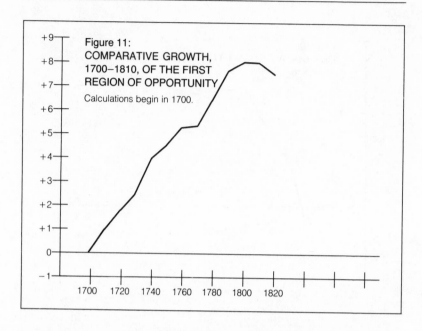

Figure 11:
COMPARATIVE GROWTH,
1700–1810, OF THE FIRST
REGION OF OPPORTUNITY
Calculations begin in 1700.

seems probable that South Carolina during these years enjoyed a more rapid economic growth per capita than any other American colony—and perhaps more than that of any other colony or county in the world.''[4]

But after 1789, and especially after 1817, another migration was on its way. It created a plethora of opportunities in a very different kind of real estate, for a very different group of people. Had the New Englanders and Carolinians of 1789 been schooled in the economics of this book they would have predicted their region's coming obsolescence. This was not to be the case. As in every age, too many were lulled into complacency by decades of experience, projecting past growth into future growth. While they slumbered in the security of old convictions, high land values slipped away like rich soil blown by a high wind.

The lesson is this: when migration turns to a new region, do not clutch the dying past. Let go and move on.

Three

The second region of opportunity, 1817–1846

EXCEPT for the period 1828–1836, one brief interlude when gray skies cleared, the twenty-six years between 1817 and 1843 were almost continuously depressed. "By 1828 the postwar depression in the West as well as the South was already ten years old with no relief in sight," writes economic historian Howard R. Smith.[1] The first urban soup kitchens in the New World appeared in 1820.

Henry Clay gives us an eyewitness account of the U.S. economy in 1824.

In casting our eyes around us, the most prominent circumstance which fixes our attention and challenges our deepest regret is the general distress which pervades the whole country. It is forced upon us by numerous facts of the most incontestable character. It is indicated by the diminished exports of native produce; by the depressed and reduced state of our foreign navigation; by our diminished commerce; by successive unthrashed crops of grain, perishing in our barns and barn-yards for want of a market; by the alarming diminution of the circulating medium; by the numerous bankruptcies, not limited to the trading classes, but extending to all orders of society; by a universal complaint of the want of employment and the consequent reduction of the wages of labor; by the ravenous pursuit after public situations, not for the sake of their honors and the performance of their public duties, but as a means of private subsistence.[2]

Another observation from 1826 reinforces Clay's account.

For the past three years the grain boats from Missouri have scarcely paid the expense of their building and transport to New Orleans. The difficulty of paying taxes, and finding money for those articles which were originally luxuries, and have come by use to be necessaries, is great.

After a short recovery ending in 1836, the economy steadily worsened. "There is abundant evidence," wrote economic historian Douglass North, "that the depression from 1839–1843 was one of the most severe in our history."[3] Once again the misery was borne unequally by different sections of the country. Areas where growth had been rapid now drew a declining share of the national population and a major share of the suffering. Other areas throughout the nation were now favored by the continuing stream of migrants. Their efforts and investments stimulated economies of the rising areas during that depressed period.

The comparative growth of counties in the second region of obsolescence declined during the first half of the nineteenth century (see Figure 12). The accompanying map shows the location of all counties within the region of obsolescence, which were largely confined to the eastern seaboard. A dot on the map represents the approximate center of an obsolescing county (see Figure 13).

It may seem paradoxical—in view of substantial growth from 1800 to 1850— that this area should be characterized as a region of obsolescence. The Old South almost doubled its population. New England slightly more than doubled and the eastern urbanized portions of New York and Pennsylvania tripled their populations. But the significance of that growth is muted by the fact that the total United States population more than quadrupled. Comparative growth of the eastern seaboard declined.

The Mississippi Valley became the major focus of the emerging region of opportunity. From 1800 to 1850 nearly ten million people migrated into that huge territory—from the Gulf of Mexico to the Canadian border, from the limits of the original colonies to the eastern border of Kansas. Those first five decades of the century

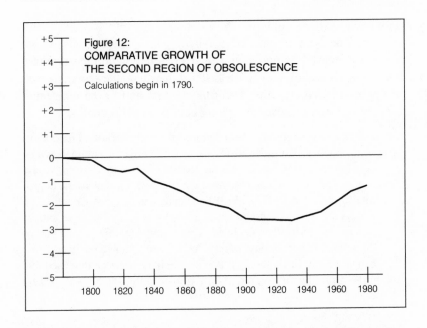

Figure 12:
COMPARATIVE GROWTH OF
THE SECOND REGION OF OBSOLESCENCE

Calculations begin in 1790.

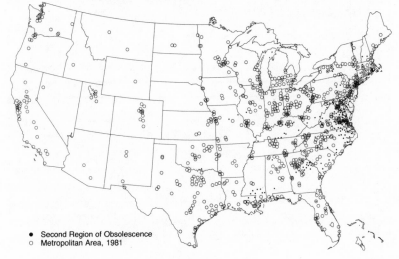

Figure 13:
THE SECOND REGION OF OBSOLESCENCE, 1817–1843
Locations of Counties

● Second Region of Obsolescence
○ Metropolitan Area, 1981

witnessed a twenty-fold growth in population, from 466,000 to 9.8 million! The New South (the southern portion of the Mississippi Valley) increased its population by 10.6 times, while the northern portion of the valley grew even faster. Growth of the second region of opportunity rose to a peak during the first half of the nineteenth century and was followed by a long decline (see Figure 14).[4]

Regions of opportunity could be more precisely identified if counties were smaller. Consider Cook County. Ideally, it should be three counties: (1) Old Chicago, within a radius of three miles from the city center; (2) New Chicago, beyond the three-mile radius to the corporate limits as of 1933; and (3) the remainder of Cook County. The comparative growth of Old Chicago rose rapidly to a point of saturation around 1850, then declined. That timing identified it as a part of the second region of opportunity. While Old Chicago declined, New Chicago rose. In 1860 only 8,000 people lived between three and five miles from the city center. By 1870 that figure was 55,000, and by

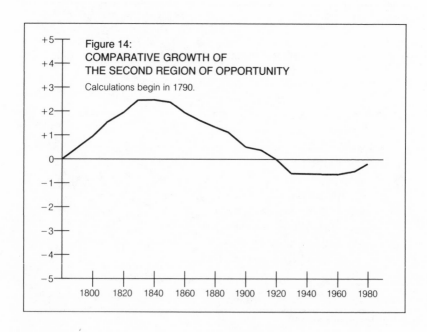

Figure 14:
COMPARATIVE GROWTH OF
THE SECOND REGION OF OPPORTUNITY
Calculations begin in 1790.

Figure 15:
THE SECOND REGION OF OPPORTUNITY, 1817–1843
Locations of Counties

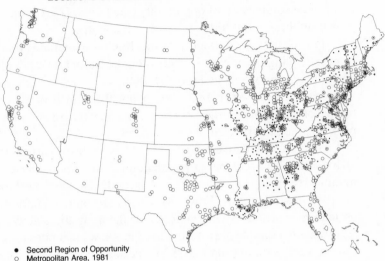

● Second Region of Opportunity
○ Metropolitan Area, 1981

1873 it was nearly 100,000. More than a twelvefold increase in only thirteen years![5] In the statistics of Cook County that spectacular rise of the next region of opportunity swamped the demographics of Chicago. It covered over the decline of the old city. Looking at the statistics of Cook County as a whole—lumping together Old and New Chicago—we see only a rising county. The marked decline of Old Chicago is completely obscured. Nor was Cook the only county so large that it harbored migrations of different vintages.

Unfortunately all the "Old Chicagos" (and all the counties in which they appear throughout the nation) are necessarily omitted from the second region of opportunity. Therefore, the region is underrepresented. (Later regions are subject to the same limitation.)

The dots in Figure 15 locate the approximate centers of all counties included in the second region of opportunity.

The growth profile of the second region of opportunity suggests an optimum period for investment, beginning around 1817 (when the migration first becomes visible) and continuing until the 1840s peak. Consider Tate County, Mississippi, near the very center of the second region of opportunity (see Figure 16). Comparative growth in this county follows the overall pattern.

Tate County grew rapidly in the 1830s—sometimes doubling or even tripling in individual years—but because Tate's population had been close to zero in 1830, by 1840 it had not risen beyond a minuscule 7,002. After 1840, following the course of the entire region of opportunity, the county's comparative growth rose to a peak and then plummeted.

Highest speculative returns should have been earned in the 1840s, when an accelerating population presumably induced maximum increases in land value. That is indeed what the data show. In his 1942 master's thesis, Edwin M. Chapman compiled information on land transactions by the largest speculators in the county.[6] The representative sample drawn from his data shows that rates of appreciation were rising during the 1830s, peaked in the 1840s, and fell thereafter (see Figure 17).

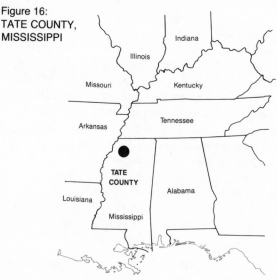

Figure 16:
TATE COUNTY,
MISSISSIPPI

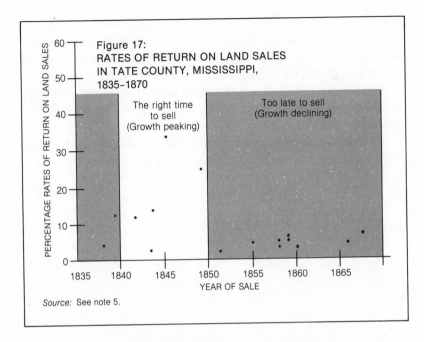

Figure 17:
RATES OF RETURN ON LAND SALES
IN TATE COUNTY, MISSISSIPPI,
1835–1870

The right time to sell (Growth peaking)

Too late to sell (Growth declining)

PERCENTAGE RATES OF RETURN ON LAND SALES

YEAR OF SALE

Source: See note 5.

There is no mistaking the sharp differences between rates of return in the 1840s and those either before or after. In the 1830s, two of the seventeen transactions brought mixed results—14 percent profit in one sale and 4 percent in another. By contrast, the 1840s delivered unambiguously high profits. Of the six sales, only one yielded less than 11 percent and that one violated two cardinal rules of my strategy: the purchase was made at the beginning of a long period of depression; the sale was made at its end. (See Chapter One.) Three other transactions during the 1840s yielded more than 25 percent, and one a whopping 100 percent. The average for all six cases was 31 percent, and this despite the severe depression from 1839 to 1843! One purchase made at the beginning of the recovery in 1844—with a subsequent sale in the following year— returned a handsome 34 percent.

These high-flying gains, however, did not extend beyond 1850. Although the 1850s were a period of unparalleled national prosperity, land investments in Tate County no longer prospered. Out of nine sales transacted after 1850, not one returned more than 6 percent. Such poor results were due to violations of one or both of two basic principles. First, sales were made when comparative growth was falling. Second, purchases were made during previous booms. One of these, made at the height of the boom in 1836, returned only 1.2 percent.

By 1873 a new region of opportunity appeared on the horizon. Once again the real-estate deck was to be reshuffled.

Four

The third region of opportunity, 1873–1900

THE third surge of migration became widely visible in the early 1870s and began a noticeable decline after 1900. Once again boundaries of the regions of opportunity and obsolescence are redrawn. The new region of opportunity bears little resemblance to its predecessor. No longer confined to the eastern third of the nation, it includes counties from coast to coast. The third region of obsolescence includes counties that had been considered part of the second region of opportunity (see Figures 18 and 19).

Comparative growth of all counties in the third region of opportunity is shown in the accompanying graph for the period 1790–1980 (Figure 20). The rise and fall of comparative growth suggest a timing strategy for investment. An optimum investment period begins around 1873, when the migration first becomes visible. It ends with the peak of comparative growth shortly after 1900.

The investment period 1873–1900 coincides with a time of instability in the American economy. After three prosperous decades (including the era of the Civil War), businessmen of 1873 were no less surprised than were their counterparts in 1929 to see business activity suddenly suffer a free fall. The crash of 1873—allegedly triggered by the failure of financiers involved in the construction of the Northern Pacific—sent convulsive tremors radi-

Figure 18:
THE THIRD REGION OF OPPORTUNITY, 1873–1900
Locations of Counties

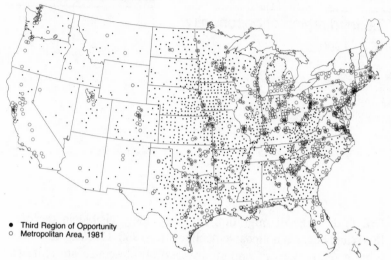

● Third Region of Opportunity
○ Metropolitan Area, 1981

Figure 19:
THE THIRD REGION OF OBSOLESCENCE, 1873–1900
Locations of Counties

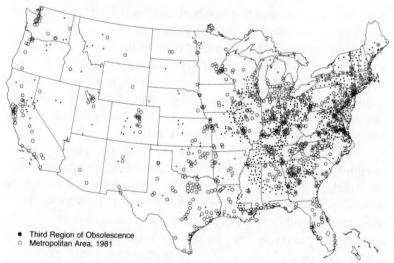

● Third Region of Obsolescence
○ Metropolitan Area, 1981

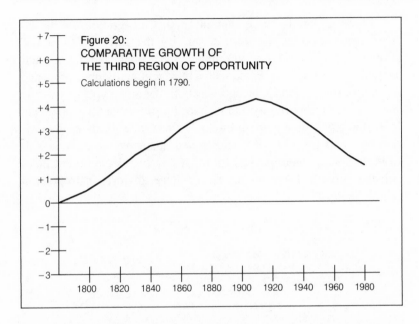

Figure 20:
COMPARATIVE GROWTH OF
THE THIRD REGION OF OPPORTUNITY
Calculations begin in 1790.

ating across all economic and social boundaries. Soon the nation became mired in the deep depression of 1873–1878. Half the steel industry shut down. The production of coal—an all-important source of energy in the nineteenth century—slowed to a dribble. Wages fell. Bread lines lengthened across the country.

During the generally unstable period 1873–1900, economic paralysis alternated with manic booms. After 1885, more then 40,000 miles of railroad track expanded the region of opportunity by opening up the Great Plains—one of the most fertile agricultural empires of the world. The accompanying boom ended unhappily eight years later with a panic and the depression of 1893–1897.

As in other periods of chronic instability, the booms and busts of 1873–1900 affected different areas unequally. Although the economy as a whole was exposed to booms and busts, in the region of opportunity the booms lifted real-estate values at a furious rate. In the region of obsolescence, depressions sank real-estate values to worrisome depths.

From negligible beginnings in 1830, Chicago became the favored destination of the third surge. By the early 1870s it had thrown off every vestige of its ambiance as a small river town. Suddenly the world was presented with a third region of opportunity and its major urban center. Chicago was both the archetypal city of the third region of opportunity and its hub. From a mere 50 residents in 1830, the city's population grew to 29,963 by 1850, more than tripled by 1860 (to 109,206), and tripled again by 1870. By 1900, 1,698,575 souls were packed into that city of relentless and indefatigable growth. From muddy river village to world metropolis in half a century!

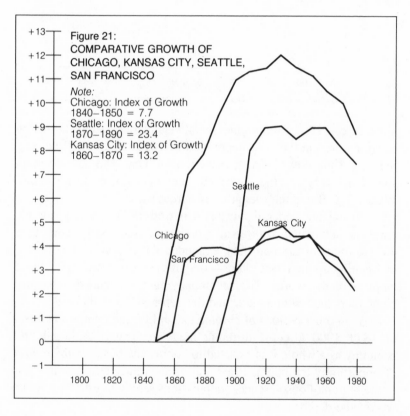

Figure 21:
COMPARATIVE GROWTH OF
CHICAGO, KANSAS CITY, SEATTLE,
SAN FRANCISCO

Note:
Chicago: Index of Growth
1840–1850 = 7.7
Seattle: Index of Growth
1870–1890 = 23.4
Kansas City: Index of Growth
1860–1870 = 13.2

By 1900 Chicago embraced markets throughout the nation and the world. It became the central supplier and market for a number of smaller cities like Cleveland, Kansas City, and Cincinnati in the East, San Francisco and Seattle in the West. Together these cities constituted one great urban system, all growing rapidly and all then declining at about the same time (see Figure 21).

The third surge also sponsored the rise of hundreds of small towns in obscure counties like Klickitat in Washington, Kootenai in Idaho, and Keweenaw in Michigan. These smaller towns provided rich and accessible sources of raw materials for burgeoning new industries (see Figures 22, 23, and 24).

In a recent best-seller, *The Coming Real Estate Crash,* considerable space was devoted to the dramatic history of Chicago's real-estate crash in 1836.[1] Beginning in 1832, investors—buyers and sellers—were overcome by a spectacular vision of Chicago's future. The meteoric rise of land prices between 1832 and 1836 reflected the maturing of that vision. In 1832 some of the best 80-

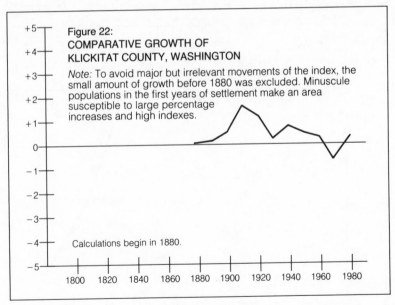

Figure 22:
COMPARATIVE GROWTH OF
KLICKITAT COUNTY, WASHINGTON

Note: To avoid major but irrelevant movements of the index, the small amount of growth before 1880 was excluded. Minuscule populations in the first years of settlement make an area susceptible to large percentage increases and high indexes.

Calculations begin in 1880.

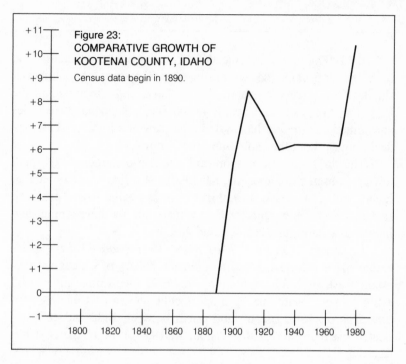

Figure 23:
COMPARATIVE GROWTH OF
KOOTENAI COUNTY, IDAHO

Census data begin in 1890.

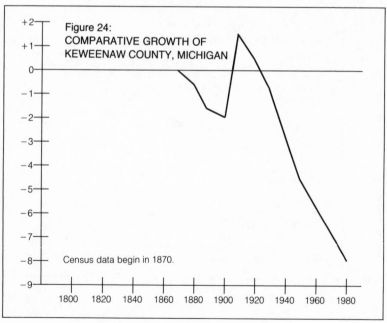

Figure 24:
COMPARATIVE GROWTH OF
KEWEENAW COUNTY, MICHIGAN

Census data begin in 1870.

by-100 lots sold for $100. By 1834 a horde of speculators drove the price up to $3,000, and in 1836 to $15,000. Then, like an acrobat on the high wire who loses his nerve, speculation came abruptly to an end. Prices plummeted from $15,000 back to $100.

Hindsight tells us that those early speculators were on to something. Between 1833 and 1933—on the average—Chicago's land values increased by 11,848 times![2] The run-up of land values follows the steep curve of comparative growth.

Is there a lesson in Chicago's land bubble of 1836? There is. A crash may signal the imminent arrival of the ideal moment to buy real estate—provided that real estate is within the emerging region of opportunity.

Five

The fourth region of opportunity, 1929–1958

AROUND the turn of the twentieth century, we embarked on a new migration—from dreary tenement-filled neighborhoods to rustic meadowlands, from the raucus din of clattering subways and screaming factory whistles to the lowing of cows and the music of birdsong. Here, midst peaceful, green communities far beyond the city boundaries, was suburbia, the promised land. This is where middle-class America longed to be.

Growing lustily from sparse beginnings, the tiny suburban fetus comprised no less than 5.4 million by 1910. In each of the following three decades it grew by more than twice the national rate.

After 1929, when the migration had become too obvious to ignore, it was accompanied—but not interrupted by—the Great Depression. Many among us can still recall that dizzying decline between 1929 and 1932, followed by nine long years of stagnation and ending only after the attack on Pearl Harbor. By the middle of 1932, industrial production had dropped to less than half its maximum output in 1929. The average wage was reduced by 60 percent. Most dividends had fallen to less than half what they had been the year before. Unemployment rose to 15.9 percent in 1931, remained in the 20–25 percent range through 1935, and as late as 1939 never dipped below 17 percent. With the end of the Depression came suburbia's most feverish growth. By 1940, most Americans dreamed of living in the suburbs. The dream, only mildly seductive at first, soon throbbed throughout the land like a titanic dynamo. In the 1940s, despite the devastation of World War II, suburbs grew by 2.4 times the national rate. After the war and throughout the 1950s, dream and reality converged in an explosion of suburban development. Census data suggest an incredible near-doubling of suburban population in a single decade. (Between 1950 and 1960 the "urban fringe" grew from 20.9 to 37.9 million.) But after 1960 that pace could no longer be sustained. Though still prodigious, the rate of growth declined to 44 percent in the 1960s. In the 1970s it declined still further, to 32 percent.

Counties participating in the extraordinary growth of the 1950s and 1960s, as well as the slowing of the 1970s, are shown in the accompanying map, "The Fourth Region of Opportunity" (Figure 25). Counties with lower than average growth during 1950–1970 are shown in the map, "The Fourth Region of Obsolescence" (Figure 26).

For me, the fourth migration is a personal experience. In 1935, when the economy was still scraping along at the bottom of the Depression, my family joined the early fugitives from New York City. In that year, I became thirteen, a bar mitzvah boy. My proud parents were prosperous enough to hold a splendid reception in my honor at what I recall as a middle-class, downtown night club. I remember the pious old men among the guests and how my father enjoyed watching them steal guilty glances at the *"naketdeh maiden"* —scantily clad chorus girls who entertained us that evening.

Our good fortune we owed to my father, by profession a pharmacist and by avocation a speculator in real estate. A restless man, he loathed nothing more than waiting for customers to walk into his drug store. To relieve his boredom he acquired the habit of perusing the classified ads, keeping a sharp lookout for good locations in which to build a new drug store. In this he was successful. Every

Figure 25:
THE FOURTH REGION OF OPPORTUNITY, 1929–1958
Locations of Counties

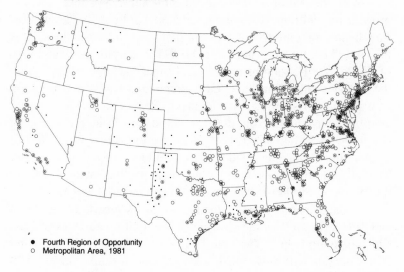

- ● Fourth Region of Opportunity
- ○ Metropolitan Area, 1981

Figure 26:
THE FOURTH REGION OF OBSOLESCENCE, 1929–1958
Locations of Counties

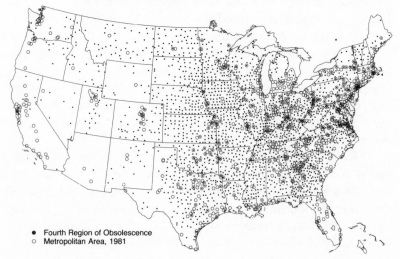

- ● Fourth Region of Obsolescence
- ○ Metropolitan Area, 1981

year or two, with awesome regularity, he would sell a store at a profit and build another.

It seemed he had a wizard's eye for good locations—until that fateful year of 1935. Soon after my bar mitzvah in February, he met his nemesis. It was a store on Aldous Street in the Bronx that "done him in." Despite my father's earnest efforts, people could not be induced to come into that store. They were being lured away by the new cut-rate chains—the Tomashevskys and the Walgreens—now springing up all over the city. These formidable competitors carried more varied merchandise. Their stores were larger, more modern, and with as many lights as a theater on Broadway. But the severest blow of all was that they cut prices—not a little but deeply—and on just those items from which small neighborhood druggists like my father had to make a living.

In desperation, my father resorted to a tactic often used by his cutthroat competitors: loss leaders—merchandise sold below cost to attract customers into the store. After school one day, he asked me to help distribute circulars for a final effort, a do-or-die sale. His loss leader was Epsom salts, at a price far below cost. (Could it have been nine cents for five pounds?) Suddenly the store was packed. There wasn't enough room for all the customers. Everyone in New York, it seemed, was stocking up on a lifetime supply of Epsom salts. At dinner, the second day of the sale, my father's voice was tinged with anxiety. He threw up his arms to the heavens and anguished, "Every package of Epsom salts I sell is pushing me into my grave."

Three days later he closed the store for good. He left for California—more specifically, for Rosemead, a tiny suburb of Los Angeles. (In a sense, all of Los Angeles was a suburb of New York, an increasingly popular alternative to Long Island.) Two weeks later, my mother, two sisters, and I received a fateful telegram. "Pack up immediately. Come to California. If we must starve at least it will be in the sunshine." And so it was that in 1935 we joined the pioneers of the fourth migration.

The fourth migration still rolls on. But for how much longer? Because the suburbs have been growing for as long as most adults can remember, it's easy to imagine the unimaginable, that growth will continue for all time. That, at least, is the *feeling*. Surely, suburbia will stop growing . . . someday. And the planet Earth will burn, freeze, or explode into cosmic debris . . . in billions of years. But nobody worries about it. In 1985, vacant land is still being surveyed, divided, and subdivided. Freeways are still filling with new migrants. And forecasters have not yet tired of predicting suburbia's future as a straight-line extrapolation of its past. "America's Suburbs Are Still Fine," [1] they tell us, and, not to worry, 80 million suburbanites can't be wrong.

On the other hand there is a nagging sense that all is not well in middle America. Like the third reel of a stupendous film, suburbia may be winding itself out sooner than expected. As early as the 1950s, unmoved by an optimistic present, alarmists warned of ill effects in the future. Ill effects? We couldn't see any. Lately, the drumbeat of negative comment has accelerated. Titles of recent magazine articles tell the story. "Aging of the Suburbs," [2] "Our Troubled Suburbs," [3] the "Trek Back to the Cities," [4] and "Suburbia: End of the Golden Age." [5] Suburbs used to be a refuge, a place for big-city folk to escape pollution, crime, high taxes, exorbitant rents, and an unpleasant environment. But in recent years the suburbs themselves have fallen prey to those same afflictions. As one author put it, suburbanites resemble the people in Boccaccio's *Decameron* who "ran away from the plague and took it with them." [6]

Suppose—just suppose—that the pessimists are right, that the core of twentieth-century America (now housing more than one-third of the nation's population) is poised on the brink of a great reversal, and that obsolescence is shooting its poison smack into our suburban neighborhoods, drying up migration, sending residents into flight, despoiling the environment, annihilating property values. The switches would be set for an economic disaster. Consider the owner of a near-typical house valued at $100,000 with a mortgage of $75,000. If market values fall by only 25 percent, the owner's equity is wiped out. It wouldn't end there. Every other kind of suburban real estate would suffer a similar fate—industrial parks, office buildings, shopping centers, apartment houses. Nor would the tidal wave of obsolescence spend itself in suburbia. Its repercussions would spread throughout the economy. Consider the impact on our banking system alone. When property values approach mortgage values, bankers become restive. When values sink still lower there is a deep sense of helplessness—like falling from an airplane without a parachute.

What, then, do the coming decades hold for suburbia? Will it continue to feed on Edenic hopes? Or has it become an 85-year-old geisha whose thick plastering of lipstick and mascara holds little allure for the coming generation. The new migrants are already studying their maps. Will they be searching for another land of promise, thereby pushing suburbia gradually, but inexorably, into the grimy obsolescence of, say, the south Bronx?

Statistics of growth are suggestive. In the graph of comparative growth, the fourth region of opportunity shows a persistent upward trend throughout the first half of the twentieth century, but the rate of rise slows in the 1960s and in the 1970s begins to stoop over (see Figure 27). Los Angeles County, the very archetype of suburbia,

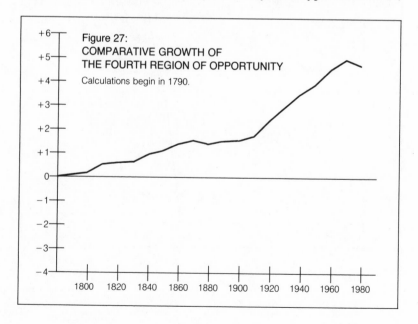

Figure 27:
COMPARATIVE GROWTH OF
THE FOURTH REGION OF OPPORTUNITY
Calculations begin in 1790.

shows the typical profile of the group as a whole (see Figure 28).
Like hundreds of other counties, King County, Washington, also
shows the typical pattern (see Figure 29).

Is that fall in comparative growth after 1970 a temporary set-
back? Or will the growth profiles of earlier regions of opportunity be

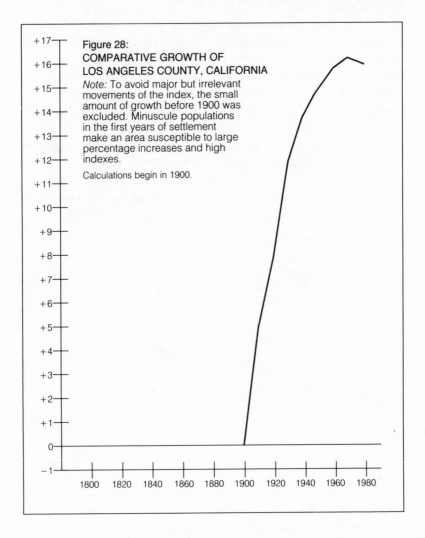

Figure 28:
COMPARATIVE GROWTH OF
LOS ANGELES COUNTY, CALIFORNIA

Note: To avoid major but irrelevant
movements of the index, the small
amount of growth before 1900 was
excluded. Minuscule populations
in the first years of settlement
make an area susceptible to large
percentage increases and high
indexes.

Calculations begin in 1900.

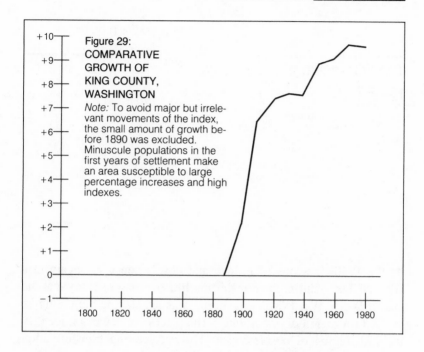

Figure 29:
COMPARATIVE
GROWTH OF
KING COUNTY,
WASHINGTON
Note: To avoid major but irrelevant movements of the index, the small amount of growth before 1890 was excluded. Minuscule populations in the first years of settlement make an area susceptible to large percentage increases and high indexes.

repeated—a sharp rise, followed by a slight downturn, then a long decline?

As a rear-view mirror cannot inform us of driving conditions ahead, yesterday's facts are an unreliable guide to the future. Past events had their origins in past conditions. But conditions change. Like a mountain stream, they're always running, meandering, digging out new channels. We need a theory that suggests the effects of different conditions, to help explain the past and forecast the future.

Six

The fifth region of opportunity, 1980–?

IN the 1980s, regions of growth and obsolescence are again in a state of flux—shifting and reshifting like the map of Europe at the end of World War I. Millions of migrants are staking out the limits of the fifth region of opportunity. The places they abandon identify the fifth region of obsolescence. The accelerating transformation signals another period of instability likely to last well past the turn of the century.

The remainder of the book explores the new regions of opportunity and obsolescence, their connections to each other and to real-estate values throughout the nation. Part Two presents the theory. It explains why each of the first four regions develops and how the fifth region can be predicted. Part Three uses the theory to make a series of forecasts for specific counties to the year 2000 and beyond. Part Four helps the investor apply the findings to individual strategies.

Part two

The theory

Seven

Predicting regions of opportunity

IN the 1980s, real-estate investors must make difficult decisions about where to expect growth in the long term. Rural America is at present the land of richest potential, but not everywhere. Only those who decide wisely will prosper.

In facing that promising future, one caution deserves major emphasis: do not extrapolate trends from one decade to the next. Not in this decade. Not in 1986. There are times when trends—even megatrends—seem limitless. Some trends seem to shoot into the social and economic stratosphere as though born to remain in flight, spearing onward and upward, seemingly indifferent to the law of gravity. Eventually, however, every trend reverses. An up trend turns down. A down trend turns up. In such moments of reversal, one decade does not foretell the next.

The 1980s are a time of transition, when trends are wavering and uncertain, when they represent conflicting forces, and when an investor can easily be misled.[1] The fourth migration is in decline but not yet ended—many suburbs are still growing. Superimposed on the fourth migration and adding to the confusion is the fifth, in an early stage. The fifth region of opportunity is where we want our investment dollars to go, but it is difficult to tell whether the growth we observe is driven by the expiring energies of the fourth migration or the vital wave of the fifth. As a result of this overlap, growth in the 1970s and early 1980s is an unreliable indicator of growth in the 1990s.

To differentiate one migration from another and to predict our target area, the emerging fifth region of opportunity, it will be helpful to apply lessons taught by scientific method.

Science calls for the union of two very different activities—observation of facts and interpretation of facts by theory. To predict the region of opportunity, a theoretical model must take into account the underlying forces responsible for migrations generally and for this migration in particular. Obviously, we cannot expect to predict with 100 percent certainty—neither in the short term nor the long term. (Tomorrow's weather cannot be predicted with absolute certainty.) Yet we have a lot to go on: detailed information on the first four migrations, clues drawn from the progress of the fifth, and, above all, a theory of migrations tested in the crucible of the last two hundred years.

Theory must answer four difficult questions. Why do migrations begin? Why do they end? How can we know when a new migration is on its way? How can we predict the next region of opportunity?

The theory of perishable economies

My central premise is this: just as the migration of birds is directed by the changing seasons, the migration of people is directed by a *changing social and economic environment.* That change is not local, but national and even international; it is not a development evolving bit by bit over many centuries but a whopping, cataclysmic, irreversible change that takes place over mere decades.

One entire economy develops as a single integrated unit, reaches a peak, and declines thereafter. As it declines, another economy emerges. The only way to understand successive migrations is to understand the successive economies in which they arise.

Successive economies are not the same as *the* economy. By

definition, *the* economy is the never-ending interaction among markets, the grand competition among suppliers and demanders. So long as interaction continues—and the presumption is that it always will—*the* economy will never end.

By contrast, an impermanent or *perishable* economy is an original, a unique and living masterpiece growing out of the *interaction of a particular people*—not only in their economic strivings (how they produce and distribute goods) but in the nature of their beliefs, theories, organizations, rituals, and values that condition economic strivings. Economists must study people. People—loving, angry, caring, joyous, problem-solving—are the central subject matter of economics, not factories, not technologies, not money. All of these are important, but they come second, as the means by which people get what they want. People, in all the diversity of their interactions, influence demands, whether for houses, computers, or nuclear missiles.

Before they can perform a symphony, musicians must tune to a common pitch. Before playing in the symphony of economic life, we the people reach a *consensus,* a broad agreement on rules of behavior and life-styles. Regardless of differences in age, sex, income, region, race, religion, political party, or class, in the symphony of economic life we all tune to the same ''A.''

Consensus is the fundamental requirement of civilized life. Specialized production—indispensable to rising living standards—is possible only when a finite number of products are produced, when consumers prefer those products above all others that are possible, and when the preferred products enhance contemporary lifestyles. Thus, consensus is the prerequisite to higher standards of living. To exist outside its pale is to wither and die.

There are many kinds of consensus, however, some briefly enduring (like the mass infatuation with New Wave, Punk Rock, or the hula hoop), some enduring for millennia (like the world's great religions). The consensus animating a perishable economy can always be identified by its special function. Like a fairy-tale hero who rescues the beauteous princess from an evil ogre, *an economy's con-*

sensus is always the solution to a problem that the previous economy could not solve. To describe this problem—and the consensus that arises to solve it—we must break in on a seamless circle of interactions. To do this, I ask the reader to extend "credit"—to accept a major proposition on faith for perhaps the next five minutes of reading time, after which it is hoped the "loan" will be repaid.

The proposition: Every economy perishes as a result of a unique problem it cannot solve. Its successor is governed by a unique consensus able to solve that problem.

Throughout the life of an economy its governing consensus serves as a scaffolding around which all social and economic changes are made. All the contrivances, plans, and maneuvers that move an economy incrementally forward; all the trends, propensities, and preferences; all the institutions, land, capital, and other resources, everything that summarizes, characterizes, or describes the essence of what an economy is and what it is trying to become— all this is controlled by the economy's unique consensus. Consensus is at the heart of every economy, defining its identity, directing its destiny.

Steadfast in its consensus, the economy becomes a veritable bulldozer programmed to scoop out, heap up, and reshape the world to its own special image. In magazines, books, television, movies, and newspapers the favored life-styles are pushed, promoted, and publicized. People experiment with the new modes. They wear trench coats, slouch, and smoke like Humphrey Bogart. At another time they exercise, breathe deeply, and eat health foods like Jane Fonda. Under the aegis of a favorable consensus, migration to a new region of opportunity begins. That region expands more than any other. The values of its real estate increase. The energies of the consensus spill out in still wider circles. Laws favorable to the consensus are passed. New industries and new technologies emerge as though by invitation. All this churning up of new ground in every enterprise and occupation is the consequence of a single consensus.

As every life seeks to preserve its identity, every consensus resists changes to *itself*. Whatever would alter it is alien, an enemy to be resisted. Ideally, the keynote of consensus is stability. But as the consensus strives to survive forevermore, stability soon hardens into rigidity.

No one consensus can be appropriate for all time: in the 1920s, the moral lessons of Horatio Alger no longer excited a generation of flappers; in the 1980s, songs of union solidarity cannot thrill an assemblage of yuppies. Before a consensus is repudiated, however, its failure is announced by the appearance of many and formidable excesses. Exceeding limits imposed by the law of diminishing returns, further "improvements"—relentlessly pursued by an economy in the grip of a fixed consensus—no longer improve anything. They become destructive, create serious imbalances. Too many migrants enter the region of opportunity; its real estate is overpriced. Expansion of the favored industries is constrained by increasing scarcities. Favored life-styles become both unaffordable and less satisfying. Government begins to frustrate other sectors of the economy. Intransigent idealists whose ideals have gone bankrupt helplessly tear apart the house they labored so long to build.

Each economy develops its own characteristic form of excess. If an economy's consensus seeks centralization, it becomes overcentralized; if if seeks decentralization, it becomes over-decentralized; if it is production-oriented, it overproduces; if consumption-oriented, it overconsumes.

Because no perishable economy is able to end its own excesses there is only one possible outcome: the old economy—all of it as a total system—will become obsolete.

To restore order, a new economy is born. It aggressively challenges the runaway excesses and therefore opposes the consensus that spawned them. Thus begins a whole new cycle. Accelerating excesses form the "key problem" of the new economy, determining its agenda and unique integration. As a key is shaped to open a lock, the new economy shapes its identity to solve its inherited key problem. Again, like a key, the "solution" it presents is the negative image of the "problem." Thus, overcentralization begets decentralization. Overproduction begets mass consumption. Overconsumption begets conservation. These oppositions are always effective. They eventually solve the key problem by ridding the land of the old economy's excesses—and of the old economy as well.

A new economy is an apocalyptic event. When we the people become convinced that traditional patterns can no longer be endured, that traditional life-styles are no longer satisfying, one economy perishes and another emerges. Once the inertia of the past is overcome, every familiar landmark is swept away in the current of comprehensive change. Like earthquakes that resolve pent-up stresses in the earth's shifting strata, a shift from one economy to another resolves the pent-up need for social and economic accommodation. Pressures from long-accumulating and steadily worsening problems are eventually resolved by great structural movements. In the crush of change, we alter *who we are* as a people, *what we hope for, how we live,* and, of special importance to the forecaster of migrations, *where we live.*

The good fortune an economy bestows on a region of opportunity during its rise is surrendered during its fall. This comedown can be ascribed to the economy's unwelcome durability. Like a perverse telephone-answering device that cannot erase its messages, every economy imprints its region of opportunity with the indelible markings of its characteristic real estate. Spatial patterns, neighborhoods, architecture, and public utility systems are developed to specifications imposed by the economy's specialized demands. Unfortunately, real estate cannot easily be returned to a virginal state for a new beginning and the region passes into a long and irreversible decline. In the very long run it will shake loose of old commitments to become part of another context, another region of opportunity, another economy. Meanwhile, it cannot easily compete with places more amenable to the embrace of a rising economy.

Now I've told you why economies perish and why each perishable economy gets its identifying consensus from unique excesses committed by its predecessor. I therefore consider the principal on my "loan" to be "paid." Payment of "interest" follows.

A succession of unique economies can be discerned, each with its own region of opportunity, each rising, reaching a peak, developing excesses and inevitably declining. Because it brackets the seedtime of the modern industrial era, I define the economy extending from 1735 to 1846 as the first. I call it the Mercantile Aristocrat.

The economy of the Mercantile Aristocrat (1735–1846) and the first region of opportunity

The American colonies were bound within the mercantile system, a centralized state apparatus for the support of the dominant role of a mother country. The reigning aristocracy in England and America exerted a firm command over that system.

To support its mercantilist policies, Britain depended on the colonies for raw materials—tobacco, lumber, fish, and grains. This dependence created a burgeoning demand for agricultural land in the New World, not for a scattering of thin-soiled small parcels but for immense stretches of lush, virgin acres, permitting the huge estates preferred by aristocrats. The region of opportunity best able to serve this economy would be located near the Atlantic, the only accessible waterway from which to conduct large-scale commerce. North and South Carolina best suited all requirements.

In England, as in its American colonies, the indigent poor no less than the landed aristocracy subscribed to the consensus of the mercantile economy. Together, at the peak of the economy's development, they embraced the proposition that what the common man did best was to labor at menial tasks, while he who stood on a pedestal of birth and breeding could better lead the nation, direct large enterprises, and ensure prosperity. Three ideal requirements were assumed by the reigning consensus of the Mercantile Aristocrat: *centralization* (an economic system centralized around the power of the king); *big business* (large-scale enterprises and government-sponsored monopolies); *inequality* (acceptance of a fixed social pyramid). Up to 1789 these three were the economy's pillars of strength.

In the period of excess after 1789, every strength degenerated into weakness, every good turned bad—in the United States as well as in Great Britain. Mindful of the advantages of centralization—and the indispensable role of the upper classes at its center—the Federalists espoused legislation favoring the growth of aristocratically controlled corporations, not for the benefit of the ruling few, they honestly believed, but to advance the general welfare. To give the nation a competitive edge in the jungle of the Western world, many would have preferred to establish a monarchy, headed by an American king, George (Washington) the First. They did their patriotic best to make America strong—their way. Had the Federalists won their campaign to keep the price of public land high and the terms of sale exacting and beset with obstacles, potential settlers would have had little chance to own their own land. They would have been nailed to their jobs in the East—in Boston, New York, and Philadelphia—trapped by the necessity to survive. For their wealthy employers, however, things would have been quite different. Trapped, potential settlers would have provided cheap labor as well as a large and accessible market and America would take its place as a proper mercantilist power. The traditional formula of the Mercantile Aristocrat would be maintained: aristocrats contributing money and influence, the common man brawn and patience. That formula grew increasingly unacceptable—not only to the common man but to the aristocrats as well.

In the United States, Thomas Jefferson, himself a Southern patrician, attacked the consensus sustaining the ruling American aristocracy (led by Alexander Hamilton and the Federalists). With indignation bursting all bonds and promising that his presidency would ring in the "revolution of 1800"—that he would fight for "those who labor in the earth . . . the chosen people of God"— Jefferson sought to bring the curtain down with a smash on the drama of the Mercantile Aristocrat.

As the new consensus increasingly took hold, Americans and Europeans poured into the second region of opportunity and the second economy began to spread itself into the generations.

The economy of the Bantam Capitalist (1789–1900) and the second region of opportunity

I call the second economy the Bantam Capitalist because its consensus aimed at a proliferation of very small capitalists drawn from the ranks of the common man.

Had an opinion poll been taken around 1817, it would undoubtedly have shown a spectacular collapse of respect for the still dominant aristocracy. Hereditary landholders, the rich and mighty who formed the privileged class of the eighteenth century, were tumbled from their places of eminence. Now ordinary laborers earning a scant $150 a year were newly esteemed, nurtured, and encouraged to swim in the capitalist stream. Many did. They became farmer-entrepreneurs who bought land, developed it as quickly as they could, and sold it at a profit.

The consensus against aristocratic privilege translated into a bull market of laborers transformed into tiny businessmen. The nation's masses were swept by a passion to make money, to become rich, to acquire farms, animals, houses, gardens, and, above all, respectability. Money was freedom. Money was security. Money was independence. The infatuation with making money soon spread like a jingle, a tune on everyone's lips. In the 1830s an Englishman remarked that he "had never overheard Americans conversing without the word *dollar* being pronounced between them."

The new consensus intended those dollars to circulate among the common people. Legislation soon appeared to reinforce all barriers against any resurgence of the privileged class. Because the federal government was the seat of centralized power—pure oxygen to the Mercantile Aristocrats interested in launching large corporations—the principal tactic in the war against the aristocrats was the assertion of states' rights. Slash power from the federal government and redistribute it to city, county, and state institutions. It happened. The resulting hodge-podge of laws and infrastructure throughout the land effectively quashed the potential for national markets. Caught in a morass of endless local variations, an aspiring corporate giant would be as helpless as a whale in a fishpond.

Putting its faith in the unlimited energies of the poor and the humble, the Bantam Capitalist was ideally served by migration to virgin lands of the Mississippi Valley, the emerging region of opportunity. The new consensus created an environment favorable to small towns and small markets. Migrants poured into the valley wherever they could find a port bordered by good land. Soon there was a profusion of isolated village-ports, each filling its hinterland with farmer-entrepreneurs. Land was cheap, fertile, and abundant. Crops could be efficiently transported to overseas markets via the ubiquitous Mississippi.

Fortune also smiled on bantam manufacturers, bantam retailers, bantam wholesalers. Thousands of small producers flourished in an era when iron mills were often no larger than an eight-by-ten-foot room attached to the blacksmith's house. Tiny family-run flour and lumber mills supplied customers limited to an area a few miles around. Within the multiplicity of small, isolated markets, local "manufacturers" could easily produce at lower costs than could larger competitors. The immense Mississippi region contained only four cities of any size—New Orleans, Cincinnati, St. Louis, and Pittsburgh (though in an important sense the valley continued on into New York State via the Erie Canal). Most of the valley was a world of small, sleepy towns. As late as 1850, Chicago was hardly more than a small town with a population of fewer than 30,000. Small was never more beautiful than in the economy of the Bantam Capitalist.

But the success of the Bantam economy soon created excesses leading to its downfall. By the middle of the nineteenth century, the economy began to choke on the changes it had wrought. The small-scale economy brought layers of costly duplications and a senseless lack of standardization. Travel by rail was a nightmare of transfers to different companies with different-gauge tracks and different rules. Factories, machinery, and all the nuts and bolts of industrial civilization were a hodge-podge of sizes and descriptions conjured up by millions of small, independent improvisers. "Yankee ingenuity" they called it. As a result of small-scale production and unnecessary layers of middlemen, prices were both variable and unduly high.

The Mississippi cradle of the Bantam Capitalist had become the center of a stifling obsolescence. Tiny villages were growing out of control. Their populations became too large and unwieldy for the institutions by which they were governed. Crime and corruption abounded. In the 1870s, those holding land in the Mississippi region would bear witness to a lengthy decline in the comparative growth of population and to plummeting investment returns. On the other hand, perspicacious real-estate investors who recognized the emerging turnabout in national aspirations and priorities could realize overflowing opportunities to prosper. Despite the confusion of overlapping trends, they would see where the favored places must be and why the emerging economy could best fulfill itself precisely there and nowhere else.

A chasm gaped between the world that was and the world that was being born. It was time to move on, to follow a new vision, to seek the new region of opportunity. Migration to the second region of opportunity dried up as Americans began streaming into the third.

The economy of the Colossus (1846–1958) and the third region of opportunity

The third economy I call the Colossus because its consensus aims at a spectacular increase in the scale of industrialization—enormous factories, giant corporations, mighty cities, vast commercial farms. The Colossus was everything the Bantam Capitalist was not.

Whereas the Bantam Capitalist distributed power far and wide in an orgy of democratic equality, the Colossus conferred power on a few millionaire captains of industry—the Rockefellers, the Vanderbilts, and the Carnegies. Where the Bantam Capitalist opposed centralization with Jeffersonian ardor, the Colossus gave centralization its highest priority. Where the Bantam Capitalist conceived a passion for small independent business, the Colossus was stirred by giant corporate structures.

Beginning around the middle of the nineteenth century, a groundswell of consensus united national and personal goals. Nationally, Americans sought to outdo the industrial achievements of other nations. They took pride in America's mighty industrial fortress, in its superior technology, its coast-to-coast railroads, and its giant factories. By the end of the century, Americans could point to industrial behemoths that dwarfed competitors everywhere in the world. Said one contemporary observer, U.S. Steel "receives and expends more money every year than any but the very greatest of the world's national governments; its debt is larger than that of many of the lesser nations of Europe; it absolutely controls the destinies of a population nearly as large as that of Maryland or Nebraska, and indirectly influences twice that number." [2] As with steel, so with oil, railroads, and banking.

On the personal level, flesh-and-blood models like John D. Rockefeller, Andrew Carnegie, and Edward Harriman were inspiring proof that rags-to-riches dreams could come true. In an age when the average family earned a dollar a day, Rockefeller was an outsized dream, but not beyond belief to readers of Horatio Alger novels. Starting from near poverty (no one need be ashamed of being poor so long as he keeps trying), men of the Colossus expected to emulate the millionaires who now lived off the cream at the top of the bottle. Why not? Weren't they once poor themselves? Rockefeller began as a $4-a-week clerk in a commission merchant's house. In 1892 his fortune was estimated to be $815,647,796.89. [3] Andrew Carnegie started out at the age of thirteen as a bobbin boy in a cotton mill at $1.20 a week and became the largest steel manufacturer in the world. From 1889 to 1899 the profits from Carnegie's industrial empire averaged $7,500,000 a year, and in 1900 spiralled to $40,000,000.[4] Edward H. Harriman, builder of a railroad empire, began his career as an office boy at $5 a week.

In this great land of ours, any man—or his children, or children's children—could become a captain of industry, or at least one of his assistants, or, short of that, a prominent investor. The common man of the Colossus economy didn't want a small farm. He wanted a place in the largest corporation he could imagine. Armed with diligence, thrift, patience, initiative, punctuality, reliability— all the copybook virtues plus a bit of luck—he could have that place. The present might be back-breaking work at $5 a week, but there was dignity in it because the future glittered with promise.

What region of opportunity would best serve the new economy? Above all, such a region must constitute a single national market. The thousands of fragmented, rural markets of the Bantam Capitalist world would never do for the Colossus. Tearing down the barriers of a small-scale economy would put companies in touch with millions of customers, giving life to giant corporations having a talent for mass production. Specialized machinery and labor would drive costs down so low that smaller competitors would be routed, leading to even greater size and even greater savings for corporations. Savings meant rapid accumulation of capital. Capital, invested and reinvested, would bring the endless industrial expansion so much prized by people of the Colossus.

The Colossus built cities. Big cities. Dense cities. Giant corporations attracted swarms of migrants, who pressed into cities like Chicago expecting to make their fortunes. While waiting for their fortunes to materialize, the new migrants fertilized the economy with cheap labor and obligingly bought back what they produced. Their tolerance of crowded conditions, back-breaking work, and hand-to-mouth penury allowed savings needed by the economy for reinvestment. Consensus, urged on by an optimistic Horatio Alger outlook, wrung from the migrants the great personal sacrifices needed to build this industrial Gargantua of the late nineteenth century.

Chicago was the fastest-growing and largest city in the new

region of opportunity. Those who invested their savings in Chicago's real estate at the end of the great depression of 1873–1878 earned remarkable profits. Even if they chose properties by throwing darts at a map of Chicago—while blindfolded—and even if they sold during any boom year of the 1880s or early 1890s, on the average they would have earned a gross return of 15 percent![5] These high returns were possible at a time when stock yields were around 4.5 percent. And think of the possibilities for those who took off the blindfolds and chose locations carefully. During the period 1877–1894, twentyfold increases in land value were not at all uncommon within Chicago's commercial loop.[6]

Migrants also flocked to rural areas, where labor was needed to satisfy industry's ravenous demands for raw materials. Mines and quarries (iron, coal, silver, mercury, iron manganese, copper, cement, soda ash) sprang to life from Minnesota to California. In regional cities of the Pacific Northwest, such as Seattle and Portland, industry mobilized to harvest abundant forests and fisheries. The penchant for smallness was gone. On the prairies of the Midwest a new, highly mechanized, and large-scale farming became an adjunct of the city—as though it were any other manufacturing operation. The city mass-produced the plows, harrows, and harvesters used on the farm and also processed the harvests. The city's lusty appetite for food and raw materials offered the farmer a ready market. (See Chapter Five.) Farmers were no longer independent, no longer small, no longer Bantam Capitalists.

Railroads welded raw-material sites and dense urban cores— the interdependent components of the new region of opportunity— into a single well-regulated machine. The great arc of steel railroad construction—and the visible rise and fall of the third region of opportunity—extended from the 1860s into the early twentieth century (see Figure 30).[7] Locations of counties in the third region of opportunity matched the map of railroad lines in 1900 (see Figure 31).

By 1920, the Colossus was running out of demands for more steel, more industrial capacity, and more railroad lines. Railroad

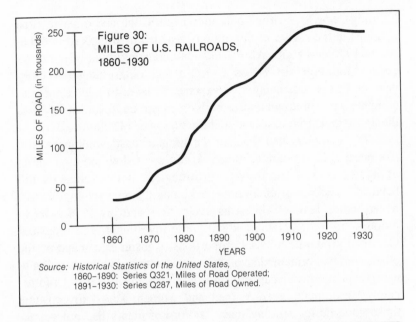

Figure 30:
MILES OF U.S. RAILROADS,
1860–1930

MILES OF ROAD (in thousands)

YEARS

Source: *Historical Statistics of the United States,*
1860–1890: Series Q321, Miles of Road Operated;
1891–1930: Series Q287, Miles of Road Owned.

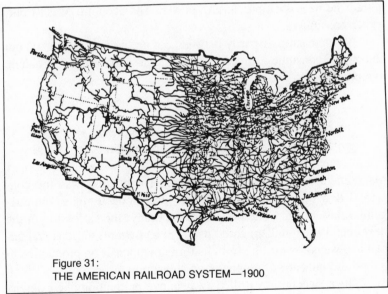

Figure 31:
THE AMERICAN RAILROAD SYSTEM—1900

building came to a virtual halt after 1920. Cook and other favored counties in the region of opportunity reached their peak growth between 1900 and 1930. After 1930 comparative growth began to recede. Migration slowed as Chicago and other industrial cities become congested, noisy, and expensive places to live. Unable to compete with suburban houses built on cheap, large, and sunny lots, the aging industrial cities entered the region of obsolescence.

The Colossus had reached the limit of its development. But like every other mature economy, it could not slow the momentum of its excesses. It obstructed. It struggled. It multiplied its imbalances. The key problem now beckoning the next economy was a never-ending and self-defeating cycle: save and invest in order to produce still more saving and still more investment. The industrial plant had grown to colossal proportions. Consumer demand on the other hand had remained small and unpromising. Who was going to use the phenomenal capacity unleashed by the system? Unfortunately, customers (average men and women) slated to consume those good things pouring from the horn of plenty had not yet acquired the necessary purchasing power. The economy wasn't nurturing consumers.

An increasing disparity between our ability to produce and our ability to consume exacerbated a single and terrible problem: overproduction.

The economy of the Little King (1900–   ) and suburbia, the fourth region of opportunity

Marx and Lenin had preached that overproduction was the congenital flaw of capitalism. It wasn't. Overproduction was the congenital flaw of only one perishable economy, the Colossus. In the next century, capitalism cured itself (in its own mysterious and unplanned ways) by turning from its former emphasis on production to a new and unheard-of emphasis on consumption.

The new economy drilled away at overproduction like a dentist at a cavity. So comprehensive was our acceptance of the new consensus urging ever greater consumption, and so complete the cure, that after almost a century, capitalism in the 1980s is suffering not from overproduction but from *overconsumption*—the diametric opposite of overproduction. Explain that if you can, Karl Marx.

Because the consumer is King in the new economy, and because the Kings are many, I call it *the economy of the Little King*. From laborers earning little more than a dollar a day around the turn of the century, America's Little Kings soon boosted themselves into the great middle class.

By what miracle did the Little Kings win their thrones? Was it an extraordinary propensity to save and invest, the age-old capitalistic formula for making us richer by driving down costs of production? On the contrary. That was precisely what did not happen. Higher savings and investment would only have aggravated the key problem of underconsumption. What we did was far more ingenious. We didn't change the method of getting what we wanted. We changed what we wanted.

To do that we commenced a little-celebrated shift in consensus. "Save and invest" was out. "Spend and consume" was in. We all learned to glorify consumption. "Don't hoard your capital as grandpa used to do" became the sage advice of the Little King.

It was difficult at first. Saving for productive purposes ran in the blood. How could a man of the Colossus, an earnest man, a man of integrity and conscience spend hard-earned capital on consumer goods? "It would be unseemly, even wicked. Buy a house, a car, a motorcycle, a boat?" Unthinkable. He didn't *need* it. That much money added to his savings would insure a better future for his children and his children's children. "Save and invest" had become the Eleventh Commandment.

Said the Little King with a smile bright as a silver dollar, "Don't worry so much. Enjoy. Play. Go on vacations—to the East coast, the West coast, Canada, Alaska, Europe, South America, Asia, Africa. And spend your capital. All of it. Spend more than your capital. Spend more than you earn."

"How?"

"Haven't you heard of credit?"

Big Borrowers and Big Spenders became the patriots who made the economy go round.

Institutions and customs rallied to support the new consensus as though born to the job. Banks grew facile at making consumer loans. Unions jacked up middle-class income to insure greater purchasing power. Congress enacted the Wagner Act to embolden the unions and expand their influence. The IRS taxed the savers and gave tax breaks to users of credit. And in our zeal to consume, we easily fell into the great American competition to outspend the Joneses.

One of the greatest obstacles to the rising consensus, however, was the lack of a suitable place to consume. Within the tight circle of the old central cities, land was expensive, lots necessarily tiny. There was no room for a Little King and his Queen to spread out, no feeling of spaciousness to inform the world of royal mastery, no space in which to accumulate wave after wave of automatic appliances and up-to-the-minute gadgetry.

Suddenly, because of an amazing invention of the Little King, lack of space ceased to be a problem. According to U.S. patent laws a patentable invention must pass three tests. It must be *useful*. It must be *novel*. And it must be a *surprise*—unlikely to be conceived and implemented by ordinary reasonable individuals. On all counts, suburbia qualified as an authentic invention.

As elegant as anything created by Leonardo da Vinci, the suburban invention was as simple as it was unique, valuable as it was bold. What the Little King accomplished was to break the monopolistic grip of the central cities on the urban land supply. And it did so by *rearranging the urban landscape*. In suburbia, employment, shopping, and public centers no longer converged in an orderly manner around a single point as in cities of the past. Now, as though conceived by a mad planner, those destination points were deposited here and there, apparently in chaotic abandon, throughout a huge domain.

But if the planner was mad, there was genius in that madness. While the old city radiated its beneficence on a tiny circle of land a few miles from the center, suburbia created a vast and welcome supply of urban land in and around the random archipelago of shopping malls, factories, and housing subdivisions. Accessible land was suddenly cheap. Gloriously cheap. Blessedly cheap. In suburbia, Little Kings and Queens could afford the houses they needed for a life dedicated to consumption. They had places to put the thousands of articles made cheap by everyone's commitment to buy them. (Items that would otherwise sell for $10 were now sold by Thrifty Drug Stores for $3.99—$2.99 on sale. And auto dealers across the country advertised fine cars that could be bought for as little as $999 . . . on credit.) Urban land in staggering abundance changed everything. To hell with apartment living. There would be no more of that. It was like moving out of a coffin. Now there was room, plenty of room. Everything would fit—automobiles, all the furniture you could wish for, even large private gardens. Such was suburbia, invention of the Little King.

Suburbia is the New City. But its name is misleading. The word *suburb* refers to a community living in the shadow of an "urb." An urb is the central city—Chicago, Detroit, Philadelphia. Suburbs are presumably dependent on urbs for services or employment opportunities, a relationship reminiscent of parent and child. That at least was how it all began. Early in the century, middle-class refugees from the big city—to escape the spectacle of unwashed immigrants as well as the stench and noise of unflagging industrial progress—built hideaway Arcadias in the country. Those were true suburbs—bedroom communities where a person could breathe clean air and relax in pastoral surroundings, but where one was almost completely dependent on the city for employment, goods, and services. Early industrial suburbs were essentially the same. Although teeming with employment opportunities, they were just as dependent on the city for most goods and services. By midcentury, however, the suburbs had changed. They weren't "sub" anything. They had become cities unto themselves, complete with industrial parks, condominiums, housing developments, shopping centers, and modern high-rises in smoky glass and concrete.

We associate that new suburban city with the automobile. Aren't the centerless suburbs, we ask, the direct result of the automobile rather than of the Little King? It's true that automobiles free us from the need to locate close to public transportation. But those omnipresent wheels were only one component in an extensive system. Every element of the system supports every other. Automobiles are the "stars" of a well-rehearsed balancing act. Twenty men with bulging muscles stretch a long rope; a smiling lady rides the rope on a bicycle; two men stand on each handlebar of the bicycle; two other ladies pose prettily as they balance on the shoulders of each man. In this perfect performance, everyone is dependent on everyone else. Should one performer sneeze or daydream the whole system could collapse. The auto was similarly dependent—on other features of the Little King economy. It was dependent, for example, on consumer credit. People of the Colossus would not have put themselves in debt for mere pleasure or convenience. And they would have looked with suspicion on any proposed legislation favoring consumer credit. A sweeping shift in consensus had to come first. That shift in emphasis, from production to consumption, would integrate all the interdependent components of the new economy—beliefs, attitudes, priorities, life-styles, customs, laws, industries, and suburbia as well. Suburbia was the work of the economy as a whole, not of the automobile, not of new credit institutions, not of any single component of the Little King.

As the new consensus washed over the mind of America, the economy devoted to spending became a roaring reality. Average Americans migrated to suburbia by the millions to preside as Little Kings and Queens over their one-sixth-acre domains. Here, in sovereign splendor, plumbers, steelworkers, and pipe fitters lived in a lavishness of life-style exceeding the most impossible dream of their parents and grandparents. They filled their single-family palaces with freezers, furnaces, home laundries, vacuum cleaners, air-conditioners, stain-resistant nylon carpets, FM radios, television sets, electric blankets, electric floor polishers, electric pencil sharpeners, electric can openers. They filled their royal carports and garages with automobiles, boats, and recreational vehicles of every type and description. ''Planned obsolescence'' accustomed us each year to discard 8 million automobiles, 100 million tires, 40 million tons of paper, 48 million cans, and 26 million bottles.[8]

So faithfully did we follow the injunction to spend and consume, and so efficiently did the American economy supply the desired consumables, that the *poverty* level of the 1970s probably exceeded the standard of living achieved by the *average* American of 1900.

The economy of the Little King had done its job only too well. Overproduction had been conquered by the 1950s and overconquered by the 1970s. The Little King was no longer the solution. It was becoming the problem. Suburbs springing out of farms in remote areas soon filled in the countryside, and then the corridors between the suburbs and the old cities. Eventually, people who believed they had escaped the city found the city crowding in around them. As idyllic suburb merged with congested metropolis, our former bucolic paradise was increasingly spoiled by congestion, loss of open space, air and water pollution, epidemic levels of crime and drug addiction.

As usual, we clutched too long to the consensus of a mature economy. In the 1960s the Little King had succeeded only too well in achieving prosperity through consumer spending. The new key problem that increasingly summoned the next economy was overconsumption and, with it, a devastating by-product: capital shortage. We were spending money we didn't have. Capital was being artificially produced by the banking system, while the economy was blowing away. In the 1980s, the key problem of overconsumption (or undersaving) becomes more urgent. Immense capital sums needed in the coming decades seal the fate of the Little King and ensure the emergence of a successor. Consider:

- Because we spend too much on consumption and not enough on investment, our capital structure is deteriorating. From 1961 to 1965 we added $55,000 of capacity per person added to the labor force (in 1958 dollars). In 1966–1970 the comparable figure was $46,000. In 1971–1982 it was $42,000. [9]

- Our support of basic research has dangerously dwindled. Between 1967 and 1980, federal funding for research in high-energy physics (in dollars adjusted for inflation) declined by 30 percent. [10] Other fields, with less obvious connections to national defense, have suffered even greater cuts.

- We are reducing aid to underdeveloped nations at the very time when starvation and economic chaos are frustrating our attempts to head off the growth of communism in those areas. The drain on capital is dramatized by the near bankruptcy of the richer underdeveloped nations. Brazil, Mexico, Argentina, Venezuela, Poland, Chile, and Nigeria owe more than $300 billion to Western banks. Most of this may never be paid. [11]

- Our infrastructure is crumbling. Two out of every five bridges in the United States are seriously deficient. Eight thousand miles of the interstate system are now beyond their engineered life, 756 urban areas with populations over 50,000 will have to spend up to $100 billion just to maintain their water systems. [12] Prisons are dangerously overcrowded, resulting in increasing numbers of riots. Yet federal, state, and local spending for upkeep of the nation's public works has been virtually halved during the last twenty years.

- The United States government is creating deficits into the distant future that range from $150 to $300 billion annually, depending on the assumptions made.

To solve these problems, and they are monstrously large, the economy of the Little King will eventually perish. In the 1970s and 1980s we are witnessing an unparalleled onslaught against its consumerist attitudes, values, priorities, institutions, industries. The battle is mounted by forces of the next economy. I call it the Caring Conserver.

The economy of the Caring Conserver
(1958–   )

Brought to life in the late 1950s by the extravagances of the Little King, the Caring Conserver is named for its unique attitudes toward conservation on the part of a growing number of people. In 1985 the consensus of this fledgling economy is still in flux and we cannot see it clearly. No one has been there and no textbooks exist to guide us beyond the frontiers of what is known.

Development cannot be quick. Like a quarterback attempting to run while being dragged down by tacklers, it will snatch progress however it can, despite controversy, accidents, miscalculations, feuds, misunderstandings, false starts. Judging from the half-century or more required by past economies to reach maturity, the ripening of the Caring Conserver will take us well past the beginning of the twenty-first century. Only then, after the fact, when we can feel the new consensus deep in the solar plexus, will we comprehend it with certainty.

In 1985 what do we know of the emerging economy? We know this much: that the Caring Conserver must solve the twofold problem of overconsumption and capital shortage. This is its mandate and its key problem. Until we are able to staunch the flow of our economic substance now bleeding away in excessive spending, until we are able to replenish our languishing capital stock with real savings—not money newly printed by the Federal Reserve—we will remain patients in intensive care, with ever diminishing prospects for a stable economic life.

What's to be done? Every new economy solves its key problem by opposing the preceding consensus. We know that in order to solve the problem of overconsumption the Caring Conserver must oppose every tenet of the consumption consensus. To conserve the huge capital sums routinely squandered by the Little King, the ardent pursuit of consumption must be opposed by an equally ardent determination to conserve.

This is what the emerging economy does. It conserves. It saves and it guards and it safeguards—by law, by propaganda, by appeal to conscience. The will to conserve extends to capital—what we save and invest to support the new priorities; to all that nature gives freely—energy, pure air and water, an unmaimed environment; to culture—historic buildings, parks, folksongs and dances, all forms of art; and to people—the Caring Conserver emboldens women and minorities, it cherishes the aged, the poor, and the handicapped everywhere in the world.

Whereas the Little King valued the poor for their *inability to save* (they spend *all* their income) gladly shoveling billions into the maw of their limitless needs, the Caring Conserver values them for a different reason: they are potential contributors to a capital-hungry economy. They can and will be treated as any other undeveloped resources to be succored, trained, and absorbed into the mainstream of economic life. Such is the faith of the Caring Conserver.

It will happen. Nurtured by the new economy, we will not waste the immense productive capacities of our women, our minorities, our senior citizens. All the former rejects—quadriplegics, high-school dropouts, the deaf, blind, homeless, and hungry—can be tomorrow's psychiatrists, computer programmers, pharmacists, writers, teachers, and scholars.

Will sacrifices be necessary? Will we be called upon to reduce our standards of living? Indeed not. We are not asked to buy one iota less of what we prefer. Rather, the Caring Conserver invites us to *change* what we prefer. Wants grow out of consensus. Our new attitudes will end our consumer orgies and, with them, our deficits and our capital shortages. At the same time a mighty ocean of savings will permit us to maintain a stable economic life. Gently, steadily, inevitably, the Little King will be edged into oblivion.

Theory suggests the shape of the new human type now emerging.

To promote spending, the Little King resolved to "give" little and "take" a lot. Demands for shorter work days and higher pay eventually escalated into the permissive society with its careless work habits, white-collar crime, easy bankruptcies, welfare frauds. The Caring Conserver reverses the Little King's formula: "Give a lot and take little" is the new tenet. We already see it happening. Increasingly, eager volunteers are applying for public service. The growing hospice movement relies almost entirely on volunteer labor. People of good will, without a cent of compensation, minister to orphans, the illiterate, the elderly, the underprivileged, the sick, the starving. Scarcely a day passes without our hearing of individuals, both rich and poor, who find meaning in service to the less fortunate. And corporations, so puritanical about the pursuit of profit in the past, now support the arts, public radio and television, a gamut of charities. Altruism, of course, is nothing new. The milestone is in the numbers. The numbers keep growing.

The Caring Conserver reverses yet another formula. Whereas the Little King maximizes purchasing power by *trading future benefits for present satisfactions*, the Caring Conserver maximizes savings and investment, *trading present satisfactions for future benefits*. Investments are "in" these days. IRA and Keogh investment programs are mandated by Congress, and they are becoming increasingly popular. Small businesses are proliferating. Business books and magazines are among the best sellers. Business consultants are a regular feature on radio and television.

Prodded by the consumption economy, advertising (the Little King's oldest profession) seduced us into a Dionysian intoxication with junk foods, cigarettes, and liquor. Nobody mentioned the little death knells under each shiny wrapper. And nobody mentioned that from today's delicious corruption of the palate would come tomorrow's costs in illness, doctors, and spiraling hospital fees. (Those Little Kings who lit up two packs of "coffin nails" a day, they didn't know? They didn't *want* to know.) At the cost of a less indulgent present, the Caring Conserver directs us to choices that promise a more salubrious future. We accept discipline, make sacrifices for longevity. We jog, meditate, take vitamins, and show a preference for whole natural foods. It's happening. The movement toward caring conservation is spreading like an anthem through the ranks. Abandoning the Little King, a chorus of millions will be picking up the new theme.

Our wholesale defection bears inescapable implications for suburbia, ancestral home of the Little King. In our vast inventory of land, suburban real estate is the one type least suited to the emerging consensus. Not only has it become expensive as a result of a century of ever increasing demands, but the very qualities that make it attractive to the Little King make it repugnant to the Caring Conserver. Whereas conservers wish to take little from life and give a lot, suburbia has become the symbol of indulgence, the place where one takes a lot and gives as little as possible. While Caring Conservers are shifting their priorities into the future, almost a century of suburban development has made it a metaphor for the spirit of ''get it now.''

A quarter of a century ago, when precursors to the Caring Conserver denounced suburbia we tuned out their vitriolic attacks. They claimed that below the slick exterior were suburbia's boring conformity, its ''automobility,'' its ''ticky-tacky'' houses, its ''sluburban'' appearance. How unfair. With nary so much as a nod or a thank-you they were railing against an economy that after half a century had finally solved the desperate problem of overproduction. In its proper season, any economy can be constructive. The Little King was appropriate . . . *then*.

What suburbia's critics could never do in the 1950s, three decades of worsening excesses are accomplishing more easily. Suburbia's index of comparative growth, reaching a peak around 1970, is beginning the decline characteristic of every region of obsolescence. *Suburbia will go down with the ship*—along with the entire system of the Little King's consumption economy.

As suburban real estate begins its long descent to the end of the line, an age-old process is revived. Let us not forget those sumptuous mansions built at the turn of the century. When the plutocrats migrated to suburbia it was the poor who commandeered their elegant turrets and cupolas. Many of these palatial homes have been rehabilitated in recent years, but not before wasting away for decades in deepest slums.

Suburbia will show a similar deterioration. Not everywhere. And not all at once. But we will see miles of 2,500-square-foot behemoths, their wide windows broken and patched, their many rooms divided and subdivided into nondescript apartments, and, betraying the indignities of poverty, the former proud front lawns will be littered by junk automobiles and broken furniture.

Suburbia, like every region of opportunity, serves a unique economy. It grew rapidly when its economy was rising. It obsolesces when its economy declines. Because every economy must inevitably yield to another, suburbia too—wunderkind of a yesteryear—will become obsolete. Its obsolescence will not be quickly terminated. Suburbia and the economy of the Little King face a long and irrevocable retirement.

Meanwhile, a new region of opportunity will rise and prosper. Because it is the fifth region of opportunity (the fifth "urb" since the beginning of the industrial era), I call it "penturbia."

Eight

Predicting penturbia—the fifth region of opportunity

DID the year 1 A.D. seem like the beginning of a new era to Romans living in that pivotal century? Probably not. Poll those toga-clad senators as they emerge from the Forum. Ask them what the world will be like in a thousand years. They will tell you, "The power, the gods and the society of Rome will prevail."

We needn't feel superior. The human propensity to project the immediate past into the indefinite future remains a constant. By the 1970s, the economy of the Caring Conserver had been alive and pulsing for more than a decade. Few noticed it. A new migration was beginning to reshape the American landscape. Most everyone, including the experts, seemed unaware of it.

For over a century, the reigning assumption—that people would continue pouring out of rural locations into the metropolitan areas—had remained the same. The trend was inexorable and the experts "proved" it. We could safely predict ever-increasing densities of urban populations. On the average, small cities would become medium-sized cities, medium-sized cities would become larger, and the largest cities would become still larger.

In 1975 the author of a well-known text on urban development asked, "Why then, do urban populations rise both relatively and absolutely, all over the globe?" [1] His answer came from the core of the profession: people *choose* the urban condition. They always do. They always will. Large cities permit greater specialization, which means low-cost mass production and distribution. The larger the city the greater its capacity to produce what people want—houses, automobiles, appliances, schools, hospitals, theaters, bowling alleys, golf courses, political rallies, and gala celebrations.

But while urban economists were explaining that migration had to proceed from rural to urban areas, people were already reversing direction and moving from urban to rural areas.

In 1975 Calvin L. Beale, an eminent demographer, was among the first formally to proclaim the change. He documented it in an obscure monograph published by the U.S. Department of Agriculture, entitled *The Revival of Population Growth in Non-metropolitan America.*[2] By 1977—long after the migration had actually begun—a spate of technical publications at last acknowledged the changing patterns.[3]

By 1978 news of the migration had filtered down to popular journals. But by unduly emphasizing population changes *among* states, economists had overlooked a vital fact: populations were also shifting *within* states—from large population centers to smaller ones, from urban to rural. The narrow selection of facts gave the impression that the migration was from Frostbelt to Sunbelt. In fact, counties favored in the fifth surge are scattered throughout most of the fifty states. In 1981 a *Newsweek* cover story, "The Small Town Boom," presented a more accurate version of what was really happening.[4] It noted a shift in preference from the big-city life-style to the slower pace of the small-town environment.

It would be simplistic to explain the current enthusiasm for small towns as regressive, a return to the life of early-nineteenth-century America. The socioeconomic circumstances of the two periods are utterly different. Small towns of the 1800s catered to the Bantam Capitalist, to an economy dominated by dirt-poor laborers aspiring to become capitalists. Small towns in the 1980s further the objectives of the Caring Conserver, of an economy dominated by an affluent generation with a unique mandate. The new economy aims to end the profligacy of its consumer-oriented predecessor, the economy of the Little King.

The insatiable hunger for consumption found its central location in *suburbia*—the fourth region developed since the outset of the modern industrial era. Efforts to subdue that hunger are sited in counties I call *penturbia*—the *fifth* region of opportunity since the beginning of industrialization.

Explaining penturbia is best accomplished by means of a conversation with a fictional character. Meet Harold Beaverton, composite student, investor, and client.

A conversation with Harold Beaverton, chairman, "XYZ Land Company"

HB: My predecessors in the company have generally assumed that land values only go up. So they kept buying and stockpiling. They never sold except for immediate development—for shopping centers, industrial parks, or the like. As a result, we own thousands of acres around the country.

Author: I take it you want to consider selling off properties in declining areas and buying others with more promising prospects?

HB: Yes. I am looking toward a managed portfolio of land—like a portfolio of stocks owned by a mutual fund. And I would like to consider shifting out of suburbia and more heavily into what you call "penturbia."

Author: You would like information on the precise location of penturbia?

HB: At your convenience.

Author: And you shall have it. My forecast of that fifth type of city is shown in Figure 32. Another map shows counties in the fifth region of obsolescence—those least favored for investment. [Figure 33.]

Figure 32:
THE FIFTH REGION OF OPPORTUNITY, 1980–2010
Locations of Counties

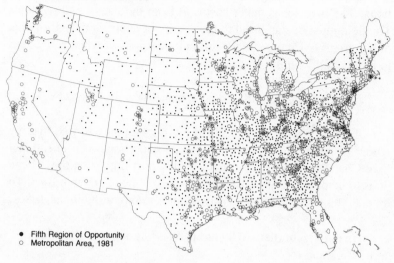

- ● Fifth Region of Opportunity
- ○ Metropolitan Area, 1981

Figure 33:
THE FIFTH REGION OF OBSOLESCENCE, 1980–2010
Locations of Counties

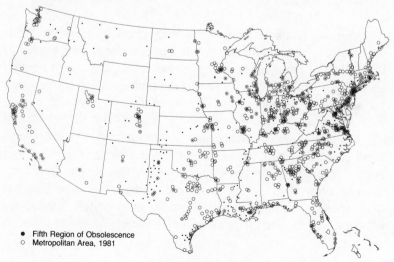

- ● Fifth Region of Obsolescence
- ○ Metropolitan Area, 1981

HB: Is *every* county in penturbia favorable for investment?

Author: Generally favorable, but there are bound to be variations. The investor is never absolved from the need for discretion. The field must be narrowed to the county or counties best fitting his or her criteria. Then come the difficult decisions of when and where to buy or sell *within* a given county.

HB: Can you help the investor make those decisions?

Author: I believe I can. Read my book. You will find that the whole of penturbia is broken down into additional classifications. [See Chapters Eleven–Fifteen.] But the most important thing I can do is to help you to reason about these investments on your own. To do that you must understand *why* people are migrating in the 1980s.

HB: All right then. Why are people migrating in the 1980s?

Author: Will you promise to hear me out even when I seem to be taking the long way round?

HB: I'll do my best.

Author: To understand why people are migrating in the 1980s we have to begin with the key problem of our times—overconsumption. For the previous economy of the Little King, consumption spending was a necessity. It solved the problem of overproduction bequeathed by the industrial Colossus of the nineteenth century. It was only after spending went out of control—by the 1960s and 1970s—that consumption became overconsumption. Today, everything about the economy of the Little King comes together in an orgy of spending. Government spends more than it can afford—on defense, on welfare, on the environment, and much more. The rest of us spend more than we can afford on automobiles, houses, appliances. . . . No need to name them all, there's no end to it.

HB: I'm sure we all spend too much. But how is that relevant to migration?

Author: Patience . . . We'll get to migration in due course. But first you'll need to grasp the relationship of overconsumption to the availability of capital. Because so many of us still *think* as Little Kings—both as individuals and as a government—we simply do not save enough to balance the immense amount of capital we need for research and development, modernization of industries, welfare programs, defense programs, the Third World, bridges and dams, and so on. It is not surprising that we suffer from an acute shortage of capital.

HB: It seems to me there is plenty of capital. Read the newspapers any day in the week. Banks are soliciting borrowers with full-page advertisements. "Rainier Bank has $400 million to lend." And they're not the only ones begging us to take their money. What makes you think we're suffering from capital shortages? Where's the evidence?

Author: The best evidence is chronically high interest rates. Interest is the price of capital. Fluctuations in interest depend on fluctuations in supply of capital. Less than a decade ago, 9 percent would have seemed exorbitant. Now, if the rate is ever as low as 9 percent people rush to take advantage of it. Furthermore, high interest rates are politically unpopular. Don't you think the Administration would lower them if they could? I call all of this hard evidence of capital shortage.

HB: I would interpret that evidence differently. The reason for high interest rates is not capital shortage but inflation—or the expectation of inflation.

Author: Yes, but what causes inflation?

HB: An imbalance between demand and supply. Either demand is too large or supply is too small. Demand grows at a gallop, supply only trots along.

Author: I like your way of putting it. Now let me ask two questions. First, *why is demand so large?* I'll tell you. Because of overconsumption: we violate the proper balance between consuming and saving, between what we want now and making adequate provision for the future. Second, *why is supply so small?* Again, the answer is overconsumption—overconsumption in the past. The capital we need now must come from previously accumulated savings, but those savings are obviously inadequate. The rest you know. Inadequate savings mean inadequate stocks of capital, which limits our capacity to produce. There aren't enough plants to produce all the things we want, not enough modern equipment in the plants we have, not enough teachers and classrooms to teach unemployed workers what they need to know about new technologies. Because of an incapacity to produce, demand outstrips supply. When demand outstrips supply we have inflation.

HB: So overconsumption is the root problem?

Author: Indeed. Overconsumption is the ultimate mischief maker. It is spending that is not for productive investment, in amounts that create imprudent debts. In this sense, overconsumption includes spending on defense and welfare as well as on automobiles and houses. Whether we spend too much in the public or the private sector, it comes to the same thing—we are living beyond our means, permissively, without discipline. Almost every chronic social and economic problem facing us at the end of the twentieth century can be traced to overconsumption.

Take the federal deficit. Like any debt, the federal deficit is the result of not paying back what has been spent. It's a lack of discipline. Either we have been spending too much or paying back too little. Spend less and the deficit goes down. The deficit can be further reduced by diverting funds from nonproductive spending to capital goods. When the supply of capital is greater, the economy is more productive. A more productive economy generates more income with which to pay taxes. With more taxes government can better afford to pay its debts.

HB: All right. All right. Suppose for a moment we agree that overconsumption is a serious problem. What does that have to do with migration?

Author: Trust me. We'll get to migration in a moment. But first I would like you to see that many people all over the country are aware of the problem. They're not taking overconsumption lightly.

HB: I don't hear economists or politicians talking about it. My friends and neighbors don't seem to be aware of it either. What I do hear about is inflation or potential inflation, high interest rates, deficits, failing banks. As for concern about overconsumption, on the contrary, the people I know seem to be spending as much as they can.

Author: That's how it *seems*. But more and more people have become conscious of a spending problem. It became evident in the 1970s—about the same time the latest migration became highly visible. Though no one used the word *overconsumption,* that's when a groundswell of feeling against unlimited consumption first appeared among masses of Americans. Let me refresh your memory. In 1976 a Louis Harris poll reported that a large majority of interviewees— almost three to one—agreed that it is "morally wrong" for Americans to consume 40 percent of the world's energy and raw materials when we constitute a mere 5½ percent of the world's population.[5] Shortly afterward, a reporter from the *Wall Street Journal* asked, "Austerity ahead?"—and answered that "the idea wins surprising acceptance among Americans." Only a minority of those interviewed by all pollsters felt that traditional life-styles could continue unchanged.[6]

HB: I remember. Remorse was rather heavy in the 1970s.

Author: Remorse is the right word. Americans felt that they were pressing on the limited supply of the world's goods, even to the detriment of their own health. I remember one person who complained at the time that he couldn't buy bread in a plastic bag, eat a hamburger, wear knit pants, or flush a toilet without being guilty of consuming some product that is either deadly to life's long-range continuance or in diminishing supply. He had to cope with his individual guilt as a modern consumer, he said, or run naked into the woods and starve.

HB: People got over those feelings. Nobody wants to wear hairshirts or deny the flesh. There's no lobby seeking to lower the standard of living.

Author: You're right about the standard of living, but wrong about overconsumption. Without guidance from philosophers, economists, or politicians, increasing numbers are doing something about the problem. Caring Conservers have found a way to deal with overconsumption by the most astonishing feat of social alchemy.

HB: Social alchemy! You're joking.

Author: Maybe half joking. The alchemy is this: Caring Conservers *change their sense of values*—by consensus. Faced with the necessity of buying less of what they prefer, people change what they prefer. They shift their preferences from things that are expensive to things that are inexpensive. Perhaps you will recognize in this the alchemist's magic: something perceived as near worthless is, presto, converted into purest gold. This can happen because, as I said, there is another sense of values. Or to put it somewhat differently, the "beholder of beauty" is growing a new pair of eyes. Caring Conservers don't turn grudgingly to their substitutes. *They adore them.*

HB: Your analysis of Caring Conservers puzzles me. If I remember my college economics, individuals are free to determine their own values and priorities, to decide what they want to buy and how much they should pay for it. In a free society we're all basically independent.

Author: In the details we're independent, yes, in the types, sizes, and prices of our purchases. The assortment of computers that fit different tastes and pocketbooks is bewildering. But why are we all coming to want computers—and at the same time? In the larger vision, wants are not independent but social. A man of the fifties wanted an eight-cylinder car. A man of the eighties wants a jogging uniform. Once all of us agree to change what we want, we are as happy living by one set of values as another. By changing what we want, we gently draw pressure away from resources made scarce by past preferences. As Caring Conservers we downgrade spending. We are pleased, oh yes, even delighted, by things that are cheap or free.

HB: I get your drift. But tell me, what cheap or free things do people substitute for spending?

Author: You have just asked *the* question of the evening. The major substitute for spending is penturbia.

HB: Are you serious?

Author: I am. More specifically, it is the life-style of "self-fulfillment" in penturbia. The way pollster and social analyst Daniel Yankelovich explains it, self-fulfillment is a movement sweeping toward an inspirational array of intangibles. Emphasis is on sharing, participation, adventure, and joy of living.[7] Though Yankelovich doesn't make the connection, self-fulfillment, with its stress on intangibles, minimizes the drain on capital. Conservation in the new economy becomes as pleasurable as profligacy was in the old.

HB: There is undoubtedly a growing interest in self-fulfillment. Even the word has popular appeal. But I'd like to hear more about the connection between self-fulfillment and penturbia.

Author: The two are inseparable. Penturbia is where the Caring Conserver can best enjoy a life of self-fulfillment, where he or she can live better on less. Self-fulfillment comes more easily at the foot of a blue-gray mountain and a few strides from a creek. The genius of the Caring Conserver thrives in the intimacy of small, rural areas where people call each other by their first names, within jogging distance of forests, mountains, and rivers, where most everyone hikes, swims, camps, and skis, and where creative, artistic, do-it-yourself projects of all kinds are "in" and win prestige from the community.

HB: Are we to become a nation of sprites and wood nymphs?

Author: Have no fear. It's true that the change will be immense. But we'll still drive our cars, live in modern houses, and continue to enjoy our stereos.

HB: Whew! That's a relief. To use a cliché, we can have our cake and eat it too.

Author: So long as it's the Caring Conserver's carrot-and-zucchini cake. This small-town recipe for living substitutes free or cheap things for the urban extravagances that drain our savings and consume our capital.

- Gifts bestowed by nature—sumptuous scenery and sheer space—substitute for expensive goods and services made necessary by the artificialities of urban life.

- Rural counties are the natural milieu of the underground economy. Productivity and savings multiply as people use "spare" time and "free" land at home to produce things they would otherwise have to buy at high prices—things expensively produced, transported, brokered, and retailed in metropolitan areas. Bartering is commonplace in penturbia. Trading expert skills and advice, penturbians can build their own homes at minimum cost. They sew their own clothes, raise their own food. And home-grown foods are regarded as a substitute for expensive health care because they are less polluted by pesticides and other chemicals.

- Closeness of jobs to homes in small towns substitutes short commutes for lengthy ones often required in metropolitan areas. (Demographers Gladys K. Bowles and Calvin L. Beale estimate that even excluding farmers and others working at home, work trips in nonmetro counties are, on the average, 40 percent shorter.)[8]

- Decrepit nineteenth-century structures rich in nostalgia (plentiful in many rural counties) are joyfully restored and substituted for costlier modern buildings. Or, on typical lots of one to five acres, Caring Conservers—aided by more flexible building and zoning codes—can substitute cheaper, rapidly installed mobile homes ("manufactured housing") for more expensive, conventional construction.

- Finally, Caring Conservers volunteer their loving labor as a substitute for expensive services in schools and hospitals and in ministering to the young, the elderly, and the handicapped.

HB: I grant you, that's a striking array of substitutes. If magnified by a population of millions, the capital savings would be enormous. But surely some of the activities you mention aren't limited to penturbia. Volunteering, for example. People volunteer everywhere—in every city and suburb throughout America.

Author: That's true. The economy of the Caring Conserver is felt throughout the nation. Migration begins in the mind, as people everywhere are increasingly dissatisfied with the squandering life of the Little King. All of us feel the problem—you, I, everyone. And we feel it wherever we happen to be—in cities, suburbs, or penturbs, in every region of the country. To solve the problem we activate the new economy. Volunteering is one way of activating the economy of the Caring Conserver. It is one of the many trends that was set in motion during the late 1950s and that became more pervasive during the 1970s. The fifth region of opportunity is not the *exclusive* home of the Caring Conserver, but it is the *ideal* home, where that economy can be best implemented. It is the region best able to serve the new requirements.

HB: Isn't it possible that what you call penturbia is simply the outward extension of suburbia, that we are merely substituting remote and cheaper land for land that has become too expensive? I would especially like to know if the migrants themselves think they are doing what you say they are doing. Do you have objective evidence of their motives?

Author: Perhaps you would be interested in a sample of 501 households studied by Professors James D. Williams and Andrew J. Sofranko. They interviewed people who had moved between 1970 and 1977 from a metropolitan area to any of 75 rapidly growing nonmetropolitan counties in the Midwest.[9]

HB: And what did they find?

Author: That the migrants are no longer looking for suburbia, that "the growth of nonmetropolitan America is not simply suburban sprawl." Twenty-five of the 75 nonmetropolitan counties studied were adjacent to metropolitan areas, but a minuscule 8 percent of the migrants had migrated from a nearby city or suburb. Another study, by Gladys K. Bowles and Calvin L. Beale, shows that only a small percentage of those migrating from metropolitan to nonmetropolitan areas continued to work in cities and suburbs. Conclusion? The present migration is not a reshuffling but an actual break with earlier patterns.[10]

HB: Even so, isn't it also possible that people are moving for the obvious reason that they need jobs? More jobs are appearing in nonmetropolitan areas—in recreation, information and energy industries, and in services for the retired.

Author: Let me refer you again to Williams and Sofranko. "Our most dramatic finding contradicts traditional migration studies that stress the importance of employment to migration. Based on probing interviews about why people move, we found instead an emphasis on the quality of life." Seventy-six percent of the migrants cited reasons other than employment as their motive for making the move.[11]

HB: But are you prepared to say that people come to these remote places because they want to solve the problem of overconsumption? That's an astounding idea.

Author: Astounding only because the concept of overconsumption is abstract and theoretical—and as individuals we can be stirred only by the concrete, the immediate, and the corporeal. Our muscles "know" that a piano is heavy, not that it is being pulled into the center of the earth by the force of gravity. Our eyes recognize the color "red," not a wavelength of .0000303 inches. But there is aways an exact translation from one to the other. Let me ask what may seem to be a frivolous question. Why do people make love?

HB: Why ask? They enjoy it.

Author: Obviously. But why do they enjoy it? There's a stark reality behind that enjoyment: the necessity to ensure the continuity of the community and the species. It is doubtful that any Don Juan ever seduced his lady with anguished appeals to promote the general welfare, and yet lovers do provide a community service. That is the exact, though abstract, truth. Behind individual motivations there are always *higher reasons*—the imperatives of the group.

HB: I see what you mean. "Higher reasons" belong in the picture even though we're not ordinarily aware of them. And in this case, by "higher reasons" you mean the necessity to solve the problem of overconsumption.

Author: Solving that problem is as necessary to the perpetuation of our economic life as having children is to the perpetuation of the species. At this time, overconsumption is our key problem. So long as it remains unsolved it's as though we were all aboard a foundering ship. If the ship goes down everyone drowns. We all try to keep the ship afloat because somewhere in our social consciousness we understand that each life can be saved only if all are saved.

HB: I see the logic of your position. But where's the evidence? If migrants were indeed acting to keep the ship upright, that is, to solve the problem of overconsumption, they would be trying to end their spendthrift ways. That isn't happening. We are a people accustomed to luxury and I don't quite see any great change coming in the near future. We like our expensive restaurants, long vacations, stylish clothing. Do you have any statistics showing that migrants to your fifth region of opportunity actually spend less than they used to?

Author: At this early point, only some intriguing clues suggest that they do. Almost half of Williams and Sofranko's respondents said that their new life-style is less expensive.[12] I can assure you that the percentage who feel that way will grow. You should bear in mind that in the 1980s we're all Little Kings in transition—and that includes the migrants. It's hard to break with the temptations of spending. But it will happen, because it must. And there is evidence that we're on our way. The same study shows that migrants are well aware of receiving valuable benefits that are abundant and free in the new areas. I quote Williams and Sofranko: "91 percent of respondents who moved from cities say the environment is healthier in their new location. About 82 percent say they now feel safer, and 87 percent say the rural area is a better place to raise children.'' [13] To solve the problem of overconsumption, Caring Conservers must increasingly substitute these free things for the goods and services bought by the Little Kings.

HB: They "must." But will they?

Author: Not "they." *We.* We will all change our ways. We always do.

HB: I'd like to believe you, but I'm more pessimistic than you are. Can a few people living in the sticks really make a major contribution to solving the problem of overconsumption? Are *they* going to pay off our federal deficits, finance the Third World, modernize our industries, repair the ruts in our streets, rebuild our bridges and dams, and satisfy the demands of the private sector?

Author: Don't be fooled by what you see today. The present trickle will accumulate into a river, then a flood. Try to imagine the eventual transformation. In the next century, most middle-class Americans will be living in the penturbs. You have difficulty imagining that, don't you? Well, it was just as hard to imagine the migrations of the past. In 1930, how many experts—let alone laymen—could have foreseen that middle-class America would soon leave the cities and move to the suburbs? Not many. The same applies to 1985. Penturbs—the fifth region of opportunity—is the new frontier.

HB: So you believe that because we're on our way toward solving the problem of overconsumption in 1985, the present capital shortage will disappear?

Author: Without a doubt. I'll let you in on a little secret. In several decades, the Caring Conservers will create a very different and world-shaking problem: *too much* capital. We'll be drowning in it. Every new economy goes too far in solving its key problem. So it was with the Mercantile Aristocrat, the Bantam Capitalist, the Colossus, and the Little King, and so it will be with the Caring Conserver. This new economy, too, will eventually be driven to its own form of excess and perish as a result of it. Meanwhile—in your own lifetime—you will see spectacular growth in penturbia.

Nine

Don't be confused by overlap

EVERY economy overlaps a preceding economy. The result is a superimposing of conflicting trends and different migratory surges.

In the 1980s there is no better example of confusion due to overlap than in the popular notion that people are migrating from Frostbelt to Sunbelt. Americans are presumably attracted by better weather. In fact, almost every one of the nation's fifty states contains rapidly growing counties favored by the Caring Conserver.

Exaggeration of the Sunbelt's importance stems from failure to consider overlap. In the 1970s, counties of both the Colossus and the Little King economies were either declining or growing at a declining rate. At the same time, counties of the Caring Conserver were rising.

In the Frostbelt, rising counties are often hidden by state population figures. Between 1970 and 1975 tiny Clinton County in New York State grew by 14.1 percent; Greene grew by 15.3 percent and Putnam by 22.4 percent. In the state totals, these extraordinary increases were obscured by the 5.2 percent decline of New York City with its 7.9 million.

The problem is one of averaging elephants and fleas. The Sunbelt states—with fewer large metropolitan areas created by the third and fourth migrations—easily show rapid gains in their state totals.

Analyses typically fail to distinguish between fourth- and fifth-surge counties within the Sunbelt. The Sunbelt too has its share of both types, each with a different forecast. For one it is down; for the other, up. Late bloomers of the fourth surge are easily confused with early bloomers of the fifth. For example, Phoenix, Houston, and San Diego are late bloomers of the fourth surge. All had rising population shares in the 1950s continuing into the 1970s.

The investor who fails to consider the overlap between fourth and fifth surges is vulnerable to a high risk.

Ten

Land can and does depreciate

ANCIENT wisdom speaks: everything in this world eventually dies—people, possessions, cultures, and societies—but not the land. Land is space on the planet. For millions of years to come, barring some rare astronomical accident, the planet will persist in its orbit around the sun. Land is indestructible. Even the IRS says so. A lathe can be written off in six years, a computer in twelve, a building in eighteen—land in an eternity. Land does not depreciate.

Except in the special world of the IRS, land can and does depreciate, as does the real estate in which it is embodied. The cause of depreciation? Obsolescence. A particular piece of land can become as obsolete as a three-year-old computer. At the end of three years the computer is still intact. Its circuits still whirl electric currents with unerring aim. But it is superseded by later, smaller, faster, more sophisticated computers. So it is with land in a region of opportunity that has become obsolete.

Such a region is like a faithful servant trained to serve one master. When a new master with a very different temperament and needs takes over, the servant, whose habits have crystallized, cannot be more than second-rate. He will be replaced. The rise of a new economy nails a lid on the past.

Obsolescence could be mitigated if adjustments to the emerging economy were made rapidly enough to match the pace of change, if changing social and economic relationships were welcomed and incorporated into the current stream of life. In the case of mature real estate, this does not happen. Adjustment is neither easy nor rapid, for it is the nature of real estate to resist change. When change is denied, obsolescence is inexorable.

In the nineteenth century, the Cockerill steel plants of southern Belgium were the most modern and productive in the world. Their location, inland and close to the coal fields, was ideal for the 1800s, but not for the 1980s. Today these plants are all but moribund. Yet they stand: monstrous structures partly sleeping, partly functioning, partly crumbling, an enormous patch of obsolescence casting a pall upon a wide area. A discouraging environment for industrialists who might consider locating there. The community suffers from chronically high levels of unemployment, innumerable dissatisfactions, and a foundering local economy.

Counties resist change for many reasons. One is that a real-estate structure is virtually anchored to the spot on which it is built. Designed for permanence, it is expected to endure. And it does endure. A building may fail in its plumbing and wiring, its floors may buckle and its plaster disintegrate, but until a more profitable use can be found for the site, it will escape the wrecking ball.

Of course, partial adjustments can be made. A structure uneconomical in its original use can be consigned to other uses. A school is converted into a factory, a warehouse into a theater, a millionaire's mansion into low-income apartments. But these are "make-do" arrangements and rarely ideal. The original structure always intrudes, always prevents total adjustment to changing circumstances.

There is another reason for resistance to change. Real-estate units are not independent entities. Civic centers, schools, downtown areas, and parks are all built to serve a community at a particular time. As an investor operating in the unique context of the Caring Conserver, I would be ill-advised to erect an industrial campus for high-tech firms in a city that does not attract high-tech professionals with the right neighborhoods, schools, galleries, shopping centers, and concert halls.

High-tech firms seek a comprehensive support system involving the choicest environment and personnel drawn from the most elite elements of society. By contrast, the "lowest-tech" firms are enmeshed in a very different system. Theirs is a world of blight, slums, poverty, despair, and crime—a fabric of social and economic relationships so tightly woven that only the human equivalent of a nuclear explosion could break its hold.

Consider the Bronx, in New York City, since World War II. Here is the machinery of obsolescence all of a piece: the unskilled and uneducated, the gangs, the dope peddlers, the prostitutes, all crowded into neighborhoods where ugly, dilapidated housing and stench-producing factories are the norm.

And here, too, are the industries offering the lowest-paying jobs for manual labor. Labor will be plentiful. Dense belts of minorities live here, poor blacks and Puerto Ricans, crowded into old buildings whose designers never imagined such an evolution. Brownstones, once the envy of the middle class, are converted into squalid rooming houses. Apartments barely adequate for one family are sublet to two or more families.

The "invisible hand" of economics beckons the area's landlords to capitalize on their two big advantages: closeness to Manhattan and cheap real estate per capita. Both result in hastening obsolescence—first, by creating more and more rental units up to the legally permissible limit and, second, by reducing the amount of service and maintenance down to the lowest permissible limit. Poverty and despair, the stealthy enemies, are inevitable.

In the Bronx, poverty and despair are a rich ore to be mined by "low-tech" firms. Contractors and subcontractors in the garment industry seek out pockets of cheap female labor to mass-produce clothing for sale around the country. They make use of the same two assets: closeness to Manhattan (where designers and buyers congregate) and obsolescence of the housing supply (where labor is cheap and plentiful). Meanwhile, the lesser demand for male labor feeds a cycle of broken homes, gangs, crime, and narcotic addictions. As Saul Bellow's Toby Winthrop describes it in *The Dean's December:* "Those people are down in the cesspool. We reach for them and try to get a hold. Hang on—hang on! They'll drown in the shit if we can't pull 'em out.'' [1]

It is the intricacy of total systems, the tangle and snarl of countless interdependencies that makes change so painfully slow. If we could somehow eliminate interdependence, we could speed the pace of change from slum-riddled decadence to modern high-tech marvels. But we can't. Interdependence is the essence of economic life.

Change would come more easily if a network of real estate wore out all at once. Then it could be replaced all at once. This does not happen. We are nagged and nudged by the need for myriad small, uneconomical changes coming at random moments. Instead of one apocalyptic fix, we jack up a thousand foundations, patch ten thousand roofs, resurface many separate miles of freeway. There is never a time, any one time when we will find it practical to rebuild everything at once.

And there's one more reason for intransigence in the face of change: the high cost of land. Favored counties develop over many decades. Their increasing rates of growth push land values ever upward. With few large acreages available, the difficulties of assembling land in a mature area add still another increment to the cost of land: absentee owners are often hard to reach and isolated "holdouts" have been known to extort exorbitant prices. High land values often persist long after an area begins to decline. What keeps values up are the poor people who seek cheap housing and who are willing to live under crowded conditions. In 1957 the price of blighted land in the Bronx was over four times greater than choice land in suburban Westchester. [2]

High land values—as distinct from rising values—are warranted only for uses serving the old pattern. But that pattern is largely irrelevant to the new economy. The new users require something different. For them, the high cost of land cannot be justified. It will constitute another impediment to growth in the mature counties.

When the economy changes, immobility, interdependence, and high land values converge to create an inhospitable environment for growth. No impediment to future development is greater than that offered by a county recently gorged on the real-estate patterns and prices of the *preceding* economy. Development must constantly respawn in new areas. Typically, a season of hibernation follows a season of rapid growth. Counties attracting population are either located on land never settled before or in areas so old, so obsolete, and so little identified with the *last* economy that they are ready for another cycle of growth.

Every new region of opportunity is located as far from obsolescing land as circumstances permit. For example, suburbs of the Little King initially had to be close to the central cities of the Colossus. The jobs were there, along with retail centers, financial markets, educational opportunities, everything needed to nurture the growing suburbs until they could sustain themselves. But umbilical ties to the mother cities were loosened as soon as the suburbs were able to supply a gamut of facilities of their own. As suburbs grew larger, more versatile, and more self-contained, proximity to the old central cities became increasingly irrelevant—even undesirable.

A mounting repulsion between new and old regions can be observed on maps of metropolitan areas. Locations of the earliest suburbs resembled the pattern of bullet holes made by a marksman shooting at a target. A definite concentric form rings the central city. In time, however, the target lost its significance. The pattern became more scattered, eccentric, and, some believed, chaotic.

Does growth beget growth? Or is every long period of growth terminated by obsolescence?

Having grown early in the century in the service of the Bantam Capitalist, major eastern cities presumably were endowed with a superior capacity for further growth. Each bustling metropolis monopolized huge markets. Accessibility to raw materials and industrial suppliers permitted lowest possible production costs.

But Boston, New York, and Philadelphia did not leap into the new industrial age. They limped into it. From 1860 to 1890, they barely kept pace with average increases in U.S. population. Fettered by the obsolete real estate and institutions of the Bantam Capitalist

economy, these cities were unprepared for hugeness. Everything
was far too small for the emerging Colossus. Most factories were
tiny, fragmented structures. Much of the retail business was con-
ducted in lofts, stables, back rooms, basements, and one-room
shops. By midcentury that small-scale economy was being rapidly
eclipsed. At a time when small businesses were daily being swal-
lowed by giant national corporations, cities catering to smallness
were unable to compete.

Note the phlegmatic growth of the great coastal cities (see Figure 34).

As the diagram shows, Chicago, a hick town in 1860, hurtled
into the industrial age as though it rightfully belonged there, inci-

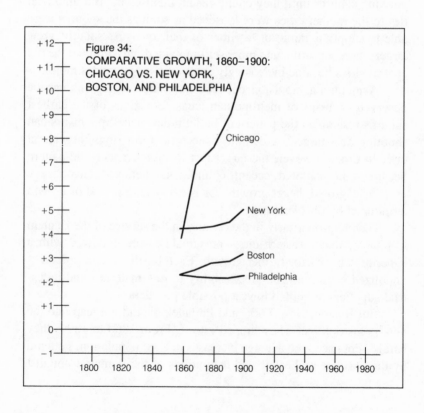

Figure 34:
COMPARATIVE GROWTH, 1860–1900:
CHICAGO VS. NEW YORK,
BOSTON, AND PHILADELPHIA

dentally mocking conventional theory, which would have left it a slumbering backwater far from the mainstream.

Partly responsible for Chicago's success was its accessibility to waterways, raw materials, and railroads, but even these advantages were largely duplicated in the eastern cities. There had to be something else, some reason for migrants and new businesses to prefer Chicago over other places. There were, in fact, two reasons. One was Chicago's central location within the emerging region of opportunity. The other was an abundance of something rare among the cities on the east coast: vacant land.

Not only was Chicago built on new land, so was its hinterland of villages, towns, and cities. Chicago and its network of interdependent areas enjoyed maximum freedom to shape the physical environment in accord with current preferences. Architects and engineers of the new age designed centralized systems supporting armies of workers along with countless machines able to move mountains of materials over half a continent. The city developed real estate that suited the emerging Colossus.

But soon it was Chicago's turn to face the opposition of a new economy. In the twentieth century, the Little King was on the rise. Promoters of subdivisions with bucolic names like "Golden Meadows," "Sleepy Hollow Estates," or "Orchard Hills," were little tempted to invest capital in the city's gray and grimy neighborhoods. Long before 1930, Chicago's growth slowed. Where growth had once tripled each decade, now it merely doubled, then less than doubled. After 1930 its comparative growth began to recede. The economy had changed, but Chicago was unable to change with it. Its cramped city lots had been laid out before people turned their dreaming around from saving all they could to spending all they could. Unresponsive, unable to compete with suburban houses built on cheap, large, and sunny lots, Chicago was now the city of obsolescence.

The economic destinies of counties do not typically swerve up and down from decade to decade. They do not ordinarily wax and wane with shifting political programs of municipal administrations, nor are they shaken off a centuries-old course by the antics of local heroes or villains. Rather, each county plows its massive furrow through history. No individual can change its ultimate destiny, but every individual can make use of its predictability, can set his or her investment clock by what can be known about that destiny. Note again the consistency of any of the three regions examined in Chapters Two–Five. The third region of opportunity, for example, rises for the first 120 years of United States history and declines for the next 70, up to 1980: a rise and fall taking 190 years! (See Figure 35.)

Once an area is gripped by obsolescence, its "corruption" continues until it is returned to the "soil." The period of decline is sustained long enough to dissipate old patterns, divest vested interests, reduce population and desirability. In the distant future a new economy will eventually give the old real estate a comparative advantage and a more honored place in contemporary life. In the 1980s, such "new" land is once again the target of development, this time by the Caring Conserver.

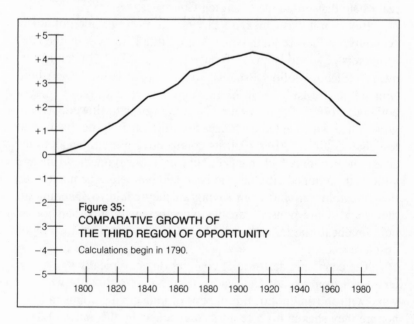

Figure 35:
COMPARATIVE GROWTH OF
THE THIRD REGION OF OPPORTUNITY

Calculations begin in 1790.

Part three

Forecasts: Seven classes of counties

Eleven

Decelerating and obsolescing counties: Classes VI and VII

I have classified counties throughout the nation in seven major classes based on their histories of population growth, each having a different potential for real-estate investment during the period from 1985 to 2010. Counties in each of the seven classifications share a common history and destiny. Classes I to IV are dominated by one or two regions of opportunity from the past. Counties in Class II, for example, flourished early in the nineteenth century as part of the second region of opportunity, then gradually obsolesced for over a hundred years. Classes VI to VII showed little promise for growth until the turn of the twentieth century.

I shall begin in reverse order, with Classes VII and VI, both belonging to the obsolescing fourth region of opportunity. A lag in timing differentiates Class VII from Class VI. VII is clearly on the decline, but VI is still rising, although at a declining rate.

To find the classifications of specific counties, see Appendix A.

Obsolescing counties: Class VII

Obsolescing counties are the furiously growing suburbs of midcentury that are now declining. More spacious counties in Class VII

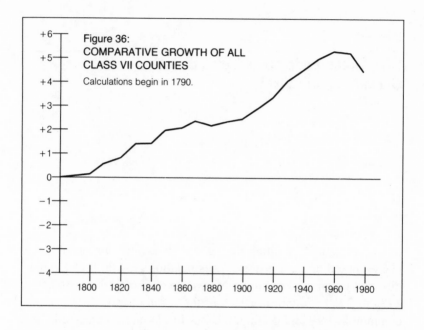

Figure 36:
COMPARATIVE GROWTH OF ALL
CLASS VII COUNTIES

Calculations begin in 1790.

may also contain older central cities established during the third migration, around the turn of the century. The class is identified by growth greater than average for 1950–1970 and slower than average for 1970–1980.

Even though counties in Class VII are designated by statistics pertaining to 1950 and later, the degree to which they share common trends for 160 years before 1950 is astonishing. Once again we see a vast, irreversible tide sweeping through almost two centuries. Class VII counties in the early nineteenth century were often lagging members of the second region of opportunity. Note the cycle from 1800 to 1880. After 1880 a second major cycle soars to a peak in the 1960s or 1970s (see Figure 36).

The map of Class VII counties shows the high proportion of counties located in metropolitan areas (Figure 37). (In terms of population, the correlation between Class VII counties and metropolitan areas is even greater.)

Figure 37:
LOCATIONS OF CLASS VII COUNTIES

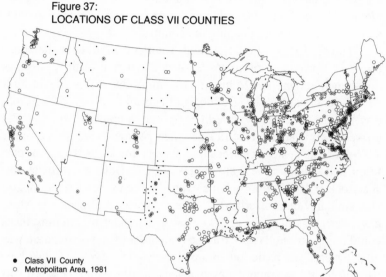

● Class VII County
○ Metropolitan Area, 1981

Facts and logic suggest a bleak outlook in the long run for most Class VII counties. These counties favored by the fourth migration and the economy of the Little King—developing rapidly after 1930—supported an economic structure geared to mass consumption. That structure was soon to become obsolete. By the 1950s, critics had begun to portray unflattering images of suburbanites as creatures extruded en masse from their culture. Lewis Mumford described the suburbs as "a multitude of uniform, unidentifiable houses, lined up inflexibly, at uniform distance, on uniform roads, in a treeless communal waste, inhabited by people of the same class, the same income, the same age group, witnessing the same television performances, eating the same tasteless pre-fabricated foods, from the same freezers, conforming in every outward and inward respect to a common mold." [1]

But the average American delighted in that conformity and its suburban setting. On March 7, 1949, William J. Levitt began selling his look-alike houses on that 1,500-acre potato farm. More than a thousand buyers waited in line, some for more than four days and nights. Those "ticky tacky boxes" represented the emerging middle-class dream then sweeping the country.[2]

The microcosm Levitt created, soon copied all over the country, was a prototype of suburbia—leading region of the consumption-minded economy. In his first assembly-line effort, Levitt built 17,500 identical houses. Bulldozers lined up and moved in formation like tanks across a battle line. On cue, a horde of street pavers arrived, followed by electricians, then by men with street signs. William Manchester describes the delivery trucks "tossing out prefabricated sidings at 8 A.M., toilets at 9:30, sinks and tubs at ten, sheetrock at 10:45, flooring at eleven."[3] The mode of consumption was similarly circumscribed. "Everything was uniform. On Mondays wash was hung in 17,500 backyards; under no circumstances could it flap on Sundays." But the high order of standardization was no deterrent. The basic four-room house sold for $6,990, a fabulous bargain for the average young marrieds of the time. To them it was no "box" but a palace for a minor monarch, his lady, and other members of the royal family.

Average Americans were Little Kings who thirsted to own and enjoy the technological marvels of their era. Suburbs were the places where that thirst could be slaked. Americans filled their carports with automobiles and their houses with freezers and furnaces, home laundries, vacuum cleaners, air conditioners, stain-resistant nylon carpets, FM radios, television sets, electric blankets, electric floor polishers, electric pencil sharpeners, and electric can openers. To titillate their palates, they purchased an unprecedented store of gourmet foods and liquors.

But the great American buffet began to pall in the 1960s and to sour in the 1970s. Suburbs springing out of farms in remote areas soon filled in the countryside to become part of vast metropolitan areas. People who believed they had escaped the city found the city crowding in around them. As the idyllic suburb merged with the congested metropolis, the "buffet" was increasingly spoiled by congestion, loss of open space, air pollution, unbalanced municipal budgets, declining standards of public service, and an epidemic of crime and drug addiction.

The simple Eden inhabited by the original Levittowners and their clones throughout the nation was now infected by galloping dissatisfactions. In the early 1970s, a fast-rising environmental movement was responsible for population ceilings and building moratoria in many areas. Self-interest was also at stake—the desire to preserve property values.

Whether out of idealism or self-interest, Los Angeles suburbanites revolted against their own bigness. In 1973 they elected a mayor who publicly renounced an earlier plan for accommodating ten million residents in the city of Los Angeles. He called the plan "insane." A notable contradiction was developing in the structure of the Little King economy. Though many clung to their aging dreams of a standardized middle-class paradise in suburbia, it was becoming increasingly obvious that the dream was dying and that no power on earth could keep it alive.

Obsolescing counties can be found in every corner of the nation, but the prototype is Los Angeles. Having risen slowly but steadily since 1860, Los Angeles' population exploded during the early and middle twentieth century. Its declining rates in the 1960s and 1970s matched the general decline of other fourth-surge counties. (See Chapter Five.)

As a result of unique factors, some Class VII counties may escape the fate of the group. King County, Washington, for example, may be accorded an economic transfusion by the rise of trade with Pacific Rim countries, especially with China. Some selected parts of Class VII counties could prove to be highly profitable, especially in the short run. In general, however, the future is likely to be grim for this class. Fourth-surge counties of the Little King are committed to patterns of the past. Counties yoked to those outdated patterns will be unable to compete for growth.

The comparative growth of individual counties in Class VII closely follows the pattern of the whole group (see Figures 38, 39, and 40).

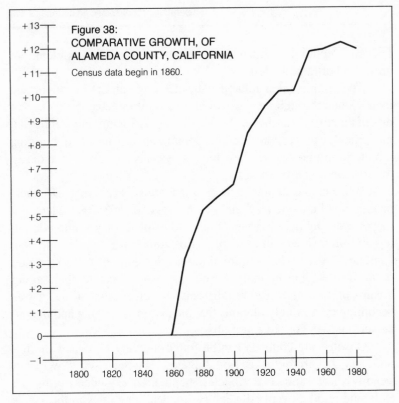

Figure 38:
COMPARATIVE GROWTH, OF
ALAMEDA COUNTY, CALIFORNIA

Census data begin in 1860.

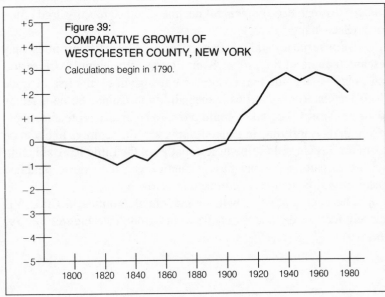

Figure 39:
COMPARATIVE GROWTH OF
WESTCHESTER COUNTY, NEW YORK

Calculations begin in 1790.

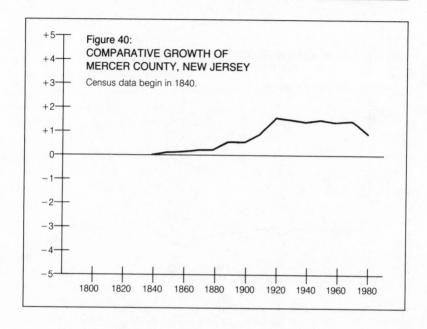

Figure 40:
COMPARATIVE GROWTH OF
MERCER COUNTY, NEW JERSEY

Census data begin in 1840.

Decelerating counties: Class VI

Decelerating counties are still growing rapidly in the 1980s, but
they are marked by impending obsolescence—the typical S-shaped
curve of deceleration. Class VI counties are identified by two conditions of comparative growth: (1) they show greater than average
growth for 1950–1970 and 1970–1980; and (2) growth slows after
1970. Although Class VI counties are identified exclusively by
post-1950 criteria, they too seem molded by a common history of
comparative growth over the entire 190 years since 1790. After
showing flat or even slightly declining growth throughout the nineteenth century (being relatively distant from metropolitan centers),
they gradually accelerate after 1900 and hit their peak in 1960 (see
Figure 41). The map shows that, like Class VII counties, Class VI
counties also tend to be located in metropolitan areas (Figure 42).
Surprisingly, Santa Clara County, home of Silicon Valley and wun-

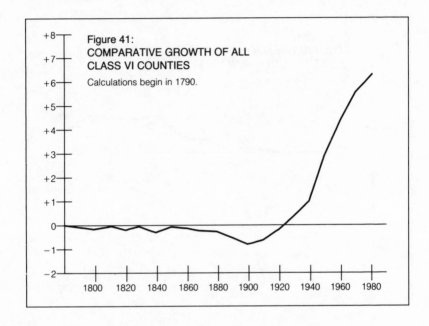

Figure 41:
COMPARATIVE GROWTH OF ALL
CLASS VI COUNTIES

Calculations begin in 1790.

Figure 42:
LOCATIONS OF CLASS VI COUNTIES

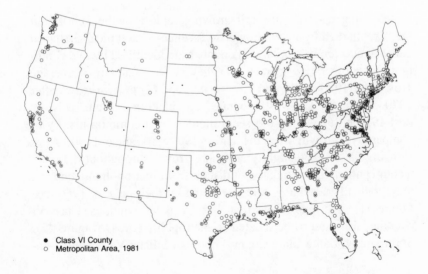

● Class VI County
○ Metropolitan Area, 1981

derkind of the nation, is one of these decelerating counties (see Figure 43).

One of the best-attended sessions at the May 1983 conference of the Urban Land Institute was devoted to "high-tech" development. The potential for this development around the nation is heightened by the exodus of high-tech firms from Silicon Valley. In a recent article, Susan Benner explains why the firms are leaving.[4] The "freeways filled with cars, the hills grew hazy behind the smog, and the driving time of some six-mile commutes lengthened to 45 minutes." Toxic chemicals were found in the public drinking

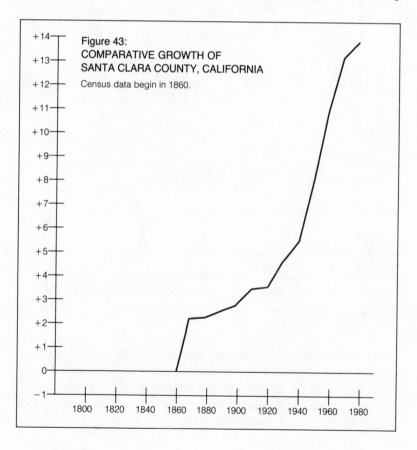

Figure 43:
COMPARATIVE GROWTH OF
SANTA CLARA COUNTY, CALIFORNIA
Census data begin in 1860.

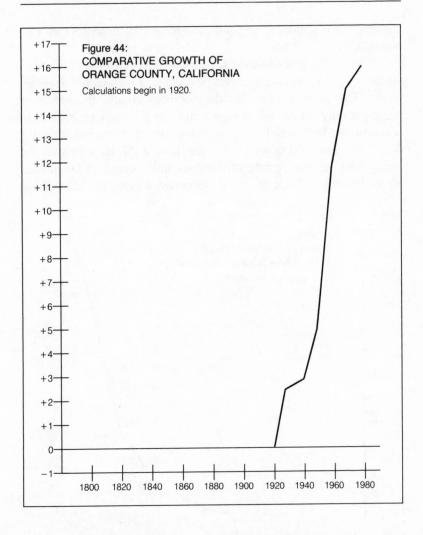

Figure 44:
COMPARATIVE GROWTH OF
ORANGE COUNTY, CALIFORNIA
Calculations begin in 1920.

water, and white-collar crime had become the order of the day (employees stole chips and circuit designs and sold them on the high-
tech black market). In addition, the price of raw land was becoming
ridiculously uncompetitive: between 8 and 12 dollars a square foot
in Santa Clara as compared with 20 cents in Austin and 65 cents in

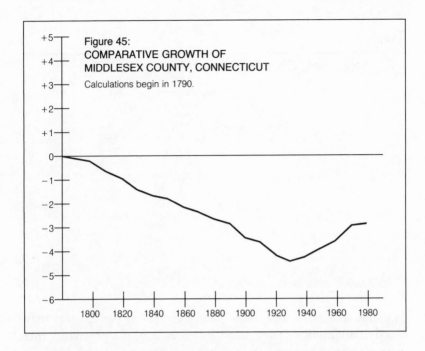

Figure 45:
COMPARATIVE GROWTH OF
MIDDLESEX COUNTY, CONNECTICUT

Calculations begin in 1790.

Colorado Springs. Moreover, raw land in Silicon Valley was virtually nonexistent. An official of the Rolm Corporation told Ms. Benner that in 1981 his company could not find the 125 acres it needed for an intended plant in South San Jose. A large number of counties like Santa Clara fall into Class VI (see Figures 44 and 45).

Twelve

Risky counties: Classes IV and V

Class V counties: Type A risk

Counties of type A risk show strong growth at present that may shortly be curtailed. They are risky because of the possibility that their present strong growth is only a masquerade—that behind today's "lion" lurks tomorrow's "mangy dog." The counties may very well be members of Class VI, but for them the decline in growth has not yet occurred. Class V counties grew rapidly during the 1970s, but they grew just as rapidly from 1950 to 1970. It is that rapid fourth-surge growth and high current land values that make them risky investment prospects for the 1980s and 1990s.

Even though the class is defined exclusively by criteria defined since 1950, (once again, with allowances for many individual variations) we see a common trend through 190 years of history. Growth of Class V counties, like that of Class VI counties, is almost flat from 1790 to 1920, followed by steady increases. Vital differences show up in the 1970s. While Class VI counties begin to slow down, Class V counties continue to accelerate (see Figure 46).[1] Like Class VI and VII counties, Class V counties also tend to be located in metropolitan areas (see Figure 47).

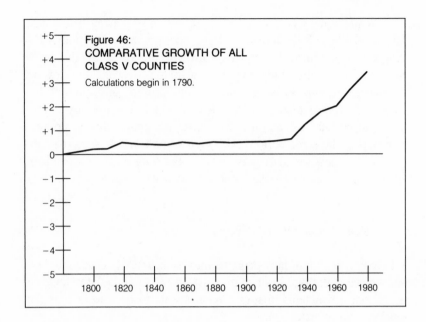

Figure 46:
COMPARATIVE GROWTH OF ALL
CLASS V COUNTIES

Calculations begin in 1790.

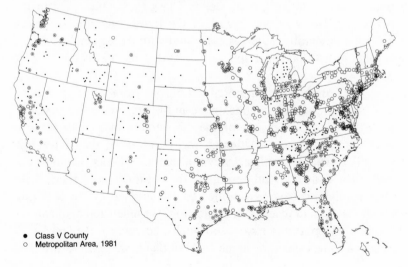

Figure 47:
LOCATIONS OF CLASS V COUNTIES

• Class V County
○ Metropolitan Area, 1981

While some Class V counties are only a step away from Class VI, other Class V counties are large enough and well enough endowed to contain valid areas of growth propelled by the latest migration. Whether they evolve toward obsolescence or toward fifth-surge growth, Class V counties may present an important disadvantage for investment. Decades of population pressures have often raised land values far above those in counties losing population during the same period. Although some Class V sites may appreciate in the short term—or even in the long term as a result of special circumstances—the evidence suggests caution.

Class IV counties: Type B risk

Whereas type A risk may drive us into bankruptcy because the winner we see is really a loser in disguise, type B risk is the reverse. It is the risk of underestimation. What seems to be a loser may, in reality, be a winner.

Type B counties show low growth at present but *may* conceivably show higher growth within the next two decades. Two conditions of comparative growth define Class IV counties: (1) in the period 1950–1970—peak years of the fourth migration—growth was on a downhill course (as compared with the national average); and (2) growth declined still further during the 1970s (see Figure 48).[2]

The *possibility* of future growth results from a particular heritage—most Class IV counties were in the third region of opportunity. They have been out of the mainstream of growth for one intervening migration. Although many are rural, they have few amenities to attract the latest surge of migrants. Others contain central cities with doubtful resources for a turnaround. Here, low-income migrants have partly filled the vacuum left by the departing middle class, and recent ''gentrification'' or redevelopment and rehabilitation programs have been unable to reverse the long-term trend. In some cases—as in the cities of San Francisco, Seattle, and

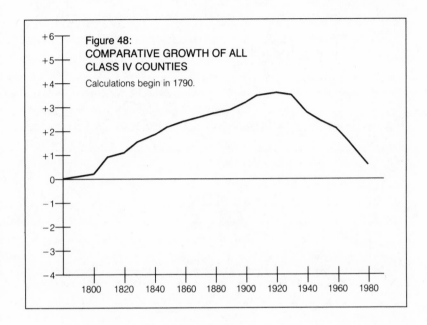

Figure 48:
COMPARATIVE GROWTH OF ALL
CLASS IV COUNTIES

Calculations begin in 1790.

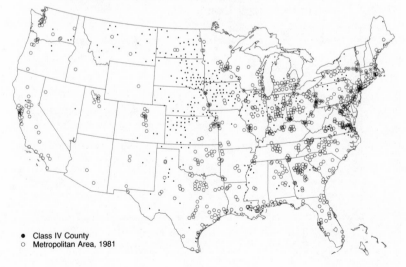

Figure 49:
LOCATIONS OF CLASS IV COUNTIES

● Class IV County
○ Metropolitan Area, 1981

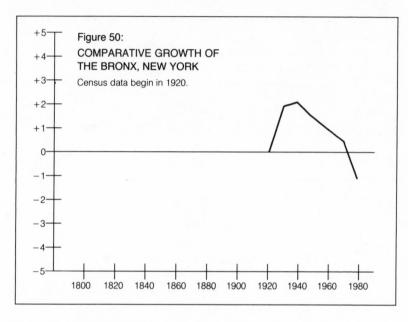

Figure 50:
COMPARATIVE GROWTH OF
THE BRONX, NEW YORK
Census data begin in 1920.

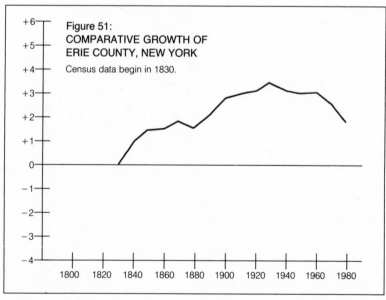

Figure 51:
COMPARATIVE GROWTH OF
ERIE COUNTY, NEW YORK
Census data begin in 1830.

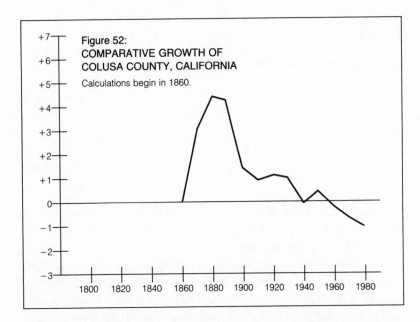

Figure 52:
COMPARATIVE GROWTH OF
COLUSA COUNTY, CALIFORNIA

Calculations begin in 1860.

New York (Manhattan)—Class IV areas have seen a recent proliferation of shops and offices because of their metropolitan and
national affiliations. Even so, the outlook is typically dimmed by
declines or decelerations in *surrounding* fourth-surge (suburban)
counties (see Figure 49).[3] Individual members of Class IV show the
typical trend (see Figures 50, 51, and 52).

Thirteen

Counties of maximum potential: Class I

WE started the classification of counties with Class VII—key to all the negative classes, from VII to IV. Now we examine Class I—key to all the positive classes, from I to III.

A first condition defining Class I counties is their less than average growth during 1950 to 1970. That lack of growth during the peak of suburban migration is their most important resource. Excluded from the great midcentury suburbanization of America, these were the backwater areas of the nation. But because they did not participate in the growth of the economy of the Little King, Class I counties are not now shackled to an obsolete suburban structure. They are unfettered by the curving superblocks, manicured lawns, and homogeneous dormitories of the swing generation. They are free of dated regional shopping centers and vast gray parking lots. They are exempt from miles of freeway congestion and air pollution. They are only slightly vulnerable to municipal deficits and drug traffic. Remoteness also insulates them from the wage demands often imposed by labor unions. Finally, they are unburdened by the Little King himself, that prisoner of belief in everything promoting consumerist values.

What these rural and semirural communities lost in growth during the fourth surge, they are now able to reclaim in the fifth. Here is a clean slate on which to write the lessons of the emerging order. Class I counties are least committed to the patterns of suburban development, least albatrossed by a spent history. They enjoy a further advantage: their land values have not soared. In some counties of Class I a temporary slowing of migration due to the deep recession of 1980–1982 brought values down to levels preceding the rapid buildup in the 1970s. It is still possible to acquire land here at bargain prices.

A Class I county is especially endowed with amenities prized by the emerging economy. One way to demonstrate a county's desirability in this regard is to compile data on resources increasingly coveted after the 1960s—view lots, proximity to outdoor recreational opportunities, and superior schools, as well as local attitudes congenial to the ethos of the postconsumption generation.

There is yet another way to identify a Class I county: Class I counties grew rapidly during the 1970s, at the same time that suburban counties gave unambiguous evidence of decline. Among all those available for migration in the United States, Class I counties have been singled out for intensive settlement.

To qualify as Class I, a county had to grow more slowly than average during 1950–1970 and a good deal faster than average during the 1970s. More precisely, it had to be among the counties containing the fastest-growing 16 percent of the national population.[1]

The shift from slow growth (or even actual loss) to rapid growth after 1970 is highly significant. Until 1970, many of the Class I counties had been obsolescing for up to a century or more. They could be jolted from their paths only by a collision with some massive object. Such an "object" was the new economy emerging in the late 1950s. By the 1970s it pressed the formerly declining counties toward a new role as prime suppliers of the new demands.

The comparative growth of Class I counties declines during most of the twentieth century and rises steeply after 1970. It is apparent that over the whole 180-year period between 1790 and 1970 Class I includes selected counties of both the second and third regions of opportunity. On the average, comparative growth of the Class I counties rises to a long plateau beginning in 1830 and falls shortly after the turn of the century (see Figure 53). The map of Class I counties shows their aversion to metropolitan locations (see Figure 54).

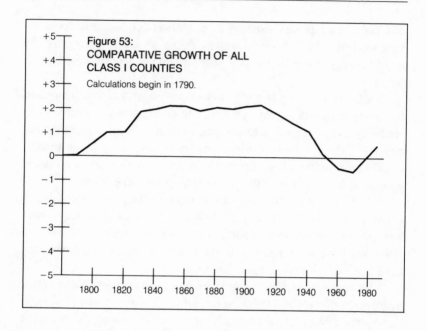

Figure 53:
COMPARATIVE GROWTH OF ALL
CLASS I COUNTIES
Calculations begin in 1790.

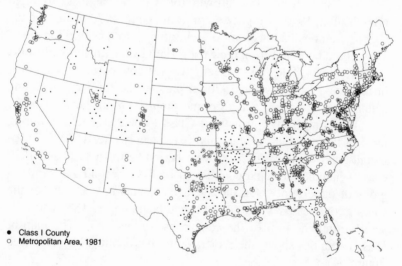

Figure 54:
LOCATIONS OF CLASS I COUNTIES

● Class I County
○ Metropolitan Area, 1981

The long decline up to 1970 and the rapid rise thereafter is well illustrated by Stevens County, near the northeastern corner of Washington State. After a steep fall in comparative growth from 1910 to 1960, the population of Stevens County rose sharply in the 1970s (see Figure 55).

Why do people come here, clear across the state from Seattle and the other old population centers? asked Bill Dietrich of the *Seattle Times*. To find out, he tells us, breathe the air and contemplate the scenery. This is spectacular mountain country. Lakes and

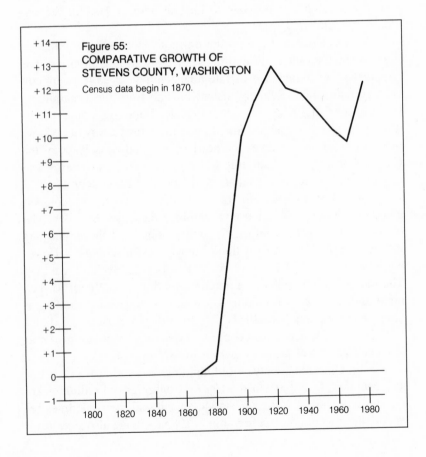

Figure 55:
COMPARATIVE GROWTH OF
STEVENS COUNTY, WASHINGTON

Census data begin in 1870.

streams abound, and the water is pure. The only congestion is from roaming deer. Nearby Ferry County—another Class I county—has a single traffic light (a yellow blinker). Olaf Heintz, recent migrant to the area, recalled, "I came over the hill down into Chewelah. The sky was totally clear. The hills were beautifully green. The farms were green, gold and brown. I knew I'd found it." [2]

As a result of sixty years of steady population loss in Stevens County, land values were low in the 1960s. As late as 1975—long after rapid migration had begun—land could still be purchased for $250 to $350 an acre. By 1983, land values had more than tripled, and it was all but impossible to buy an acre of land in Stevens County for under $1,000.

Stevens County also serves to illustrate another factor influencing investment values during the era of the Caring Conserver. The county has an abundance of late-nineteenth- and early-twentieth-century real estate. Suitably distant in time from the streamlining styles of the Little King, it sports antiquated buildings that now have nostalgic appeal. Using old structures is more than a way of embracing history. It also relieves the newly awakened conscience of the Caring Conserver. Substituting old for new conserves energy and raw materials otherwise "squandered" on new construction.

Sarah Lee Pilley, wife of a retired Marine Corps colonel, bought a 1900s-era farmhouse overlooking the Colville Valley. She converted the upstairs into their family home and the downstairs into what Bill Dietrich calls the "valley's best restaurant." He records her account of the venture: "'It was horribly rundown . . . The interior was derelict, the porch crumbling . . . We all worked night and day, for five months—just in time to open at the beginning of the recession in 1981.'" [3] But Pilley's Roadhouse didn't fail. Its success was ensured by an expanding population of migrants attracted to Caring Conserver life-styles.

Estimating the supply of old buildings is another way to classify counties. In the age of the Caring Conserver old buildings are not only valuable for their nostalgic appeal and for sometimes reducing the cost of construction, but in 1985 there are also significant tax benefits: a *20 percent tax offset on the cost of rehabilitating structures 40 years old or older.*[4] I call counties that have a large inventory of old real estate "A" counties, those with a smaller inventory "B" counties.

Because of the unavailability of data, the inventory of old buildings is estimated on the basis of population. In any year, the housing supply as well as commercial and industrial real estate should correspond roughly to the size of population. Class IA counties had larger populations and Class IB counties had smaller populations in 1930 or before than they had in 1970. Either the IB counties were not favored for growth in previous migrations (perhaps because of locational deficiencies), or they began their period of growth after 1930—after the third surge had already peaked.

In satisfying increasing demands for raw materials from its forests and fields, Stevens grew from 10,543 in 1900 to 25,297 in 1910. Then, as with many other third-surge counties, Stevens was

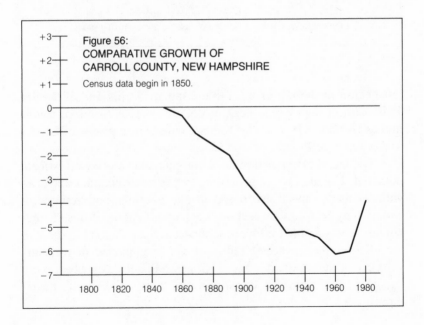

Figure 56:
COMPARATIVE GROWTH OF
CARROLL COUNTY, NEW HAMPSHIRE
Census data begin in 1850.

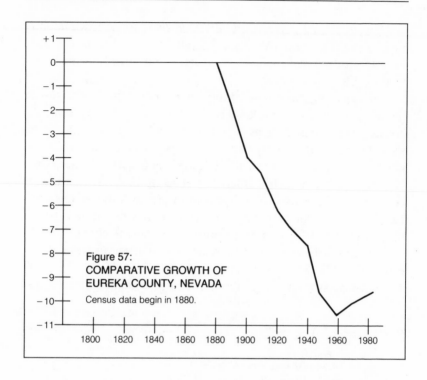

Figure 57:
COMPARATIVE GROWTH OF
EUREKA COUNTY, NEVADA
Census data begin in 1880.

left behind in the era of the Little King. It declined to 17,405 in 1970—lower than its old peak of 25,297—and is therefore classified as IA. Other IA counties followed the typical profile of Class I as a whole (see Figures 56 and 57).

The Class I designation does not guarantee a good investment potential. Unique factors pertaining to particular counties and sites within counties must also be taken into account. For example, a county may be Class I based on the general criteria of this chapter but yet be unsuitable for investment because population increases in the 1970s reflect a heavy influx of the unemployed or migrants working at substandard wages. (Chapter Sixteen describes every county in the region of opportunity in terms of 39 fundamental traits.)

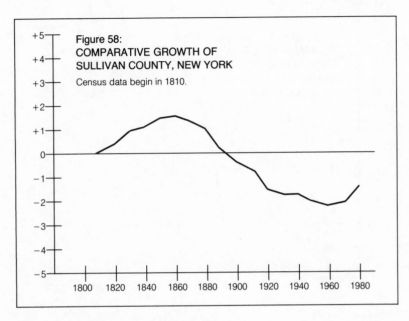

Figure 58:
COMPARATIVE GROWTH OF
SULLIVAN COUNTY, NEW YORK

Census data begin in 1810.

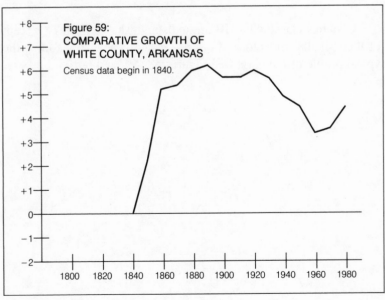

Figure 59:
COMPARATIVE GROWTH OF
WHITE COUNTY, ARKANSAS

Census data begin in 1840.

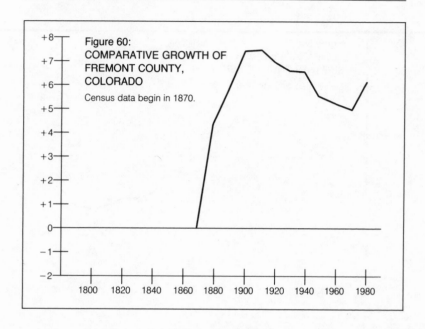

Figure 60:
COMPARATIVE GROWTH OF
FREMONT COUNTY,
COLORADO

Census data begin in 1870.

Counties classified as IB are indistinguishable from IA except for their smaller inventory of old real estate. They, too, follow the typical profile of the class (see Figures 58, 59, and 60).

Fourteen

Comparison of counties in classes I, II, and III

DURING the peak years of suburban migration—1950–1970—Class I, II, and III counties grew more slowly than the national average. After 1970, prompted by the rise of the new economy, the growth of all three speeded up, I more than II, II more than III.

Class II counties are counties of moderate growth potential. They grew more rapidly during the 1970s than the average of all counties, but less rapidly than the counties in Class I.[1] The comparative growth profile of Class II counties suggests an overwhelming presence of counties formerly in the second region of opportunity (unlike Class I, in which the third region is also heavily represented). As is typical of the second region as a whole, growth of Class II counties peaks in the 1840s and thereafter begins a long downward slide until 1970 (see Figure 61). Class II counties are heavily represented in the Mississippi Valley (location of the second region of opportunity). (See Figure 62.)

Class III counties from 1950 to 1970 showed minimum potential. But before 1970 they were indistinguishable from Class I or II. (All three classes grew less rapidly than the average.) Their differences became visible only after 1970. Though Class III counties continued to lag behind the national average, after the 1970 turning point they lagged less.[2]

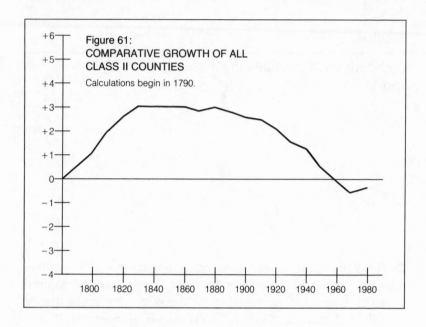

Figure 61:
COMPARATIVE GROWTH OF ALL
CLASS II COUNTIES

Calculations begin in 1790.

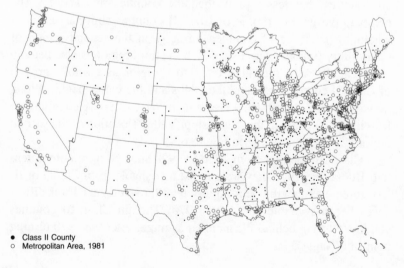

Figure 62:
LOCATIONS OF CLASS II COUNTIES

● Class II County
○ Metropolitan Area, 1981

The comparative growth profile of Class III counties most resembles that of Class IV, but differs in the 1970s. Although both continue to decline in the 1970s, Class IV dives steeply while Class III declines at a decreasing rate (see Figure 63). Class III counties are located throughout the nation, with lesser concentration in the West (see Figure 64).

Old real estate: A and B counties

Old real estate is a useful commodity in the now-rising economy. (See Chapter Eight.) As in Class I, the presence of differing amounts of old buildings is noted in Classes II and III. Again, "A" signifies the greater inventory of old buildings. The accompanying graphs illustrate the comparative growth rates of counties in Classes IIA, IIB, IIIA, and IIIB (see Figures 65, 66, 67, and 68).

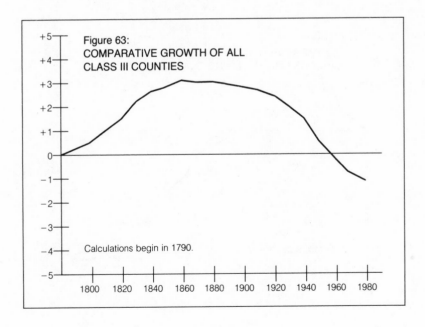

Figure 63:
COMPARATIVE GROWTH OF ALL
CLASS III COUNTIES

Calculations begin in 1790.

Figure 64:
LOCATIONS OF CLASS III COUNTIES

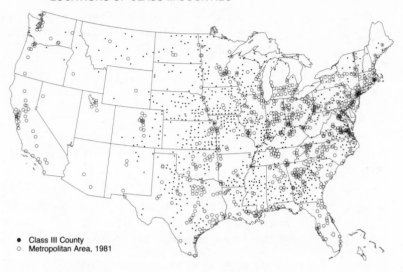

● Class III County
○ Metropolitan Area, 1981

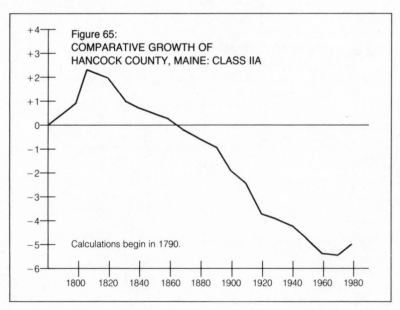

Figure 65:
COMPARATIVE GROWTH OF
HANCOCK COUNTY, MAINE: CLASS IIA

Calculations begin in 1790.

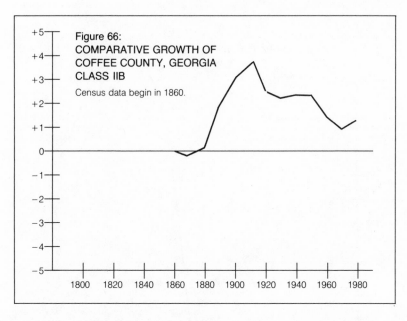

Figure 66:
COMPARATIVE GROWTH OF
COFFEE COUNTY, GEORGIA
CLASS IIB

Census data begin in 1860.

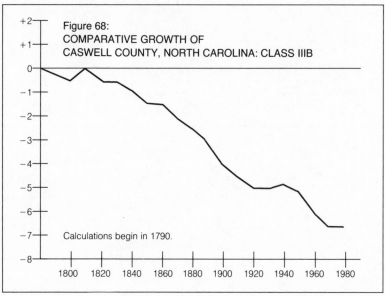

Figure 68:
COMPARATIVE GROWTH OF
CASWELL COUNTY, NORTH CAROLINA: CLASS IIIB

Calculations begin in 1790.

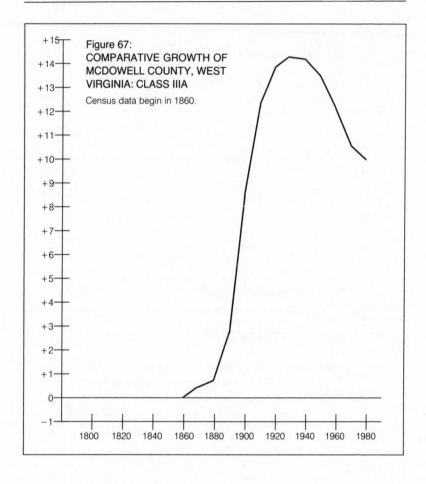

Figure 67:
COMPARATIVE GROWTH OF
MCDOWELL COUNTY, WEST
VIRGINIA: CLASS IIIA

Census data begin in 1860.

Will differences among Classes I, II, and III continue into the future?

The three classes are recognized by their differences in comparative growth during the 1970s. We need to know if there are deeper social and economic differences explaining the observed trends that are likely to be sustained in succeeding years. There are, in fact, profound differences among the three classes.

Life-style

Of the three classes, Class I counties are most specifically adapted to the life-style associated with the Caring Conserver. (See Chapter Eight.) Migration to penturbia, the fifth region of opportunity, is neither rural nor urban. It is rural-urban. Residents of Class I, in the heart of penturbia, are neither farmers nor city-dwellers. They show a preference for a rural life-style—homes on large lots—but earn their living in the cities as urbanites, often commuting long distances. Consider the following findings based on the 1980 census.

Farm population as a percent of total population

Class I	7.4%
Class II	9.6%
Class III	14.4%

Average value of farm land per acre

Class I	$688
Class II	$716
Class III	$746

Urban population as a percent of total population

Class I	22.6%
Class II	24.9%
Class III	26.3%

Percent of individuals commuting to work outside county

Class I	30.8%
Class II	26.9%
Class III	21.6%

Number of in-county jobs per hundred population

Class I	5.7%
Class II	6.1%
Class III	6.7%

Income

Residents of Class I counties are richer on the average than those in Class II—who are richer than residents of Class III counties.

Percent of families at the poverty level

Class I	13.3%
Class II	13.8%
Class III	14.4%

Percent of households earning less than $10,000 per year

Class I	37.8%
Class II	39.0%
Class III	40.3%

Percent of households earning $20,000–$29,999

Class I	18.6%
Class II	18.1%
Class III	17.3%

Percent of households earning $30,000–49,999

Class I	9.2%
Class II	8.5%
Class III	8.1%

Average value of owner-occupied houses

Class I	$34,844
Class II	$30,822
Class III	$27,579

Average monthly rent (residential)

Class I	$188
Class II	$173
Class III	$164

Minorities

The smallest percentage of Blacks reside in Class I, followed by Class II and Class III.

Percent Black

Class I	6.9%
Class II	9.2%
Class III	11.3%

Age

Class I counties have the smallest percentage of population over 65, Class III counties the highest.

Percent of Population Over 65

Class I	13.1%
Class II	13.7%
Class III	15.8%

Despite evident disparities in rates of growth and socioeconomic characteristics among the three classes, no one should assume that *every* Class II or Class III county is less sound a candidate for investment than *any* in Class I. Counties vary. As a class, I shows greater potential than II, II more than III. But some properties in Class II may prove to be more profitable than others in Class I, and some in Class III may be authentic "sleepers." For the next decade or two, the astute investor must recognize the potential of particular sites to satisfy requirements of today's rising economy. The value of pastureland in certain counties of generally low potential may be multiplied by many times its purchase price as tomorrow's haven for Caring Conservers.

Fifteen

Three forecasts for
1986–2010

Forecast 1. Current population densities of metropolitan areas cannot be sustained. Counties in Classes VI and VII are destined to decline.

Forecast 2. A vast redistribution of wealth lies ahead. Every parcel of real estate in America will be affected—mansions, townhouses, yuppie condos, suburban ranch houses, neighborhood shopping centers, regional centers, lofts, industrial parks, mobile-home parks, and office buildings—whether one or one hundred stories high. Properties lying within the vast reaches of population decline will drop in value or rise lethargically. Those within the area of increasing populations will rise in value.

Forecast 3. Penturbia—consisting of counties in Classes I, II, and III—will become increasingly important, I more than II and II more than III. (See Figure 69.)

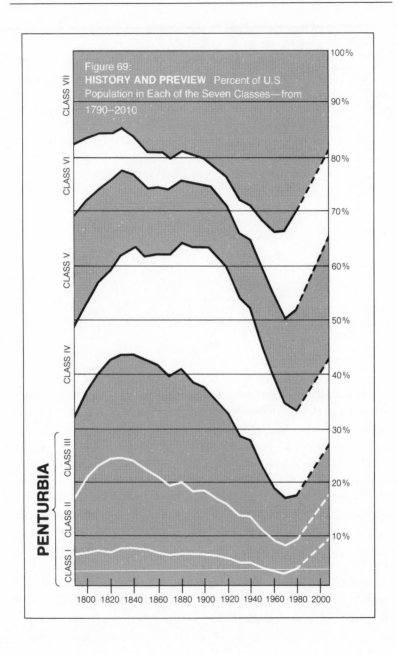

Figure 69:
HISTORY AND PREVIEW Percent of U.S. Population in Each of the Seven Classes—from 1790–2010

Review of the theory behind the forecasts

1. The comparative growth of counties is not haphazard, but typically reveals consistent long-run trends—decades of rise or fall sometimes stretching into a century or more.

2. Large groups of counties rise together as great regions of opportunity and fall together as regions of obsolescence. Rising counties are destinations for lengthy migrations. Falling counties are the places where the migrations originate. In 1985, Class I, II, and III counties represent a minor share of the national population. But it wasn't always so. Over a century ago, counties in these three classes contained nearly half the United States population, the peak having been in 1840 (44 percent), when the counties were members of the second and third regions of opportunity. (See Figure 69.)

3. Every region of opportunity serves a unique economy. A new economy crystallizes a gamut of social and economic changes around a central vision—a general consensus on value, attitudes, and priorities.

4. No economy can continue indefinitely, but is inevitably corrupted when the general consensus on which it is based continues for too long. The late-nineteenth-century Colossus economy was based on a consensus affirming the supreme value of maximum production for industrial expansion. It eventually gave rise to *overproduction*. The twentieth-century consensus on shifting priorities to maximum consumption—economy of the Little King—eventually generated *overconsumption*. The most recent economy, based on a consensus of conservation to build up vitally needed human and material capital, will in time fall victim to rampant *overconservation*.

5. Each new economy serves a fundamental function—to restrain, combat, and finally exorcise the excesses of its predecessor. To do that, its consensus always challenges and negates the preceding consensus.

6. As every economy is functional (serving to solve the problem created by its predecessor), so is every region of opportunity. The location and resources of each new region are designed to serve one and only one economy. And because each economy is antithetical to its predecessor's, each region of opportunity necessarily shifts to very different locations, possessing very different resources.

7. The new locations are found in a different set of counties. Counties in the preceding region of opportunity are typically at a disadvantage. Real estate that has vigorously participated in the life of any economy is unlikely to make a comeback in the *very next* economy. At least one economy must intervene, for real estate cannot readily adapt to new conditions. Once a pattern develops, it lingers long after the original impetus for it is gone. This inability of real estate to adjust to new conditions accounts for the typically long decline of counties once a mature peak is reached.

8. For almost a century Class VI and VII counties have been stars in the consumer economy of the Little King. They are ill-prepared to serve the conserving economy now ascending. Classes I, II, and III, already distant from their nineteenth-century peaks and possessing the locations and resources to accommodate conservation, are now ready to assume the burden of growth.

Part four

Applications

Sixteen

An opportunity atlas

"AH, Pend Oreille County, Washington. Interesting name . . . has a good sound to it. It's also Class IA in *Regions of Opportunity*. And it's within commuting distance of a company offering exactly the kind of job I've been hoping for. But what sort of a place is it?"

Our investor sets out to get salient facts about Pend Oreille. Forewarned by Chapters Thirteen and Fourteen, she knows that suitability for investment doesn't depend on the sevenfold classification alone, that it is essential to consider a county's detailed characteristics. Is the county filled with poverty-stricken individuals unable to find employment in the metropolitan areas? Does it represent mainstream Americans? Does it provide important services? What are its special problems?

Our resourceful seeker visits the library and looks up Pend Oreille County in the 1983 *County and City Data Book*. She finds that in 1980 8.4 percent of Pend Oreille's total population were under five years of age, and that there were 93.2 physicians per 100,000 population, and that 28.6 percent of the households earned between $10,000 and $19,999 annual income. Becoming increasingly confused, she finds 213 additional bits of information—raw statistics that are relevant, no doubt, but, to her, inscrutable.

This chapter puts those statistics into perspective, making it possible for anyone to acquire an instant and valuable insight into particular counties. Consider any of those county traits—like the 8.4 percent of the population under five years of age. By itself 8.4 percent does not mean very much. Is it a lot or a little? Or is it something in between? To make it more useful, the 8.4 percent needs to be compared to corresponding values in other counties of the region of opportunity (the counties of Classes I–III). We need to know if 8.4 is relatively high, low, or average for the group as a whole. If a trait in one county is close to the average of the region it is given an index of 5 in the table at the end of this chapter.

Indexes greater than 5 are above average.
9 very far above average
8 far above average
7 above average
6 slightly above average

Indexes lower than 5 are below average.
4 slightly below average
3 below average
2 far below average
1 very far below average[1]

The inscrutable statistics our investor looked up for Pend Oreille County can now be decoded. Here is the way the county stands.

Percent of population under five years of age	7
Physicians per capita	8
Percent of households with annual incomes of $10,000–$19,999	2
Percent of persons below the poverty level	4
Percent of households with annual incomes of $50,000 or over	2
Percent of wholesale jobs	1

Interpretation. These six traits of Pend Oreille depict a rural county peopled by young families with low but not desperately low incomes. One may speculate about the above-average presence of physicians despite the predominantly lower-income character of the county. Perhaps it is explained by a high order of scenic and recreational amenities appealing to the Caring Conserver. Physicians, too, may opt for the new life-style, may be glad to accept a reduced income in order to live in this scenically beautiful and less pressured environment. Notice that the county is in Class I, attracting unusual numbers of migrants in the 1970s despite declining growth in preceding decades or centuries.

A table of traits for every county in penturbia

In addition to the six traits listed so far, this chapter supplies others of general interest to real-estate investors, business executives, regional planners, county administrators, and those deciding where to settle.

What can we learn about a county from a table of comparative traits? Plenty. More than the casual visitor might find by going there. Notice how our knowledge of Pend Oreille is powerfully expanded by considering a larger number of traits. (The numbers preceding the names of the traits correspond with the order of the traits in the table at the end of this chapter.)

1. Population	4
2. Land Area	7

Interpretation. The county's "small" population, large land area, and consequent "low" density suggests that it is still at an early stage in its development. It will be necessary, however, to find out if the county's land area is available for private settlement. Is there perhaps a large federal park—or reservoir or marsh—that preempts much of the land?

3. Median House Value	6
4. Median Gross Rent	4
5. Average Farm Value per Acre	4

Interpretation. Real-estate values are reasonable. Farm land is inexpensive—perhaps it is largely pasture or cropland with limited growing season and fertility.

9. Percent of Population 65 and Over   3

Interpretation. There are probably few facilities for retired people. Yet one requirement is already in place: the higher than average number of physicians per capita already noted.

11. Percent Earning under $10,000   6
12. Percent Earning $10,000–$19,999   2
13. Percent Earning $20,000–$29,999   7
14. Percent Earning $30,000–$49,999   5
15. Percent Earning over $50,000   2

Interpretation. The high percentage of people earning $20,000–$29,999 sticks out like a skyscraper on a desert, raising an interesting question. Does this moderate-income bracket represent recent arrivals—distinctly different from lower-income, long-time residents? Note that because of the likely "underground" or trading economy, $20,000–$29,999 may represent a higher standard of living than the same income in a metropolitan area.

16. Percent Completed High School   8
17. Percent Completed College or More   6
18. Ratio of Families to Population   5
19. Percent Married Couples   7
20. Percent of Husbandless Families   2

Interpretation. The county attracts mainstream Americans, permanent residents with respectable, but not rare, educational attainments who plan on more or less traditional families. This interpretation is further supported by the large number of children in the population.

21. Percent Black	3
22. Percent Spanish	4
23. Percent American Indian	6
24. Percent Asian	3

Interpretation. Minorities tend to be attracted to more populous places. American Indians are different. Perhaps they were here first.

25. Percent Urban	2
26. Percent Rural-Farm	3
27. Percent Farmers	4
28. Percent Working Out of the County	6

Interpretation. We would expect to find in Pend Oreille many people who prefer a rural life-style, who are noncommercial farmers or part-time farmers living on large lots or acreages and who are often employed part-time in urban occupations. Other data tell us that in Pend Oreille many are employed outside the county. Some work in retail and manufacturing establishments (see numbers 29–33 below). Others may be self-employed within the county in cottage industries, as computer programmers, craftsmen, writers, and so on. The county's land quality probably does not justify extensive commercial farming.

29. Ratio of Jobs to Population	1
30. Percent of Jobs in Manufacturing	7
31. Percent in Wholesaling	1
32. Percent in Retailing	9
33. Percent in Services	5

Interpretation. Relative to population, very few jobs are available locally, so many work outside the county. As population grows we can expect more jobs. (A growing county provides an attractive labor pool for new firms and stimulates the local construction industry. The present small population and work force compel wholesalers to locate elsewhere. The same circumstances encourage local retailing. But where residents tend to be self-sufficient or trade their services, service establishments are likely to be in lesser demand. And how about the unusual degree of manufacturing? Abundant forests in the county may support wood-products industries.

35. Crimes per Capita	9
36. Local Expenditures to Fight Crime	5

Interpretation. We see a flaw in Utopia: an unusually high crime rate, and perhaps too little money to fight it. Potential residents and investors need to know why. Is it perhaps extreme socioeconomic disparities among county residents—a newly arrived affluent group living among old-time residents at the bitter edge of poverty?

Now it is your turn. The table of traits that follows is a powerful tool permitting you to obtain an initial insight into a county's character. But you will, of course, need to verify your interpretations with additional information. Pay special attention to patterns of income, socioeconomic status, and age.

All data were drawn from a computer tape of the 1983 *County and City Data Book* covering the years between 1977 and 1982. The abbreviated labels of the traits are defined below. All Class I and II counties are listed in the first part of the table; and all Class III counties are listed after them. Counties are arranged alphabetically by states, which are also in alphabetical order. See Appendixes A and B for a listing of all counties in the United States and the classes (I–VII) to which they have been assigned. An asterisk within the table means that data needed to calculate the index were not available.

Traits of counties in the fifth region of opportunity

Size of County

1. Population (as of April 1, 1980)

2. Land Area (in square miles, 1980)

Real-Estate Values

3. Med House Val (median value of housing units occupied by owners—condominiums not included, 1980)

4. Med Gross Rent (median gross rent for renter-occupied housing, units paid in cash rent, 1980)

5. Av Farm Val/Acre (average value of farm land and buildings per acre, 1978)

Ages of Population

6. % Under 5 (number of persons under 5 years old divided by total population, 1980)

7. % 5–17 (number of persons 5–17 years old divided by total population, 1980)

8. % 18 and Over (number of persons 18 years old and over divided by total population, 1980)

9. % 65 and Over (number of persons 65 years old and over divided by total population, 1980)

Incomes

10. % Poverty (number of families below poverty level in 1979 divided by all families, 1980)

11. % Under $10,000 (number of households with less than $10,000 income in 1979 divided by all households, 1980)

12. % $10–19,999 (number of households with income of $10,000 to $19,999 in 1979 divided by all households, 1980)

13. % $20–29,999 (number of households with income of $20,000 to $29,999 in 1979 divided by all households, 1980)

14. % $30–49,999 (number of households with income of $30,000 to $49,999 in 1979 divided by all households, 1980)

15. % Over $50,000 (number of households with income of $50,000 or over in 1979 divided by all households, 1980)

Socioeconomic Status

16. % Completed HS (number of persons 25 years old and over who completed 4 years of high school and did not complete college divided by total population, 1980)

17. % College or More (number of persons 25 years old and over who completed 4 or more years of college divided by total population, 1980)

18. Families/Pop (number of families divided by total population, 1980)

19. % Married Couples (number of married-couple families divided by total number of families, 1980)

20. % W/O Husband (number of female-headed families divided by total number of families, 1980)

Minorities

21. % Black (Black population divided by total population, 1980)

22. % Spanish (Spanish-origin population divided by total population, 1980)

23. % Amer Indian (population of American Indians, Eskimos, and Aleuts divided by total population, 1980)

24. % Asian (population of Asian and Pacific Islanders divided by total population, 1980)

Rural-Urban

25. % Urban (urban population divided by total population, 1980)

26. % Rural (rural farm population divided by total population, 1980)

27. % Farmers (percent of operators residing on farms operated in 1978)

28. % Out of County (number of residents who worked outside county of residence divided by workers reporting county and state of work, 1980)

Economic Base

29. Jobs/Pop (sum of manufacturing, wholesale, retail, and service employees as of March 1977 divided by total population, 1980)

30. % Manufacturing (number of manufacturing employees as of March 1977 divided by total population, 1980)

31. % Wholesale (number of employees in wholesale trade as of March 1977 divided by total population, 1980)

32. % Retail (number of employees in retail trade as of March 1977 divided by total population, 1980)

33. % Service (number of employees in service trade as of March 1977 divided by population, 1980)

County Conditions

34. Physicians/Cap (number of physicians per 100,000 residents, 1980)

35. Crimes/Cap (number of offenses known to police per 100,000 residents, 1980)

36. $ Police/Crimes (direct general expenditure for police protection by local government in 1977 divided by number of property crimes known to police, 1981)

37. $ Educ/Enrollment (direct general expenditure for education by local government divided by school enrollment of children 3 years and over, 1980)

38. Carpool or Transit (whichever is higher: workers carpooling to work or workers using public transportation as a percentage of workers reporting means of transportation to work, 1980)

39. Pop Density (population per square mile, 1980)

Economic Indicators For Class IA, IB, IIA, And IIB Counties	SIZE OF COUNTY		REAL-ESTATE VALUES			AGES OF POPULATION				INCOMES					
	Population	Land Area	Med House Val	Med Gross Rent	Av Farm Val./Acre	% Under 5	% 5-17	% 18 and Over	% 65 and Over	% Poverty	% Under $10,000	% $10–19,999	% $20–29,999	% $30–49,999	% Over $50,000
ALABAMA															
Bibb IIA	4	4	2	2	2	6	8	2	4	7	6	5	5	4	2
Blount IB	6	4	5	4	5	3	6	5	3	6	5	6	5	5	2
Cherokee IIA	5	4	4	3	4	3	4	6	3	6	6	6	5	2	3
Chilton IB	6	4	4	2	4	5	6	4	4	6	6	7	4	3	3
Cleburne IIA	4	4	3	2	3	4	6	5	3	5	5	7	6	3	2
Cullman IIB	8	5	5	5	7	3	5	5	3	6	6	5	4	4	4
De Kalb IB	8	5	3	4	6	4	5	5	4	6	7	4	4	3	3
Elmore IB	7	4	7	3	4	4	7	4	2	5	3	4	8	7	7
Fayette IIA	5	4	3	3	3	5	5	5	5	6	6	6	4	3	3
Franklin IIB	6	4	4	3	4	3	4	6	4	5	6	3	4	5	4
Henry IIA	4	4	3	1	4	6	6	4	5	7	7	4	4	3	3
Houston IB	9	4	6	7	5	6	7	3	2	5	3	6	6	6	7
Jackson IB	8	6	5	6	6	6	7	4	1	5	4	5	7	5	3
Lamar IIA	4	4	3	1	4	4	6	5	5	5	6	5	6	2	2
Marion IB	6	5	3	2	3	3	6	5	4	5	6	8	3	2	3
Marshall IIB	9	4	5	4	7	2	5	6	3	5	6	5	4	5	3
Pike IIA	6	4	3	2	3	2	4	7	5	8	9	1	2	2	3
St. Clair IB	7	4	5	7	6	6	7	3	2	4	3	5	8	6	4
Shelby IB	9	5	9	9	7	7	6	3	1	3	1	1	9	9	9
Tallapoosa IIB	7	4	3	2	3	3	7	4	4	5	5	6	5	4	2
Walker IB	9	5	3	6	6	5	6	5	3	5	5	3	6	6	4
Winston IB	5	4	3	3	5	4	6	4	2	6	6	5	5	3	4
ARIZONA															
Gila IB	6	9	6	8	2	7	7	3	3	4	5	2	8	7	2
ARKANSAS															
Baxter IB	5	4	7	8	4	1	1	9	9	3	6	9	2	1	3
Benton IB	9	5	8	8	8	3	3	7	6	2	3	9	5	4	6
Boone IB	5	4	6	6	4	3	2	8	7	5	7	6	2	3	4
Carroll IA	4	4	6	5	4	2	1	9	9	6	8	8	1	2	2
Cleburne IA	4	4	7	5	4	2	2	8	8	7	8	7	1	3	2
Cleveland IIA	3	4	2	1	5	3	7	5	7	5	8	1	6	4	1
Conway IIA	5	4	3	3	4	5	7	4	5	5	7	4	3	4	3
Craighead IB	8	5	5	8	7	4	3	7	2	4	4	8	5	4	6
Crawford IB	6	4	4	6	6	7	7	3	3	5	4	9	4	3	3
Drew IIA	4	5	4	3	6	6	5	4	4	5	6	3	4	6	3
Faulkner IB	7	4	8	7	4	3	3	7	2	3	4	6	6	5	5
Franklin IA	4	4	3	4	4	3	6	5	6	6	7	9	2	2	1
Fulton IA	4	4	4	4	2	2	2	8	9	7	9	7	1	1	2

SOCIO-ECONOMIC STATUS					MINORITIES				RURAL-URBAN				ECONOMIC BASE					COUNTY CONDITIONS					
% Completed HS	% College or More	% Married Couples	Families/Pop	% W/O Husband	% Black	% Spanish	% Amer Indian	% Asian	% Urban	% Rural	% Farmers	% Out of County	Jobs/Pop	% Manufacturing	% Wholesale	% Retail	% Services	Physicians/Cap	Crimes/Cap	$ Police/Crimes	$ Educ/Enrollment	Carpool or Transit	Pop Density
2	1	3	2	8	8	4	4	3	6	2	2	8	2	8	2	9	2	2	1	7	3	9	4
3	2	8	8	3	3	4	4	3	3	3	4	9	2	5	6	3	6	2	2	5	2	9	6
2	2	8	6	4	5	4	4	3	2	4	4	8	2	5	6	8	2	3	3	5	3	9	5
3	2	7	5	5	6	4	4	4	4	2	3	9	2	5	3	7	5	3	5	5	2	9	5
1	2	8	6	4	4	4	4	4	5	3	3	9	1	9	5	8	2	4	2	5	3	9	4
3	3	8	7	3	3	4	4	4	4	4	4	5	4	6	3	5	7	5	5	5	2	6	7
2	2	8	6	5	3	4	4	3	6	4	5	5	2	7	6	2	6	3	4	5	2	7	6
5	5	3	4	7	8	4	4	4	5	2	2	9	1	4	2	6	8	5	8	4	2	8	6
2	3	7	5	5	6	4	4	6	6	2	3	5	3	8	5	7	2	4	3	5	2	6	4
3	2	9	6	5	4	4	4	3	7	3	3	7	3	6	4	8	2	5	5	5	4	8	5
2	4	5	1	9	9	5	4	3	8	3	3	7	4	8	9	1	3	3	3	5	2	6	4
4	7	6	2	8	8	4	4	8	9	2	2	2	9	4	6	2	8	9	9	5	3	5	8
3	2	8	6	4	4	4	5	3	7	3	3	4	2	8	3	7	5	4	4	5	2	8	5
2	2	7	6	4	6	4	4	3	4	3	3	5	2	9	5	7	2	3	2	5	3	8	4
2	2	8	7	4	3	4	4	6	6	3	3	5	2	9	6	4	3	3	2	5	2	6	5
4	4	8	5	6	3	4	4	4	8	2	3	5	7	6	6	4	5	5	7	5	2	6	8
1	6	1	1	9	9	4	4	3	9	2	3	2	6	5	6	2	7	5	6	5	1	5	5
4	2	7	6	4	5	4	4	4	4	2	2	9	1	5	3	5	6	2	4	5	2	7	6
4	9	6	7	3	5	4	4	7	7	2	2	9	2	7	7	4	3	4	5	5	1	5	7
3	4	5	2	8	8	4	4	8	8	2	2	3	4	9	2	7	6	5	6	5	2	8	6
3	2	7	4	6	4	4	4	4	5	2	2	5	4	4	3	7	5	5	5	5	2	7	7
2	2	8	6	4	3	4	4	4	5	3	3	4	3	9	7	3	3	3	3	5	3	5	5
7	3	5	5	5	3	9	9	7	9	2	1	2	*	*	*	*	*	5	7	5	7	4	4
8	6	9	8	2	3	4	5	4	6	2	2	2	5	7	1	7	8	9	3	5	2	5	5
7	7	9	8	2	3	4	5	7	8	3	4	3	5	6	4	4	8	8	5	5	2	4	7
7	6	9	7	4	3	4	4	4	7	4	5	1	9	4	7	3	5	9	5	5	2	5	5
7	6	9	7	4	3	4	4	4	4	7	7	2	4	5	4	2	9	6	5	5	2	4	4
5	3	9	8	2	3	4	4	3	5	4	5	4	2	4	2	8	6	7	2	5	3	8	5
3	2	7	7	3	6	4	4	4	2	3	4	9	*	*	*	*	*	3	2	5	3	9	4
4	3	6	5	6	6	4	4	3	7	4	4	3	3	8	5	6	4	4	4	5	2	7	5
3	8	5	5	6	4	4	4	7	8	2	2	2	8	5	5	5	6	9	6	5	1	4	7
5	1	7	6	4	3	4	6	6	7	2	3	9	*	*	*	*	*	3	7	4	2	6	6
2	7	4	2	8	8	4	4	2	8	2	3	2	4	7	2	9	2	5	2	5	2	6	4
4	8	2	6	4	5	4	4	5	8	2	3	4	5	5	2	5	8	4	7	5	1	7	6
5	2	7	6	4	3	4	5	5	5	4	5	6	2	5	3	8	3	2	2	5	3	6	4
6	2	9	8	3	3	4	5	4	2	7	9	6	*	*	*	*	*	5	2	5	2	6	4

Economic Indicators For Class IIA, IB, IIA, And IIB Counties		SIZE OF COUNTY		REAL-ESTATE VALUES			AGES OF POPULATION				INCOMES					
		Population	Land Area	Med House Val	Med Gross Rent	Av Farm Val./Acre	% Under 5	% 5–17	% 18 and Over	% 65 and Over	% Poverty	% Under $10,000	% $10–19,999	% $20–29,999	% $30–49,999	% Over $50,000
Grant	IA	4	4	4	4	5	3	7	4	3	5	4	4	7	6	4
Greene	IB	6	4	3	4	5	4	4	6	5	5	6	8	3	2	3
Hempstead	IA	5	5	2	3	4	6	4	5	7	6	8	2	4	3	2
Hot Spring	IB	5	4	4	3	5	5	4	6	5	5	5	4	6	4	3
Howard	IIA	4	4	2	2	4	6	4	5	8	4	7	7	3	2	4
Independence	IB	6	5	5	7	4	5	4	6	5	4	6	7	4	2	2
Izard	IA	4	4	5	3	3	1	1	9	9	7	9	5	1	1	2
Johnson	IA	4	4	3	4	4	4	3	7	8	6	8	7	1	2	3
Lawrence	IIA	5	4	2	3	5	3	4	7	7	8	9	5	1	1	2
Little River	IA	4	4	3	2	4	7	8	2	4	6	6	1	4	8	8
Logan	IIA	5	5	3	2	4	3	7	5	7	8	9	4	1	2	3
Lonoke	IA	6	5	6	5	7	6	9	2	2	5	4	4	6	6	5
Madison	IIA	4	5	3	2	3	4	4	6	6	7	9	9	1	1	2
Marion	IA	4	4	5	6	3	2	3	8	9	8	9	5	1	2	4
Miller	IIB	7	4	3	5	5	7	6	3	4	6	6	5	5	4	4
Montgomery	IA	3	5	2	1	4	1	2	9	8	8	9	7	1	1	2
Newton	IA	3	5	3	1	3	6	6	4	4	9	9	1	1	1	1
Perry	IA	3	4	2	3	5	3	8	4	5	4	7	5	4	3	1
Pike	IIA	4	4	2	2	5	3	4	6	7	6	7	6	2	3	2
Polk	IA	4	5	3	2	5	3	5	6	8	8	9	6	1	1	4
Pope	IB	7	5	6	6	5	4	5	6	3	5	5	5	5	5	5
Randolph	IA	4	4	3	2	4	4	6	5	6	7	8	8	1	1	5
Scott	IIA	4	5	2	1	3	2	5	6	7	8	9	3	1	1	2
Searcy	IIA	4	4	2	2	2	3	4	7	7	9	9	1	1	1	1
Sebastian	IIB	9	4	5	7	5	5	4	6	3	3	3	7	6	6	7
Sevier	IA	4	4	3	3	5	3	6	5	6	5	6	4	5	4	1
Sharp	IA	4	4	5	8	2	1	2	9	9	8	9	7	1	1	5
Stone	IA	4	4	3	3	3	3	4	7	6	9	9	1	1	1	2
Van Buren	IA	4	5	6	5	3	2	3	8	8	7	8	8	1	2	2
White	IB	8	6	5	5	4	3	5	6	4	6	7	5	3	3	3
Yell	IIA	4	5	3	4	4	2	4	7	7	6	8	7	2	2	3
CALIFORNIA																
Amador	IB	5	4	9	9	3	1	1	9	7	2	2	5	9	7	6
Imperial	IB	9	9	9	9	9	8	9	1	1	4	2	6	6	8	9
Modoc	IIB	4	9	8	6	2	5	3	6	4	4	4	3	5	8	7
Sierra	IA	3	5	9	7	2	1	1	9	5	3	3	3	7	8	5
Siskiyou	IIB	7	9	9	8	3	5	2	7	4	3	3	6	7	6	6
COLORADO																
Archuleta	IA	3	7	9	9	2	5	9	2	1	6	4	6	4	5	8

SOCIO-ECONOMIC STATUS					MINORITIES				RURAL-URBAN				ECONOMIC BASE					COUNTY CONDITIONS					
% Completed HS	% College or More	Families/Pop	% Married Couples	% W/O Husband	% Black	% Spanish	% Amer Indian	% Asian	% Urban	% Rural	% Farmers	% Out of County	Jobs/Pop	% Manufacturing	% Wholesale	% Retail	% Services	Physicians/Cap	Crimes/Cap	$ Police/Crimes	$ Educ/Enrollment	Carpool or Transit	Pop Density
5	3	8	8	2	4	4	5	8	5	2	2	9	2	7	2	9	3	2	2	5	3	8	4
3	3	8	6	4	3	4	4	2	8	4	3	2	4	8	3	5	6	7	6	5	2	4	5
6	4	6	3	7	9	4	4	2	8	3	4	3	5	4	9	1	6	4	5	5	2	5	5
5	4	8	6	4	5	4	5	3	7	2	2	7	3	6	2	8	4	4	5	5	2	8	5
4	3	6	5	6	7	4	4	5	6	4	5	2	4	9	2	9	3	6	2	5	3	3	4
4	4	8	6	4	3	4	5	6	5	3	3	2	6	6	7	2	5	7	4	5	2	5	5
6	6	9	8	2	3	4	4	2	2	5	7	5	1	3	2	9	2	6	2	5	3	7	4
3	4	8	7	4	3	4	4	6	6	3	4	2	2	6	1	9	6	5	2	5	2	6	4
2	2	8	6	5	3	4	5	3	7	4	4	4	3	5	5	5	5	4	3	5	3	6	5
4	3	4	4	6	8	4	4	2	6	2	3	4	*	*	*	*	*	4	3	5	2	7	4
3	2	5	6	4	3	4	5	5	7	5	6	4	2	6	2	9	3	4	2	5	2	6	4
4	3	5	6	4	4	4	5	8	3	3	8	2	6	7	4	3	4	3	*	5	2	8	5
4	2	9	8	2	3	4	5	3	2	8	9	7	1	5	2	7	7	3	2	5	3	8	4
8	4	9	8	3	3	4	5	3	2	5	6	6	1	4	3	5	8	7	2	5	2	7	4
5	3	5	1	9	8	4	5	6	9	2	2	9	*	*	*	*	*	6	9	5	3	4	6
4	4	9	8	2	3	4	5	7	2	4	6	5	*	*	*	*	*	2	2	5	3	9	4
3	3	8	8	2	3	4	4	2	2	7	8	9	1	2	1	1	9	5	2	5	3	9	4
5	2	7	7	3	3	4	5	2	2	5	5	9	1	2	2	5	9	2	3	5	2	9	4
4	3	8	7	3	4	4	5	2	2	5	4	6	2	6	7	7	1	4	2	5	2	7	4
4	4	8	6	4	3	4	5	7	6	5	6	2	3	7	4	7	4	5	3	5	2	3	4
4	7	6	6	5	3	4	5	6	8	2	3	2	7	5	4	5	6	8	7	5	3	4	5
2	2	8	6	4	3	4	4	3	7	4	5	2	2	9	3	8	3	5	4	5	2	6	4
3	1	8	8	2	3	4	5	3	5	5	7	3	1	7	2	9	2	4	2	5	2	5	4
2	3	8	7	2	3	4	5	2	2	6	7	3	1	7	8	3	2	3	2	5	3	8	4
7	7	7	4	7	4	4	5	9	9	2	2	1	9	6	6	2	7	9	9	4	2	5	9
5	4	7	6	4	4	4	5	3	6	3	4	5	4	6	4	8	2	7	3	5	2	6	4
7	5	9	8	2	3	4	5	3	5	4	4	6	2	3	3	9	2	5	3	5	3	7	4
2	3	9	7	2	3	4	5	2	2	5	8	3	2	3	6	8	1	4	3	5	3	8	4
7	3	9	8	3	3	4	4	3	2	4	5	5	*	*	*	*	*	3	4	4	2	8	4
3	4	5	7	4	4	4	4	5	7	3	4	3	4	5	5	5	6	7	5	5	1	4	5
5	2	8	7	3	3	4	5	6	4	5	6	6	*	*	*	*	*	6	4	5	2	5	4
9	9	9	8	2	3	6	5	8	2	2	2	3	*	*	*	*	*	9	7	5	6	5	5
2	4	1	3	7	3	9	5	9	9	2	1	1	9	3	7	3	6	7	9	5	6	6	4
9	8	7	6	3	3	6	6	6	7	5	6	2	5	3	3	6	6	3	8	5	8	3	3
9	9	7	6	3	3	7	6	7	2	2	2	4	*	*	*	*	*	3	9	5	9	4	3
9	9	7	6	3	3	6	7	8	6	2	2	1	6	4	3	7	5	8	9	5	9	3	4
6	9	7	6	4	3	9	4	8	2	2	3	2	7	4	1	4	9	5	8	5	5	7	3

Economic Indicators For Class IIA, IB, IIA, And IIB Counties

		SIZE OF COUNTY		REAL-ESTATE VALUES			AGES OF POPULATION				INCOMES					
		Population	Land Area	Med House Val	Med Gross Rent	Av Farm Val./Acre	% Under 5	% 5-17	% 18 and Over	% 65 and Over	% Poverty	% Under $10,000	% $10-19,999	% $20-29,999	% $30-49,999	% Over $50,000
Custer	IA	3	5	8	6	2	7	3	5	4	6	6	8	5	2	2
Delta	IB	5	6	9	8	5	4	3	7	8	3	7	2	6	3	4
Elbert	IA	3	8	9	8	1	7	9	2	1	2	1	2	9	9	9
Fremont	IB	6	7	9	7	2	2	2	8	8	3	5	6	5	5	4
Garfield	IB	5	9	9	9	4	7	2	6	1	1	1	1	9	9	9
Gunnison	IB	4	9	9	9	3	1	1	9	1	1	3	4	6	8	9
Hinsdale	IA	3	6	9	8	6	2	1	9	1	1	1	9	2	3	9
La Plata	IA	5	8	9	9	2	4	2	8	1	3	3	4	7	7	9
Mineral	IIA	3	5	8	9	2	5	3	7	1	1	1	9	5	9	2
Morgan	IIB	5	7	9	8	3	8	5	4	3	2	2	7	6	8	8
Ouray	IA	3	4	9	9	2	4	3	7	2	2	3	7	5	4	9
Park	IA	3	9	9	9	1	8	6	3	1	3	1	4	9	9	8
Routt	IA	4	9	9	9	2	6	1	8	1	1	1	2	9	9	9
San Miguel	IA	3	7	9	9	2	8	1	8	1	4	3	8	7	4	4
Teller	IA	3	4	9	9	2	3	7	4	1	2	1	4	8	9	8
Weld	IB	9	9	9	9	4	7	4	5	1	3	2	5	8	8	8
Yuma	IIA	4	9	8	4	2	8	4	4	6	6	6	3	4	6	6
FLORIDA																
Calhoun	IIA	4	4	1	2	5	5	7	4	6	8	8	2	3	3	2
Gilchrist	IA	3	3	4	7	5	3	8	4	2	6	8	3	3	2	3
Hamilton	IIA	4	4	2	2	5	8	9	1	4	9	8	3	2	2	2
Holmes	IA	4	4	2	4	5	3	6	5	5	9	9	5	1	2	2
Jackson	IIB	7	5	2	2	5	4	6	5	4	7	8	4	2	2	3
Jefferson	IA	4	4	2	2	6	8	8	2	4	9	9	1	2	4	6
Lafayette	IA	3	4	3	2	5	8	7	2	3	7	7	5	3	2	5
Levy	IB	5	6	4	4	5	3	4	7	6	7	8	7	1	2	3
Liberty	IA	3	5	2	2	5	7	4	5	3	7	8	1	4	2	2
Sumter	IB	5	4	4	6	6	1	3	8	7	6	7	6	2	4	2
Suwannee	IA	5	4	3	4	6	6	7	3	4	8	7	5	3	3	2
Taylor	IB	4	6	2	3	3	5	7	4	3	7	7	1	5	8	5
Union	IB	4	3	3	2	6	1	1	9	1	5	6	9	3	2	1
Wakulla	IB	4	4	3	6	7	7	8	2	2	6	6	6	5	4	2
Walton	IB	5	6	3	4	4	2	3	8	6	8	8	3	2	4	3
Washington	IA	4	4	2	3	3	2	7	5	6	8	9	4	1	2	2
GEORGIA																
Appling	IB	4	4	2	3	4	8	9	1	2	9	8	6	1	2	3
Banks	IA	4	3	2	1	6	4	6	5	2	3	4	9	5	2	3
Barrow	IB	5	3	6	5	7	5	7	3	2	4	4	7	6	5	6
Bartow	IB	7	4	5	6	5	4	8	3	1	3	2	9	7	6	2
Ben Hill	IA	4	3	3	2	6	7	6	4	4	7	8	3	3	3	3

SOCIO-ECONOMIC STATUS					MINORITIES				RURAL-URBAN				ECONOMIC BASE					COUNTY CONDITIONS					
% Completed HS	% College or More	Families/Pop	% Married Couples	% W/O Husband	% Black	% Spanish	% Amer Indian	% Asian	% Urban	% Rural	% Farmers	% Out of County	Jobs/Pop	% Manufacturing	% Wholesale	% Retail	% Services	Physicians/Cap	Crimes/Cap	$ Police/Crimes	$ Educ/Enrollment	Carpool or Transit	Pop Density
9	9	8	7	3	3	5	5	2	2	6	8	5	*	*	*	*	*	6	8	5	5	5	3
9	8	8	7	3	3	7	5	5	4	3	5	3	4	3	4	7	5	7	8	5	5	5	4
9	9	6	9	1	3	5	5	9	2	5	8	9	1	3	8	1	6	1	2	5	7	6	3
9	8	3	5	5	3	7	5	4	9	2	2	2	4	4	1	9	6	8	8	5	5	5	4
9	9	3	7	3	3	6	5	7	7	2	2	3	9	2	2	3	9	9	9	5	9	9	4
3	9	1	5	3	3	5	5	6	9	2	2	1	9	2	1	2	9	8	9	5	1	9	3
9	9	8	3	3	3	5	4	2	2	3	3	2	7	2	1	1	9	9	9	5	2	3	3
8	9	1	4	5	3	8	7	5	7	2	3	1	9	3	1	3	9	9	9	5	4	6	4
9	9	6	8	1	3	5	4	2	2	2	2	2	*	*	*	*	*	9	9	5	9	8	3
7	7	5	7	3	3	8	5	5	9	5	5	1	9	3	8	3	3	5	8	5	7	3	4
8	9	7	9	1	3	6	4	9	2	5	5	3	*	*	*	*	*	5	3	6	9	4	3
9	9	6	9	1	3	5	5	9	2	2	2	9	2	2	1	2	9	3	9	5	7	8	3
8	9	1	7	2	3	5	5	6	7	2	3	1	9	2	1	8	9	9	9	5	7	9	3
7	9	1	5	3	3	5	6	9	2	2	3	2	*	*	*	*	*	9	8	5	9	5	3
9	9	8	7	3	3	4	4	2	6	2	2	9	2	2	1	9	5	9	8	5	3	8	4
5	9	2	5	5	3	9	4	9	9	4	3	4	7	4	5	4	6	8	9	5	4	6	5
8	7	7	9	1	3	5	5	4	6	9	9	1	8	3	9	2	2	4	2	5	9	5	3
3	3	5	4	7	6	4	5	2	6	3	3	6	3	5	7	6	2	4	3	5	5	6	4
6	3	6	6	4	4	4	4	5	2	5	7	9	*	*	*	*	*	1	5	5	7	8	4
3	2	2	1	9	9	4	5	2	2	3	4	2	*	*	*	*	*	5	7	5	7	5	4
3	2	7	5	5	3	4	5	4	4	4	5	9	1	5	4	7	3	2	2	5	5	7	4
4	3	3	2	9	8	4	4	5	5	4	3	4	6	4	9	3	2	4	4	5	7	7	5
3	6	1	1	9	9	4	4	8	5	3	3	7	2	3	7	2	7	3	4	5	6	9	4
4	4	6	6	4	4	4	4	3	2	8	9	8	*	*	*	*	*	1	2	5	6	5	4
6	4	7	3	7	6	4	4	5	2	3	3	8	3	3	4	7	4	5	9	5	6	5	4
3	3	4	4	6	5	4	4	2	2	2	2	9	*	*	*	*	*	3	2	5	8	9	3
5	3	6	4	6	7	5	4	4	3	3	3	7	4	3	1	4	9	3	9	5	8	6	5
5	2	5	3	7	7	4	4	8	6	6	6	4	5	4	6	6	4	4	2	5	6	6	5
4	4	5	1	9	7	4	4	7	8	2	2	2	6	6	2	8	5	5	7	5	6	6	4
8	2	1	2	8	9	5	5	9	2	2	3	6	1	3	9	1	1	9	2	5	3	8	5
5	4	5	4	6	7	4	4	2	2	2	2	9	*	*	*	*	*	2	3	5	5	9	4
4	6	8	4	7	5	4	5	8	5	2	3	8	2	4	3	7	6	3	7	5	4	7	4
5	2	7	4	6	6	4	5	5	5	3	3	7	2	3	5	5	6	4	3	5	9	8	4
1	2	3	3	7	7	4	4	6	5	6	5	6	*	*	*	*	*	4	3	5	7	6	5
2	1	8	5	4	4	4	4	2	2	4	5	9	*	*	*	*	*	2	4	5	2	9	5
1	3	6	3	7	6	4	4	2	6	2	2	7	4	9	4	6	4	3	7	5	3	8	8
1	2	6	3	7	5	4	4	4	5	2	2	5	6	8	4	3	7	4	8	5	7	8	7
2	3	4	1	9	9	4	4	3	9	2	2	2	7	6	5	5	4	4	9	5	2	4	6

Economic Indicators For Class IIA, IB, IIA, And IIB Counties

		SIZE OF COUNTY		REAL-ESTATE VALUES			AGES OF POPULATION				INCOMES					
		Population	Land Area	Med House Val	Med Gross Rent	Av Farm Val./Acre	% Under 5	% 5–17	% 18 and Over	% 65 and Over	% Poverty	% Under $10,000	% $10–19,999	% $20–29,999	% $30–49,999	% Over $50,000
Berrien	IIA	4	4	3	4	5	5	7	3	2	7	5	8	3	4	3
Brantley	IA	4	4	2	3	5	7	9	1	1	5	4	9	5	3	1
Bryan	IB	4	4	5	5	4	9	9	1	1	6	3	9	7	3	3
Bulloch	IIB	6	4	8	7	6	3	3	7	1	6	5	6	3	5	5
Butts	IA	4	3	4	5	4	5	6	5	2	4	4	4	6	7	4
Candler	IIA	3	3	4	2	5	3	7	5	7	9	9	2	1	2	6
Carroll	IB	8	4	6	6	6	4	7	4	2	4	3	7	6	6	4
Charlton	IB	3	5	2	4	4	8	9	1	1	7	4	8	5	5	2
Coffee	IIB	5	4	4	2	6	8	8	2	2	8	8	6	1	2	7
Coweta	IB	7	4	6	7	9	6	8	3	2	4	3	2	8	8	9
Crawford	IA	3	3	4	2	5	6	9	1	1	6	3	4	8	6	3
Dawson	IA	3	3	5	5	8	5	6	4	2	6	5	8	4	3	3
Decatur	IIA	5	4	3	3	6	8	9	1	3	7	6	8	2	3	6
Echols	IIA	3	4	1	1	4	9	9	1	2	8	6	8	3	2	1
Emanuel	IIA	5	4	2	1	4	8	7	2	3	9	8	4	2	2	6
Evans	IIB	3	3	4	3	4	7	8	2	3	8	7	6	3	2	4
Franklin	IIA	4	3	4	1	6	2	5	7	4	6	6	7	4	2	2
Gordon	IB	6	3	4	7	6	4	8	3	1	3	2	9	6	5	4
Haralson	IIB	5	3	4	2	5	2	7	4	3	4	4	8	5	3	4
Harris	IA	4	4	5	4	7	3	6	6	3	5	4	2	7	7	9
Hart	IIA	5	3	4	2	5	4	7	4	3	4	4	9	2	4	3
Heard	IA	3	3	2	2	4	4	8	3	3	4	4	8	5	4	2
Jackson	IIA	5	3	4	5	7	4	7	4	2	4	4	8	6	4	3
Jasper	IA	3	3	5	2	5	7	6	4	4	6	4	5	7	5	3
Jeff Davis	IB	4	3	3	2	5	6	9	2	1	5	4	9	4	4	4
Johnson	IIA	4	3	2	1	3	8	6	3	5	9	8	2	4	2	2
Lamar	IIB	4	3	3	3	6	4	7	4	3	4	4	8	4	7	4
Lanier	IIB	3	3	2	4	5	8	9	1	3	9	9	3	1	2	2
Laurens	IIA	6	5	4	4	4	6	7	3	3	6	6	3	6	5	5
Lee	IA	4	3	9	7	7	8	9	1	1	5	1	1	9	9	5
Lincoln	IIA	3	3	3	1	4	5	7	3	3	5	5	7	6	3	3
Long	IA	3	3	2	9	3	9	7	2	1	8	8	1	6	2	1
Madison	IA	4	3	4	4	6	5	7	3	1	4	4	9	5	3	3
Mitchell	IIA	5	4	3	2	7	8	9	1	2	9	7	1	5	5	7
Monroe	IA	4	3	4	3	4	3	6	5	3	4	3	6	7	6	6
Montgomery	IIA	3	3	2	1	4	5	5	5	3	7	9	4	1	3	3
Morgan	IIA	4	3	5	1	4	6	9	2	3	6	5	4	5	5	5
Murray	IA	5	3	5	7	7	7	9	1	1	3	3	9	6	4	5
Newton	IB	6	3	6	6	6	5	9	2	2	3	1	8	9	8	5
Oconee	IA	4	3	9	9	5	5	7	4	1	2	1	2	9	9	9
Oglethorpe	IIA	4	4	3	2	5	3	9	3	3	5	6	3	7	4	2

SOCIO-ECONOMIC STATUS					MINORITIES				RURAL-URBAN				ECONOMIC BASE					COUNTY CONDITIONS					
% Completed HS	% College or More	Families/Pop	% Married Couples	% W/O Husband	% Black	% Spanish	% Amer Indian	% Asian	% Urban	% Rural	% Farmers	% Out of County	Jobs/Pop	% Manufacturing	% Wholesale	% Retail	% Services	Physicians/Cap	Crimes/Cap	$ Police/Crimes	$ Educ/Enrollment	Carpool or Transit	Pop Density
2	2	6	4	6	6	4	4	3	7	5	5	5	6	6	8	1	5	4	9	4	3	5	4
3	1	5	6	4	4	4	4	2	2	5	5	9	1	4	4	2	9	1	3	5	3	9	4
2	1	4	4	6	7	4	4	3	2	2	2	9	3	3	1	2	9	2	7	5	2	9	4
1	8	1	3	8	8	4	4	6	7	3	2	2	8	3	6	4	4	7	6	5	1	6	5
2	2	1	1	9	9	5	4	4	6	2	2	8	*	*	*	*	*	2	3	5	3	9	6
1	5	3	2	8	9	4	4	3	8	5	4	5	7	3	9	1	4	5	2	5	3	4	5
2	6	3	3	7	7	4	4	4	6	2	2	4	5	7	3	5	7	7	6	5	3	7	8
2	1	2	1	9	9	4	4	2	2	2	2	8	*	*	*	*	*	4	4	5	3	9	4
1	3	3	2	9	8	4	4	5	7	5	4	2	7	5	8	3	3	7	8	5	2	6	5
2	5	4	2	9	8	4	4	2	6	2	2	6	4	7	2	8	4	7	6	5	3	7	7
1	2	2	2	8	9	4	4	3	2	3	3	9	*	*	*	*	*	2	1	5	6	9	4
1	1	8	7	4	3	4	7	2	2	2	4	9	*	*	*	*	*	1	8	5	4	8	4
2	3	2	1	9	9	4	4	4	7	4	2	3	6	6	8	2	4	6	7	5	2	6	5
2	1	4	5	6	7	4	6	2	2	5	4	9	*	*	*	*	*	1	*	*	5	8	3
1	3	3	1	9	9	4	4	3	7	4	3	2	5	7	7	3	4	4	6	5	5	7	4
2	2	3	1	9	9	4	4	3	6	3	3	4	*	*	*	*	*	3	1	6	2	6	5
1	4	8	4	6	5	4	4	3	2	4	4	8	4	6	3	9	3	5	3	5	2	8	6
2	2	6	4	6	4	4	4	3	4	2	2	4	4	9	3	4	8	4	7	5	2	5	7
2	3	7	4	7	4	4	4	2	7	2	2	6	3	9	2	6	6	4	5	5	3	7	6
3	7	6	3	7	9	5	4	5	2	2	2	9	2	4	1	2	9	3	7	5	2	7	5
1	3	6	4	6	8	4	4	3	5	3	3	7	2	9	5	4	4	3	2	5	2	7	7
1	1	5	3	6	7	4	4	2	2	2	3	9	*	*	*	*	*	4	3	5	3	9	4
1	3	6	3	7	5	4	4	2	4	3	3	9	3	7	7	4	4	3	5	5	2	7	6
1	5	3	1	9	9	4	4	3	2	4	3	7	*	*	*	*	*	2	4	5	2	9	4
1	3	5	4	6	6	4	4	3	7	4	4	3	6	8	7	3	4	2	3	5	3	3	5
1	2	4	1	9	9	4	4	2	6	4	4	8	2	9	8	2	4	2	1	9	2	9	4
2	3	3	2	9	9	4	4	2	7	2	2	8	*	*	*	*	*	4	5	5	2	8	6
1	1	2	4	7	8	4	4	3	8	4	4	9	1	4	2	7	7	5	6	5	4	7	4
2	5	3	1	9	9	4	4	5	8	3	3	2	7	6	8	1	6	9	7	5	3	7	5
3	4	3	4	6	8	4	4	7	3	3	2	9	*	*	*	*	*	2	3	5	5	5	5
2	3	4	2	8	9	5	4	3	2	3	3	8	1	9	5	3	7	3	3	5	3	9	5
2	2	3	2	7	8	5	4	3	2	3	3	9	*	*	*	*	*	2	*	*	2	9	4
2	3	8	5	5	5	4	4	3	2	4	3	9	*	*	*	*	*	2	3	5	2	8	6
1	2	1	1	9	9	4	4	3	8	4	3	5	7	4	9	1	6	4	9	5	2	8	5
2	5	2	1	9	9	4	4	5	6	2	2	7	*	*	*	*	*	4	9	5	1	9	5
1	2	1	2	8	9	4	4	7	2	5	4	9	6	5	5	3	7	3	*	*	2	9	4
1	4	2	1	9	9	4	4	3	5	5	3	5	4	5	7	2	6	3	9	5	2	8	5
1	1	6	5	5	3	4	4	3	2	2	2	7	2	9	7	4	3	2	5	5	2	5	6
2	4	3	2	8	8	4	4	4	6	2	2	9	3	6	1	9	5	3	8	5	3	8	8
2	9	6	5	4	5	4	4	4	2	3	2	9	1	6	5	1	9	4	*	*	1	5	6
1	5	5	2	8	9	5	4	2	2	4	4	9	1	6	6	4	4	2	*	*	2	9	4

Economic Indicators For Class IIA, IB, IIA, And IIB Counties

		SIZE OF COUNTY		REAL-ESTATE VALUES			AGES OF POPULATION				INCOMES					
		Population	Land Area	Med House Val	Med Gross Rent	Av Farm Val./Acre	% Under 5	% 5–17	% 18 and Over	% 65 and Over	% Poverty	% Under $10,000	% $10–19,999	% $20–29,999	% $30–49,999	% Over $50,000
Pickens	IIB	4	3	3	5	8	3	5	6	4	5	6	6	4	3	4
Pierce	IA	4	3	4	2	7	7	9	2	2	8	7	7	3	3	2
Pike	IA	4	3	3	3	6	6	7	3	3	3	2	2	9	7	6
Putnam	IA	4	3	5	2	5	3	7	4	2	7	5	2	6	7	7
Rabun	IB	4	3	6	4	8	1	3	8	5	5	7	5	3	3	5
Schley	IIA	3	3	3	2	3	6	9	1	3	9	6	8	1	5	3
Screven	IIA	4	4	3	1	3	8	6	3	4	9	9	2	1	2	4
Seminole	IB	4	3	4	2	7	6	8	3	4	7	8	2	2	6	3
Toombs	IIB	5	3	4	3	5	7	8	2	2	9	8	4	2	2	4
Towns	IB	3	3	6	3	7	1	1	9	7	8	9	4	1	1	4
Twiggs	IIA	4	3	2	1	4	8	9	1	2	5	5	6	3	2
Union	IA	4	3	4	4	8	1	5	7	6	9	9	3	1	1	4
Walton	IB	6	3	6	4	7	6	9	2	2	5	4	6	7	5	6
Wheeler	IIA	3	3	1	1	4	8	8	2	5	9	9	2	1	2	1
White	IB	4	3	6	5	9	2	3	7	3	6	6	5	5	2	6
Worth	IA	4	4	5	2	7	5	9	2	2	8	5	6	5	4	5

IDAHO

Adams	IIB	3	7	6	2	2	6	7	3	3	4	3	8	7	6	3
Bear Lake	IIA	3	6	8	7	2	9	8	1	3	3	2	7	9	7	2
Benewah	IA	3	5	7	5	5	8	7	2	2	2	2	2	9	8	8
Boise	IA	3	8	9	6	2	8	5	3	1	3	2	9	8	4	6
Bonner	IB	5	8	9	9	5	8	4	4	2	6	6	4	4	4	4
Camas	IIA	3	6	6	4	2	5	8	3	3	4	2	9	2	5	4
Cassia	IIB	5	9	8	6	4	9	9	1	1	4	3	8	5	6	5
Custer	IIA	3	9	8	2	3	9	4	3	2	6	6	8	3	2	4
Franklin	IIA	4	4	8	8	4	9	9	1	3	2	1	9	6	3	2
Fremont	IA	4	8	8	7	3	9	9	1	1	5	3	9	6	3	4
Gem	IB	4	4	8	7	3	8	6	3	5	4	5	1	6	7	4
Idaho	IIB	4	9	8	5	2	8	7	3	3	4	2	9	7	7	3
Jefferson	IB	4	6	9	8	6	9	9	1	1	5	2	9	7	6	1
Latah	IIB	6	6	9	7	5	3	1	9	1	2	4	5	5	8	5
Oneida	IIA	3	6	6	5	2	9	8	1	7	5	7	9	4	1	1
Boger	IB	3	7	9	8	3	9	9	1	1	4	2	8	7	8	7
Teton	IA	3	4	7	7	5	9	9	1	1	7	5	9	3	3	1
Valley	IB	3	9	9	9	2	6	4	5	1	2	1	9	8	8	4
Washington	IIA	4	7	6	5	2	8	6	3	8	6	8	4	2	3	4

ILLINOIS

Bond	IIA	4	3	5	6	9	3	2	8	6	3	4	2	8	7	8
Clinton	IIB	6	4	8	9	9	7	7	3	3	2	1	7	9	9	5
	IIA															

SOCIO-ECONOMIC STATUS					MINORITIES				RURAL-URBAN				ECONOMIC BASE					COUNTY CONDITIONS					
% Completed HS	% College or More	Families/Pop	% Married Couples	% W/O Husband	% Black	% Spanish	% Amer Indian	% Asian	% Urban	% Rural	% Farmers	% Out of County	Jobs/Pop	% Manufacturing	% Wholesale	% Retail	% Services	Physicians/Cap	Crimes/Cap	$ Police/Crimes	$ Educ/Enrollment	Carpool or Transit	Pop Density
1	3	8	5	5	3	4	4	3	2	2	2	6	2	9	4	5	5	7	3	5	4	9	5
2	2	5	4	7	6	4	4	3	5	5	5	8	3	4	9	2	4	5	4	5	2	7	5
2	4	4	5	5	8	5	4	3	2	4	4	9	*	*	*	*	*	2	2	5	3	8	5
2	5	3	1	9	9	4	4	2	8	3	2	4	3	8	6	5	3	2	6	5	5	8	4
2	7	9	5	6	3	4	4	3	2	2	2	2	*	*	*	*	*	7	2	5	9	8	4
2	3	2	1	9	9	4	4	2	2	5	4	8	*	*	*	*	*	1	*	1	7	4	
1	3	3	1	9	9	4	4	5	5	4	4	4	*	*	*	*	*	3	2	5	3	8	4
2	3	3	2	9	9	5	4	3	7	5	3	6	6	3	9	3	2	5	5	5	2	7	5
1	4	4	1	9	8	4	4	5	9	3	2	4	7	5	8	3	3	7	3	5	2	8	6
2	6	8	7	3	3	4	4	4	2	2	3	7	*	*	*	*	*	3	1	9	4	7	5
1	1	1	1	9	9	5	4	3	2	2	2	9	*	*	*	*	*	2	1	9	2	9	4
1	4	9	6	4	3	4	4	3	2	3	3	4	*	*	*	*	*	6	1	6	3	6	4
1	3	4	3	7	7	4	4	6	7	2	2	8	2	9	3	7	4	4	6	5	3	9	7
1	3	3	3	8	9	4	4	2	2	5	6	9	*	*	*	*	*	2	1	7	4	8	4
3	5	7	6	4	4	4	4	6	2	3	3	8	3	7	1	9	5	4	4	5	3	6	5
2	3	3	2	8	9	4	4	9	6	6	3	8	3	5	9	1	2	4	6	5	4	8	5
8	7	7	8	2	3	4	4	3	2	6	8	2	*	*	*	*	*	5	6	5	4	3	3
8	5	3	9	2	3	4	5	4	8	3	6	5	6	3	4	7	4	4	6	5	4	9	4
7	5	5	6	3	3	4	8	3	6	4	3	2	3	8	2	9	2	4	6	5	6	4	4
8	8	7	7	3	3	5	4	5	2	2	3	8	*	*	*	*	*	1	7	5	7	5	3
9	7	7	7	3	3	4	5	7	4	2	3	2	5	4	2	6	8	7	9	5	3	3	4
9	9	7	9	1	3	4	4	9	2	9	9	1	*	*	*	*	*	9	3	5	8	3	3
7	5	2	7	3	3	7	4	6	8	6	5	4	*	*	*	*	*	7	9	5	4	3	4
9	8	5	8	2	3	4	4	3	2	9	8	2	3	2	3	5	8	5	5	5	8	9	3
8	5	1	9	1	3	5	4	3	8	8	8	5	5	3	6	6	3	2	4	5	4	7	4
7	6	1	9	2	3	5	5	8	6	4	5	4	5	3	9	2	4	3	6	5	4	4	4
8	4	7	7	3	3	5	5	9	7	6	5	4	*	*	*	*	*	3	6	5	3	4	4
8	7	5	8	2	3	4	5	4	5	7	6	2	4	5	7	3	4	7	4	5	3	3	3
6	4	1	8	2	3	6	5	5	4	8	7	8	*	*	*	*	*	2	4	5	3	9	4
5	9	1	7	3	3	4	4	9	9	3	3	2	8	3	3	6	6	8	8	5	1	4	4
8	7	3	8	2	3	4	4	5	2	7	9	3	*	*	*	*	*	3	7	5	6	7	3
8	6	2	6	4	3	7	7	4	9	6	5	5	*	*	*	*	*	3	9	5	6	4	3
8	9	1	9	1	3	4	4	7	2	8	9	3	5	2	1	6	9	3	3	5	5	9	4
9	9	6	8	2	3	5	5	9	2	2	3	1	*	*	*	*	*	8	9	5	5	3	3
6	8	6	7	3	3	7	5	9	9	8	7	2	8	3	9	1	3	3	6	5	5	3	4
4	6	5	7	3	3	4	4	4	6	7	6	6	6	3	7	2	7	5	2	5	2	4	5
5	2	3	7	3	3	4	4	7	7	6	4	8	5	3	9	1	3	4	3	5	2	6	6

Economic Indicators For Class IIA, IB, IIA, And IIB Counties		SIZE OF COUNTY		REAL-ESTATE VALUES			AGES OF POPULATION				INCOMES					
		Population	Land Area	Med House Val	Med Gross Rent	Av Farm Val./Acre	% Under 5	% 5–17	% 18 and Over	% 65 and Over	% Poverty	% Under $10,000	% $10–19,999	% $20–29,999	% $30–49,999	% Over $50,000
Cumberland	IIA	4	3	5	4	9	5	5	4	5	2	2	8	7	5	7
Edwards	IIA	3	3	3	3	8	5	1	8	8	2	4	6	7	4	6
Effingham	IB	6	4	9	8	9	8	6	3	3	1	1	4	9	9	9
Franklin	IIA	7	3	3	6	7	2	2	8	8	3	6	1	6	7	5
Jefferson	IIB	6	4	5	8	6	5	3	7	6	3	3	3	8	7	7
Jersey	IIB	5	3	6	7	9	4	5	6	3	1	1	5	9	9	6
Johnson	IA	4	3	4	4	4	1	2	9	6	4	5	6	4	5	4
Marion	IIB	7	4	4	7	7	5	3	6	6	3	3	4	7	7	6
Mason	IIB	5	4	7	8	9	5	6	4	5	3	2	5	8	9	8
Menard	IA	4	3	9	9	9	5	5	5	5	2	1	3	9	9	7
Mercer	IIA	5	4	8	9	9	4	7	4	3	2	1	2	9	9	8
Pope	IIA	3	3	2	3	4	1	4	7	8	5	7	6	3	5	1
Putnam	IIA	3	3	9	9	9	6	5	4	2	1	1	1	9	9	8
Randolph	IIB	6	4	7	7	8	4	1	8	5	1	1	2	9	9	6
Washington	IIA	4	4	7	8	9	4	2	7	8	2	2	4	8	8	8
Williamson	IIA	8	4	5	8	6	2	2	8	6	2	3	3	8	7	4
Woodford	IIB	6	4	9	9	9	7	7	3	2	1	1	1	9	9	9
INDIANA																
Boone	IIB	6	4	9	9	9	4	7	4	2	1	1	2	9	9	9
Crawford	IA	4	3	3	5	4	6	6	4	4	6	6	6	4	5	2
Dearborn	IIB	6	3	9	8	7	6	8	2	2	2	1	3	9	9	6
Franklin	IIA	5	3	8	7	9	7	9	1	2	2	1	8	8	9	4
Fulton	IIB	5	3	7	8	9	5	3	6	5	2	2	7	8	7	7
Greene	IIA	6	4	3	5	7	3	3	7	7	3	4	4	7	5	3
Harrison	IB	5	4	8	8	7	7	7	3	1	2	1	8	9	8	4
Jefferson	IIB	6	3	7	9	7	5	4	6	2	3	2	7	7	7	6
Lawrence	IIB	7	4	4	6	5	4	5	5	3	2	2	7	8	8	4
Marshall	IIB	7	4	8	9	9	6	6	4	3	2	1	6	9	9	7
Newton	IB	4	3	8	9	9	8	7	2	3	2	1	3	9	9	7
Noble	IIB	6	3	6	8	9	8	7	3	2	2	1	9	9	8	3
Ohio	IA	3	2	7	5	7	5	5	5	4	2	3	1	8	8	5
Owen	IA	4	3	4	7	7	3	7	4	4	3	3	8	7	6	3
Parke	IIA	4	4	4	6	7	2	6	6	6	2	3	5	8	7	3
Posey	IB	5	3	9	9	9	7	6	4	2	2	1	1	9	9	8
Ripley	IIB	5	4	7	7	8	6	8	2	4	2	2	8	7	6	4
Spencer	IIA	5	3	7	6	8	5	5	5	4	2	2	2	9	9	7
Switzerland	IIA	3	3	4	5	6	5	5	5	5	4	6	7	5	3	3
Warrick	IB	7	3	9	9	9	7	8	2	1	1	1	1	9	9	9
Washington	IIB	5	4	5	7	6	7	7	3	3	3	4	9	5	4	4
White	IIB	5	4	7	9	9	6	4	5	4	1	1	8	9	8	5

SOCIO-ECONOMIC STATUS					MINORITIES				RURAL-URBAN				ECONOMIC BASE					COUNTY CONDITIONS					
% Completed HS	% College or More	% Married Couples	Families/Pop	% W/O Husband	% Black	% Spanish	% Amer Indian	% Asian	% Urban	% Rural	% Farmers	% Out of County	Jobs/Pop	% Manufacturing	% Wholesale	% Retail	% Services	Physicians/Cap	Crimes/Cap	$ Police/Crimes	$ Educ/Enrollment	Carpool or Transit	Pop Density
6	3	6	7	3	3	4	4	4	2	9	8	9	4	4	9	1	2	5	3	5	5	4	5
8	3	8	7	3	3	4	4	2	2	8	7	4	*	*	*	*	*	4	2	5	3	3	5
7	4	3	7	4	3	4	4	2	7	6	5	2	9	4	5	5	6	7	6	5	4	4	6
6	3	8	5	6	3	4	4	3	8	3	2	6	4	3	4	5	6	5	5	5	6	3	7
6	6	7	5	5	4	4	4	4	8	4	4	2	9	4	7	1	8	6	9	5	7	7	6
6	3	3	7	3	3	4	4	5	7	5	4	9	3	3	6	6	3	4	6	5	3	4	6
6	4	5	8	3	4	4	4	2	2	6	6	8	3	3	8	5	1	2	1	5	4	4	4
6	4	7	4	7	4	4	4	8	8	3	3	3	9	4	6	5	5	8	8	5	7	4	6
7	4	7	6	3	3	4	4	4	7	5	4	8	6	3	8	3	3	4	5	5	7	7	5
8	8	7	8	3	3	4	4	3	2	6	5	9	4	3	9	1	4	3	3	5	7	7	5
9	4	6	8	2	3	4	4	6	4	7	7	8	4	3	9	2	2	2	2	5	8	4	5
4	2	5	5	4	4	4	4	3	2	6	8	8	*	*	*	*	*	2	5	5	5	8	4
8	5	7	8	2	3	4	4	2	2	6	5	8	*	*	*	*	*	4	3	5	8	3	5
6	3	2	7	3	4	4	4	8	8	5	4	2	4	7	3	8	3	5	3	5	4	5	6
5	3	6	7	2	3	4	4	6	4	8	8	7	*	*	*	*	*	4	1	6	3	3	4
7	7	7	5	6	3	4	4	4	9	2	2	7	6	4	3	4	8	7	5	5	6	4	8
8	8	4	8	2	3	4	4	5	4	4	4	9	*	*	*	*	*	3	2	5	4	8	6
9	9	6	8	3	3	4	4	7	8	4	3	9	6	3	3	7	5	9	4	5	3	4	7
4	2	6	5	5	3	4	4	3	2	4	6	9	1	3	3	7	5	1	8	4	4	9	5
6	5	4	5	5	3	4	4	8	7	3	3	8	3	7	5	5	5	6	5	5	4	6	8
4	3	2	7	2	3	4	4	7	4	6	6	9	1	4	6	6	2	2	7	5	2	5	5
9	4	8	7	3	3	4	4	7	5	7	6	4	5	7	6	6	2	4	4	5	3	4	5
8	3	8	7	4	3	4	4	5	6	4	4	8	4	4	3	9	2	5	9	5	4	8	6
7	2	6	7	3	3	4	4	4	3	6	6	9	3	4	8	2	4	3	2	5	2	8	6
6	7	3	5	6	3	4	4	7	9	4	4	3	7	5	3	8	3	8	3	5	3	6	7
7	3	8	6	5	3	4	4	7	8	3	3	4	4	6	2	8	3	9	6	5	3	6	7
8	6	6	7	3	3	5	4	4	6	6	4	5	*	*	*	*	*	5	4	5	4	3	7
8	3	5	7	3	3	4	4	5	2	6	4	8	6	5	9	3	2	3	*	5	5	4	5
7	3	5	7	4	3	4	4	3	6	6	4	6	6	7	7	4	4	5	9	5	3	4	7
5	3	6	6	4	3	4	4	7	2	6	7	9	*	*	*	*	*	1	2	5	3	6	6
7	3	6	7	3	3	4	4	7	4	6	6	9	*	*	*	*	*	3	*	5	2	7	5
9	4	7	7	3	3	4	4	3	4	6	5	9	*	*	*	*	*	3	*	5	5	6	5
7	5	6	7	3	3	4	4	5	6	4	3	8	4	6	7	5	3	3	*	6	3	3	6
5	3	4	7	3	3	4	4	6	0	7	6	6	4	8	6	5	3	4	3	5	3	7	6
6	4	4	8	2	3	4	4	6	3	7	5	8	5	4	6	4	5	2	5	4	3	5	5
5	2	6	7	4	3	4	4	7	2	9	9	7	*	*	*	*	*	3	*	5	4	8	5
8	8	6	8	3	3	4	4	9	8	2	2	9	*	*	*	*	*	6	9	5	3	4	7
5	2	6	6	4	3	4	4	3	5	7	7	6	2	8	5	7	2	3	*	5	3	7	5
9	4	7	7	3	3	4	4	7	4	6	4	5	7	5	6	4	5	3	9	5	7	4	5

Economic Indicators For Class IIA, IB, IIA, And IIB Counties	SIZE OF COUNTY		REAL-ESTATE VALUES			AGES OF POPULATION				INCOMES					
	Population	Land Area	Med House Val	Med Gross Rent	Av Farm Val./Acre	% Under 5	% 5–17	% 18 and Over	% 65 and Over	% Poverty	% Under $10,000	% $10–19,999	% $20–29,999	% $30–49,999	% Over $50,000
Whitley IIB	5	3	8	7	9	6	6	4	2	1	1	5	9	9	3
IOWA															
Clarke IIA	4	4	4	6	6	4	2	7	7	5	6	6	3	4	4
Dallas IIB	6	4	9	8	9	6	5	5	4	1	1	3	9	9	9
Dickinson IB	4	3	9	8	9	5	1	8	7	1	1	8	7	8	9
Louisa IIA	4	3	7	9	9	6	6	4	4	2	1	6	9	9	7
Marion IIB	6	4	8	8	8	5	2	7	5	2	1	7	8	9	4
Mills IIA	4	4	7	8	9	6	5	5	3	2	1	9	9	6	9
KANSAS															
Butler IIA	7	7	8	7	4	6	4	5	3	1	1	3	9	9	8
Coffey IA	4	4	3	9	3	5	2	7	9	2	4	3	7	8	5
Gray IIA	3	5	7	5	4	9	4	4	3	2	1	8	9	7	8
Harvey IIB	6	4	7	8	6	4	1	8	6	1	1	7	9	9	5
Jackson IIA	4	4	3	6	4	5	6	4	6	2	2	3	9	7	5
Jefferson IA	4	4	7	6	5	3	7	5	5	2	1	2	9	9	6
Kearny IIB	3	5	7	5	2	9	8	1	1	2	1	9	9	8	9
Miami IIA	5	4	6	5	6	4	5	5	6	1	1	4	9	9	9
Osage IIA	4	4	5	5	3	4	4	6	7	2	2	6	8	7	4
Pottawatomie IA	4	5	7	7	3	7	3	6	5	2	2	8	8	6	3
Thomas IIB	3	6	8	4	3	8	2	6	3	2	2	5	7	8	8
KENTUCKY															
Adair IIA	4	3	3	2	4	2	5	6	6	9	9	3	1	1	3
Allen IIA	4	3	3	2	4	3	3	7	6	6	8	1	5	3	2
Anderson IA	4	3	7	8	8	5	6	4	3	2	1	8	9	8	2
Barren IIB	6	4	5	3	6	3	4	7	5	5	6	5	5	3	3
Breathitt IIA	4	4	1	2	3	9	9	1	2	9	9	1	1	5	5
Breckinridge IIA	4	4	3	3	4	5	6	4	4	8	8	3	3	3	3
Butler IIA	4	4	2	1	3	5	5	5	5	7	8	5	3	2	1
Carter IA	5	3	4	4	3	7	8	2	2	8	8	3	3	3	2
Casey IIA	4	4	2	1	4	5	7	4	4	9	9	2	1	1	3
Clark IIB	6	3	8	7	8	6	6	4	2	4	2	2	8	9	7
Clinton IIA	4	3	2	2	5	3	5	6	5	9	9	1	1	1	1
Edmonson IIA	4	3	2	2	3	5	7	4	3	8	9	5	2	1	1
Elliott IIA	3	3	3	2	3	9	9	1	2	9	9	2	1	3	1
Estill IIA	4	3	2	3	3	5	8	3	4	9	8	2	5	2	3
Gallatin IIA	3	3	5	6	5	6	8	3	2	6	5	1	7	8	4
Garrard IIA	4	3	6	1	5	3	3	7	5	7	7	6	4	2	2
Grant IA	4	3	5	6	5	6	8	2	3	4	2	5	8	6	4

SOCIO-ECONOMIC STATUS					MINORITIES				RURAL-URBAN				ECONOMIC BASE					COUNTY CONDITIONS					
% Completed HS	% College or More	Families/Pop	% Married Couples	% W/O Husband	% Black	% Spanish	% Amer Indian	% Asian	% Urban	% Rural	% Farmers	% Out of County	Jobs/Pop	% Manufacturing	% Wholesale	% Retail	% Services	Physicians/Cap	Crunes/Cap	$ Police/Crimes	$ Educ/Enrollment	Carpool or Transit	Pop Density
9	3	6	8	3	3	4	4	3	4	7	5	7	7	6	9	1	3	3	2	5	3	4	6
9	4	8	8	2	3	4	4	6	8	9	9	3	7	4	4	7	4	4	5	5	6	7	4
9	8	6	7	3	3	4	4	3	6	6	5	9	6	4	7	5	3	5	7	5	7	6	5
9	9	8	8	2	3	4	4	3	5	6	5	3	9	4	2	1	9	6	7	5	8	3	5
9	4	6	7	3	3	4	4	6	2	8	7	8	*	*	*	*	*	2	8	5	8	5	4
7	6	3	8	3	3	4	4	8	9	5	5	3	6	5	5	7	3	5	6	5	6	7	5
8	6	2	8	3	3	4	4	3	7	8	7	5	*	*	*	*	*	4	6	5	6	4	5
9	8	7	8	3	3	4	5	6	8	4	3	8	5	4	2	7	6	4	7	5	7	6	5
8	5	8	9	1	3	4	5	4	6	8	8	2	3	2	6	6	3	2	5	5	5	6	4
7	7	6	9	2	3	4	4	4	2	9	8	2	8	2	9	1	2	1	2	5	9	3	4
8	9	4	8	3	3	6	4	7	9	4	4	3	7	5	4	8	3	9	7	5	5	3	6
9	5	6	8	2	3	4	7	4	5	9	9	8	*	*	*	*	*	3	2	5	5	8	4
9	7	7	8	2	3	4	5	5	2	7	7	9	*	*	*	*	*	3	5	5	7	8	4
7	7	5	9	1	3	8	5	3	2	7	6	3	*	*	*	*	*	1	7	5	9	3	3
9	6	5	8	3	4	4	4	4	7	6	6	7	4	4	5	5	5	6	8	5	4	6	5
9	4	7	9	2	3	4	5	5	4	7	7	9	*	*	*	*	*	3	4	5	5	8	4
9	8	6	8	2	3	4	4	9	5	7	6	8	4	3	7	5	3	5	4	5	7	6	4
7	9	2	8	2	3	4	4	3	9	6	6	2	9	2	7	2	7	7	8	5	9	3	4
1	2	8	6	4	4	4	4	3	5	9	9	6	2	4	2	9	4	4	3	5	2	9	5
2	2	8	6	4	3	4	4	3	6	7	9	5	*	*	*	*	*	3	2	5	5	5	5
4	3	8	6	5	4	4	4	4	7	5	6	9	3	6	4	6	5	3	4	5	4	9	6
2	4	8	6	5	4	4	4	3	7	8	7	2	8	5	6	3	6	9	2	5	5	4	6
1	3	2	3	7	3	4	4	4	4	3	2	3	*	*	*	*	*	3	2	5	2	7	5
2	2	7	6	4	4	4	4	3	2	9	9	7	2	3	3	9	2	3	3	5	3	8	4
1	1	7	5	4	3	4	4	4	2	6	7	8	1	6	6	6	3	2	3	5	3	7	4
1	1	6	5	6	3	4	4	2	5	4	4	7	2	5	1	9	3	2	3	5	2	8	6
1	2	8	6	4	3	4	4	2	2	9	9	5	2	6	9	2	2	4	2	5	2	8	5
5	5	6	4	7	4	4	4	4	9	4	3	5	8	6	4	5	6	6	7	5	2	5	8
1	1	8	4	7	3	4	4	3	2	9	9	3	2	7	3	8	3	4	3	5	5	8	5
1	2	7	7	3	3	4	5	2	2	8	8	9	*	*	*	*	*	3	4	4	2	9	5
1	2	6	5	4	3	4	4	2	2	7	8	9	*	*	*	*	*	4	2	5	3	9	4
1	2	5	4	7	3	4	4	2	4	3	4	7	1	5	2	8	4	3	2	5	3	9	6
2	2	6	5	4	3	4	5	2	2	7	7	9	*	*	*	*	*	2	7	4	2	5	4
3	3	9	7	3	4	4	4	3	6	9	8	8	*	*	*	*	*	3	3	5	3	6	5
4	2	6	6	4	3	4	4	3	4	8	8	9	*	*	*	*	*	2	5	5	5	7	5

Economic Indicators For Class IIA, IB, IIA, And IIB Counties

County	Class	Population	Land Area	Med House Val	Med Gross Rent	Av Farm Val./Acre	% Under 5	% 5–17	% 18 and Over	% 65 and Over	% Poverty	% Under $10,000	% $10–19,999	% $20–29,999	% $30–49,999	% Over $50,000
Grayson	IA	5	4	3	4	4	5	6	4	4	8	8	5	1	3	4
Greenup	IIB	7	3	6	8	4	5	8	3	1	3	2	2	9	9	7
Harlan	IIA	7	4	1	2	6	8	8	2	2	9	7	1	5	4	4
Henderson	IIB	7	4	7	9	8	5	5	5	2	2	1	5	8	9	8
Henry	IIA	4	3	5	3	8	2	5	6	4	6	5	6	5	4	4
Hopkins	IIB	7	4	4	7	6	5	4	5	4	4	3	1	8	9	7
Johnson	IA	5	3	5	7	5	6	7	3	2	8	7	1	4	6	6
Knox	IA	6	3	2	4	4	7	9	1	3	9	9	1	2	2	1
Larue	IIB	4	3	4	4	5	3	4	6	5	8	7	6	3	4	1
Laure	IIB	7	4	6	6	7	7	8	2	2	8	6	7	4	3	3
Lawrence	IA	4	3	5	5	3	6	8	2	4	9	9	1	2	6	3
Lee	IIA	3	3	2	3	2	6	7	3	6	9	9	1	1	2	3
Letcher	IA	6	3	1	2	4	8	9	1	2	9	8	2	4	3	3
Lewis	IIA	4	4	3	2	3	8	9	1	2	9	9	4	1	2	1
Lincoln	IIB	5	3	3	2	5	6	7	3	4	9	8	5	2	2	2
Livingston	IA	4	3	4	7	5	3	3	7	5	4	5	5	7	4	2
Lyon	IIA	3	3	7	3	5	1	1	9	7	4	3	5	7	7	5
McCreary	IA	4	4	1	3	3	8	9	1	2	9	9	1	1	1	2
Magoffin	IA	4	3	4	2	3	9	9	1	1	9	9	1	2	3	3
Menifee	IA	3	3	3	2	4	6	9	2	2	9	9	4	2	1	1
Mercer	IIA	5	3	6	6	7	4	4	6	4	5	4	4	8	7	2
Metcalfe	IIA	4	3	3	1	4	3	5	6	5	9	9	3	1	2	3
Montgomery	IB	5	3	6	4	7	7	7	3	2	7	6	7	3	4	4
Morgan	IIA	4	3	5	2	5	7	8	2	3	9	9	1	1	2	4
Muhlenberg	IIA	6	4	4	7	4	6	5	5	4	4	4	1	7	9	6
Nelson	IIB	5	4	6	5	6	8	9	1	2	5	3	7	7	6	5
Ohio	IIA	5	4	4	6	5	6	5	4	4	6	4	2	8	7	2
Owen	IIA	4	3	3	1	4	6	4	5	6	8	8	2	3	3	2
Owsley	IIA	3	3	1	1	3	6	8	2	4	9	9	1	1	1	1
Perry	IA	6	3	2	4	4	8	9	1	1	9	6	2	5	6	6
Powell	IB	4	3	4	5	4	8	9	1	1	9	8	4	3	2	2
Pulaski	IB	7	4	5	5	6	4	5	5	3	7	8	2	2	3	3
Rockcastle	IIA	4	3	1	1	4	4	8	3	3	9	9	3	1	1	2
Russell	IA	4	3	3	2	6	2	5	7	5	9	9	1	1	2	2
Scott	IB	5	3	9	7	9	6	5	5	2	4	2	6	8	6	7
Shelby	IA	5	3	8	7	9	3	5	6	3	4	2	2	9	8	8
Simpson	IIB	4	3	6	5	8	6	6	4	4	5	4	4	8	4	5
Taylor	IB	5	3	6	5	6	3	3	7	3	6	5	6	6	4	3
Trimble	IIA	3	3	6	7	6	4	7	4	2	4	4	7	6	5	3
Union	IIA	4	3	4	6	8	5	8	3	2	3	2	1	8	9	8
Wayne	IIA	4	4	2	1	4	6	7	3	3	9	9	4	1	1	2

% Completed HS	% College or More	Families/Pop	% Married Couples	% W/O Husband	% Black	% Spanish	% Amer Indian	% Asian	% Urban	% Rural	% Farmers	% Out of County	Jobs/Pop	% Manufacturing	% Wholesale	% Retail	% Services	Physicians/Cap	Crimes/Cap	$ Police/Crimes	$ Educ/Enrollment	Carpool or Transit	Pop Density
1	2	7	6	4	3	4	4	2	4	8	8	4	2	5	5	6	4	4	4	5	3	9	5
5	4	7	7	3	3	4	4	4	8	2	2	9	*	*	*	*	*	2	3	5	2	3	8
1	2	4	2	8	4	4	4	4	4	2	1	1	3	3	3	7	5	8	6	4	3	8	7
5	5	7	3	7	4	4	4	4	9	3	2	4	8	5	4	3	7	9	9	5	2	6	7
5	3	7	5	4	4	4	4	5	2	9	8	9	2	4	3	9	3	6	3	5	2	7	5
4	3	7	5	6	4	4	4	4	8	2	2	3	8	4	5	3	7	9	6	5	3	4	7
2	3	6	5	5	3	4	4	4	4	2	2	5	*	*	*	*	*	7	2	5	3	8	7
1	3	4	2	8	3	4	4	3	3	2	2	6	2	5	1	8	6	2	5	4	2	5	6
3	2	8	6	5	4	4	4	3	4	8	8	9	2	4	3	9	3	2	2	5	4	9	5
2	2	6	6	5	3	4	4	7	3	4	4	4	6	4	7	1	9	3	6	4	4	4	7
1	2	4	5	5	3	4	4	2	2	3	3	7	2	4	2	9	4	7	4	4	6	8	5
1	2	6	3	7	3	4	4	2	2	3	3	4	*	*	*	*	*	4	2	5	3	5	5
1	2	5	4	6	3	4	4	3	3	1	1	4	2	2	4	6	7	5	2	5	2	8	7
1	1	4	5	5	3	4	4	3	2	8	7	7	*	*	*	*	*	2	3	4	2	9	4
1	1	7	5	5	4	4	4	2	3	8	8	9	*	*	*	*	*	3	3	4	3	8	6
6	2	9	7	3	3	4	4	2	2	4	5	9	*	*	*	*	*	3	3	5	3	4	4
8	3	4	8	2	4	4	4	2	2	5	5	9	*	*	*	*	*	3	4	4	2	6	5
1	1	2	2	8	3	4	4	3	2	2	2	4	1	4	1	9	4	5	3	4	7	8	5
1	1	3	5	4	3	4	4	4	2	4	3	5	*	*	*	*	*	1	2	5	3	9	5
1	1	5	7	4	3	4	4	9	2	8	8	9	*	*	*	*	*	1	2	5	2	9	4
4	5	8	6	5	4	4	4	5	7	6	7	7	7	5	9	1	2	5	4	5	3	6	6
1	2	8	6	3	4	4	4	3	2	9	9	6	1	4	5	7	4	2	2	4	3	4	5
2	3	7	4	7	4	4	4	2	6	5	4	4	*	*	*	*	*	6	3	5	3	7	7
1	2	7	6	4	3	4	4	2	2	7	7	3	2	3	3	9	2	5	2	5	3	7	5
3	2	7	6	4	4	4	4	4	6	3	3	3	5	3	6	5	4	4	3	5	3	7	6
4	4	2	4	7	4	4	4	2	5	5	5	6	4	5	3	6	7	4	6	5	2	6	6
3	2	8	7	3	3	4	4	4	5	5	5	4	2	5	2	9	3	2	3	5	3	7	5
2	3	6	6	3	3	4	4	2	2	9	9	7	*	*	*	*	*	3	4	4	3	8	4
1	2	6	6	4	3	4	4	2	2	7	6	5	*	*	*	*	*	1	2	5	2	8	4
1	2	3	4	6	3	4	4	2	4	1	1	2	4	2	6	5	4	7	5	5	3	6	7
1	1	4	4	7	3	4	4	3	5	2	3	9	1	3	1	8	7	3	3	5	2	9	6
2	3	7	5	5	3	4	4	5	5	5	5	1	6	5	4	6	4	8	4	5	2	6	6
1	2	7	5	6	3	4	4	3	2	7	7	8	1	2	4	8	4	4	3	5	3	8	5
1	2	8	4	5	3	4	4	2	2	9	8	3	2	7	2	8	6	3	3	5	2	7	6
3	6	4	5	6	4	4	4	3	8	5	5	7	*	*	*	*	*	4	4	5	3	6	6
4	7	6	5	5	5	4	4	3	5	8	7	8	5	4	6	5	4	5	6	4	2	6	6
4	3	7	2	8	6	4	4	4	9	7	6	3	8	7	5	4	5	4	5	5	5	3	6
2	4	8	5	6	4	4	4	5	7	7	6	2	5	8	3	7	3	7	4	5	3	9	6
4	2	8	7	3	3	4	4	2	2	9	8	9	*	*	*	*	*	3	2	4	3	6	5
4	2	1	5	6	7	4	4	4	7	4	3	2	3	4	7	4	4	5	5	5	2	4	5
1	2	7	4	6	3	4	4	2	6	6	7	3	2	6	3	8	3	5	5	4	5	6	5

Economic Indicators For Class IIA, IB, IIA, And IIB Counties

		SIZE OF COUNTY		REAL-ESTATE VALUES			AGES OF POPULATION				INCOMES					
		Population	Land Area	Med House Val	Med Gross Rent	Av Farm Val./Acre	% Under 5	% 5–17	% 18 and Over	% 65 and Over	% Poverty	% Under $10,000	% $10–19,999	% $20–29,999	% $30–49,999	% Over $50,000
Webster	IIA	4	3	2	4	6	5	4	6	7	5	5	1	7	7	6
Whitley	IA	6	4	3	5	3	6	7	4	3	9	9	2	2	2	4
Wolfe	IIA	3	3	2	1	2	8	7	2	3	9	9	1	1	2	1
Woodford	IB	4	3	9	8	9	4	8	3	1	2	1	2	9	9	8
LOUISIANA																
Assumption	IIA	5	3	6	2	8	9	9	1	1	7	3	1	8	9	6
Beauregard	IB	6	6	5	7	5	7	9	2	1	5	4	1	6	9	8
Caldwell	IIA	4	4	2	2	6	6	7	3	6	8	9	1	2	5	5
Cameron	IIB	4	7	6	7	5	8	7	2	1	3	1	1	8	9	9
De Soto	IIA	5	5	3	2	4	6	7	3	6	8	7	2	3	6	7
Grant	IA	4	4	2	2	6	5	8	3	5	7	7	1	5	6	3
La Salle	IB	4	4	2	3	6	6	5	4	5	7	6	2	5	5	5
Lincoln	IIB	7	4	8	8	5	2	1	9	2	6	6	1	4	8	8
Natchitoches	IIB	7	7	5	4	6	7	6	3	3	9	8	2	3	4	6
Red River	IIA	4	3	4	1	5	8	8	2	5	9	9	1	2	4	3
Sabine	IA	5	5	2	1	5	6	6	4	6	8	7	4	2	3	6
St. Martin	IB	7	5	7	2	7	9	9	1	1	7	3	3	7	8	6
Tangipahoa	IB	9	5	7	5	9	9	7	2	2	8	7	1	4	6	7
Union	IIA	5	5	3	2	5	5	5	5	6	7	8	3	3	3	6
Vermilion	IIB	7	6	6	4	8	8	8	2	2	5	4	1	7	8	9
West Feliciana	IIA	4	3	9	2	5	1	1	9	1	9	7	1	4	6	9
MAINE																
Franklin	IIB	5	8	6	7	3	3	6	5	3	2	3	8	6	5	3
Hancock	IIA	7	7	7	9	3	2	3	8	6	3	5	9	3	3	2
Kennebec	IIB	9	5	8	8	5	3	5	6	3	2	2	8	7	6	4
Knox	IIA	6	3	7	9	4	2	3	8	7	3	5	8	4	3	5
Lincoln	IA	5	4	9	9	6	3	3	7	6	4	4	9	4	3	3
Oxford	IIB	8	9	6	6	3	3	6	5	5	3	4	9	5	4	3
Waldo	IA	6	5	6	8	4	5	6	4	3	6	6	9	2	1	2
Washington	IIA	6	9	4	7	2	5	4	6	5	7	8	6	2	2	1
MARYLAND																
Caroline	IIB	5	3	7	7	9	3	5	6	4	3	4	5	7	7	5
Garrett	IB	5	4	7	7	7	5	7	3	3	4	4	9	5	3	4
Queen Annes	IB	5	3	9	8	9	3	3	7	3	2	1	2	9	9	9
Worcester	IB	6	4	8	8	9	2	2	9	4	3	3	6	6	7	8
MASSACHUSETTS																
Dukes	IB	4	3	9	9	9	1	1	9	8	2	3	9	4	6	7

SOCIO-ECONOMIC STATUS					MINORITIES				RURAL-URBAN				ECONOMIC BASE					COUNTY CONDITIONS					
% Completed HS	% College or More	Families/Pop	% Married Couples	% W/O Husband	% Black	% Spanish	% Amer Indian	% Asian	% Urban	% Rural	% Farmers	% Out of County	Jobs/Pop	% Manufacturing	% Wholesale	% Retail	% Services	Physicians/Cap	Crimes/Cap	$ Police/Crimes	$ Educ/Enrollment	Carpool or Transit	Pop Density
4	2	7	6	4	4	4	4	3	6	4	4	8	3	3	5	3	8	2	2	5	4	5	5
1	4	5	3	8	3	4	4	5	7	2	2	4	7	5	4	3	8	8	6	5	2	5	6
1	2	6	2	8	3	4	4	3	2	7	7	6	*	*	*	*	*	3	3	5	5	9	4
4	9	6	5	5	5	4	4	4	7	6	4	8	*	*	*	*	*	8	6	5	2	5	7
1	2	1	3	6	9	5	4	2	3	2	1	9	1	4	8	5	2	2	3	5	3	9	6
4	6	2	5	5	6	4	4	6	7	3	3	7	3	4	2	8	5	5	5	5	3	6	4
2	3	4	3	7	7	5	4	4	2	2	3	7	1	3	5	8	2	4	6	5	9	6	4
2	2	4	7	2	4	5	4	4	2	3	3	4	7	3	2	1	9	3	*	*	8	4	4
2	4	3	1	9	9	4	4	4	5	2	3	7	2	4	3	8	3	2	4	5	3	8	4
3	3	5	4	6	7	5	4	5	2	2	2	9	1	4	4	8	3	3	2	5	4	8	4
4	5	6	5	5	5	4	5	7	5	2	2	4	3	5	9	4	1	5	2	5	4	3	4
1	9	1	1	9	9	4	4	8	9	2	2	3	7	4	6	5	4	7	7	5	1	5	7
2	9	1	1	9	9	5	4	5	7	2	2	3	*	*	*	*	*	5	6	5	3	7	5
2	2	3	1	9	9	4	4	3	2	3	3	5	3	5	6	7	2	5	*	*	3	8	4
4	3	5	3	6	7	7	6	3	5	2	2	5	2	5	3	4	8	4	4	6	5	9	4
1	2	1	2	8	9	5	4	7	6	2	2	9	2	6	8	6	2	2	3	5	3	7	5
2	6	1	1	9	9	4	4	4	6	2	2	5	*	*	*	*	*	5	6	5	2	5	7
3	4	5	4	6	9	4	4	3	4	2	3	9	1	5	8	2	5	4	6	5	3	6	4
1	3	4	4	6	6	5	4	8	7	3	3	5	4	3	6	3	7	5	5	5	4	7	5
3	5	1	1	9	9	4	4	4	2	2	2	6	*	*	*	*	*	7	3	5	6	9	4
8	8	2	4	6	3	4	4	5	3	2	2	3	7	8	2	1	9	9	7	5	4	7	4
9	9	5	5	6	3	4	4	3	5	2	1	2	6	4	2	8	5	9	8	5	4	8	4
7	9	2	3	7	3	4	4	7	9	2	2	2	8	4	4	6	6	9	8	5	3	6	8
9	9	4	4	7	3	4	4	4	7	2	2	2	7	4	3	6	7	9	8	5	3	5	7
9	9	7	5	5	3	4	4	2	2	2	2	6	6	3	1	6	9	9	6	5	7	7	6
8	6	5	4	6	3	4	4	6	5	2	2	3	5	7	2	6	7	7	5	5	6	7	4
7	8	4	4	6	3	4	4	6	5	2	2	7	3	6	5	6	4	7	6	5	2	6	5
7	6	4	4	6	3	4	6	4	3	2	2	1	3	5	2	9	2	6	6	5	6	6	4
3	5	6	2	7	7	4	4	3	2	5	4	8	4	5	6	3	5	3	7	5	8	5	6
5	3	4	6	4	3	4	4	4	2	3	3	4	6	4	4	4	8	6	9	4	8	6	5
5	8	7	5	5	6	4	4	3	2	3	2	9	4	3	8	3	4	3	7	4	8	7	6
4	7	5	2	8	8	4	4	9	5	3	2	4	9	3	2	2	9	6	9	5	9	9	6
9	9	3	2	8	4	4	5	3	2	2	2	1	*	*	*	*	*	9	9	5	9	4	7

Economic Indicators For Class IIA, IB, IIA, And IIB Counties	SIZE OF COUNTY		REAL-ESTATE VALUES			AGES OF POPULATION				INCOMES					
	Population	Land Area	Med House Val	Med Gross Rent	Av Farm Val./Acre	% Under 5	% 5–17	% 18 and Over	% 65 and Over	% Poverty	% Under $10,000	% $10–19,999	% $20–29,999	% $30–49,999	% Over $50,000
Nantucket IA	3	2	9	9	9	1	1	9	8	1	1	3	9	9	9
MICHIGAN															
Alcona IB	4	4	6	7	3	1	3	8	9	5	8	7	2	2	2
Antrim IA	4	4	7	9	5	4	5	5	6	2	3	8	7	5	5
Arenac IB	4	3	6	8	5	4	7	4	4	4	5	5	6	5	3
Charlevoix IIA	5	4	7	9	4	6	6	4	3	2	3	5	7	7	4
Cheboygan IB	5	5	6	8	3	4	7	4	4	4	4	8	5	4	2
Emmet IB	5	4	8	9	3	3	5	5	3	2	3	4	7	8	7
Hillsdale IIB	7	4	5	9	7	5	6	4	3	2	2	6	8	7	6
Ionia IIB	8	4	5	9	6	7	7	3	1	2	1	4	9	9	6
Kalkaska IA	4	4	6	9	4	9	8	2	2	4	3	6	8	5	4
Leelanau IB	4	3	9	9	7	2	5	6	4	2	1	7	8	8	8
Manistee IIA	5	4	5	8	4	2	4	7	6	2	3	5	7	6	4
Mason IIB	5	4	5	7	4	4	3	7	5	3	3	8	7	6	3
Missaukee IA	4	4	4	8	4	7	8	2	3	4	5	9	4	3	2
Montcalm IIB	7	5	4	8	5	6	8	3	3	3	3	6	8	6	4
Oceana IB	5	4	4	9	5	7	8	2	3	3	3	7	7	5	5
Osceola IA	5	4	3	7	3	6	8	3	4	3	4	8	5	4	2
Sanilac IIB	7	5	5	9	7	5	7	3	4	3	2	7	7	6	6
Tuscola IIB	8	5	7	9	9	6	9	1	1	2	1	3	9	9	6
Wexford IB	5	4	5	8	4	5	6	4	4	3	4	8	4	5	6
MINNESOTA															
Aitkin IIA	4	8	7	3	2	3	3	7	9	5	8	6	2	2	1
Becker IIB	6	7	8	7	3	6	8	3	5	5	5	7	5	4	5
Beltrami IIB	6	9	7	8	2	6	4	5	2	5	6	5	4	5	4
Benton IIB	5	3	9	9	5	9	7	2	2	2	2	7	9	7	4
Cook IIB	3	7	8	6	3	2	2	8	5	2	3	4	6	9	5
Crow Wing IIB	7	6	8	7	2	5	4	5	6	4	5	5	6	4	3
Dodge IIB	4	4	9	8	9	9	7	2	3	2	1	6	9	8	7
Douglas IB	6	4	9	7	4	5	3	6	6	3	5	6	6	4	4
Hubbard IB	4	5	6	3	2	5	6	4	7	6	6	7	3	3	4
Itasca IIB	7	9	7	8	2	7	6	3	3	2	2	2	9	8	3
Kanabec IB	4	4	7	7	4	7	8	2	5	3	4	7	5	5	4
Kandiyohi IIB	6	5	9	9	7	6	3	7	4	2	2	8	7	7	8
Meeker IIB	5	4	8	7	7	7	6	4	7	3	3	6	7	6	7
Mille Lacs IIB	5	4	7	7	4	7	6	3	7	3	5	5	7	4	4
Otter Tail IIA	8	8	7	8	4	3	3	7	8	4	5	6	4	4	6
Pine IIA	5	7	7	6	3	7	6	3	6	4	6	6	5	4	2
Steele IIB	6	4	9	9	9	7	4	5	3	2	1	6	9	8	6

% Completed HS	% College or More	Families/Pop	% Married Couples	% W/O Husband	% Black	% Spanish	% Amer Indian	% Asian	% Urban	% Rural	% Farmers	% Out of County	Jobs/Pop	% Manufacturing	% Wholesale	% Retail	% Services	Physicians/Cap	Crimes/Cap	$ Police/Crimes	$ Educ/Enrollment	Carpool or Transit	Pop Density
9	9	2	2	8	3	4	4	9	9	1	1	1	*	*	*	*	*	9	9	5	9	3	8
8	3	9	7	2	3	4	4	5	2	2	4	8	*	*	*	*	*	5	9	5	3	5	4
8	7	7	7	3	3	4	5	4	2	2	2	7	6	5	2	1	9	3	8	5	7	6	5
5	2	6	6	4	3	4	4	3	2	4	4	7	*	*	*	*	*	2	8	4	5	6	5
8	8	5	5	5	3	4	6	4	6	2	2	4	7	5	1	1	9	8	9	5	4	3	5
8	5	6	6	5	3	4	5	7	5	2	2	3	7	4	2	8	6	4	9	5	4	4	4
8	9	2	5	5	3	4	6	4	5	2	2	2	9	3	2	3	9	9	9	5	7	3	5
8	5	4	6	4	3	4	4	6	4	5	4	5	4	7	6	3	5	3	8	5	4	4	6
7	3	1	5	6	4	5	4	5	6	4	3	7	4	7	2	9	3	3	8	5	5	7	7
7	3	6	7	3	3	4	5	5	2	2	2	6	4	3	3	8	5	3	9	5	8	5	4
9	9	6	8	2	3	4	5	5	2	3	3	9	4	3	1	2	9	6	5	5	5	3	5
8	5	5	6	4	3	4	5	5	6	2	2	2	5	6	2	6	6	7	9	5	4	8	5
8	6	6	6	4	3	4	5	6	6	3	3	2	7	5	2	7	7	9	9	5	9	6	5
7	3	7	8	2	3	4	4	8	2	5	5	8	2	3	3	9	2	2	6	5	3	4	4
7	4	5	6	5	3	4	4	8	4	3	3	5	5	6	5	7	2	4	8	5	8	6	6
7	4	4	7	4	3	6	5	4	2	4	4	8	*	*	*	*	*	4	7	5	3	5	5
7	4	5	6	4	3	4	5	5	2	3	4	5	2	8	3	7	5	3	8	5	6	5	5
7	3	5	6	4	3	5	4	5	2	7	6	4	3	7	8	4	2	3	7	5	5	4	5
7	3	3	6	4	3	5	4	5	3	4	3	8	3	5	8	5	2	4	6	5	5	5	6
7	6	6	5	6	3	4	4	6	7	2	2	2	9	5	2	4	9	9	9	4	4	5	5
8	4	8	7	2	3	4	5	4	2	4	7	3	*	*	*	*	*	5	9	5	9	3	4
6	5	3	6	3	3	4	8	5	5	7	6	2	6	4	3	6	7	7	9	5	5	4	4
4	9	1	4	6	3	4	9	9	7	3	3	2	8	3	2	7	7	8	9	5	5	6	4
6	7	1	7	3	3	4	4	8	8	7	5	9	8	4	6	4	5	3	5	5	3	8	6
9	9	5	7	3	3	4	8	9	2	2	1	2	*	*	*	*	*	9	9	5	9	7	3
8	7	5	6	4	3	4	5	5	6	3	2	2	8	3	3	7	6	8	9	5	7	4	5
8	5	5	8	2	3	4	4	6	4	9	8	8	5	3	9	3	2	3	7	5	8	5	5
7	6	4	8	2	3	4	5	9	5	7	6	1	9	3	5	4	6	9	7	5	6	4	5
7	8	6	7	3	3	4	5	4	4	3	5	5	*	*	*	*	*	6	8	5	7	4	4
8	7	5	7	3	3	4	6	5	4	2	2	2	6	3	2	8	6	7	6	5	8	5	4
6	4	5	7	3	3	4	4	9	5	8	8	5	4	4	4	9	2	6	5	5	5	5	4
7	7	3	8	2	3	4	4	8	8	6	5	1	*	*	*	*	*	9	7	5	5	7	5
7	4	4	8	2	3	4	4	6	6	9	8	4	6	3	5	8	2	5	6	5	8	4	5
6	4	4	7	3	3	4	6	9	4	7	7	4	6	4	3	9	3	7	9	5	9	5	5
7	6	5	8	2	3	4	4	4	5	8	8	2	6	3	3	8	5	8	5	5	6	4	4
6	4	3	6	3	3	4	5	9	2	7	8	5	5	3	1	9	3	3	8	5	7	4	4
7	8	4	8	2	3	4	4	7	9	6	5	2	9	5	3	7	6	7	6	5	6	3	6

Economic Indicators For Class IIA, IB, IIA, And IIB Counties

		SIZE OF COUNTY		REAL-ESTATE VALUES			AGES OF POPULATION				INCOMES					
		Population	Land Area	Med House Val	Med Gross Rent	Av Farm Val./Acre	% Under 5	% 5–17	% 18 and Over	% 65 and Over	% Poverty	% Under $10,000	% $10–19,999	% $20–29,999	% $30–49,999	% Over $50,000
Todd	IIA	5	5	5	5	4	8	8	2	6	7	7	7	2	3	3
Wabasha	IIB	5	4	9	7	7	7	6	4	6	3	2	6	8	7	7
Wadena	IIB	4	4	5	4	3	6	7	3	7	6	7	5	3	3	2
MISSISSIPPI																
Alcorn	IB	6	3	5	4	4	5	6	4	3	5	6	5	4	4	6
Claiborne	IA	4	4	3	1	3	8	5	4	3	9	9	1	1	8	4
Clarke	IIA	4	4	3	3	3	7	7	3	5	7	7	7	4	2	3
Clay	IIB	5	3	4	5	4	9	8	2	3	8	5	7	4	3	4
Covington	IIA	4	3	3	2	5	7	9	1	4	9	9	1	2	3	3
Greene	IIA	4	5	2	1	4	9	9	1	3	8	9	4	3	1	1
Itawamba	IB	5	4	4	4	4	3	5	6	4	4	6	9	4	1	3
Lafayette	IB	6	4	8	8	4	2	1	9	2	6	6	4	4	6	4
Lamar	IB	5	4	8	9	4	7	9	2	1	5	4	6	7	6	5
Lauderdale	IIB	9	5	6	4	3	6	5	5	3	6	6	3	4	6	6
Lawrence	IIA	4	4	4	5	3	8	9	2	3	6	6	2	4	8	3
Lee	IB	8	4	7	7	5	6	7	4	2	4	4	8	6	4	6
Lincoln	IIB	6	4	4	4	3	7	8	2	4	7	6	3	5	5	3
Madison	IA	7	5	7	7	5	9	9	1	2	9	6	1	4	7	6
Marion	IIB	5	4	4	2	4	8	8	2	3	8	8	2	4	3	3
Marshall	IA	6	5	4	1	4	8	9	1	2	9	8	3	4	2	3
Neshoba	IIA	5	4	4	2	4	7	8	2	5	8	8	4	2	3	4
Pike	IIA	6	3	4	2	4	8	8	2	4	8	8	2	2	3	5
Pontotoc	IIA	5	4	4	3	4	5	6	4	5	6	7	5	4	2	3
Prentiss	IIB	5	3	3	3	3	4	6	5	4	5	7	6	3	2	3
Scott	IIB	5	4	2	2	4	7	9	2	3	9	8	5	2	3	4
Simpson	IIB	5	4	3	5	4	7	8	2	4	7	7	3	4	4	2
Stone	IIB	4	4	3	5	5	5	7	4	2	5	4	7	5	7	2
Tippah	IIA	5	4	2	3	5	5	6	4	6	8	8	9	1	1	2
Tishomingo	IA	5	4	4	6	4	3	3	7	4	3	5	8	4	3	2
Union	IIA	5	3	4	2	4	5	5	5	5	6	7	6	3	2	3
Warren	IIB	8	4	7	7	3	8	8	2	2	5	3	1	7	9	6
Wayne	IIB	5	5	3	2	4	9	9	1	2	9	9	2	2	3	2
MISSOURI																
Andrew	IIA	4	4	7	7	6	6	4	5	5	2	2	8	8	6	6
Barry	IA	5	5	5	3	4	3	2	8	9	4	8	6	2	3	3
Benton	IA	4	5	3	5	3	1	1	9	9	6	8	5	1	2	4
Bollinger	IIA	4	4	2	2	3	4	4	6	7	9	9	6	1	1	1
Callaway	IB	6	5	7	8	5	4	3	6	3	2	1	4	9	8	4
Cape Girardeau	IIB	8	4	8	8	6	2	1	9	3	2	3	4	8	7	7

% Completed HS	% College or More	Families/Pop	% Married Couples	% W/O Husband	% Black	% Spanish	% Amer Indian	% Asian	% Urban	% Rural	% Farmers	% Out of County	Jobs/Pop	% Manufacturing	% Wholesale	% Retail	% Services	Physicians/Cap	Crimes/Cap	$ Police/Crimes	$ Educ/Enrollment	Carpool or Transit	Pop Density
5	4	3	8	2	3	4	4	5	5	9	9	3	4	4	7	5	2	5	5	5	6	4	4
7	5	4	8	2	3	4	4	7	4	8	7	5	6	4	5	7	4	7	6	5	8	4	5
5	6	3	7	3	3	4	4	4	7	7	7	3	8	3	8	4	3	6	6	5	8	3	4
3	4	7	4	6	5	4	4	6	8	2	2	2	6	8	3	4	7	7	9	5	2	9	7
1	8	1	1	9	9	4	4	8	2	2	2	3	*	*	*	*	*	3	3	5	1	9	4
3	2	5	2	8	9	4	4	4	4	3	3	5	2	9	5	5	4	3	2	5	2	9	4
2	5	2	1	9	9	4	4	6	7	2	2	3	4	9	4	3	7	4	4	5	2	7	5
2	3	3	2	8	9	4	4	3	2	3	4	7	2	6	9	3	2	4	1	5	2	8	5
3	2	3	5	5	7	4	4	2	2	3	4	9	*	*	*	*	*	3	1	6	3	9	4
2	2	8	6	4	4	4	4	9	4	4	3	8	1	9	3	8	2	3	2	6	8	9	5
1	9	1	2	8	8	4	4	9	6	2	2	2	*	*	*	*	*	8	9	5	1	7	5
4	8	5	5	5	5	4	4	9	4	2	2	9	*	*	*	*	*	2	2	5	2	5	5
6	6	3	1	9	9	4	4	9	9	2	2	1	9	4	7	2	7	9	8	5	3	9	8
3	3	4	3	7	9	4	4	2	2	3	3	7	*	*	*	*	*	4	1	9	2	8	4
5	7	6	3	8	7	4	4	4	8	2	2	2	9	6	8	1	7	9	8	5	2	6	8
4	5	4	2	8	9	4	4	5	7	2	2	4	5	4	5	3	8	7	4	5	2	5	5
2	9	1	1	9	9	4	4	6	8	2	2	9	2	5	7	3	4	4	8	5	1	9	6
3	3	4	2	8	9	4	4	4	6	3	3	4	4	5	6	6	3	5	3	5	2	7	5
1	3	1	1	9	9	4	4	6	5	2	3	8	1	6	4	8	3	3	1	9	1	9	5
2	4	5	3	7	7	4	9	3	5	3	4	4	3	7	4	5	5	4	1	7	1	6	5
3	6	3	1	9	9	4	4	4	6	2	2	2	7	4	6	4	5	9	8	5	4	7	7
3	3	7	5	5	6	4	4	4	5	5	4	6	1	9	2	8	4	5	*	*	2	8	5
2	2	7	4	6	5	4	4	2	6	3	3	5	3	7	5	7	3	3	2	5	8	9	6
2	3	4	2	8	9	4	4	3	7	3	4	5	3	8	4	7	3	3	2	5	3	9	5
3	3	4	3	7	9	4	4	2	5	3	3	6	*	*	*	*	*	3	2	5	2	8	5
4	6	1	4	6	8	4	4	2	6	2	3	5	3	6	3	8	3	4	1	9	9	4	4
3	2	6	4	6	6	4	4	3	5	3	4	4	2	8	5	2	7	4	1	9	2	7	5
4	2	9	6	4	4	4	4	2	3	2	2	3	2	9	6	5	3	6	*	*	2	9	5
3	4	8	5	5	6	4	4	3	6	4	4	5	3	8	6	4	4	6	2	5	3	8	5
3	9	2	1	9	9	4	4	9	8	2	1	2	9	4	7	3	6	9	8	5	2	7	7
2	2	3	2	8	9	4	4	2	5	2	3	5	2	6	3	8	4	3	2	5	2	8	4
8	6	8	8	2	3	4	4	3	7	8	8	9	2	2	6	6	4	3	4	5	3	4	5
8	3	9	8	2	3	4	4	6	4	8	8	4	4	7	5	5	4	4	2	5	5	5	5
6	3	9	8	2	3	4	4	3	2	8	8	4	3	3	8	6	1	1	3	5	4	3	4
2	1	8	8	2	3	4	4	2	2	8	9	8	1	6	9	4	1	2	4	5	4	9	4
5	6	2	6	4	4	4	4	9	8	5	5	7	5	3	2	8	4	4	9	5	1	8	5
5	9	3	6	5	4	4	4	6	9	3	3	2	9	4	6	3	6	9	9	5	2	5	7

Economic Indicators For Class IIA, IB, IIA, And IIB Counties

		SIZE OF COUNTY		REAL-ESTATE VALUES			AGES OF POPULATION				INCOMES					
		Population	Land Area	Med House Val	Med Gross Rent	Av Farm Val./Acre	% Under 5	% 5–17	% 18 and Over	% 65 and Over	% Poverty	% Under $10,000	% $10–19,999	% $20–29,999	% $30–49,999	% Over $50,000
Carter	IA	3	4	1	2	3	6	6	4	6	8	9	3	1	1	2
Cedar	IA	4	4	4	3	3	1	1	9	9	4	9	3	1	2	3
Christian	IA	5	4	6	6	5	5	7	4	2	3	3	8	6	4	5
Clinton	IA	4	4	7	6	6	4	8	4	5	2	2	2	9	9	5
Cole	IB	8	3	9	9	4	4	2	8	2	1	1	3	9	9	8
Crawford	IB	5	5	3	4	3	5	5	5	7	4	7	6	3	3	2
Dallas	IIA	4	4	2	3	3	3	3	7	9	6	9	2	1	2	6
De Kalb	IIA	3	4	2	4	5	3	3	7	9	5	7	4	3	5	3
Dent	IA	4	5	3	4	2	4	3	7	7	6	8	5	3	2	2
Douglas	IA	4	5	3	3	3	4	5	6	6	8	9	2	1	1	3
Hickory	IA	3	3	4	4	3	1	1	9	9	8	9	2	1	1	2
Howe	IIB	6	5	4	3	3	3	4	7	6	7	9	5	1	1	4
Iron	IIB	4	4	3	3	3	5	5	5	7	5	7	3	6	2	2
Laclede	IB	5	5	4	5	3	4	5	6	5	5	8	6	2	2	5
Lafayette	IIA	6	4	5	6	7	3	3	7	7	2	2	4	8	8	5
Lawrence	IIA	6	4	4	3	5	4	4	6	8	4	7	6	4	2	3
McDonald	IIA	4	4	2	2	5	4	6	5	5	8	8	8	1	1	4
Madison	IA	4	4	2	2	3	2	2	8	9	7	9	3	2	1	5
Miller	IA	5	4	5	4	3	5	4	6	6	4	6	7	4	3	2
Moniteau	IIA	4	3	3	3	4	4	3	7	7	2	5	6	4	5	5
Morgan	IA	4	4	5	3	4	2	2	9	9	6	8	5	2	2	2
Newton	IB	7	4	5	4	5	3	5	6	4	4	5	9	3	4	4
Oregon	IIA	4	5	1	2	2	2	4	7	9	9	9	1	1	1	1
Ozark	IA	3	5	3	1	2	3	2	8	8	8	9	4	1	1	3
Perry	IIB	4	4	6	7	5	7	5	4	7	3	4	8	6	3	2
Polk	IA	5	4	3	4	4	2	2	8	8	4	8	5	2	2	5
Ralls	IIA	4	4	4	5	6	6	4	5	6	2	2	7	9	6	4
Randolph	IIA	5	4	3	6	5	5	1	8	7	3	5	3	6	6	5
Ray	IA	5	4	6	7	6	4	7	4	4	2	1	4	9	9	6
Reynolds	IIA	3	5	2	3	3	5	6	5	5	8	8	4	3	1	1
Ripley	IA	4	4	2	2	3	4	3	7	8	9	9	2	1	1	1
St. Clair	IIA	4	4	2	2	4	1	2	8	9	8	9	2	1	3	2
St. Francois	IIB	4	4	7	6	4	6	7	3	3	2	1	7	9	8	4
Ste. Genevieve	IIB	9	4	9	9	9	2	4	7	2	1	1	1	9	9	9
Stoddard	IIA	6	5	3	4	8	2	4	7	7	5	8	5	2	2	3
Stone	IA	4	4	8	5	4	1	1	9	9	5	7	9	2	2	4
Taney	IB	5	4	8	7	3	1	1	9	9	3	6	8	3	3	3
Texas	IIA	5	6	3	2	3	4	4	6	7	6	9	5	1	1	3
Warren	IA	4	4	8	8	7	5	5	5	6	2	2	2	8	9	8
Washington	IIB	4	5	2	3	2	8	9	1	2	7	7	8	2	2	2
Wayne	IA	4	5	1	3	3	1	3	8	9	8	9	1	1	1	3

SOCIO-ECONOMIC STATUS					MINORITIES				RURAL-URBAN				ECONOMIC BASE					COUNTY CONDITIONS					
% Completed HS	% College or More	Families/Pop	% Married Couples	% W/O Husband	% Black	% Spanish	% Amer Indian	% Asian	% Urban	% Rural	% Farmers	% Out of County	Jobs/Pop	% Manufacturing	% Wholesale	% Retail	% Services	Physicians/Cap	Crimes/Cap	$ Police/Crimes	$ Educ/Enrollment	Carpool or Transit	Pop Density
3	3	6	7	3	3	4	5	2	2	4	5	4	2	5	1	6	8	1	2	5	7	5	4
7	3	9	8	2	3	4	5	4	6	6	8	3	3	5	3	9	2	3	2	5	5	4	4
8	3	9	7	3	3	4	5	4	5	6	7	9	2	6	7	6	2	2	*	*	2	6	5
9	5	5	7	3	3	4	4	3	5	6	6	9	5	3	5	5	6	2	7	5	4	5	5
6	9	1	5	5	5	4	4	8	9	2	2	2	9	4	5	4	7	9	6	5	2	8	8
3	3	7	7	3	3	4	4	5	2	4	4	8	3	5	2	8	5	2	4	5	2	6	4
6	2	8	8	2	3	4	5	3	2	8	9	7	2	3	4	8	3	3	3	5	3	4	4
9	4	8	8	2	3	4	4	5	3	9	9	8	4	2	9	1	8	1	3	5	5	3	4
3	3	8	7	3	3	4	4	7	6	5	6	4	5	6	5	3	7	4	6	5	3	7	4
4	3	8	8	2	3	4	5	2	5	9	9	5	2	5	3	9	2	2	2	5	3	4	4
8	3	9	9	1	3	4	4	2	2	9	9	4	*	*	*	*	*	1	*	*	8	6	4
5	3	8	7	3	3	4	5	3	5	6	7	1	8	5	7	4	4	4	5	5	4	5	5
4	3	5	8	3	3	4	5	6	2	3	3	3	3	7	2	8	6	4	2	5	7	6	4
6	3	8	7	4	3	4	5	4	7	5	6	2	7	5	3	6	6	4	8	5	3	4	5
8	5	6	7	3	4	4	4	7	8	7	6	7	5	4	6	6	4	4	3	5	4	6	5
7	4	8	7	3	3	4	4	4	7	6	7	7	3	5	3	8	3	6	4	5	3	4	5
6	3	8	7	3	3	4	5	4	2	7	8	8	2	6	7	4	3	1	1	5	1	8	4
3	2	9	6	4	3	4	4	7	7	4	4	4	3	5	2	9	2	4	2	5	4	7	4
6	3	7	7	3	3	4	4	7	5	6	7	6	8	3	2	1	9	2	*	*	5	9	5
6	4	6	7	3	3	4	4	3	5	8	8	7	3	7	4	8	2	3	2	5	5	7	4
7	3	9	8	2	3	4	5	4	2	8	7	6	5	3	8	1	8	3	5	5	2	8	4
8	5	8	8	3	3	4	5	5	7	4	5	8	3	5	3	6	7	3	6	4	3	4	6
5	2	8	6	4	3	4	4	4	2	9	9	4	*	*	*	*	*	2	2	5	4	5	4
6	3	9	7	3	3	4	5	4	2	8	9	8	2	3	1	8	8	4	*	*	4	8	4
2	2	4	8	2	3	4	4	7	8	7	7	4	7	4	3	8	3	6	2	5	2	8	5
6	5	5	8	2	3	4	5	3	6	8	9	6	4	4	8	4	2	3	2	5	3	5	4
7	3	9	9	2	3	4	4	2	2	9	9	9	1	8	8	1	9	1	9	6	1	3	4
8	5	3	6	5	4	4	4	7	9	4	4	2	8	4	5	4	6	6	3	5	4	5	5
8	3	7	8	2	3	4	5	5	5	6	6	9	3	3	7	6	2	3	4	5	3	9	5
3	1	8	8	2	3	4	4	3	2	5	6	4	2	5	5	4	6	2	4	5	8	7	4
2	1	8	5	5	3	4	4	4	2	5	5	3	1	5	4	8	2	2	3	5	3	5	4
6	4	8	8	2	3	4	5	4	2	8	9	5	3	2	5	9	1	5	*	*	4	5	4
4	2	3	8	2	3	4	4	3	6	5	5	6	4	9	2	7	5	3	4	5	2	8	4
7	9	5	4	6	5	4	4	9	9	1	1	7	9	4	5	1	9	7	9	5	4	9	9
3	3	8	6	4	3	4	4	4	5	6	5	3	5	6	6	6	2	3	1	8	5	4	5
8	8	9	9	1	3	4	5	6	2	6	6	6	3	4	1	1	9	4	*	*	4	6	5
9	9	9	8	2	3	4	5	5	3	3	3	2	8	3	2	3	9	5	*	*	2	4	5
5	3	8	7	3	3	4	4	5	2	7	8	3	3	7	2	9	2	3	1	5	4	7	4
5	3	6	8	2	4	4	4	3	4	6	5	9	5	5	3	6	6	3	3	5	2	9	5
1	1	4	5	5	3	4	4	2	3	2	3	8	1	4	2	6	8	2	8	5	3	9	4
2	1	9	7	3	3	4	5	3	2	3	4	3	2	6	1	9	5	2	3	5	4	9	4

Economic Indicators For Class IIA, IB, IIA, And IIB Counties		SIZE OF COUNTY		REAL-ESTATE VALUES			AGES OF POPULATION				INCOMES					
		Population	Land Area	Med House Val	Med Gross Rent	Av Farm Val./Acre	% Under 5	% 5–17	% 18 and Over	% 65 and Over	% Poverty	% Under $10,000	% $10–19,999	% $20–29,999	% $30–49,999	% Over $50,000
Webster	IA	5	4	4	5	4	7	8	3	4	5	6	8	3	3	3
Wright	IIA	4	4	2	3	3	4	4	6	7	8	9	5	1	1	5
MONTANA																
Broadwater	IA	3	6	7	5	2	8	5	3	3	4	3	9	4	5	7
Carbon	IIA	3	9	7	4	2	5	2	7	8	3	4	9	5	3	5
Jefferson	IA	3	8	9	6	1	6	9	2	1	1	1	8	9	8	9
Musselshell	IIA	3	8	2	3	1	7	4	5	6	6	7	4	5	2	3
Park	IIB	4	9	8	6	2	4	2	7	5	2	3	5	8	7	6
Richland	IB	4	9	9	9	2	9	4	3	2	2	1	6	9	9	8
Rosebud	IA	4	9	9	7	1	9	9	1	1	5	2	1	9	9	7
Sanders	IB	4	9	6	2	2	7	5	4	4	3	5	8	4	3	4
Stillwater	IIA	3	8	9	6	2	6	3	6	6	4	5	6	6	5	2
Yellowstone	IB	3	3	6	3	1	1	1	9	1	1	4	9	4	1	6
NEBRASKA																
Box Butte	IA	4	6	9	9	2	9	2	5	3	1	1	4	9	9	9
Cass	IIA	5	4	7	8	7	5	6	4	3	1	1	7	9	9	5
Chase	IIA	3	5	5	5	3	8	5	4	6	5	5	7	3	5	4
Dakota	IB	4	3	8	9	6	9	7	2	2	2	1	8	9	8	6
Dawson	IIB	5	6	7	7	5	8	4	4	5	2	1	9	9	7	4
Lincoln	IB	6	9	9	9	2	8	5	4	3	1	1	4	9	9	8
Madison	IIB	6	4	8	9	5	7	1	7	5	2	2	5	7	9	8
Stanton	IIA	3	4	8	6	5	9	8	1	3	4	1	7	8	8	6
Washington	IIB	4	3	9	7	9	4	6	4	3	2	1	3	9	9	8
NEVADA																
Elko	IB	4	9	9	8	1	6	7	3	1	2	1	7	8	9	9
Esmeralda	IIA	3	9	1	9	1	4	1	9	2	1	2	4	7	9	8
Eureka	IA	3	9	2	9	1	8	3	5	1	9	7	3	3	6	5
Lincoln	IA	3	9	6	8	3	9	9	1	3	3	2	9	5	7	3
Pershing	IB	3	9	8	8	1	8	2	7	2	4	2	7	3	9	7
Storey	IA	3	3	9	9	9	5	1	9	1	2	1	3	9	9	4
NEW HAMPSHIRE																
Belknap	IB	7	3	9	9	7	3	3	7	4	2	2	9	8	6	7
Carroll	IA	6	5	9	9	4	1	1	9	7	2	3	9	4	4	8
Grafton	IIB	9	8	8	9	4	1	1	9	3	2	2	9	6	6	8
Merrimack	IB	9	5	9	9	6	2	3	7	3	1	1	8	9	8	8
Sullivan	IIB	6	4	8	9	5	3	5	6	4	2	2	8	8	6	5

% Completed HS	% College or More	Families/Pop	% Married Couples	% W/O Husband	% Black	% Spanish	% Amer Indian	% Asian	% Urban	% Rural	% Farmers	% Out of County	Jobs/Pop	% Manufacturing	% Wholesale	% Retail	% Services	Physicians/Cap	Crimes/Cap	$ Police/Crimes	$ Educ/Enrollment	Carpool or Transit	Pop Density
6	2	6	8	2	3	4	4	6	4	7	8	8	2	6	6	6	2	4	3	5	3	5	5
4	2	8	7	3	3	4	4	5	5	8	9	3	4	5	7	6	2	3	*	*	5	4	4
9	7	5	8	2	3	4	5	4	2	8	7	2	*	*	*	*	*	5	6	5	6	4	3
9	9	6	7	3	3	4	5	9	2	6	8	4	5	2	1	8	7	4	3	5	9	3	3
8	9	2	6	3	3	4	5	8	2	4	3	9	*	*	*	*	*	5	4	5	5	6	3
9	6	6	8	2	3	4	4	3	2	7	6	2	5	2	3	9	2	2	4	5	7	3	3
9	9	7	8	2	3	4	4	3	9	4	4	2	9	3	2	6	8	8	5	5	7	3	3
6	6	3	8	2	3	5	5	8	8	6	5	2	*	*	*	*	*	7	7	5	8	4	4
7	6	1	5	4	3	4	9	3	5	4	4	1	3	2	1	9	3	4	3	5	9	5	3
8	8	5	8	2	3	4	5	8	2	4	5	2	3	5	1	9	3	4	4	5	9	8	3
9	8	7	8	2	3	4	5	2	2	8	8	4	*	*	*	*	*	5	6	5	9	3	3
4	9	1	5	8	3	4	4	2	2	1	1	9	1	*	*	*	*	1	*	*	1	9	3
9	7	3	8	2	3	5	5	8	9	5	4	1	*	*	*	*	*	6	9	5	6	3	4
9	6	6	8	2	3	4	4	7	6	7	5	9	*	*	*	*	*	4	5	5	5	8	5
9	8	5	9	1	3	4	5	3	2	9	8	1	9	2	9	1	2	2	2	5	9	3	3
8	4	3	5	5	3	5	5	9	9	3	3	8	*	*	*	*	*	2	9	5	3	4	6
8	8	7	8	2	3	5	4	6	9	5	5	1	9	5	8	2	5	4	8	5	7	3	4
9	7	5	7	3	3	6	4	6	9	4	3	1	9	2	3	4	8	7	9	5	6	3	4
8	7	3	7	3	3	4	4	4	9	4	3	2	9	3	7	2	7	7	7	5	8	4	6
7	4	4	9	1	3	4	4	9	2	9	9	9	*	*	*	*	*	2	3	5	1	3	4
8	8	4	8	2	3	4	4	4	7	8	7	8	6	3	3	4	9	5	4	5	6	3	5
8	8	2	3	5	3	8	9	8	8	3	2	1	*	*	*	*	*	8	9	5	6	9	3
9	9	8	6	2	3	7	4	6	2	1	3	9	*	*	*	*	*	1	9	5	9	3	3
7	5	2	8	2	3	7	6	9	2	5	8	2	*	*	*	*	*	7	6	5	9	6	3
7	7	1	6	3	3	7	6	9	2	2	2	1	*	*	*	*	*	5	4	5	8	8	3
9	2	4	6	2	3	8	8	9	2	4	4	2	*	*	*	*	*	5	9	5	8	3	3
9	9	4	6	3	3	5	6	9	2	2	1	9	8	2	1	1	9	1	8	5	9	9	3
8	9	4	4	6	3	4	4	4	7	2	1	4	9	4	1	7	8	9	9	5	4	6	7
9	9	7	5	5	3	4	4	4	2	2	1	4	9	3	1	2	9	9	9	5	4	4	4
6	9	1	4	6	3	4	4	9	7	2	2	2	9	4	1	3	9	9	7	5	3	5	5
8	9	2	4	6	3	4	4	6	8	2	1	4	9	4	3	4	8	9	8	5	3	6	7
8	8	5	4	5	3	4	4	4	9	2	2	5	6	7	4	8	3	9	8	5	2	6	6

Economic Indicators For Class IA, IB, IIA, And IIB Counties

		SIZE OF COUNTY		REAL-ESTATE VALUES			AGES OF POPULATION				INCOMES					
		Population	Land Area	Med House Val	Med Gross Rent	Av Farm Val./Acre	% Under 5	% 5–17	% 18 and Over	% 65 and Over	% Poverty	% Under $10,000	% $10–19,999	% $20–29,999	% $30–49,999	% Over $50,000
NEW MEXICO																
Catron	IA	3	9	2	2	1	8	6	3	4	7	8	4	2	2	2
Colfax	IIA	4	9	6	4	1	6	8	2	4	5	6	4	5	5	4
Grant	IIB	5	9	6	6	1	9	8	1	2	4	2	2	9	7	4
Hidalgo	IB	3	9	2	2	1	9	9	1	1	6	3	2	9	5	2
Lincoln	IB	4	9	9	9	1	4	4	6	3	5	4	4	4	7	8
Rio Arriba	IIB	6	9	5	3	1	9	9	1	1	9	8	5	2	2	1
Socorro	IA	4	9	6	5	1	9	8	1	1	9	8	6	2	2	5
Torrance	IA	3	9	3	3	1	8	8	2	3	8	7	8	1	3	3
NEW YORK																
Allegany	IIB	8	6	4	7	3	4	4	6	2	3	3	8	6	4	2
Columbia	IIB	8	4	8	8	7	1	4	7	6	2	2	7	7	7	7
Greene	IB	7	4	7	9	5	1	3	8	7	3	4	6	7	5	5
Ontario	IIA	9	4	8	9	5	2	5	6	2	1	1	5	9	9	7
Oswego	IIB	9	5	6	9	3	5	7	3	1	2	1	6	9	9	3
Schoharie	IIA	6	4	6	8	4	1	4	8	4	3	3	8	6	4	3
Sullivan	IB	9	5	8	9	8	2	2	8	6	3	5	6	4	5	5
NORTH CAROLINA																
Alleghany	IIB	4	3	5	4	6	2	2	8	6	6	8	9	1	2	4
Ashe	IIB	5	4	6	3	8	2	3	8	5	8	8	7	1	1	2
Avery	IIB	4	3	4	6	8	2	4	7	2	5	7	9	2	1	2
Beaufort	IIB	7	5	5	5	8	5	5	5	3	7	6	5	4	3	4
Brunswick	IB	6	5	6	8	7	4	7	4	2	7	5	5	6	4	3
Chatham	IIB	6	5	6	7	6	2	3	8	2	2	2	9	7	6	3
Cherokee	IIB	5	4	4	2	6	2	4	7	6	8	9	4	1	1	2
Chowan	IIB	4	3	6	6	7	4	4	6	5	8	7	5	4	2	6
Clay	IB	3	3	5	3	7	2	2	9	7	8	9	7	1	2	3
Currituck	IA	4	3	6	9	7	3	4	6	3	6	5	8	3	6	1
Dare	IB	4	3	9	9	8	1	1	9	3	2	3	8	4	5	7
Davie	IB	5	3	8	7	7	2	6	6	2	3	2	5	8	8	8
Franklin	IIB	6	4	4	4	6	2	4	7	4	6	6	5	4	4	2
Hoke	IB	5	3	4	8	5	9	9	1	1	7	5	7	6	3	2
Iredell	IIB	9	4	7	6	7	2	5	6	2	2	2	8	8	6	5
Jackson	IIB	5	4	7	6	9	1	1	9	2	5	7	7	3	2	4
Johnston	IIB	9	5	5	5	8	3	5	6	2	6	6	7	4	3	3
Lincoln	IB	7	3	7	6	8	3	6	5	1	2	1	9	8	7	3
Macon	IB	5	4	8	5	9	1	1	9	8	5	7	9	1	2	5
Montgomery	IIB	5	4	3	3	4	4	5	5	3	3	5	9	5	2	2
Moore	IB	8	4	8	7	6	2	3	8	5	3	3	7	5	6	9

SOCIO-ECONOMIC STATUS					MINORITIES				RURAL-URBAN				ECONOMIC BASE					COUNTY CONDITIONS					
% Completed HS	% College or More	Families/Pop	% Married Couples	% W/O Husband	% Black	% Spanish	% Amer Indian	% Asian	% Urban	% Rural	% Farmers	% Out of County	Jobs/Pop	% Manufacturing	% Wholesale	% Retail	% Services	Physicians/Cap	Crimes/Cap	$ Police/Crimes	$ Educ/Enrollment	Carpool or Transit	Pop Density
6	8	5	5	3	3	9	5	2	2	6	8	1	*	*	*	*	*	3	3	5	9	6	3
6	8	2	3	6	3	9	5	7	9	3	2	1	7	3	1	9	7	9	8	5	6	6	3
5	7	3	5	6	3	9	5	5	8	2	2	1	*	*	*	*	*	9	8	5	4	6	4
4	3	1	5	5	3	9	4	9	9	3	3	2	*	*	*	*	*	3	3	6	9	9	3
8	9	6	4	6	3	9	5	3	7	2	3	2	9	2	1	3	9	8	8	5	9	3	3
3	4	1	1	8	3	9	9	2	4	2	2	8	2	3	1	9	5	7	2	5	9	9	3
3	8	1	3	6	3	9	9	9	9	2	3	1	4	3	1	5	9	4	3	5	4	9	3
6	5	4	5	5	3	9	5	7	2	4	5	7	*	*	*	*	*	3	4	5	9	5	3
6	7	1	5	5	3	4	4	7	4	2	3	4	3	5	3	7	5	5	5	5	5	5	5
7	9	4	3	6	4	4	4	5	3	2	2	6	4	4	4	6	5	8	7	5	8	9	7
8	6	4	3	7	4	4	4	5	4	2	2	7	6	4	2	2	9	5	8	5	9	9	6
8	9	2	4	6	3	4	4	7	6	2	2	7	9	3	2	8	6	9	7	5	9	6	8
6	5	1	3	6	3	4	4	6	6	2	2	5	3	5	2	9	4	5	7	5	7	7	8
6	6	1	5	4	3	4	4	7	4	3	3	7	*	*	*	*	*	5	5	5	7	7	5
7	8	1	3	6	4	5	4	9	4	2	2	4	9	2	2	1	9	8	9	5	9	9	6
2	2	9	5	5	3	4	4	2	2	4	6	4	3	8	2	8	4	6	2	5	4	9	5
2	2	9	5	5	3	4	4	4	2	4	7	3	3	8	4	7	3	3	2	5	4	9	5
3	5	4	5	5	3	4	4	2	2	2	2	6	3	3	2	2	9	9	4	5	3	9	6
4	4	5	2	9	9	4	4	3	4	4	3	2	8	5	8	2	5	8	6	5	5	8	5
4	3	7	4	6	8	4	4	5	3	2	2	6	2	3	4	8	3	5	5	5	6	8	5
3	8	7	3	6	8	4	4	4	3	4	4	8	3	9	8	3	3	6	5	5	4	9	5
3	2	9	4	6	3	4	5	5	2	2	2	2	3	7	2	8	3	8	3	5	4	8	5
3	4	6	1	9	9	4	4	9	8	3	3	3	*	*	*	*	*	9	8	5	5	6	6
3	6	9	6	4	3	4	4	2	2	3	4	8	*	*	*	*	*	7	3	5	4	8	5
5	1	7	4	5	6	4	5	8	2	3	2	9	*	*	*	*	*	3	4	5	6	8	5
8	9	8	5	5	4	4	4	2	2	2	1	1	9	2	1	2	9	5	8	5	3	3	5
4	6	8	6	5	5	4	4	2	3	3	3	9	2	9	4	8	2	5	4	5	2	8	7
2	3	3	1	9	9	4	4	3	3	5	3	9	*	*	*	*	*	3	3	5	3	9	6
2	3	1	1	9	9	5	9	7	4	2	2	8	1	9	3	5	5	3	8	5	4	9	5
4	5	7	3	7	7	4	4	4	6	2	2	4	6	8	5	4	6	8	8	5	4	6	8
2	8	1	4	7	3	5	9	5	2	2	2	4	2	6	1	7	9	9	4	5	2	8	5
3	3	7	2	8	7	4	4	4	5	5	4	7	6	5	9	1	5	5	6	5	5	7	7
3	4	8	5	5	5	4	4	3	3	2	2	8	4	8	7	4	4	6	3	5	3	7	8
5	7	9	6	4	3	4	4	5	3	2	2	3	4	4	1	8	8	7	3	5	4	6	5
2	3	5	1	8	8	4	4	3	3	2	2	3	2	9	3	7	3	4	8	5	5	8	5
5	9	7	2	8	7	4	5	5	5	2	2	3	8	5	1	1	9	9	7	5	6	6	6

Economic Indicators For Class IIA, IB, IIA, And IIB Counties		SIZE OF COUNTY		REAL-ESTATE VALUES			AGES OF POPULATION				INCOMES					
		Population	Land Area	Med House Val	Med Gross Rent	Av Farm Val./Acre	% Under 5	% 5–17	% 18 and Over	% 65 and Over	% Poverty	% Under $10,000	% $10–19,999	% $20–29,999	% $30–49,999	% Over $50,000
Nash	IIB	9	4	8	7	8	4	6	5	2	6	4	4	6	6	7
Pender	IB	5	5	4	5	7	4	7	4	3	7	7	4	4	4	4
Perquimans	IIA	4	3	3	4	8	4	3	7	6	8	8	5	3	2	1
Person	IIB	6	3	5	4	5	3	5	6	2	5	4	7	7	5	1
Richmond	IIB	7	4	3	4	5	4	6	5	2	4	4	6	6	5	2
Rutherford	IIB	8	4	4	5	6	3	5	6	4	3	4	8	6	3	3
Stokes	IB	6	4	7	5	6	3	7	4	1	3	2	8	8	5	3
Surry	IIB	8	4	5	4	7	2	4	7	3	3	4	8	5	4	4
Swain	IIA	4	4	4	3	7	3	5	5	5	9	9	8	1	1	2
Union	IB	9	4	8	7	8	4	8	3	1	2	1	6	9	8	8
Vance	IIB	6	3	5	4	7	4	7	4	2	7	6	7	3	3	4
Watauga	IB	6	3	9	8	7	1	1	9	1	5	8	3	2	4	4
Yancey	IIA	4	3	4	5	7	2	4	7	5	8	8	9	1	1	2
NORTH DAKOTA																
Cass	IIB	9	8	9	9	5	6	1	8	1	1	1	3	9	9	9
McKenzie	IIA	3	9	8	9	2	9	8	1	2	4	2	6	7	9	8
Mercer	IA	4	6	9	9	2	9	5	3	2	2	1	2	9	9	6
Morton	IA	5	8	9	7	2	9	7	2	2	2	1	5	9	9	5
Stark	IIB	5	7	9	9	2	8	6	3	1	2	1	5	8	9	6
Williams	IIB	5	9	9	8	2	8	3	5	2	2	1	3	9	9	9
OHIO																
Adams	IA	5	4	4	7	6	6	8	2	3	8	8	3	3	3	2
Brown	IIA	6	4	7	8	8	7	8	2	3	4	3	5	8	6	4
Carroll	IIB	5	3	8	7	6	6	7	3	2	2	1	7	9	8	4
Darke	IIB	8	4	7	8	9	7	7	3	3	2	1	9	8	8	6
Fulton	IIB	7	3	9	9	9	7	8	2	2	2	1	4	9	9	9
Gallia	IIA	6	4	8	9	5	5	4	6	3	4	3	4	8	7	5
Guernsey	IIA	7	4	5	7	4	6	4	5	4	2	3	6	8	6	3
Highland	IIB	6	4	5	7	9	6	5	4	5	4	4	8	5	4	4
Hocking	IIA	5	4	5	5	5	5	6	4	3	3	3	9	8	4	2
Holmes	IB	6	4	9	7	8	9	9	1	2	5	2	7	8	7	6
Jackson	IIA	6	3	4	7	4	5	6	4	3	5	6	6	5	4	3
Lawrence	IIB	8	4	7	8	5	6	7	4	2	4	3	3	8	7	3
Logan	IIB	7	4	7	8	9	6	5	5	4	2	2	8	7	6	4
Madison	IIB	6	4	9	8	9	5	5	5	1	2	1	4	9	9	7
Meigs	IIA	5	4	4	5	3	5	5	5	3	5	5	5	6	4	2
Morgan	IIA	4	3	5	5	3	6	7	3	5	4	4	7	7	4	3
Morrow	IB	5	3	7	9	8	7	9	2	1	2	1	9	9	8	3
Perry	IIA	6	3	3	5	6	7	8	2	2	3	3	9	8	5	2

SOCIO-ECONOMIC STATUS					MINORITIES				RURAL-URBAN				ECONOMIC BASE					COUNTY CONDITIONS					
% Completed HS	% College or More	Families/Pop	% Married Couples	% W/O Husband	% Black	% Spanish	% Amer Indian	% Asian	% Urban	% Rural	% Farmers	% Out of County	Jobs/Pop	% Manufacturing	% Wholesale	% Retail	% Services	Physicians/Cap	Crunes/Cap	$ Police/Crimes	$ Educ/Enrollment	Carpool or Transit	Pop Density
3	6	5	1	9	9	4	4	7	7	3	2	4	*	*	*	*	*	2	9	5	6	5	8
3	3	4	2	8	9	4	4	8	2	3	3	9	2	4	9	2	3	2	6	5	4	9	4
2	2	6	3	7	9	4	4	2	2	5	4	9	2	3	7	6	2	2	5	5	4	7	5
3	3	6	2	8	9	4	5	3	5	4	3	3	6	7	9	1	3	4	5	5	7	8	6
3	3	4	1	9	8	4	5	4	7	2	2	2	5	7	2	8	6	4	8	5	5	6	7
3	4	8	3	7	6	4	4	4	6	2	2	3	4	9	4	6	4	6	5	5	4	7	7
3	2	8	5	5	4	4	4	2	5	5	5	9	*	*	*	*	*	3	3	5	3	9	6
2	2	8	4	6	4	4	4	3	4	3	3	3	*	*	*	*	*	6	4	5	5	8	8
2	4	6	1	9	3	4	9	4	2	2	2	3	8	5	1	6	9	5	3	5	6	9	4
3	4	5	5	6	7	4	4	5	4	3	2	7	4	7	8	1	5	5	6	5	2	7	8
2	3	3	1	9	9	4	4	4	7	3	2	2	8	7	5	6	4	6	9	4	3	5	9
2	9	1	4	6	3	4	4	5	6	3	3	2	8	4	3	3	9	9	7	5	1	6	7
3	3	9	4	5	3	4	4	5	2	3	5	7	1	8	1	9	5	7	*	*	4	9	5
7	9	1	6	4	3	4	5	8	9	3	2	2	9	3	9	1	7	9	9	5	3	9	5
6	4	2	7	2	3	4	9	6	2	9	9	3	*	*	*	*	*	3	8	5	6	3	3
5	6	4	9	1	3	4	5	9	6	7	6	2	3	2	8	4	3	5	2	5	9	7	4
5	6	3	7	2	3	4	5	6	9	6	4	7	*	*	*	*	*	3	7	5	4	3	4
4	8	1	7	2	3	4	4	4	9	5	4	1	9	3	5	3	8	9	9	5	4	3	4
8	7	3	7	3	3	4	7	6	9	4	5	1	9	3	7	3	6	8	8	5	6	3	4
3	2	5	5	5	3	4	4	3	3	7	6	4	2	5	3	9	2	4	7	5	6	5	5
5	2	4	6	4	3	4	4	4	3	6	6	9	3	4	5	8	2	4	3	5	3	7	6
8	2	6	7	3	3	4	4	6	4	3	4	9	3	5	2	9	4	3	2	5	2	4	6
8	3	5	7	3	3	4	4	5	5	6	5	6	6	4	8	2	4	4	6	5	4	4	7
8	4	4	8	3	3	6	4	5	7	6	4	6	8	7	8	2	4	5	6	5	7	4	7
5	4	4	5	5	4	4	4	8	4	3	3	4	5	3	8	3	4	9	6	5	5	5	6
7	4	4	4	6	3	4	4	6	7	3	3	3	7	6	2	4	9	8	4	5	2	4	7
7	3	6	5	5	3	4	4	4	6	6	5	6	4	6	5	7	3	6	4	5	3	5	6
7	3	6	5	5	3	4	4	3	5	2	2	7	4	6	2	9	3	4	2	5	2	5	6
1	2	1	8	2	3	4	4	2	3	9	6	5	2	7	5	7	3	4	3	5	2	8	6
5	3	6	3	7	3	4	4	3	7	2	2	4	4	6	4	6	4	4	3	5	4	4	6
7	2	6	4	6	3	4	4	3	9	2	2	9	*	*	*	*	*	3	6	5	3	4	8
8	4	6	6	4	3	4	4	5	6	4	3	4	8	5	8	1	6	7	6	5	6	5	7
7	3	3	5	5	4	4	4	6	7	4	3	9	4	4	6	6	3	6	4	5	5	5	6
6	2	7	5	5	3	4	4	3	5	2	3	9	3	3	2	9	2	4	4	5	4	7	6
8	2	5	7	4	4	4	4	4	2	4	6	6	*	*	*	*	*	2	4	5	4	5	5
8	2	6	8	2	3	4	4	6	3	6	5	9	2	6	1	9	4	3	4	5	3	4	6
7	2	4	5	5	3	4	4	3	5	3	3	9	.1	7	1	9	5	2	5	5	3	6	6

Economic Indicators For Class IIA, IB, IIA, And IIB Counties		SIZE OF COUNTY		REAL-ESTATE VALUES			AGES OF POPULATION				INCOMES					
		Population	Land Area	Med House Val	Med Gross Rent	Av Farm Val./Acre	% Under 5	% 5-17	% 18 and Over	% 65 and Over	% Poverty	% Under $10,000	% $10-19,999	% $20-29,999	% $30-49,999	% Over $50,000
Pike	IIB	5	4	5	7	6	5	8	3	4	7	6	6	4	4	3
Shelby	IIB	7	3	8	9	9	8	8	2	1	2	1	7	9	9	6
Union	IB	6	4	9	9	9	5	7	4	2	2	1	8	9	9	8
Vinton	IA	4	3	3	6	4	7	7	3	3	6	6	6	4	3	2
Washington	IIB	9	4	8	8	4	5	5	5	2	2	1	7	9	8	5
OKLAHOMA																
Adair	IB	5	4	2	2	4	5	9	2	4	9	9	2	1	1	2
Atoka	IIA	4	6	2	1	2	2	3	7	6	8	9	1	1	1	4
Beckham	IA	5	5	3	7	2	7	1	7	8	4	5	1	6	6	9
Blaine	IIA	4	5	4	4	4	6	3	6	8	5	5	1	7	7	8
Bryan	IIA	6	5	2	3	2	3	2	8	7	6	8	3	1	3	3
Canadian	IB	8	5	9	9	7	8	8	2	1	1	1	1	9	9	9
Carter	IIA	7	5	4	5	2	5	3	6	6	4	5	2	6	7	7
Cherokee	IB	6	5	6	5	4	5	5	5	3	7	8	4	1	3	3
Choctaw	IIA	4	5	2	1	2	5	6	4	8	8	9	1	1	2	3
Creek	IA	8	5	5	6	4	6	7	4	3	3	3	4	8	7	5
Custer	IIA	5	6	7	6	4	5	1	9	4	4	4	2	6	8	8
Delaware	IB	5	5	5	4	4	2	4	7	8	7	9	6	1	2	2
Garfield	IIB	8	6	8	9	6	7	2	7	4	1	1	5	8	9	9
Garvin	IIA	6	5	3	4	3	3	3	7	8	3	6	3	5	4	4
Grady	IA	7	6	6	7	4	6	5	5	4	4	4	4	6	8	7
Haskell	IIA	4	4	2	1	3	3	4	6	8	7	9	2	1	4	3
Jefferson	IIA	3	5	1	1	2	5	3	7	9	6	9	2	2	2	5
Johnston	IA	4	4	2	2	2	3	4	6	8	9	9	1	1	2	2
Latimer	IIA	4	5	2	2	2	3	4	7	6	9	9	2	1	3	2
Le Flore	IA	7	8	2	2	3	5	6	4	6	6	8	5	2	2	3
Lincoln	IA	5	5	3	3	3	5	6	5	6	4	5	6	6	4	3
Logan	IA	5	5	6	3	4	5	4	5	5	3	3	6	6	7	7
Love	IA	3	4	3	3	3	4	5	6	7	5	5	4	5	6	7
McClain	IA	5	4	7	6	4	4	8	3	3	3	2	2	8	9	4
McCurtain	IA	6	8	2	2	4	7	9	2	4	8	8	3	2	3	2
McIntosh	IA	4	4	3	1	3	1	2	9	9	8	9	3	2	1	3
Major	IIA	4	5	6	5	4	6	3	6	7	3	2	4	7	8	9
Marshall	IA	4	3	3	2	2	1	1	9	9	5	8	4	1	3	5
Mayes	IB	6	4	5	6	5	6	5	5	5	4	5	5	6	5	3
Murray	IIA	4	3	3	2	2	4	4	6	8	4	5	8	4	3	5
Muskogee	IIA	9	5	4	5	4	6	4	5	5	6	6	3	4	6	5
Noble	IIA	4	5	5	6	4	5	2	7	7	2	3	7	5	8	7
Nowata	IIA	4	4	2	2	3	4	3	7	7	3	4	7	6	4	4
Osage	IA	7	9	5	3	2	6	4	6	3	2	2	4	8	8	7

SOCIO-ECONOMIC STATUS					MINORITIES				RURAL-URBAN				ECONOMIC BASE					COUNTY CONDITIONS					
% Completed HS	% College or More	Families/Pop	% Married Couples	% W/O Husband	% Black	% Spanish	% Amer Indian	% Asian	% Urban	% Rural	% Farmers	% Out of County	Jobs/Pop	% Manufacturing	% Wholesale	% Retail	% Services	Physicians/Cap	Crimes/Cap	$ Police/Crimes	$ Educ/Enrollment	Carpool or Transit	Pop Density
4	4	4	5	5	3	4	4	7	4	3	3	6	*	*	*	*	*	6	7	4	4	6	5
7	3	4	7	3	3	4	4	7	7	5	4	4	5	9	3	6	5	6	9	5	3	3	7
8	5	5	7	3	3	4	4	7	5	5	4	7	4	7	7	3	5	5	3	5	3	4	6
4	2	4	6	4	3	4	4	3	2	2	3	8	1	8	3	8	3	1	2	5	3	5	4
8	6	5	6	4	3	4	4	6	7	2	2	5	7	5	5	3	7	6	6	5	4	5	7
2	4	3	4	7	3	4	9	5	2	5	6	5	1	7	2	8	4	3	4	5	4	8	5
3	3	3	5	5	4	4	9	3	5	7	8	4	3	3	7	6	2	3	5	5	3	6	4
5	7	7	7	4	3	5	5	8	9	4	4	2	9	3	4	7	4	7	7	5	3	3	4
6	7	5	6	4	4	4	9	7	6	5	6	3	*	*	*	*	*	6	7	5	6	3	4
4	8	6	4	5	3	4	9	9	7	4	4	4	5	4	8	2	4	5	8	4	2	4	5
8	9	6	8	3	3	5	7	9	9	2	2	9	4	3	2	8	7	5	9	4	3	3	6
6	7	7	5	6	5	4	8	5	9	2	2	1	*	*	*	*	*	8	7	5	4	5	5
2	9	4	3	7	3	4	9	6	6	3	4	4	3	3	2	9	4	5	6	5	1	5	5
3	3	5	3	7	6	4	9	2	7	4	5	3	3	3	2	4	9	3	7	5	3	8	4
6	4	8	6	4	4	4	8	6	8	2	2	9	3	5	4	7	4	4	6	5	3	5	6
4	9	2	6	4	4	5	7	8	9	3	3	2	9	3	3	5	8	7	9	5	2	3	4
6	3	9	7	3	3	4	9	3	3	5	6	8	*	*	*	*	*	3	5	4	5	5	5
8	9	6	7	4	4	4	5	9	9	2	2	1	9	3	7	3	6	9	9	5	4	3	6
5	5	8	7	4	4	4	7	6	8	4	5	3	*	*	*	*	*	4	6	5	5	4	5
5	7	7	7	4	4	4	6	7	8	3	4	6	5	4	6	4	5	8	9	4	4	5	5
3	4	9	6	5	3	4	9	4	5	7	8	5	*	*	*	*	*	3	3	5	4	4	4
5	4	7	5	5	3	6	6	4	2	6	6	6	4	4	4	9	2	3	3	5	3	7	4
3	3	6	3	7	3	4	9	2	6	4	6	7	1	3	6	7	3	3	5	5	2	6	4
4	6	4	6	5	3	4	9	6	6	5	6	4	*	*	*	*	*	2	2	5	7	5	4
3	4	7	5	5	3	4	9	6	7	3	4	7	*	*	*	*	*	3	2	5	3	6	4
7	3	8	8	3	4	4	6	5	5	5	6	9	2	4	3	8	3	3	3	5	2	7	4
6	7	4	6	5	6	4	5	3	8	3	3	8	2	4	4	8	3	4	8	4	2	5	5
5	3	8	6	4	4	4	8	8	2	7	8	8	*	*	*	*	*	2	4	5	3	7	4
6	5	7	8	3	3	4	7	6	7	4	5	9	3	3	2	9	3	4	6	5	4	6	5
3	3	4	3	7	5	4	9	4	6	3	4	2	*	*	*	*	*	2	5	5	4	6	4
5	5	9	5	5	4	4	9	5	8	5	6	7	2	3	1	9	4	4	5	4	5	5	4
7	6	9	8	2	3	4	5	6	7	8	8	4	5	3	6	8	1	2	7	5	8	3	4
6	5	9	6	5	3	4	9	4	6	3	4	3	4	4	3	5	8	3	6	5	3	4	4
6	5	8	7	3	3	4	9	5	5	4	4	4	3	6	2	9	3	2	6	5	3	6	5
5	6	6	5	5	3	4	8	3	9	3	4	5	4	2	3	8	5	5	5	5	3	6	4
6	7	6	3	8	6	4	9	7	9	2	2	2	8	4	6	4	5	9	9	5	5	4	7
8	5	7	7	3	3	4	8	4	8	4	6	4	*	*	*	*	*	3	8	5	5	4	4
6	3	7	8	3	4	4	9	3	7	5	7	8	2	4	7	7	2	2	5	5	3	9	4
8	6	8	7	4	5	4	9	4	7	3	3	9	2	4	7	3	5	2	6	5	2	5	4

Economic Indicators For Class IA, IB, IIA, And IIB Counties

		SIZE OF COUNTY		REAL-ESTATE VALUES			AGES OF POPULATION				INCOMES					
		Population	Land Area	Med House Val	Med Gross Rent	Av Farm Val./Acre	% Under 5	% 5–17	% 18 and Over	% 65 and Over	% Poverty	% Under $10,000	% $10–19,999	% $20–29,999	% $30–49,999	% Over $50,000
Pawnee	IA	4	4	5	5	3	4	4	6	6	2	4	3	6	7	8
Pontotoc	IIA	6	5	5	4	3	3	1	8	7	4	7	2	5	4	5
Pottawatomie	IA	8	5	5	6	4	4	4	6	5	3	5	3	7	6	5
Pushmataha	IA	4	7	1	1	2	2	6	6	8	9	9	2	1	1	6
Sequoyah	IA	6	4	3	3	4	5	9	2	3	6	7	6	3	2	2
Stephens	IIB	7	5	6	7	3	5	2	7	6	2	3	4	8	8	7
Wagoner	IB	7	4	9	7	6	8	9	1	1	2	2	1	9	9	8
Washita	IIA	4	6	3	7	5	6	2	7	7	3	2	6	7	8	8
Woodward	IB	5	6	8	9	2	9	3	4	2	2	1	2	9	9	9
OREGON																
Columbia	IB	6	4	9	9	9	7	7	3	2	2	1	1	9	9	8
Harney	IIB	3	9	7	8	1	7	5	4	1	2	1	7	9	9	6
Morrow	IA	3	9	9	9	2	8	7	2	1	2	1	3	9	9	9
Union	IB	5	9	9	9	3	7	5	5	3	3	2	5	8	7	6
Wallowa	IIA	3	9	9	6	2	5	3	7	5	2	4	6	6	5	7
PENNSYLVANIA																
Adams	IIB	9	4	9	9	9	3	5	6	2	1	1	9	9	8	5
Butler	IIB	9	5	9	9	8	3	5	6	2	1	1	3	9	9	8
Clarion	IIB	7	4	7	7	4	3	3	7	2	2	2	3	9	8	5
Clearfield	IIA	9	6	5	7	5	4	6	5	4	2	2	7	8	6	5
Columbia	IIB	8	4	6	8	7	1	2	9	4	2	2	9	7	5	2
Franklin	IIB	9	5	9	8	9	2	5	6	3	1	1	8	9	9	5
Fulton	IIB	4	4	6	6	4	5	7	4	2	4	3	9	6	3	2
Greene	IIA	7	4	5	6	5	4	5	5	4	3	3	3	8	7	4
Indiana	IIB	9	5	8	9	5	3	2	8	2	2	2	5	9	8	6
Juniata	IIB	5	3	5	6	7	5	5	5	3	3	3	9	7	4	3
Perry	IB	6	4	7	8	7	5	6	4	2	1	1	9	9	6	3
Snyder	IIB	6	3	6	8	7	3	4	7	2	2	1	9	8	5	4
Wayne	IIA	6	5	8	8	6	3	4	6	6	3	4	8	5	4	5
Wyoming	IB	5	3	7	9	5	6	8	3	2	2	2	9	8	5	5
SOUTH CAROLINA																
Anderson	IB	9	5	6	6	6	4	5	6	2	3	2	7	8	7	4
Bamberg	IIA	4	3	3	3	3	5	8	3	2	9	8	3	2	2	4
Barnwell	IIA	5	4	4	3	4	8	9	1	2	6	5	5	5	5	4
Calhoun	IIA	4	3	4	2	5	6	8	2	2	7	7	6	2	5	3
Cherokee	IIB	7	3	5	5	6	4	8	3	2	3	3	7	8	6	3
Chesterfield	IIB	7	5	3	4	3	6	8	2	2	6	5	8	4	3	3
Colleton	IIA	6	6	4	5	4	5	9	2	2	8	7	6	3	3	3

SOCIO-ECONOMIC STATUS					MINORITIES				RURAL-URBAN				ECONOMIC BASE					COUNTY CONDITIONS					
% Completed HS	% College or More	Families/Pop	% Married Couples	% W/O Husband	% Black	% Spanish	% Amer Indian	% Asian	% Urban	% Rural	% Farmers	% Out of County	Jobs/Pop	% Manufacturing	% Wholesale	% Retail	% Services	Physicians/Cap	Crimes/Cap	$ Police/Crimes	$ Educ/Enrollment	Carpool or Transit	Pop Density
8	6	9	7	3	3	4	8	6	4	4	4	8	3	3	2	4	9	3	3	5	2	7	4
4	9	7	5	6	4	4	9	8	8	3	3	2	7	4	3	7	6	9	6	5	3	4	5
7	6	6	6	5	3	4	9	8	9	2	3	6	7	3	2	8	5	8	9	5	3	6	6
4	4	7	6	5	3	4	9	2	5	5	7	3	1	3	1	9	2	3	4	5	4	5	4
3	4	6	5	5	3	4	9	3	6	3	3	8	2	3	1	9	4	2	4	5	4	7	5
7	7	9	7	3	3	5	6	5	9	3	3	2	*	*	*	*	*	6	8	5	3	4	5
6	7	6	7	3	4	4	8	3	7	2	2	9	1	4	2	9	2	2	4	5	1	6	6
7	4	8	8	2	3	5	5	7	5	6	7	5	3	3	5	4	6	2	4	5	5	3	4
7	6	7	8	2	3	5	5	9	9	4	3	3	9	3	4	6	6	7	8	5	6	3	4
9	5	6	6	3	3	4	5	9	6	2	2	7	3	7	2	7	7	3	8	5	9	5	6
9	8	5	8	2	3	5	6	9	8	4	5	1	*	*	*	*	*	8	6	5	9	3	3
8	7	5	7	2	3	6	5	9	2	5	5	3	*	*	*	*	*	3	8	5	9	5	3
8	9	4	6	4	3	4	5	8	8	4	3	1	8	4	4	6	5	9	8	5	7	4	4
9	9	8	7	2	3	4	4	3	2	6	7	1	5	4	4	6	5	6	7	5	9	3	3
5	7	4	6	4	3	4	4	7	4	3	2	8	6	6	3	3	8	5	4	4	5	5	8
8	7	4	6	4	3	4	4	6	6	2	2	5	7	5	6	4	4	6	5	5	4	5	9
6	5	1	6	4	3	4	4	6	3	2	2	4	7	4	3	6	6	3	5	4	4	4	6
7	3	5	5	5	3	4	4	4	5	2	2	4	6	5	5	5	5	6	4	5	8	6	6
7	6	3	5	5	3	4	4	4	7	2	2	4	7	6	5	4	5	8	5	5	4	5	8
6	6	6	6	4	3	4	4	7	6	3	2	3	6	6	3	7	5	8	5	5	6	5	9
4	3	6	6	3	3	4	4	3	2	4	5	8	*	*	*	*	*	2	5	4	5	9	4
5	5	4	4	6	3	4	4	5	3	2	3	6	2	3	3	8	5	7	4	5	9	4	6
6	6	1	6	4	3	4	4	5	5	2	2	4	5	5	3	7	5	6	4	5	3	5	8
6	2	6	7	3	3	4	4	4	2	4	4	7	*	*	*	*	*	3	3	4	4	8	5
7	3	6	6	3	3	4	4	4	2	3	3	9	2	4	3	9	2	3	5	4	5	9	6
6	5	2	8	3	3	4	4	4	4	3	3	6	6	6	5	6	4	5	3	4	4	5	7
8	5	5	5	4	3	4	4	4	3	3	3	5	5	5	2	4	9	6	3	4	9	5	5
8	6	4	6	5	3	4	4	5	2	3	2	7	*	*	*	*	*	5	5	4	5	7	6
2	6	7	3	7	7	4	4	6	8	2	2	4	6	8	2	6	6	9	9	4	2	5	9
1	4	1	1	9	9	4	4	3	8	2	2	5	3	6	6	4	4	4	3	5	1	9	5
2	4	2	1	9	9	4	4	5	9	2	2	4	3	9	1	9	3	4	4	5	2	9	5
2	5	2	1	9	9	4	4	2	2	3	3	9	2	4	9	1	3	3	5	5	2	9	5
2	4	4	2	8	7	4	4	7	8	2	2	5	4	8	1	8	6	4	9	5	2	8	7
1	3	3	1	9	9	4	4	2	5	2	2	5	3	9	4	8	2	3	5	5	2	9	5
2	4	2	1	9	9	4	4	3	4	2	2	4	5	6	5	2	8	4	8	5	2	9	4

Economic Indicators For Class I A, IB, IIA, And IIB Counties	SIZE OF COUNTY		REAL-ESTATE VALUES			AGES OF POPULATION				INCOMES					
		Population	Land Area	Med House Val	Med Gross Rent	Av Farm Val./Acre	% Under 5	% 5–17	% 18 and Over	% 65 and Over	% Poverty	% Under $10,000	% $10–19,999	% $20–29,999	% $30–49,999	% Over $50,000
Darlington	IIB	8	4	6	3	5	7	8	2	1	7	5	3	5	7	5
Edgefield	IIA	4	4	5	3	5	7	8	2	2	8	7	2	5	4	6
Greenwood	IIB	8	4	6	4	3	3	5	6	2	3	3	4	8	7	6
Hampton	IIA	4	4	3	1	4	8	9	1	2	9	8	2	4	2	7
Jasper	IB	4	4	4	3	3	9	9	1	2	9	8	4	2	3	2
Kershaw	IIB	7	5	7	5	4	5	8	3	1	5	2	5	7	8	6
Marion	IIA	6	4	4	3	8	9	9	1	1	8	7	5	3	2	3
Marlboro	IIA	6	4	3	3	5	7	9	1	2	8	7	7	3	3	3
Oconee	IIB	8	4	5	4	5	4	5	5	2	3	3	8	7	4	4
Orangeburg	IIB	9	6	5	4	4	5	8	3	2	9	7	3	4	4	4
SOUTH DAKOTA																
Custer	IA	3	7	7	7	1	6	5	5	3	3	2	9	8	5	3
Fall River	IIA	3	8	5	8	1	7	2	7	7	4	4	6	7	5	7
Lincoln	IIA	4	4	8	4	6	9	5	3	6	3	2	7	8	7	6
Union	IIA	4	4	6	4	6	9	4	3	5	3	3	9	6	4	3
TENNESSEE																
Bedford	IIA	6	4	5	5	5	4	4	6	5	4	4	8	5	4	5
Benton	IB	4	3	5	5	3	2	3	8	7	4	7	4	6	2	2
Bledsoe	IB	4	3	2	3	4	3	7	4	2	9	8	5	3	2	4
Cannon	IA	4	3	4	3	6	4	3	7	5	5	6	8	2	3	4
Chester	IB	4	3	4	3	4	2	2	8	4	8	7	2	5	3	3
Claiborne	IA	5	4	5	2	6	4	6	4	2	9	9	2	1	2	2
Clay	IIA	3	3	4	1	3	3	4	7	5	9	9	3	1	1	3
Cocke	IIB	6	4	3	3	5	3	6	5	2	9	8	5	2	1	2
Decatur	IIA	4	3	4	3	3	3	3	8	7	6	8	5	3	2	3
De Kalb	IA	4	3	4	3	5	4	3	7	5	8	8	7	2	2	3
Dickson	IB	6	4	5	7	4	3	7	4	3	3	3	6	8	5	5
Dyer	IIB	6	4	4	5	8	4	5	5	5	4	6	6	4	4	5
Fayette	IIA	5	5	5	1	5	8	9	1	3	9	7	4	3	4	5
Franklin	IIB	6	4	6	5	8	3	4	6	3	5	4	7	6	5	4
Grainger	IIA	4	3	3	2	6	4	6	5	2	8	7	9	2	1	2
Greene	IIB	8	4	5	4	8	2	4	7	2	6	6	8	4	2	3
Hardin	IB	5	4	4	4	4	3	5	6	4	7	7	6	4	2	3
Henderson	IB	5	4	4	4	4	6	3	6	4	5	6	9	3	2	2
Henry	IIA	6	4	5	4	5	3	2	8	8	4	6	7	4	3	3
Hickman	IA	4	4	3	6	3	2	5	7	3	4	5	8	5	3	2
Houston	IIA	3	3	3	4	3	3	5	6	5	5	7	3	3	5	3
Humphreys	IIB	4	4	6	4	3	4	6	4	3	3	3	2	9	8	1
Jackson	IIA	4	3	4	1	4	2	4	7	6	9	9	2	3	2	2

SOCIO-ECONOMIC STATUS					MINORITIES				RURAL-URBAN				ECONOMIC BASE					COUNTY CONDITIONS					
% Completed HS	% College or More	Families/Pop	% Married Couples	% W/O Husband	% Black	% Spanish	% Amer Indian	% Asian	% Urban	% Rural	% Farmers	% Out of County	Jobs/Pop	% Manufacturing	% Wholesale	% Retail	% Services	Physicians/Cap	Crimes/Cap	$ Police/Crimes	$ Educ/Enrollment	Carpool or Transit	Pop Density
2	5	2	1	9	9	4	4	3	6	2	2	4	5	7	6	3	6	5	9	5	3	6	8
1	5	2	2	8	9	5	4	7	6	2	2	9	2	9	6	6	2	4	7	5	2	9	5
2	8	5	1	9	9	4	4	8	8	2	1	2	8	8	3	7	5	9	9	5	2	5	8
2	3	2	1	9	9	4	4	2	4	2	2	4	6	5	8	1	7	4	2	5	3	8	5
2	3	1	1	9	9	4	4	5	2	2	2	9	5	2	1	5	9	4	7	5	2	9	4
3	7	4	2	8	9	4	4	5	5	2	2	4	4	9	2	6	7	7	7	5	4	8	5
1	3	1	1	9	9	4	4	6	7	3	2	3	4	8	7	3	4	7	7	5	2	9	6
1	3	1	1	9	9	4	5	5	7	2	2	4	2	9	4	6	5	5	9	5	2	9	6
2	5	7	4	6	5	4	4	3	6	2	2	4	3	8	3	7	5	8	7	5	3	7	6
2	7	1	1	9	9	4	4	8	6	2	2	3	6	5	4	4	7	7	9	4	2	7	6
8	8	4	7	2	3	4	6	3	2	4	5	3	3	4	1	9	6	3	8	5	4	5	3
8	9	1	5	6	3	5	8	3	9	3	4	1	6	3	3	9	3	5	2	5	6	4	3
8	6	5	9	1	3	4	4	5	4	9	9	8	4	4	8	2	6	2	2	5	5	3	4
8	6	5	7	2	3	4	5	6	4	8	8	8	4	5	5	1	9	2	2	5	7	3	4
4	3	7	4	6	5	4	4	3	8	4	5	3	6	8	4	1	9	6	3	5	5	6	6
4	2	9	6	4	3	4	4	3	5	3	3	7	2	6	2	9	3	4	3	5	2	6	5
1	2	2	4	5	4	4	4	4	2	4	5	7	*	*	*	*	*	2	2	5	2	9	4
3	2	8	6	4	3	4	4	3	2	7	7	7	*	*	*	*	*	4	2	5	4	8	5
2	3	3	5	6	5	4	4	4	7	3	4	7	2	7	4	8	2	3	2	5	1	8	5
1	2	7	5	6	3	4	4	3	3	6	6	7	2	7	5	4	6	3	2	5	4	8	6
1	2	8	3	7	3	4	4	2	2	8	8	7	1	9	1	8	5	4	*	*	5	8	5
2	2	7	2	8	3	4	4	4	5	4	4	5	3	7	1	9	5	2	5	5	2	8	6
3	2	9	5	6	4	4	4	2	2	5	5	5	3	9	3	8	3	4	2	5	3	7	5
2	2	9	5	5	3	4	4	3	6	5	6	6	8	6	1	1	9	5	5	5	2	9	5
3	3	7	5	5	4	4	4	2	5	4	4	7	5	6	2	7	5	6	2	5	3	9	6
2	2	7	3	8	6	4	4	2	9	3	2	2	7	6	5	4	6	8	7	5	2	5	6
1	2	1	1	9	9	4	4	2	2	4	3	8	1	8	7	5	3	3	3	5	3	8	5
3	5	6	6	4	4	4	4	7	4	4	4	6	3	5	3	9	2	6	6	5	2	7	6
1	1	8	6	5	3	4	4	3	2	6	8	9	1	7	4	8	2	2	3	5	1	9	6
3	5	7	4	6	3	4	4	4	5	5	7	2	5	7	4	4	6	8	4	5	2	4	7
3	2	8	5	5	4	4	4	3	6	3	3	4	3	8	3	8	3	4	4	5	3	8	5
2	2	9	5	6	5	4	4	3	5	5	5	5	3	8	4	6	3	3	3	5	2	6	5
4	3	9	5	6	5	4	4	4	7	4	4	2	5	7	6	5	4	7	8	5	2	4	5
2	2	6	5	5	4	4	4	3	4	5	5	8	1	9	3	4	7	3	4	5	4	9	4
3	3	8	4	6	4	4	4	3	2	3	4	9	1	8	1	8	6	5	3	5	3	9	5
5	3	7	5	5	4	4	4	4	5	3	4	3	5	8	2	7	5	5	3	5	3	9	4
1	2	9	5	5	3	4	4	3	2	7	8	8	*	*	*	*	*	2	*	*	2	9	5

Economic Indicators For Class IA, IB, IIA, And IIB Counties

		SIZE OF COUNTY		REAL-ESTATE VALUES			AGES OF POPULATION				INCOMES					
		Population	Land Area	Med House Val	Med Gross Rent	Av Farm Val./Acre	% Under 5	% 5–17	% 18 and Over	% 65 and Over	% Poverty	% Under $10,000	% $10–19,999	% $20–29,999	% $30–49,999	% Over $50,000
Jefferson	IB	6	3	5	3	9	1	4	7	2	5	5	9	4	3	2
Johnson	IIA	4	3	3	4	6	3	6	5	4	9	9	9	1	1	1
Lauderdale	IA	5	4	3	3	7	6	6	4	5	8	8	7	2	2	3
Lawrence	IIA	6	4	5	4	5	4	6	4	4	5	4	8	6	3	3
Lewis	IB	4	3	2	1	4	9	6	2	2	7	8	7	2	1	2
McMinn	IIB	7	4	5	4	7	4	5	6	3	5	4	4	7	5	3
McNairy	IB	5	4	3	4	3	4	4	6	5	6	7	7	3	2	2
Macon	IA	4	3	4	6	5	4	4	6	4	5	5	8	4	2	3
Madison	IIB	9	4	7	6	5	5	3	6	4	5	4	2	7	7	5
Marion	IIB	5	4	3	5	6	5	7	4	2	6	5	7	5	4	5
Marshall	IIA	5	3	4	5	4	3	3	7	6	3	5	8	6	3	4
Maury	IIB	8	4	6	6	6	4	4	6	3	5	3	6	8	6	5
Meigs	IA	3	3	6	6	6	5	8	3	1	4	3	6	6	8	2
Monroe	IB	6	4	4	4	7	4	7	4	2	6	6	8	3	2	5
Moore	IA	3	3	6	6	5	4	6	4	3	4	3	7	7	5	2
Morgan	IB	4	4	3	2	4	4	8	3	2	9	8	6	3	2	2
Overton	IIA	4	4	3	3	5	3	6	5	4	9	8	6	1	2	2
Perry	IIA	3	3	2	2	3	2	4	7	6	4	6	9	3	1	2
Pickett	IIA	3	3	3	4	5	4	3	6	6	9	9	7	1	1	1
Polk	IIA	4	4	2	3	6	3	8	3	2	7	6	8	5	2	1
Rhea	IB	5	3	4	6	5	5	7	4	2	6	5	6	5	4	3
Robertson	IB	6	4	7	6	8	4	6	4	3	4	2	5	8	7	5
Sevier	IB	7	4	8	8	7	3	4	6	2	4	4	7	5	4	5
Smith	IIA	4	3	5	6	4	3	3	7	5	3	4	8	6	5	4
Stewart	IIA	4	4	3	5	3	2	3	8	6	7	8	6	3	1	2
Tipton	IIB	6	4	6	6	7	7	8	2	2	6	5	3	5	6	5
Trousdale	IIA	3	3	5	8	6	5	2	8	4	2	2	8	9	6	4
Union	IA	4	3	4	5	6	4	7	4	2	8	7	9	1	2	2
Van Buren	IB	3	3	3	1	4	8	6	3	2	5	6	9	2	2	3
Warren	IIB	6	4	4	4	7	5	4	6	3	5	6	9	3	2	4
Wayne	IIB	4	5	2	2	3	5	7	4	3	6	6	9	3	2	2
Weakley	IIA	6	4	4	6	6	1	1	9	6	4	7	7	4	2	3
White	IIB	5	3	4	2	6	3	4	7	5	5	7	7	4	2	3
TEXAS																
Anderson	IA	7	6	4	5	4	4	1	8	6	5	5	2	6	7	7
Archer	IA	3	5	4	5	2	4	5	5	4	1	2	6	8	8	9
Austin	IA	4	4	8	9	8	4	3	7	8	4	4	1	7	8	9
Bandera	IA	3	5	7	7	2	1	1	9	8	3	4	7	5	7	6
Bastrop	IA	5	5	4	6	5	5	4	6	7	5	6	2	5	5	6
Blanco	IA	3	5	6	4	3	1	2	9	9	2	5	7	3	5	7

SOCIO-ECONOMIC STATUS					MINORITIES				RURAL-URBAN				ECONOMIC BASE					COUNTY CONDITIONS					
% Completed HS	% College or More	Families/Pop	% Married Couples	% W/O Husband	% Black	% Spanish	% Amer Indian	% Asian	% Urban	% Rural	% Farmers	% Out of County	Jobs/Pop	% Manufacturing	% Wholesale	% Retail	% Services	Physicians/Cap	Crimes/Cap	$ Police/Crimes	$ Educ/Enrollment	Carpool or Transit	Pop Density
3	4	7	5	5	4	4	4	4	4	4	5	8	*	*	*	*	*	4	3	5	2	6	8
2	1	9	2	8	3	4	4	6	2	6	7	3	*	*	*	*	*	5	4	5	3	9	5
2	2	3	2	9	9	4	4	3	5	4	3	2	3	9	6	4	3	3	5	5	4	7	5
2	2	7	6	4	3	4	4	2	6	5	4	2	3	9	4	7	3	5	4	5	2	7	6
3	3	2	6	5	3	4	4	2	7	3	3	3	2	9	2	7	5	4	2	5	1	7	5
3	3	8	5	5	4	4	4	3	7	2	3	3	6	8	3	5	7	6	5	5	2	5	7
3	2	9	6	5	4	4	4	3	4	3	4	6	2	9	5	5	4	3	2	5	2	6	5
1	1	9	6	4	3	4	4	2	5	8	8	7	2	9	3	8	2	2	2	5	2	8	5
4	8	4	1	9	9	4	4	6	9	2	2	2	9	4	7	2	7	9	9	4	2	8	8
2	2	7	5	6	4	4	4	4	5	2	2	9	3	6	4	7	3	4	4	5	2	9	5
5	3	8	4	7	5	4	4	4	8	5	6	2	4	9	3	7	4	6	2	5	2	6	5
4	4	7	3	7	7	4	4	5	9	3	4	2	7	6	4	5	6	8	8	5	2	6	7
2	2	7	6	3	3	4	4	2	2	3	4	9	*	*	*	*	*	4	6	5	2	8	5
1	2	6	4	5	4	4	4	3	5	3	4	8	3	6	3	8	4	4	2	5	2	8	5
4	5	8	7	2	4	4	4	2	2	7	9	9	*	*	*	*	*	1	1	5	2	6	5
2	1	5	3	7	3	4	4	7	2	2	2	9	*	*	*	*	*	3	3	5	3	9	5
1	2	8	5	5	3	4	4	2	4	5	5	5	2	7	6	4	4	3	4	5	3	8	5
4	1	9	5	5	3	4	4	3	2	5	5	6	1	9	2	8	3	3	1	5	5	8	4
1	2	9	5	4	3	4	5	2	2	6	8	4	*	*	*	*	*	4	2	5	3	8	4
2	2	7	5	5	3	4	4	3	2	2	2	9	*	*	*	*	*	4	2	5	5	9	5
2	3	6	4	7	4	4	4	6	5	2	2	3	2	9	1	9	4	3	3	5	2	9	6
5	2	7	5	6	6	4	4	2	7	6	5	8	3	6	6	5	3	4	8	5	2	8	6
4	5	9	6	4	3	4	4	3	4	3	3	6	9	3	1	2	9	5	5	5	2	6	6
3	2	9	6	4	4	4	4	4	4	8	8	7	2	7	7	5	3	3	4	5	2	9	5
3	2	9	7	3	3	4	4	5	2	5	5	7	*	*	*	*	*	2	5	5	3	9	4
3	2	4	3	7	8	4	4	7	4	3	3	9	3	4	6	7	2	4	2	5	3	8	6
2	3	8	4	5	6	4	4	2	8	7	8	4	4	9	7	5	2	2	4	5	3	7	5
1	1	8	6	4	3	4	4	2	2	4	6	9	*	*	*	*	*	2	3	5	4	9	5
2	1	8	4	5	3	4	4	6	2	4	5	9	1	9	1	4	1	2	3	5	2	9	4
4	2	8	5	5	4	4	4	4	6	4	4	2	5	9	4	5	6	5	5	5	3	5	6
2	1	7	6	5	3	4	4	2	2	5	5	7	1	9	2	9	2	2	1	7	4	9	4
2	5	5	6	4	4	4	4	4	5	5	4	4	4	7	7	5	2	5	4	5	1	4	6
2	3	9	5	5	3	4	4	2	5	5	6	3	3	9	6	2	6	5	5	5	2	6	5
4	4	1	4	6	7	6	4	9	7	2	3	2	*	*	*	*	*	6	6	5	3	5	5
6	4	8	9	2	3	4	5	3	2	5	4	9	*	*	*	*	*	3	4	5	8	4	4
3	4	5	6	3	6	6	4	2	7	4	7	7	5	3	5	5	5	5	3	5	6	6	4
8	9	9	8	2	3	8	4	6	2	4	6	8	1	3	1	7	9	4	4	5	9	7	4
3	6	5	5	5	7	8	4	4	8	3	4	8	2	4	2	9	3	4	5	5	4	7	4
5	9	8	8	3	3	7	4	2	2	6	8	5	7	2	7	7	2	6	3	5	3	3	4

Economic Indicators For Class IA, IB, IIA, And IIB Counties

County	Class	SIZE OF COUNTY		REAL-ESTATE VALUES			AGES OF POPULATION				INCOMES					
		Population	Land Area	Med House Val	Med Gross Rent	Av Farm Val./Acre	% Under 5	% 5–17	% 18 and Over	% 65 and Over	% Poverty	% Under $10,000	% $10–19,999	% $20–29,999	% $30–49,999	% Over $50,000
Bosque	IA	4	6	3	3	3	1	1	9	9	4	7	3	4	4	3
Brown	IB	6	5	3	7	3	4	3	7	8	3	6	4	4	5	7
Burleson	IA	4	4	2	3	4	4	3	7	8	5	6	1	6	5	5
Burnet	IB	4	6	7	8	3	1	1	9	9	4	6	6	4	3	6
Caldwell	IIA	5	4	2	5	4	4	8	3	5	7	6	3	4	5	5
Callahan	IA	4	5	2	4	2	2	2	8	9	3	4	4	6	7	4
Camp	IIA	4	3	3	5	4	7	3	6	7	5	5	1	7	6	8
Cass	IA	6	5	3	6	3	6	5	4	6	5	5	1	7	8	4
Cherokee	IIA	7	6	2	5	4	3	3	7	8	5	6	1	6	5	6
Clay	IIA	4	6	2	5	2	2	2	8	8	2	4	2	7	7	9
Cooke	IIA	5	5	6	8	4	5	4	6	5	3	2	3	8	8	6
Dimmit	IB	4	7	1	2	2	9	9	1	1	9	8	3	2	2	8
Ellis	IA	8	5	6	7	4	6	7	3	4	3	2	1	9	9	7
Erath	IA	5	6	4	7	3	2	1	9	9	3	6	4	3	4	9
Franklin	IA	3	3	3	5	3	4	2	8	9	3	6	1	7	6	7
Freestone	IA	4	5	3	6	4	5	3	6	9	4	7	1	4	5	9
Frio	IB	4	6	1	3	3	9	9	1	2	9	8	3	2	3	5
Gillespie	IB	4	6	9	8	4	1	1	9	9	3	5	9	4	3	6
Glasscock	IIA	3	5	3	1	2	9	9	1	1	7	2	7	4	7	9
Grimes	IIA	4	5	3	6	5	6	4	5	8	9	7	1	4	4	8
Guadalupe	IB	7	5	7	8	5	4	6	4	2	4	2	3	8	8	5
Hamilton	IIA	3	5	2	2	2	1	1	9	9	5	9	2	3	1	6
Harrison	IIB	8	5	5	7	4	6	6	4	4	5	3	3	8	8	5
Hemphill	IA	3	5	8	9	1	9	4	2	1	1	1	2	9	9	9
Henderson	IA	7	5	6	5	4	2	2	8	7	3	4	4	7	6	7
Hood	IA	4	4	9	9	4	3	1	9	5	1	1	1	9	9	9
Hopkins	IA	5	5	3	8	4	4	3	7	8	4	5	6	4	5	7
Houston	IA	5	6	3	2	4	1	1	9	8	8	9	1	2	4	5
Hudspeth	IIA	3	9	1	5	1	9	9	1	1	9	8	6	2	3	5
Hunt	IIB	8	5	3	8	4	2	3	8	5	4	4	3	6	7	6
Irion	IA	3	6	3	7	1	3	8	4	6	4	2	7	5	8	9
Jasper	IB	6	5	3	7	5	5	8	3	4	4	4	2	8	6	7
Kaufman	IIA	7	5	4	6	4	3	6	5	5	3	3	1	7	9	8
Kendall	IB	4	4	9	9	4	1	5	7	6	3	2	1	7	9	9
Lamar	IIA	7	5	2	5	3	3	5	6	7	6	7	4	3	5	4
Lampasas	IB	4	5	5	6	2	4	5	5	7	5	6	4	3	6	4
Lee	IA	4	4	5	8	4	4	6	5	8	5	6	1	6	7	6
Limestone	IIA	5	5	1	3	2	3	1	9	9	7	9	2	1	3	6
Live Oak	IA	4	6	4	6	3	8	4	4	4	5	2	2	7	9	9
Llano	IB	4	5	8	6	3	1	1	9	9	2	5	6	3	6	9
Madison	IA	4	4	5	6	5	1	1	9	6	6	8	1	3	5	5

% Completed HS	% College or More	Families/Pop	% Married Couples	% W/O Husband	% Black	% Spanish	% Amer Indian	% Asian	% Urban	% Rural	% Farmers	% Out of County	Jobs/Pop	% Manufacturing	% Wholesale	% Retail	% Services	Physicians/Cap	Crimes/Cap	$ Police/Crimes	$ Educ/Enrollment	Carpool or Transit	Pop Density
5	7	9	8	2	3	6	4	8	5	4	6	6	*	*	*	*	*	7	4	5	5	7	4
5	8	6	5	5	4	7	4	4	9	2	3	1	8	4	4	3	8	7	8	5	2	3	5
2	4	5	4	6	8	8	4	3	5	5	7	7	*	*	*	*	*	3	6	5	2	7	4
6	7	9	8	2	3	7	4	6	7	3	4	5	4	3	1	8	8	8	5	5	3	4	4
1	5	1	4	6	6	9	4	9	9	3	3	8	3	3	3	8	4	5	5	5	3	7	5
6	6	9	8	2	3	5	4	9	5	5	6	9	*	*	*	*	*	3	2	5	3	3	4
5	3	6	4	6	8	4	4	2	8	3	4	7	*	*	*	*	*	4	4	5	3	6	5
5	4	7	5	6	8	4	4	2	4	2	3	8	4	5	1	9	6	5	3	5	3	6	5
3	6	4	4	6	7	5	4	8	8	3	3	3	4	6	4	5	6	9	5	5	3	5	5
5	3	9	7	3	3	4	4	5	6	6	7	9	1	4	3	9	2	3	8	4	4	4	4
6	5	6	6	4	4	5	5	5	8	4	4	2	8	5	4	6	5	6	6	5	6	6	5
1	2	1	3	7	3	9	5	4	9	2	2	3	*	*	*	*	*	5	2	5	4	6	4
5	5	4	5	5	6	7	4	6	8	2	2	8	4	6	2	6	7	4	8	5	3	6	6
4	9	6	7	3	3	6	4	9	9	5	6	3	6	3	6	5	4	5	6	5	1	8	4
6	3	9	8	2	4	4	4	7	3	4	6	9	*	*	*	*	*	4	3	5	4	5	4
4	4	6	5	6	7	5	4	9	8	3	4	5	3	3	3	8	3	5	4	5	4	4	4
1	4	1	3	7	3	9	4	7	9	3	3	2	*	*	*	*	*	2	2	5	4	3	4
6	8	9	8	2	3	8	4	3	8	6	7	2	9	3	6	5	4	9	3	5	4	4	4
2	5	1	9	1	3	9	4	2	2	9	9	6	*	*	*	*	*	1	1	6	8	4	3
2	6	4	1	8	8	7	4	2	8	4	5	4	4	4	6	5	4	6	6	5	3	5	4
5	6	4	5	5	4	9	4	8	9	3	3	9	4	5	4	7	4	6	7	5	3	5	6
4	7	9	8	2	3	5	4	8	7	8	9	3	5	3	4	8	4	5	2	5	2	3	4
4	7	4	2	8	9	5	4	5	8	2	2	6	4	5	5	4	6	7	8	5	4	5	6
4	4	6	9	1	3	8	4	6	9	5	3	2	*	*	*	*	*	4	7	5	8	5	4
5	5	9	7	3	5	4	4	4	5	2	3	7	3	4	2	8	6	3	6	5	4	6	5
8	9	9	8	2	3	5	4	8	4	3	3	9	3	3	1	7	8	2	6	4	3	9	5
4	6	8	6	4	5	4	4	4	8	5	6	2	7	4	9	3	3	7	7	5	5	3	5
5	4	1	2	8	9	5	4	4	6	3	4	2	3	4	4	4	7	5	4	5	5	4	4
1	4	1	5	4	3	9	5	3	2	6	4	2	2	2	5	5	6	1	1	7	8	5	3
4	8	5	5	5	6	5	4	6	9	2	3	4	6	6	2	8	5	5	9	4	2	5	6
6	7	8	8	2	3	9	4	2	2	3	6	6	*	*	*	*	*	1	1	6	9	3	3
4	3	6	6	5	7	4	4	2	5	2	2	6	5	6	2	8	5	5	5	5	4	7	5
4	6	3	4	6	7	5	4	6	8	3	3	8	4	4	2	8	4	8	6	5	4	7	5
7	9	7	7	3	3	8	5	8	6	4	5	9	5	3	1	7	9	9	3	5	3	5	4
4	6	6	3	7	6	4	5	7	9	2	3	1	7	6	4	6	5	9	9	4	6	3	5
5	8	7	6	4	3	8	4	9	8	4	4	8	6	3	3	9	2	4	6	5	2	5	4
2	5	4	7	3	6	6	4	3	7	6	8	4	6	3	8	2	4	3	7	5	2	5	4
3	3	2	1	9	8	5	4	5	8	3	4	3	*	*	*	*	*	5	5	5	3	5	4
2	6	7	8	2	3	9	4	3	5	5	5	6	*	*	*	*	*	2	5	5	6	7	4
8	9	9	9	2	3	5	5	6	6	3	4	4	5	3	6	5	4	5	2	5	2	4	4
1	5	1	3	7	8	7	4	5	6	4	4	4	4	2	5	9	2	6	6	4	1	5	4

Economic Indicators For Class IA, IB, IIA, And IIB Counties		SIZE OF COUNTY		REAL-ESTATE VALUES			AGES OF POPULATION				INCOMES					
		Population	Land Area	Med House Val	Med Gross Rent	Av Farm Val./Acre	% Under 5	% 5–17	% 18 and Over	% 65 and Over	% Poverty	% Under $10,000	% $10–19,999	% $20–29,999	% $30–49,999	% Over $50,000
Marion	IIA	4	3	2	4	4	4	3	7	8	9	8	3	3	3	2
Matagorda	IB	7	6	7	9	5	9	5	3	2	3	1	1	9	9	9
Medina	IIB	5	7	2	2	4	6	8	2	4	7	5	5	5	5	4
Milam	IIA	5	6	2	4	4	5	5	5	8	7	7	1	7	6	3
Montague	IIA	4	5	2	5	2	2	1	9	9	3	6	5	4	4	4
Morris	IIB	4	3	2	4	4	4	3	7	8	9	8	3	3	3	2
Nacogdoches	IB	7	5	7	7	4	3	1	9	3	4	6	3	3	6	8
Navarro	IIA	6	6	2	4	3	3	3	7	9	5	7	2	4	5	8
Newton	IIB	4	5	1	4	3	6	9	2	4	6	6	1	8	5	3
Panola	IA	5	5	4	6	4	6	3	6	6	4	3	2	9	7	5
Polk	IA	5	6	4	6	4	6	3	6	8	6	7	2	3	5	5
Rains	IA	3	3	2	2	4	2	1	9	8	5	7	7	2	3	9
Real	IIB	3	4	2	2	2	1	9	4	7	9	9	1	2	2	2
Red River	IIA	4	6	1	1	3	3	4	7	9	8	9	2	1	2	5
Roberts	IA	3	5	4	8	1	6	9	2	3	2	1	5	7	9	9
Rockwell	IA	4	3	9	9	8	4	8	3	1	2	1	1	9	9	9
Sabine	IA	4	4	1	2	5	2	2	8	9	7	9	3	2	1	4
San Augustin	IIA	4	4	2	1	5	2	5	6	9	8	8	3	1	4	7
San Jacinto	IA	4	4	3	8	7	4	7	4	5	8	7	1	5	8	3
San Saba	IIA	3	6	2	2	3	2	3	8	9	7	9	3	1	3	5
Schleicher	IA	3	7	2	3	2	8	5	3	4	5	3	3	7	7	9
Shackelford	IIA	3	5	2	6	2	6	2	7	9	2	4	2	7	6	9
Shelby	IIA	5	5	2	2	5	3	4	7	8	7	8	2	3	5	4
Somervell	IA	3	3	4	9	3	8	3	5	5	2	2	1	9	9	9
Starr	IB	5	6	1	1	2	9	9	1	1	9	9	1	1	2	2
Stephens	IIA	4	5	3	6	2	5	2	7	7	3	5	5	6	3	7
Sterling	IIA	3	5	2	3	2	8	5	3	5	5	4	2	5	7	9
Titus	IB	5	3	4	8	4	7	4	5	6	2	3	2	8	8	8
Trinity	IA	4	4	2	3	5	2	3	8	9	6	8	2	3	3	5
Tyler	IB	4	5	3	5	5	4	5	6	8	4	6	2	5	6	5
Upshur	IB	6	4	4	7	4	6	5	5	5	3	3	3	8	7	7
Van Zandt	IA	6	5	4	5	4	2	3	8	8	3	5	2	7	5	5
Waller	IB	5	4	8	9	8	2	3	8	2	5	2	1	8	9	9
Washington	IIA	5	4	8	4	7	2	1	8	8	4	5	2	6	5	9
Williamson	IA	9	6	9	9	5	7	9	2	1	2	1	1	9	9	8
Wilson	IA	4	5	3	3	4	5	9	2	4	6	4	5	6	6	6
Wise	IA	5	5	4	5	4	3	6	5	4	3	2	2	8	9	8
Wood	IA	5	4	4	6	4	2	1	9	9	3	6	2	6	5	6
Young	IA	5	5	4	7	2	4	1	8	8	2	3	4	6	6	9

SOCIO-ECONOMIC STATUS					MINORITIES				RURAL-URBAN				ECONOMIC BASE					COUNTY CONDITIONS					
% Completed HS	% College or More	Families/Pop	% Married Couples	% W/O Husband	% Black	% Spanish	% Amer Indian	% Asian	% Urban	% Rural	% Farmers	% Out of County	Jobs/Pop	% Manufacturing	% Wholesale	% Retail	% Services	Physicians/Cap	Crimes/Cap	$ Police/Crimes	$ Educ/Enrollment	Carpool or Transit	Pop Density
4	2	6	2	7	9	4	4	2	5	2	2	9	1	4	1	8	6	4	4	5	2	7	4
3	6	3	4	5	6	9	4	9	9	2	2	3	5	3	4	6	6	6	9	5	6	8	5
2	3	3	7	3	3	9	4	2	8	4	5	7	6	3	5	2	9	3	6	5	4	8	4
3	3	5	4	6	6	8	4	4	8	4	5	3	*	*	*	*	*	5	4	5	3	7	4
4	4	8	8	3	3	4	5	5	8	4	5	3	6	3	4	6	5	6	6	5	5	3	4
4	2	6	2	7	9	4	4	2	5	2	2	9	1	4	1	8	6	4	4	5	2	7	4
2	9	1	3	7	7	5	4	9	9	3	3	2	7	4	3	6	6	9	7	5	1	4	5
3	7	6	3	7	7	5	4	7	9	2	3	2	7	4	6	4	5	9	9	4	6	4	5
3	1	5	4	6	8	4	4	3	2	2	2	9	1	7	5	7	3	2	3	5	5	9	4
4	5	7	5	5	7	4	4	2	6	3	4	5	3	3	2	9	3	3	4	5	4	5	4
3	5	8	6	4	6	5	6	6	4	2	2	4	4	4	5	5	5	4	5	5	7	6	4
4	2	9	8	2	4	4	5	3	2	5	7	9	*	*	*	*	*	1	6	5	4	6	4
3	4	7	6	5	3	9	5	4	2	6	5	4	*	*	*	*	*	4	2	5	1	3	3
2	5	7	4	6	7	5	5	6	6	4	5	5	4	5	9	2	2	4	3	5	4	9	4
6	9	8	9	1	3	5	5	2	2	8	5	5	*	*	*	*	*	1	5	5	9	3	3
7	9	7	8	2	4	5	4	5	8	2	2	9	2	4	2	9	3	5	7	5	2	5	8
2	3	9	6	4	6	5	4	2	2	3	3	5	*	*	*	*	*	2	2	5	4	6	4
1	4	6	3	8	9	4	5	2	6	3	3	5	3	3	1	7	8	4	1	6	4	8	4
3	2	7	6	4	7	4	4	2	2	2	2	9	*	*	*	*	*	2	3	5	4	8	4
4	8	8	7	3	3	9	4	7	8	7	8	2	*	*	*	*	*	6	3	5	4	3	3
3	8	7	8	2	3	9	4	5	2	7	7	4	*	*	*	*	*	6	5	5	6	3	3
4	7	8	8	2	3	6	4	4	2	3	4	3	*	*	*	*	*	5	2	5	5	3	3
3	3	7	3	7	7	4	4	3	5	4	5	4	4	7	3	7	6	3	4	5	4	6	4
4	5	7	8	3	3	7	5	3	2	5	4	3	*	*	*	*	*	4	2	5	2	9	4
1	1	1	2	8	3	9	4	6	8	2	2	2	*	*	*	*	*	2	2	5	6	9	4
5	5	8	6	5	4	6	4	9	9	2	3	2	7	4	6	6	3	4	5	5	2	3	4
4	6	7	9	1	3	9	4	2	2	8	4	1	*	*	*	*	*	7	2	5	8	3	3
4	5	6	6	4	6	5	4	7	8	3	3	3	8	4	6	4	6	7	5	5	4	7	5
3	5	8	4	6	7	4	4	5	5	3	4	7	3	3	4	8	2	3	2	5	5	7	4
4	5	8	7	4	6	4	4	.3	4	2	2	8	2	5	1	8	7	3	3	5	5	8	4
5	5	7	6	4	6	4	4	3	5	3	3	9	1	3	2	9	3	2	6	4	2	5	5
5	4	9	8	2	4	5	4	3	5	4	6	8	3	4	4	7	4	2	4	5	3	6	5
2	8	1	4	6	9	6	4	6	7	3	3	9	*	*	*	*	*	4	6	5	2	6	5
3	7	3	4	6	8	5	4	9	8	4	6	2	8	4	7	2	7	7	4	5	7	4	5
4	9	4	7	3	4	8	4	9	9	2	2	9	2	4	2	7	6	4	5	5	3	6	6
2	2	4	6	3	3	9	4	3	5	6	7	9	*	*	*	*	*	3	4	5	2	8	4
5	3	8	8	2	3	6	4	4	6	5	5	6	2	3	5	7	4	3	5	5	2	5	4
5	5	8	7	3	5	4	4	4	6	3	4	5	4	3	5	6	4	3	3	5	4	4	5
5	6	9	7	3	3	5	4	7	9	2	3	2	6	5	5	4	6	6	3	5	3	3	4

Economic Indicators For Class IA, IB, IIA, And IIB Counties	SIZE OF COUNTY		REAL-ESTATE VALUES			AGES OF POPULATION				INCOMES					
	Population	Land Area	Med House Val	Med Gross Rent	Av Farm Val./Acre	% Under 5	% 5–17	% 18 and Over	% 65 and Over	% Poverty	% Under $10,000	% $10–19,999	% $20–29,999	% $30–49,999	% Over $50,000
UTAH															
Beaver	IIA	3 9	8 6 2			9 8 1 5				3 4 9 4 6 2					
Cache	IB	8 6	9 8 7			9 4 1 1				2 2 9 7 7 5					
Duchesne	IA	4 9	9 9 3			9 9 1 1				3 1 9 9 9 6					
Emery	IA	4 9	9 9 2			9 9 1 1				2 1 2 9 9 4					
Garfield	IIA	3 9	8 6 2			9 7 1 3				3 3 9 7 3 1					
Juab	IA	3 9	8 9 2			9 9 1 3				2 1 9 9 3 6					
Kane	IA	3 9	9 7 1			9 9 1 2				4 5 9 5 2 2					
Millard	IA	4 9	9 9 2			9 9 1 3				4 4 8 5 5 3					
Piute	IIA	3 5	7 9 2			9 9 1 7				3 6 9 2 1 8					
Rich	IA	3 6	9 9 1			9 8 1 1				4 2 3 9 7 9					
Sanpete	IA	4 8	9 7 2			9 8 1 4				4 6 7 4 3 2					
Sevier	IA	8 9	9 4 9			9 1 3 2				2 7 9 6 4 8					
Summit	IA	4 8	9 9 3			9 8 1 1				1 1 3 9 9 9					
Uintah	IB	5 9	9 9 1			9 9 1 1				3 1 3 9 9 8					
Wasatch	IA	4 6	9 9 3			9 9 1 1				2 2 8 8 8 6					
Wayne	IA	3 9	9 3 2			9 8 1 4				8 7 7 3 1 7					
VERMONT															
Addison	IB	6 5	9 9 5			4 5 5 1				3 2 9 6 6 5					
Bennington	IIB	6 4	9 9 6			3 4 7 5				2 2 9 6 6 7					
Caledonia	IIA	5 4	6 7 3			5 5 5 3				3 4 9 4 3 3					
Essex	IIA	3 4	3 6 3			7 6 4 3				4 5 9 3 1 2					
Grand Isle	IA	3 2	9 9 6			6 5 5 2				3 2 9 6 7 4					
Lamoille	IB	4 4	9 9 5			5 4 6 2				3 4 9 4 2 5					
Orange	IA	5 4	8 8 4			7 5 4 3				3 4 9 4 2 2					
Orleans	IIA	5 4	5 7 4			6 7 3 3				5 5 9 2 3 3					
Windsor	IIB	8 5	8 9 5			2 3 7 4				2 2 8 8 7 7					
VIRGINIA															
Alleghany	IIA	4 4	6 5 3			2 7 4 2				2 1 7 9 8 6					
Amelia	IIA	3 3	6 6 5			3 6 5 3				2 3 8 7 5 5					
Amherst	IIB	6 4	7 8 4			2 4 7 2				2 1 7 9 8 3					
Appomattox	IB	4 3	6 7 3			3 6 5 3				2 2 6 8 8 8					
Augusta	IB	8 6	8 8 7			2 5 7 2				2 1 8 8 8 7					
Bath	IIA	3 4	4 9 3			1 2 8 4				3 4 4 4 9 5					
Bedford	IA	6 5	8 7 5			3 5 6 2				2 1 8 8 8 4					
Bland	IIA	3 3	5 5 3			1 2 8 3				4 2 9 5 2 2					
Botetourt	IB	5 4	9 7 5			2 5 6 2				2 1 3 9 9 6					
Buckingham	IIA	4 4	3 3 4			2 8 4 4				6 7 7 2 2 4					
Caroline	IA	4 4	7 8 6			4 8 3 1				5 3 6 7 7 4					

	SOCIO-ECONOMIC STATUS					MINORITIES				RURAL-URBAN				ECONOMIC BASE					COUNTY CONDITIONS					
% Completed HS	% College or More	Families/Pop	% Married Couples	% W/O Husband		% Black	% Spanish	% Amer Indian	% Asian	% Urban	% Rural	% Farmers	% Out of County	Jobs/Pop	% Manufacturing	% Wholesale	% Retail	% Services	Physicians/Cap	Crimes/Cap	$ Police/Crimes	$ Educ/Enrollment	Carpool or Transit	Pop Density
9	3	4	9	2		3	5	5	9	2	2	3	1	*	*	*	*	*	6	2	5	6	3	3
4	9	1	8	2		3	4	4	9	9	3	2	2	7	4	2	8	5	9	4	5	1	6	5
5	5	1	8	2		3	4	6	8	6	6	5	2	5	3	5	4	6	4	6	5	7	4	3
6	3	1	9	1		3	5	5	9	2	2	3	2	*	*	*	*	*	3	9	5	9	9	3
8	7	3	9	2		3	4	6	5	2	2	4	2	4	4	1	4	9	5	9	5	8	5	3
8	6	1	9	2		3	4	4	2	9	2	3	3	7	4	2	8	5	6	7	5	9	7	3
9	8	2	8	2		3	4	5	3	2	2	2	5	*	*	*	*	*	6	4	5	6	3	3
8	8	1	9	2		3	5	5	9	2	4	7	1	4	3	6	6	3	4	6	5	9	4	3
9	7	4	9	1		3	4	5	2	2	4	8	3	*	*	*	*	*	1	4	5	9	3	3
7	6	1	9	1		3	4	5	9	2	8	8	6	*	*	*	*	*	1	6	5	9	9	3
7	7	1	8	2		3	5	5	9	4	2	4	3	2	3	3	9	2	7	3	5	3	6	4
7	2	8	2	3		4	5	3	7	2	2	1	9	3	3	7	6	4		9	5	4	8	4
7	9	1	8	2		3	5	5	5	5	3	4	6	9	2	1	1	9	8	9	5	9	6	3
5	5	1	7	3		3	5	9	7	6	3	3	2	9	2	7	1	9	3	8	5	6	7	3
7	8	1	8	3		3	4	5	4	8	2	3	7	7	3	1	5	9	6	8	5	7	7	4
8	7	4	9	1		3	4	5	6	2	4	9	2	*	*	*	*	*	1	*	*	8	6	3
5	9	1	4	5		3	4	4	7	4	4	3	4	5	5	5	4	7	8	*	*	3	4	5
7	9	3	3	7		3	4	4	6	5	2	1	2	9	5	1	5	9	9	*	*	5	7	5
7	9	3	4	6		3	4	4	4	5	3	3	2	7	4	3	7	5	9	*	*	4	6	5
6	4	4	5	5		3	4	4	7	2	2	2	9	*	*	*	*	*	6	*	*	3	9	4
7	9	5	5	4		3	4	5	6	2	4	4	9	*	*	*	*	*	4	*	*	2	9	5
6	9	1	4	5		3	4	4	4	2	2	2	3	*	*	*	*	*	9	*	*	3	6	5
7	9	3	5	5		3	4	4	5	2	3	3	8	3	4	3	4	8	9	*	*	3	6	5
6	6	3	5	5		3	4	4	5	4	4	4	2	7	4	3	1	9	7	9	5	5	7	5
8	9	4	4	6		3	4	4	5	4	2	2	5	9	4	7	1	9	9	6	6	5	5	5
4	4	6	6	3		3	4	4	2	2	2	2	9	*	*	*	*	*	9	5	5	3	5	5
2	3	4	2	7		9	4	4	2	2	6	6	9	2	5	8	3	2	4	3	5	5	9	4
2	5	1	4	6		7	4	4	5	8	2	2	9	2	3	3	5	8	3	6	5	3	7	6
2	3	6	5	5		8	4	4	4	2	3	4	8	3	7	2	9	4	3	4	5	3	8	5
4	5	6	6	4		4	4	4	5	2	3	3	9	2	5	6	1	8	9	3	5	3	6	6
3	5	3	4	6		5	4	4	3	2	2	3	3	*	*	*	*	*	7	3	5	6	9	4
3	6	8	6	3		5	4	4	8	2	4	4	9	1	5	9	1	8	6	3	5	4	7	5
4	2	4	5	5		4	4	4	2	2	5	6	9	*	*	*	*	*	2	2	5	2	9	4
6	7	8	6	4		4	4	4	6	2	3	3	9	*	*	*	*	*	3	4	5	3	5	5
1	2	2	2	8		9	5	4	3	2	3	4	9	1	6	6	3	6	5	2	5	3	9	4
2	2	2	1	8		9	4	5	4	2	2	2	9	2	5	1	3	9	2	4	5	5	9	5

Economic Indicators For Class IA, IB, IIA, And IIB Counties

		SIZE OF COUNTY		REAL-ESTATE VALUES			AGES OF POPULATION				INCOMES					
		Population	Land Area	Med House Val	Med Gross Rent	Av Farm Val./Acre	% Under 5	% 5–17	% 18 and Over	% 65 and Over	% Poverty	% Under $10,000	% $10–19,999	% $20–29,999	% $30–49,999	% Over $50,000
Carroll	IIB	5	4	4	3	5	1	4	7	4	5	6	9	3	2	2
Clarke	IB	4	3	9	9	8	1	4	8	4	2	1	8	7	9	9
Craig	IIA	3	3	6	4	4	1	3	8	3	2	3	9	7	2	2
Cumberland	IA	3	3	5	4	4	2	9	2	4	8	6	8	1	4	2
Essex	IA	4	3	8	7	6	2	5	7	6	4	2	9	6	5	8
Fauquier	IB	6	4	9	9	9	3	7	4	1	2	1	1	9	9	9
Floyd	IIA	4	3	6	3	4	2	2	8	6	4	6	8	5	3	1
Fluvanna	IA	4	3	7	7	5	4	6	5	3	5	3	8	7	6	3
Franklin	IB	6	4	7	5	4	2	4	7	2	2	2	9	7	5	5
Goochland	IIB	4	3	9	9	8	1	4	8	2	3	1	1	8	9	9
Greene	IA	3	3	9	9	6	6	6	4	1	3	1	8	9	5	7
Greensville	IIA	4	3	4	2	5	5	9	1	2	6	6	6	4	4	2
Highland	IIA	3	3	6	9	3	4	1	9	6	4	5	3	5	7	5
Isle of Wigh	IIB	5	3	8	8	8	3	6	5	1	4	1	4	9	8	8
King William	IA	4	3	9	5	6	3	7	4	2	3	1	4	9	9	9
Lee	IA	5	4	3	4	5	4	6	4	4	8	8	5	2	2	2
Louisa	IA	4	4	6	8	5	3	6	5	3	4	4	6	6	5	4
Madison	IIA	4	3	8	7	6	2	5	6	5	5	2	9	6	3	4
Middlesex	IA	3	3	8	7	8	1	1	9	9	3	6	5	2	5	6
Orange	IB	4	3	8	8	7	2	5	6	4	4	3	6	6	7	5
Page	IIB	5	3	6	6	8	3	3	7	4	3	5	8	4	3	4
Patrick	IIA	4	4	5	4	4	1	5	7	4	3	5	7	7	2	2
Pittsylvania	IIB	9	6	5	4	4	2	6	6	2	4	3	8	7	4	4
Prince Edwar	IIB	4	3	6	7	4	1	1	9	3	7	6	5	4	4	5
Rappahannock	IIA	3	3	8	7	8	1	3	8	4	3	3	4	6	7	8
Russell	IB	6	4	6	7	4	4	6	4	2	5	4	5	7	6	3
Shenandoah	IIB	5	4	8	8	7	1	3	8	5	3	3	9	5	4	4
Washington	IIB	7	4	7	7	8	2	5	6	2	4	4	7	6	3	7
Westmoreland	IIB	4	3	7	8	7	2	4	7	7	5	4	7	4	6	8
Wise	IA	7	3	5	8	7	6	6	4	2	4	3	4	8	6	5
Wythe	IIB	5	4	5	5	5	2	5	6	3	3	4	9	5	3	4
Chesapeake	IB	9	3	9	9	9	6	8	2	1	3	1	4	9	9	7
Lynchburg	IB	9	2	8	8	1	1	1	9	4	3	2	5	6	9	9
Manassas	IB	4	2	9	9	1	9	6	2	1	1	1	1	9	9	9
Norton	IIB	3	2	7	9	1	4	5	6	3	5	5	2	3	9	7
Poquoson	IB	4	2	9	9	1	2	9	2	1	1	1	1	9	9	9

WASHINGTON

Ferry	IA	3	9	8	3	2	9	8	1	1	8	3	7	7	6	2
Grays Harbor	IIB	9	8	9	9	9	6	3	6	3	2	2	2	8	9	8
Klickitat	IB	4	8	8	7	2	7	6	4	3	2	2	4	9	9	6

SOCIO-ECONOMIC STATUS					MINORITIES				RURAL-URBAN				ECONOMIC BASE					COUNTY CONDITIONS					
% Completed HS	% College or More	Families/Pop	% Married Couples	% W/O Husband	% Black	% Spanish	% Amer Indian	% Asian	% Urban	% Rural	% Farmers	% Out of County	Jobs/Pop	% Manufacturing	% Wholesale	% Retail	% Services	Physicians/Cap	Crimes/Cap	$ Police/Crimes	$ Educ/Enrollment	Carpool or Transit	Pop Density
2	2	9	6	4	3	4	4	2	2	4	4	9	1	8	2	6	7	2	2	5	3	9	6
5	9	4	4	6	5	4	4	9	2	4	3	9	3	8	2	8	6	5	6	5	3	8	6
4	4	8	5	4	3	5	4	2	2	3	5	9	*	*	*	*	*	1	2	5	4	9	4
1	3	2	1	8	9	4	4	5	2	4	5	9	*	*	*	*	*	2	2	5	3	7	4
2	8	3	2	8	9	4	5	9	2	3	2	6	9	5	2	9	2	8	6	5	4	9	5
5	9	3	5	4	6	4	4	8	3	3	3	8	*	*	*	*	*	7	5	5	3	8	6
2	4	8	7	3	4	4	4	2	2	6	8	8	1	6	1	8	7	3	2	5	3	9	5
3	7	4	3	6	9	4	4	2	2	3	3	9	*	*	*	*	*	4	3	5	3	9	5
3	3	5	5	5	6	4	4	3	3	4	3	8	2	9	3	6	5	4	4	5	3	9	5
2	8	2	3	7	9	4	4	3	2	2	3	9	*	*	*	*	*	4	4	5	6	8	5
3	6	7	5	5	5	4	4	2	2	2	3	9	1	2	1	9	3	2	3	5	5	9	5
1	1	2	1	9	9	4	4	2	2	3	3	9	*	*	*	*	*	7	5	5	6	9	5
6	5	9	6	2	3	4	4	4	2	8	9	7	*	*	*	*	*	3	2	5	5	9	4
3	5	4	2	7	9	4	4	3	4	4	2	9	*	*	*	*	*	2	5	5	3	8	6
3	8	5	3	7	9	4	6	9	6	3	2	9	*	*	*	*	*	5	3	5	4	9	5
1	2	7	3	7	3	4	4	3	2	5	5	7	2	4	3	8	3	4	2	5	3	9	6
2	3	4	2	7	9	4	4	5	2	3	3	9	1	7	6	4	5	5	5	5	4	9	5
2	6	5	3	5	7	5	4	2	2	4	5	9	1	5	8	1	7	4	5	5	5	8	5
5	7	7	5	6	9	4	4	7	2	2	2	6	6	3	8	2	6	7	2	5	5	9	6
3	7	5	3	6	7	4	4	3	3	3	3	7	5	6	4	4	7	5	5	5	4	8	5
2	2	7	4	6	3	4	4	5	4	3	3	7	5	6	1	6	9	4	4	5	3	9	6
2	2	8	6	4	5	4	4	7	2	4	5	8	1	9	7	3	4	4	3	5	2	9	5
1	2	6	3	7	9	4	4	3	3	4	3	9	1	9	5	2	7	8	5	5	3	8	6
1	8	1	1	9	9	4	4	9	6	3	3	5	9	4	6	6	2	7	4	5	1	6	5
3	7	5	4	4	5	4	4	2	2	3	5	9	*	*	*	*	*	6	2	5	2	5	4
1	2	8	6	4	3	4	4	3	3	4	4	7	1	5	5	5	5	3	2	5	3	9	6
4	5	7	4	5	3	4	4	2	3	3	3	5	7	6	3	1	9	5	3	5	4	7	5
2	5	7	5	5	3	4	4	3	3	3	5	8	3	5	8	2	6	6	4	5	3	7	7
3	5	5	2	8	9	4	4	9	2	3	2	8	3	5	6	6	3	3	6	5	3	9	6
1	3	6	4	6	3	4	4	8	5	2	1	5	5	3	8	4	4	9	3	5	6	7	8
3	4	7	4	7	4	4	4	4	5	3	3	4	5	5	5	7	4	7	4	5	2	9	6
5	6	4	2	8	8	4	4	9	9	2	1	9	4	3	6	3	7	6	8	5	3	9	9
3	9	2	1	9	8	4	4	9	9	1	1	2	9	7	4	3	8	1	9	5	4	9	9
7	9	3	5	6	5	4	4	9	9	1	1	9	*	*	*	*	*	1	9	5	8	8	9
2	6	3	1	9	4	4	4	6	9	1	1	7	*	*	*	*	*	1	9	4	4	9	9
5	9	6	8	2	3	4	4	9	9	1	1	9	*	*	*	*	*	1	5	5	3	7	9
7	8	2	3	5	3	4	9	9	2	2	4	2	1	7	1	9	4	5	9	5	4	5	3
8	5	5	4	5	3	4	7	9	9	2	2	1	8	6	2	7	6	7	9	5	6	9	5
8	5	6	7	3	3	5	7	9	4	4	4	3	2	8	2	9	2	6	5	5	5	5	4

Economic Indicators For Class IA, IB, IIA, And IIB Counties

		SIZE OF COUNTY		REAL-ESTATE VALUES			AGES OF POPULATION				INCOMES					
		Population	Land Area	Med House Val	Med Gross Rent	Av Farm Val./Acre	% Under 5	% 5–17	% 18 and Over	% 65 and Over	% Poverty	% Under $10,000	% $10–19,999	% $20–29,999	% $30–49,999	% Over $50,000
Lewis	IB	8	9	9	9	9	6	5	4	4	3	2	4	7	8	7
Pend Oreille	IA	4	7	6	4	4	7	8	2	3	4	6	2	7	5	2
San Juan	IB	3	3	9	9	9	1	1	9	7	2	2	7	7	7	9
Stevens	IA	6	9	9	7	3	9	9	1	2	4	2	7	7	7	6
Whatcom	IB	9	9	9	9	9	4	2	8	2	2	2	3	8	9	9
WEST VIRGINIA																
Barbour	IIA	4	3	5	6	3	4	5	6	5	6	6	7	4	3	1
Berkeley	IB	7	3	9	8	8	5	5	5	2	3	2	3	8	8	5
Calhoun	IIA	3	3	4	1	2	6	4	5	6	8	9	5	1	2	2
Clay	IIA	4	3	2	4	3	8	9	1	3	9	9	6	1	1	1
Doddridge	IIA	3	3	3	2	2	4	7	4	6	6	8	6	2	3	1
Fayette	IIA	8	4	6	6	4	6	5	5	4	5	5	5	5	5	2
Grant	IIB	4	4	6	6	3	5	7	4	3	8	6	6	5	2	3
Greenbrier	IIA	7	6	7	7	5	4	4	6	5	4	6	5	5	4	5
Hampshire	IA	4	4	6	5	4	4	8	3	3	5	6	7	3	4	4
Hardy	IIA	4	4	5	4	3	2	4	7	4	7	7	8	4	1	2
Jefferson	IB	6	3	9	8	9	4	5	5	2	3	1	8	8	8	5
Lincoln	IB	5	4	4	4	3	7	9	1	2	8	7	4	5	3	2
Mercer	IIB	9	3	8	6	4	4	4	6	3	4	4	4	6	7	6
Mineral	IIB	5	3	6	4	3	4	6	5	3	4	3	8	6	6	5
Monongalia	IIB	9	3	9	9	5	2	1	9	1	2	5	2	5	8	7
Monroe	IIA	4	4	6	3	4	4	6	5	5	7	6	8	5	2	1
Morgan	IB	4	3	7	6	6	3	4	6	4	5	4	4	8	4	5
Pendleton	IIA	3	4	7	5	4	4	2	7	6	7	8	8	2	2	1
Pleasants	IIA	3	3	8	6	3	4	7	4	2	4	2	3	9	8	5
Pocahontas	IIA	4	5	4	5	2	3	3	7	7	3	6	7	3	5	3
Preston	IIA	6	4	5	4	3	7	6	4	3	6	5	6	6	3	6
Randolph	IIB	6	6	7	6	3	3	4	7	4	5	5	7	5	4	5
Ritchie	IIA	4	4	3	2	2	5	3	6	7	5	7	7	2	3	2
Roane	IIA	4	4	6	3	3	6	3	6	5	6	7	6	3	2	4
Summers	IIA	4	3	6	3	3	5	2	7	4	8	8	3	3	2	5
Taylor	IIA	4	3	4	3	4	4	5	5	5	4	5	7	5	4	2
Tucker	IIA	4	4	4	4	3	3	5	6	6	5	6	7	3	3	2
Tyler	IIA	4	3	7	5	3	4	8	3	4	4	3	2	9	5	3
Upshur	IB	5	3	9	7	4	4	4	6	3	4	5	6	5	5	2
Wirt	IIA	3	3	5	5	3	2	8	4	4	6	7	5	5	3	1
WISCONSIN																
Adams	IB	4	4	7	9	4	1	2	9	7	3	5	7	5	4	3
Barron	IIB	7	5	8	8	5	6	4	6	6	2	4	8	5	4	4

SOCIO-ECONOMIC STATUS					MINORITIES				RURAL-URBAN				ECONOMIC BASE					COUNTY CONDITIONS					
% Completed HS	% College or More	Families/Pop	% Married Couples	% W/O Husband	% Black	% Spanish	% Amer Indian	% Asian	% Urban	% Rural	% Farmers	% Out of County	Jobs/Pop	% Manufacturing	% Wholesale	% Retail	% Services	Physicians/Cap	Crimes/Cap	$ Police/Crimes	$ Educ/Enrollment	Carpool or Transit	Pop Density
8	6	5	6	4	3	4	5	9	7	3	3	2	*	*	*	*	*	7	9	5	5	4	4
8	6	5	7	2	3	4	6	3	2	3	4	6	1	7	1	9	5	8	9	5	5	5	4
9	9	9	7	3	3	4	4	9	2	2	2	2	8	3	2	1	9	9	9	5	4	3	5
9	5	4	7	3	3	4	8	4	4	4	4	3	3	5	3	7	5	4	8	5	2	5	4
8	9	2	5	5	3	5	6	9	9	2	2	1	9	3	3	7	6	9	9	5	3	9	5
3	4	3	4	6	3	4	4	3	4	2	3	6	1	3	2	9	2	8	3	5	3	7	5
5	6	4	4	6	4	4	4	7	5	2	2	5	4	5	2	8	4	9	7	4	6	8	9
3	2	7	2	8	3	4	4	8	2	2	3	5	*	*	*	*	*	6	2	5	6	7	4
1	1	3	4	6	3	4	4	2	2	2	2	9	*	*	*	*	*	2	2	5	4	9	5
4	5	4	5	4	3	4	4	4	2	2	4	9	*	*	*	*	*	4	2	5	5	9	4
3	3	4	2	8	5	4	4	5	4	2	1	7	3	3	2	8	4	7	3	5	7	6	7
2	3	6	6	4	3	4	4	3	2	3	4	4	3	3	6	2	8	9	2	5	7	9	4
4	6	6	4	6	4	4	4	5	4	2	2	3	7	3	2	2	9	8	2	5	4	7	5
4	6	5	5	5	3	4	4	4	2	4	4	7	*	*	*	*	*	4	4	4	4	8	4
3	2	7	3	6	3	4	4	2	2	4	5	4	2	7	6	5	4	3	2	5	6	8	4
3	9	2	4	6	5	4	4	7	3	3	2	7	6	3	1	1	9	4	8	4	2	9	8
2	1	5	5	5	3	4	4	2	2	2	2	9	1	3	1	9	2	2	2	5	4	9	5
4	6	6	3	7	4	4	4	8	7	2	1	4	9	3	7	1	8	9	4	5	3	7	9
7	3	6	5	5	3	4	4	5	7	2	2	9	4	4	1	1	9	3	3	5	6	9	7
2	9	1	4	6	3	4	4	9	8	2	1	2	7	3	2	3	9	9	6	5	1	9	9
5	4	6	5	5	3	4	4	2	2	4	6	9	*	*	*	*	*	4	2	4	4	9	4
5	5	6	7	3	3	4	4	2	2	2	2	8	3	3	7	1	9	5	5	4	5	7	5
3	4	6	4	5	3	4	4	2	2	7	9	4	1	8	4	2	9	3	2	5	9	9	4
6	3	3	4	6	3	4	4	2	2	2	2	6	*	*	*	*	*	4	3	5	7	8	6
3	5	6	3	6	3	4	4	2	2	4	5	4	4	4	2	1	9	5	2	5	6	9	4
4	2	4	6	4	3	4	4	4	3	3	3	6	*	*	*	*	*	3	3	5	7	8	5
4	5	3	4	6	3	4	4	3	6	2	2	2	5	4	5	5	6	9	4	5	5	6	4
5	2	6	4	6	3	4	4	5	2	3	3	6	1	7	2	9	3	2	2	5	7	9	4
4	3	6	5	5	3	4	5	3	4	3	3	7	2	6	4	8	2	8	2	5	4	8	5
4	2	2	2	8	4	5	4	7	6	2	2	6	2	3	2	8	5	6	3	5	5	6	5
6	3	5	3	7	3	4	4	5	7	2	2	8	*	*	*	*	*	5	3	5	3	7	7
5	3	5	4	5	3	4	4	4	2	2	3	5	3	6	1	2	9	5	3	5	7	9	4
6	3	5	7	3	3	4	4	4	3	2	3	9	*	*	*	*	*	3	2	5	4	9	5
4	6	2	6	5	3	4	4	4	6	2	2	3	5	4	5	8	3	5	3	5	5	6	6
4	2	6	5	5	3	4	4	9	2	4	5	9	*	*	*	*	*	1	2	5	5	9	4
8	4	5	7	2	3	4	5	5	2	4	4	7	*	*	*	*	*	3	9	5	4	3	4
7	6	5	7	3	3	4	4	5	5	7	6	2	8	4	4	7	4	8	3	5	7	4	5

Economic Indicators For Class IA, IB, IIA, And IIB Counties		SIZE OF COUNTY		REAL-ESTATE VALUES			AGES OF POPULATION				INCOMES					
		Population	Land Area	Med House Val	Med Gross Rent	Av Farm Val./Acre	% Under 5	% 5–17	% 18 and Over	% 65 and Over	% Poverty	% Under $10,000	% $10–19,999	% $20–29,999	% $30–49,999	% Over $50,000
Bayfield	IIA	4	7	7	7	3	4	5	6	7	3	6	6	4	3	2
Burnett	IA	4	5	7	6	2	3	3	7	8	4	7	8	2	2	2
Door	IB	5	4	9	9	5	6	2	7	6	1	1	8	8	7	9
Dunn	IIB	6	5	8	9	4	3	1	9	3	2	3	7	6	6	7
Florence	IA	3	4	7	6	2	4	6	5	8	4	7	4	4	4	2
Forest	IIA	4	6	5	6	2	4	8	4	7	5	7	9	2	2	1
Green	IIB	6	4	9	8	8	5	5	5	4	2	1	5	9	8	9
Juneau	IIA	5	5	5	6	4	6	5	5	6	2	5	8	3	4	4
Lincoln	IIB	5	5	7	6	3	4	7	4	6	2	3	8	7	4	5
Marathon	IIB	9	7	9	9	4	6	7	3	2	1	1	4	9	9	8
Marquette	IA	4	4	7	8	6	3	3	7	8	3	5	9	4	3	5
Menominee	IB	3	3	3	1	3	9	9	1	1	6	3	9	2	4	1
Oconto	IIB	6	6	6	6	5	5	7	4	5	2	4	8	6	5	3
Pierce	IIB	6	4	9	9	5	5	4	6	2	2	1	5	8	9	8
Polk	IB	6	5	8	8	5	5	6	4	6	2	3	7	7	6	4
St. Croix	IB	7	5	9	9	6	7	8	2	2	1	1	1	9	9	9
Sawyer	IB	4	6	7	8	3	3	5	6	8	5	7	6	2	3	3
Trempealeau	IIB	5	5	7	5	4	3	7	4	7	2	3	9	5	5	5
Washburn	IB	4	5	7	6	2	5	4	6	7	3	5	9	3	3	2
Waupaca	IIB	7	5	8	8	6	5	4	6	8	2	2	8	7	7	5
Waushara	IA	5	4	7	7	5	3	3	7	8	2	5	7	5	4	4
WYOMING																
Big Horn	IIA	4	9	8	5	2	9	7	2	4	3	3	8	6	7	3
Converse	IA	4	9	9	9	1	9	8	1	1	1	1	1	9	9	9
Crook	IIA	3	9	9	9	1	9	7	2	1	2	1	8	9	9	8
Johnson	IB	3	9	9	9	1	7	4	5	4	1	1	4	7	9	9
Lincoln	IA	4	9	9	9	2	9	9	1	1	3	1	3	9	9	8
Platte	IA	4	8	9	9	1	9	5	3	1	2	1	1	9	9	7
Sheridan	IB	5	9	9	9	2	7	3	6	3	1	1	1	9	9	9
Sweetwater	IB	7	9	9	9	1	9	6	1	1	1	1	1	9	9	9
Uinta	IA	4	9	9	9	1	9	7	1	1	1	1	1	9	9	9

SOCIO-ECONOMIC STATUS					MINORITIES				RURAL-URBAN				ECONOMIC BASE					COUNTY CONDITIONS					
% Completed HS	% College or More	Families/Pop	% Married Couples	% W/O Husband	% Black	% Spanish	% Amer Indian	% Asian	% Urban	% Rural	% Farmers	% Out of County	Jobs/Pop	% Manufacturing	% Wholesale	% Retail	% Services	Physicians/Cap	Crunes/Cap	$ Police/Crimes	$ Educ/Enrollment	Carpool or Transit	Pop Density
8	9	6	6	3	3	4	8	8	2	2	5	7	*	*	*	*	*	3	6	5	9	4	4
8	4	8	6	3	3	4	7	3	2	4	5	3	3	4	1	9	2	2	3	5	7	3	4
8	8	6	7	3	3	4	5	8	7	6	6	1	7	6	2	7	7	8	7	5	6	6	5
4	8	1	7	2	3	4	4	9	7	7	7	3	7	3	4	7	4	4	8	5	2	4	5
8	4	5	6	3	3	4	4	2	2	4	4	9	*	*	*	*	*	1	5	5	8	3	4
6	3	3	6	4	3	4	7	6	2	2	2	3	2	7	1	9	5	3	9	5	6	8	4
8	6	4	7	3	3	4	4	5	8	8	7	3	9	4	7	2	6	9	6	5	7	3	5
7	3	4	6	3	3	4	5	6	4	6	5	4	6	4	2	8	6	4	5	5	7	3	4
6	5	4	7	3	3	4	4	4	8	3	3	2	7	6	3	6	6	7	7	5	5	5	4
7	6	3	7	3	3	4	4	6	8	5	4	2	8	5	7	2	6	9	6	5	4	9	6
8	4	8	8	2	3	4	4	6	2	7	6	7	3	4	4	8	2	3	7	5	6	5	4
1	1	1	1	9	3	4	9	2	2	1	1	2	*	*	*	*	*	3	9	5	7	8	4
7	3	4	7	2	3	4	5	3	5	6	6	5	2	6	4	6	5	4	6	5	6	3	4
5	8	1	7	3	3	4	4	6	6	7	6	8	7	3	4	8	3	5	5	5	4	6	6
8	6	5	6	3	3	4	5	4	2	6	7	4	6	4	3	8	4	6	7	5	9	5	5
8	8	2	8	2	3	4	4	8	5	6	5	8	7	4	3	4	8	5	6	5	5	7	6
8	8	7	5	5	3	4	9	5	2	2	3	2	7	3	1	6	9	5	8	5	7	4	4
7	5	3	6	3	3	4	4	3	2	8	8	3	6	5	7	5	3	4	3	5	8	3	5
8	6	6	6	3	3	4	5	3	2	3	4	4	7	3	3	8	5	9	4	5	9	5	4
8	5	3	7	3	3	4	4	4	6	5	5	3	7	5	4	6	5	6	7	5	8	3	6
7	5	7	7	2	3	5	4	5	2	5	6	7	4	3	4	8	4	4	7	5	5	5	4
8	7	4	9	2	3	5	5	5	2	5	5	2	*	*	*	*	*	5	4	5	9	5	3
7	7	3	8	2	3	6	5	5	9	3	3	2	5	2	1	7	9	4	9	5	9	9	3
8	7	6	8	2	3	4	4	5	2	8	9	3	3	3	2	8	6	4	3	5	9	4	3
9	9	5	7	3	3	4	5	2	9	4	4	2	9	3	1	5	9	8	8	5	8	4	3
8	6	2	8	2	3	5	5	7	5	5	5	2	*	*	*	*	*	3	7	5	6	8	3
9	7	4	9	1	3	6	5	3	8	4	4	1	5	3	2	6	8	3	6	5	6	7	4
9	9	3	6	4	3	5	5	7	9	3	2	2	9	3	3	4	8	9	9	5	7	5	4
7	7	2	7	2	3	7	5	8	9	2	1	1	8	2	2	2	9	6	9	5	9	9	3
8	5	1	8	2	3	5	5	3	8	3	2	4	7	2	2	8	6	8	9	4	6	9	4

Economic Indicators For Class IIIA And IIIB Counties		SIZE OF COUNTY		REAL-ESTATE VALUES			AGES OF POPULATION				INCOMES					
		Population	Land Area	Med House Val	Med Gross Rent	Av Farm Val./Acre	% Under 5	% 5–17	% 18 and Over	% 65 and Over	% Poverty	% Under $10,000	% $10–19,999	% $20–29,999	% $30–49,999	% Over $50,000
ALABAMA																
Barbour	IIIA	5	5	3	1	3	6	9	2	4	9	9	2	2	3	4
Butler	IIIA	5	5	2	1	3	7	7	3	6	8	9	5	1	1	5
Chambers	IIIA	7	4	3	3	5	4	7	4	5	5	6	5	6	4	2
Choctaw	IIIA	4	5	2	2	3	8	9	1	3	9	9	1	3	5	3
Clarke	IIIA	6	6	3	3	2	8	9	1	3	8	7	1	5	6	5
Clay	IIIA	4	4	2	1	3	4	7	4	6	7	8	6	2	2	2
Coffee	IIIB	7	4	6	5	4	4	6	5	2	5	4	5	7	6	4
Conecuh	IIIA	4	5	1	1	3	7	7	3	6	9	9	2	1	1	5
Coosa	IIIA	4	4	2	2	2	3	7	4	4	8	8	8	2	1	2
Covington	IIIA	6	6	2	2	3	2	3	7	7	6	8	4	3	2	3
Crenshaw	IIIA	4	4	1	1	3	5	5	5	7	9	9	1	1	2	3
Escambia	IIIB	7	5	3	3	7	6	7	3	3	6	7	3	4	3	
Geneva	IIIA	5	4	2	1	4	4	6	5	5	7	8	4	3	2	4
Greene	IIIA	4	4	2	1	3	8	9	1	7	9	9	1	1	1	3
Hale	IIIA	4	4	2	1	3	9	9	1	6	9	9	1	1	2	3
Lawrence	IIIB	6	4	4	3	5	5	9	1	2	8	6	2	7	5	2
Limestone	IIIB	7	4	5	7	6	5	7	3	2	5	3	5	6	7	6
Lowndes	IIIA	4	5	2	1	3	9	9	1	2	9	9	1	1	2	2
Macon	IIIB	5	4	4	5	3	4	6	5	4	9	9	1	1	4	3
Marengo	IIIA	5	6	3	1	3	7	9	1	4	9	8	1	4	7	4
Monroe	IIIA	5	6	3	2	4	8	9	1	4	8	7	2	4	5	4
Perry	IIIA	4	5	2	1	3	8	9	1	6	9	9	1	1	2	3
Pickens	IIIA	5	5	2	1	3	7	8	2	5	9	8	4	3	2	2
Randolph	IIIA	5	4	2	2	3	5	6	5	6	7	8	4	2	2	1
Sumter	IIIA	4	5	2	1	3	9	9	1	5	9	9	1	1	5	3
Washington	IIIB	4	6	1	3	3	8	9	1	2	8	6	2	8	4	2
ARKANSAS																
Arkansas	IIIB	5	6	6	3	7	6	3	6	5	5	6	3	3	5	9
Ashley	IIIB	5	5	3	4	7	7	8	2	3	7	7	1	7	6	3
Bradley	IIIA	4	4	2	2	5	4	4	6	8	9	9	3	2	1	3
Calhoun	IIIA	3	4	2	2	3	4	3	7	7	8	9	4	2	1	2
Chicot	IIIA	4	4	1	2	6	9	9	1	6	9	9	1	1	2	6
Clark	IIIA	5	5	4	3	5	2	1	9	5	5	7	2	4	4	4
Clay	IIIA	5	4	2	2	6	2	3	8	8	8	9	2	1	1	4
Columbia	IIIB	5	5	3	2	4	4	3	7	6	7	7	3	3	3	6
Crittenden	IIIA	8	4	6	7	7	9	9	1	1	9	7	1	5	5	5
Cross	IIIA	5	4	5	5	6	9	9	1	3	7	6	6	4	3	7
Dallas	IIIA	4	4	2	3	6	5	5	5	7	4	6	8	2	2	6
Desha	IIIA	5	5	4	2	5	9	9	1	4	8	9	1	2	4	8

	SOCIO-ECONOMIC STATUS					MINORITIES				RURAL-URBAN				ECONOMIC BASE					COUNTY CONDITIONS					
	% Completed HS	% College or More	Families/Pop	% Married Couples	% W/O Husband	% Black	% Spanish	% Amer Indian	% Asian	% Urban	% Rural	% Farmers	% Out of County	Jobs/Pop	% Manufacturing	% Wholesale	% Retail	% Services	Physicians/Cap	Crimes/Cap	$ Police/Crimes	$ Educ/Enrollment	Carpool or Transit	Pop Density
	2	4	3	1	9	9	5	4	6	8	2	3	3	5	5	5	3	8	4	6	5	2	8	4
	2	4	4	1	9	9	4	4	3	7	3	3	3	4	7	3	6	6	4	7	5	2	8	4
	3	3	5	1	9	9	4	4	2	8	2	2	5	*	*	*	*	*	5	5	5	1	8	6
	2	2	2	2	9	9	4	4	3	2	2	3	3	*	*	*	*	*	3	2	5	2	9	4
	2	4	2	1	9	9	4	4	2	7	2	2	3	4	6	1	9	4	5	3	5	2	8	4
	3	2	6	5	5	7	4	4	2	2	3	3	6	2	9	1	9	4	4	3	5	2	9	4
	4	7	7	4	6	7	4	4	8	9	3	3	7	4	6	2	7	5	5	6	5	2	6	6
	2	2	3	1	9	9	4	4	2	5	4	4	7	2	6	7	2	7	3	1	7	2	7	4
	3	1	5	3	7	9	4	4	3	2	2	3	9	1	9	9	1	2	2	4	5	2	9	4
	3	3	8	4	7	6	4	4	7	8	3	3	2	6	7	6	4	4	6	5	5	3	5	5
	1	3	5	1	9	8	4	4	3	4	4	4	7	2	6	9	2	2	3	2	5	2	9	4
	4	3	2	1	9	9	4	6	3	8	2	2	4	6	5	5	6	4	6	4	5	2	8	5
	3	2	7	4	6	6	4	5	3	6	4	4	7	4	5	9	1	3	3	4	5	2	6	5
	1	4	1	1	9	9	5	4	2	2	2	3	5	2	4	7	4	3	3	7	5	3	9	4
	1	2	1	1	9	9	5	4	4	4	3	3	8	1	6	7	5	3	4	2	5	3	9	4
	2	1	5	5	5	7	4	4	3	3	4	4	9	*	*	*	*	*	3	4	5	2	9	5
	3	4	6	5	6	6	4	4	7	6	3	3	8	3	6	3	8	5	4	5	5	2	9	7
	1	2	1	1	9	9	5	4	2	2	3	3	9	1	6	2	9	1	2	5	4	3	9	4
	1	9	1	1	9	9	4	4	6	8	2	2	5	2	3	2	7	7	8	9	5	1	8	5
	2	4	1	1	9	9	5	4	3	7	2	3	4	4	6	3	8	3	3	5	5	2	7	4
	3	3	2	1	9	9	4	5	2	5	2	2	2	3	8	5	5	3	4	2	5	2	8	4
	1	4	1	1	9	9	5	4	4	6	3	3	6	2	3	9	3	2	2	5	5	2	8	4
	2	2	3	1	9	9	4	4	3	3	2	3	6	3	6	9	3	2	3	2	5	2	9	4
	2	3	6	3	8	8	4	4	3	6	2	3	6	2	8	6	4	4	4	3	5	2	9	5
	1	4	1	1	9	9	4	4	7	7	2	3	2	3	6	5	7	3	6	4	5	2	8	4
	2	1	2	3	7	8	4	8	2	2	2	3	7	*	*	*	*	*	2	1	6	3	9	4
	4	4	7	4	6	7	4	4	5	9	4	3	1	9	5	9	2	4	5	5	5	3	3	4
	4	3	4	3	7	8	4	4	3	8	2	2	1	*	*	*	*	*	3	4	5	3	3	4
	3	4	7	3	7	9	4	4	4	9	3	3	3	3	8	3	7	4	3	4	5	4	5	4
	4	1	5	3	7	8	4	4	4	2	2	3	8	*	*	*	*	*	1	2	5	3	3	4
	1	2	1	1	9	9	4	4	7	9	3	2	3	3	4	7	4	4	6	5	5	4	6	4
	2	9	2	4	6	8	4	4	6	9	2	2	2	6	5	2	7	5	5	5	5	1	4	4
	2	2	9	6	4	3	4	4	3	7	5	4	2	3	6	8	4	3	3	2	5	3	5	5
	4	5	4	2	8	9	4	5	6	8	2	2	2	5	5	4	4	7	5	3	5	2	4	5
	2	2	1	1	9	9	4	4	8	9	2	1	7	*	*	*	*	*	6	9	5	2	6	7
	2	3	2	3	7	8	4	4	2	7	4	3	4	4	6	6	5	4	4	5	5	3	6	5
	4	4	4	3	7	9	4	4	3	8	2	2	5	4	7	3	9	3	5	7	5	3	8	4
	2	4	1	1	9	9	4	4	3	9	3	2	2	6	4	7	4	4	4	6	5	5	6	4

Economic Indicators For Class IIIA And IIIB Counties		SIZE OF COUNTY		REAL-ESTATE VALUES			AGES OF POPULATION				INCOMES					
		Population	Land Area	Med House Val	Med Gross Rent	Av Farm Val./Acre	% Under 5	% 5-17	% 18 and Over	% 65 and Over	% Poverty	% Under $10,000	% $10-19,999	% $20-29,999	% $30-49,999	% Over $50,000
Jackson	IIIA	5	4	4	3	6	5	5	5	5	8	8	6	1	2	6
Jefferson	IIIB	9	5	4	6	6	7	7	3	3	7	6	1	5	8	4
Lafayette	IIIA	4	4	1	1	5	7	7	3	8	9	9	1	2	3	1
Lincoln	IIIA	4	4	2	1	6	4	4	6	4	8	8	3	2	3	3
Mississippi	IIIA	8	5	4	7	8	9	8	1	2	8	7	6	2	3	3
Nevada	IIIA	4	4	1	1	5	6	5	5	8	8	8	3	3	2	2
Quachita	IIIB	6	5	2	1	4	5	3	6	7	6	7	3	4	4	4
Prairie	IIIA	4	4	3	3	7	3	7	5	5	8	9	4	1	2	4
St. Francis	IIB	6	4	4	4	6	9	9	1	3	9	9	1	2	2	4
Union	IIA	8	6	3	3	5	5	4	6	6	6	7	2	4	6	6
Woodruff	IIA	4	4	2	2	5	7	8	2	7	9	9	2	1	1	4
COLORADO																
Baca	IIA	3	9	3	3	2	4	5	6	4	6	7	5	2	5	7
Cheyenne	IIA	3	8	3	3	1	9	2	5	6	5	6	7	3	3	6
Conejos	IIIA	3	7	2	2	2	9	9	1	2	9	9	6	1	1	1
Costilla	IIIA	3	6	2	1	1	6	8	3	4	9	9	1	1	1	3
Crowley	IIIA	3	5	1	3	1	2	2	8	9	5	9	5	1	1	1
Huerfano	IIIA	3	8	2	4	1	5	5	5	8	6	8	2	2	4	2
Kiowa	IIIA	3	8	1	3	1	6	1	9	5	5	3	7	6	5	9
Kit Carson	IIIA	3	9	7	5	2	6	6	4	4	7	3	8	6	5	7
Las Animas	IIIA	4	9	6	4	1	4	3	7	8	6	7	3	3	5	2
Lincoln	IIIA	3	9	6	4	1	2	1	9	8	3	5	7	5	4	6
Logan	IIB	5	8	8	7	2	6	3	6	3	2	2	8	7	7	8
Phillips	IIIA	3	4	6	3	3	5	3	7	9	4	5	5	4	5	8
Prowers	IIIA	4	8	5	5	2	9	7	2	3	6	5	2	7	6	4
Saguache	IIIA	3	9	3	3	2	9	6	3	3	9	9	4	1	3	2
San Juan	IIIA	3	3	8	9	9	9	2	3	1	2	2	9	9	5	1
Sedgwick	IIIA	3	4	3	2	3	3	3	7	8	2	3	9	4	3	4
Washington	IIIA	3	9	5	2	2	4	3	7	5	5	4	8	6	5	2
FLORIDA																
Franklin	IIB	3	4	2	3	6	4	7	4	5	9	9	2	1	2	3
Gadsden	IIB	7	4	2	1	6	8	9	1	3	9	7	5	2	4	4
Madison	IIIA	4	5	2	1	6	6	9	2	5	9	9	5	1	3	2
GEORGIA																
Atkinson	IIIA	3	3	1	1	4	8	9	1	2	9	9	3	1	1	4
Baker	IIIA	3	3	2	1	6	8	8	1	3	9	7	4	3	2	3
Bleckley	IIIB	4	3	4	1	4	3	4	6	2	5	5	2	6	7	5
Brooks	IIIA	4	4	2	2	5	7	9	1	5	9	9	1	2	2	3

SOCIO-ECONOMIC STATUS					MINORITIES				RURAL-URBAN				ECONOMIC BASE					COUNTY CONDITIONS					
% Completed HS	% College or More	Families/Pop	% Married Couples	% W/O Husband	% Black	% Spanish	% Amer Indian	% Asian	% Urban	% Rural	% Farmers	% Out of County	Jobs/Pop	% Manufacturing	% Wholesale	% Retail	% Services	Physicians/Cap	Crimes/Cap	$ Police/Crimes	$ Educ/Enrollment	Carpool or Transit	Pop Density
2	4	6	3	7	6	4	4	2	7	3	3	2	6	5	4	7	4	7	7	5	2	5	5
4	7	2	1	9	9	4	4	7	9	2	1	1	7	4	4	4	7	9	9	5	3	8	7
2	2	2	1	8	9	4	4	2	5	3	3	6	1	7	2	7	6	2	2	5	6	9	4
2	2	1	2	8	9	4	4	3	2	4	3	7	*	*	*	*	*	2	1	5	4	4	4
2	3	3	1	9	8	4	4	8	9	2	2	1	6	6	4	3	7	5	9	5	4	5	6
4	3	6	3	7	9	4	4	3	7	3	5	5	2	7	3	8	4	4	2	5	4	6	4
5	5	6	2	8	9	4	4	3	8	2	2	2	5	6	2	7	6	5	4	5	3	4	5
2	2	7	6	4	6	4	4	4	2	7	5	6	3	4	8	5	2	2	4	5	4	5	4
1	3	1	1	9	9	4	4	7	8	3	2	2	7	5	4	4	7	3	9	5	4	7	5
6	6	6	2	8	8	4	4	4	8	2	2	1	8	5	6	3	7	9	8	5	4	4	5
1	3	4	1	9	9	4	4	3	6	4	3	2	3	6	9	2	2	5	4	5	3	7	4
7	8	8	7	2	3	6	4	8	2	9	9	1	7	2	8	3	3	5	4	5	9	4	3
9	8	7	8	2	3	5	4	2	2	9	9	1	*	*	*	*	*	4	4	5	9	3	3
2	4	1	4	5	3	9	5	5	2	3	6	4	2	5	9	1	6	3	2	5	5	8	4
2	5	4	2	7	3	9	4	9	2	4	7	3	*	*	*	*	*	3	1	6	8	5	3
7	5	8	5	4	3	9	4	9	2	6	9	4	*	*	*	*	*	1	2	5	8	3	3
4	7	5	2	8	3	9	5	8	9	4	4	3	6	2	2	4	9	8	8	5	8	4	3
9	6	9	9	1	3	5	4	4	2	9	9	1	*	*	*	*	*	1	2	5	9	3	3
8	7	7	7	2	3	6	4	3	7	9	9	1	9	2	9	1	5	5	6	5	9	5	3
7	7	3	2	8	3	9	4	8	9	3	4	3	5	2	2	8	6	5	9	5	6	6	3
9	6	8	7	3	3	4	4	2	2	8	9	1	*	*	*	*	*	2	3	5	9	3	3
8	7	4	6	4	3	6	4	9	9	6	6	2	9	3	8	2	6	8	8	5	9	4	4
9	8	7	8	2	3	5	4	9	2	8	9	1	8	2	8	5	3	6	2	5	9	3	4
6	7	3	4	6	3	9	5	5	9	3	4	1	9	3	4	5	6	5	9	5	8	5	4
5	6	4	4	5	3	9	5	4	2	6	7	4	*	*	*	*	*	5	9	5	8	7	3
8	9	1	4	5	3	9	5	9	2	1	1	2	*	*	*	*	*	9	4	5	9	9	3
9	7	8	8	2	3	8	4	9	2	5	8	2	*	*	*	*	*	3	4	5	9	3	4
8	7	8	8	2	3	5	4	3	2	9	9	3	*	*	*	*	*	1	5	5	9	4	3
2	4	5	3	7	6	5	5	2	6	2	1	2	5	4	9	1	3	5	7	5	8	8	4
2	3	1	1	9	9	4	4	7	7	2	2	7	3	3	7	6	2	7	8	5	4	9	7
2	3	3	1	9	9	4	4	2	5	4	5	4	2	5	6	4	4	4	5	5	7	8	4
1	1	2	2	8	8	4	4	4	2	7	6	8	1	7	7	4	2	2	1	9	4	8	4
1	1	2	1	9	9	4	4	2	2	8	6	9	*	*	*	*	*	1	2	5	3	9	4
2	4	2	2	8	8	4	4	9	8	3	3	7	*	*	*	*	*	3	2	5	3	9	5
1	3	2	1	9	9	4	4	8	6	4	4	7	2	4	8	4	3	3	3	5	3	7	5

Economic Indicators For Class IIIA And IIB Counties

County	Class	SIZE OF COUNTY		REAL-ESTATE VALUES			AGES OF POPULATION				INCOMES					
		Population	Land Area	Med House Val	Med Gross Rent	Av Farm Val./Acre	% Under 5	% 5–17	% 18 and Over	% 65 and Over	% Poverty	% Under $10,000	% $10–19,999	% $20–29,999	% $30–49,999	% Over $50,000
Burke	IIIA	5	5	4	1	3	9	9	1	3	9	8	2	3	2	4
Clay	IIIA	3	3	1	1	4	6	7	3	7	9	9	1	1	2	6
Clinch	IIIA	3	5	2	1	3	7	9	1	1	8	8	2	5	2	2
Colquitt	IIIB	6	4	3	3	6	6	8	2	3	6	7	4	4	3	4
Cook	IIIB	4	3	2	3	6	6	9	1	3	6	6	9	1	2	7
Crisp	IIIB	5	3	4	4	8	8	8	2	3	9	7	3	4	4	5
Dodge	IIIA	4	4	2	1	4	4	8	3	4	9	8	3	2	3	4
Dooly	IIIA	4	3	3	2	6	9	9	1	4	9	8	5	1	2	5
Early	IIIA	4	4	3	1	5	7	9	1	4	9	9	1	2	4	6
Elbert	IIIA	5	3	4	2	3	5	5	5	4	6	6	6	6	2	2
Fannin	IIIA	4	3	2	3	4	2	3	8	6	8	9	4	2	1	2
Glascock	IIIA	3	3	1	1	4	3	3	7	7	7	7	3	2	5	8
Grady	IIIA	5	4	3	3	5	6	8	2	4	9	8	3	3	2	3
Greene	IIIA	4	3	2	2	3	8	7	2	5	8	8	7	2	2	1
Hancock	IIIA	4	4	1	1	3	7	9	1	3	9	9	4	1	1	4
Irwin	IIIA	4	3	3	2	6	5	8	2	5	8	8	4	1	5	5
Jefferson	IIIA	5	4	2	1	4	7	9	1	4	9	9	2	1	2	4
Jenkins	IIIA	4	3	3	1	4	6	8	2	3	9	9	1	2	1	3
McIntosh	IIIB	3	4	1	6	3	4	9	1	2	9	8	3	3	2	1
Macon	IIIA	4	3	2	2	5	8	9	1	3	9	8	2	2	2	7
Marion	IIIA	3	3	2	1	3	4	9	1	3	9	8	6	1	3	2
Meriwether	IIIA	5	4	2	2	4	7	8	2	3	7	6	4	4	5	3
Miller	IIIA	3	3	4	1	6	6	8	2	4	9	8	5	1	4	3
Pulaski	IIIA	4	3	5	1	5	5	7	3	4	8	7	1	6	4	3
Quitman	IIIA	3	3	2	1	4	4	9	2	5	9	9	1	1	1	3
Randolph	IIIA	4	4	1	1	4	7	6	3	7	9	9	1	1	1	6
Sumter	IIIA	6	4	5	4	6	5	7	3	3	7	6	5	3	5	6
Talbot	IIIA	3	3	1	1	3	5	8	3	4	7	6	7	2	4	4
Tattnall	IIIA	4	4	3	2	4	5	3	6	3	9	9	2	1	2	3
Taylor	IIIA	3	3	2	1	4	3	8	3	4	9	8	2	2	4	9
Telfair	IIIA	4	4	2	1	4	7	6	4	6	9	9	3	2	2	3
Terrell	IIIA	4	3	3	2	6	8	9	1	4	9	8	1	2	5	5
Thomas	IIIB	7	4	4	5	5	5	8	3	3	7	5	6	4	3	8
Treutlen	IIIA	3	3	1	1	3	6	9	2	4	9	8	3	1	3	7
Turner	IIIA	4	3	4	3	7	9	9	1	3	9	8	4	2	3	7
Ware	IIIB	6	5	3	4	5	6	7	3	3	7	6	3	4	4	7
Warren	IIIA	3	3	2	1	3	5	8	2	5	9	8	7	1	3	2
Washington	IIIA	5	4	2	1	4	6	8	2	3	8	7	3	3	4	5
Webster	IIIA	3	3	3	1	3	6	9	2	3	9	9	1	1	3	7
Wilcox	IIIA	3	3	1	2	7	5	6	4	6	9	8	2	3	3	2
Wilkes	IIIA	4	4	3	2	3	4	5	6	5	7	7	3	4	2	5

SOCIO-ECONOMIC STATUS					MINORITIES				RURAL-URBAN				ECONOMIC BASE					COUNTY CONDITIONS					
% Completed HS	% College or More	Families/Pop	% Married Couples	% W/O Husband	% Black	% Spanish	% Amer Indian	% Asian	% Urban	% Rural	% Farmers	% Out of County	Jobs/Pop	% Manufacturing	% Wholesale	% Retail	% Services	Physicians/Cap	Crimes/Cap	$ Police/Crimes	$ Educ/Enrollment	Carpool or Transit	Pop Density
1	3	1	1	9	9	5	4	7	6	3	2	4	2	7	5	6	3	5	9	5	3	9	4
1	5	2	1	9	9	4	4	6	2	3	3	5	*	*	*	*	*	7	3	5	5	9	4
1	2	2	1	8	9	4	4	4	8	2	2	2	1	9	4	8	2	3	3	5	4	7	4
2	4	4	2	8	8	4	4	7	8	4	3	3	6	5	4	3	7	7	7	5	3	5	6
1	2	4	2	8	9	4	4	6	7	4	3	5	6	6	8	1	9	3	7	5	5	4	6
2	4	3	1	9	9	4	4	3	9	3	2	3	9	4	6	4	6	5	9	5	3	6	6
2	2	4	2	9	8	4	4	3	6	4	3	6	7	4	2	9	2	4	1	5	3	6	5
1	3	1	1	9	9	5	4	6	5	4	4	5	4	4	7	1	8	3	1	7	4	7	4
1	3	2	1	9	9	5	4	7	8	5	4	3	*	*	*	*	*	2	3	5	3	7	4
2	3	6	2	8	9	4	4	4	6	2	3	3	6	7	8	2	4	5	4	5	3	6	5
3	2	9	6	5	3	4	4	5	2	2	2	8	2	6	1	9	3	3	4	5	4	8	5
1	1	5	4	7	6	5	4	2	2	5	4	9	*	*	*	*	*	1	*	*	7	8	4
1	2	4	1	9	9	4	4	4	8	5	4	5	4	6	6	5	4	4	3	5	2	7	5
1	2	2	1	9	9	4	4	5	5	2	2	3	3	8	9	1	4	4	2	5	3	9	4
1	2	1	1	9	9	4	4	2	2	2	2	9	*	*	*	*	*	3	1	9	3	9	4
2	2	4	2	8	9	4	4	3	7	7	6	8	3	4	9	2	2	2	3	5	3	6	4
1	2	1	1	9	9	4	4	3	3	3	2	4	2	7	7	5	2	4	2	5	2	9	5
1	2	2	1	9	9	4	4	2	8	5	4	4	*	*	*	*	*	5	5	5	3	7	4
1	2	2	1	9	9	4	4	7	2	2	1	8	4	4	1	5	9	1	8	5	2	9	4
1	3	1	1	9	9	5	4	6	6	3	2	4	2	7	8	3	3	2	2	6	3	8	5
1	2	2	1	9	9	4	4	3	2	4	4	8	*	*	*	*	*	7	1	8	6	9	4
1	2	2	1	9	9	4	4	3	4	2	2	6	2	9	1	9	2	4	1	9	2	8	5
2	3	5	2	9	8	4	4	2	2	8	6	7	*	*	*	*	*	5	3	5	3	7	4
2	4	4	1	9	9	4	4	7	8	4	3	5	*	*	*	*	*	7	5	5	2	9	5
1	2	2	1	9	9	4	4	3	2	3	2	9	*	*	*	*	*	1	1	8	2	9	4
1	2	1	1	9	9	4	4	6	8	4	2	3	5	5	9	1	4	3	2	5	2	8	4
1	8	1	1	9	9	4	4	6	9	3	2	2	8	4	8	3	4	7	9	5	2	7	6
1	3	1	1	9	9	4	4	3	2	3	3	9	1	5	9	1	1	2	1	6	3	9	4
3	2	1	2	8	9	4	4	7	5	5	4	6	3	4	8	4	3	4	2	5	2	6	5
1	3	2	1	9	9	4	4	3	2	3	3	6	2	6	8	2	3	4	3	5	4	9	4
1	3	4	1	9	9	4	4	2	6	5	5	6	7	4	9	1	3	4	4	5	5	7	4
1	4	1	1	9	9	5	4	2	8	4	2	4	*	*	*	*	*	3	5	5	2	9	5
2	6	3	1	9	9	4	4	4	8	3	2	2	8	5	9	1	5	9	8	5	5	6	6
1	2	3	1	9	9	4	4	6	8	3	4	8	1	6	1	9	2	4	1	9	3	8	4
1	3	2	1	9	9	4	4	5	8	5	4	3	8	4	9	1	3	5	4	5	4	5	5
2	5	4	1	9	8	4	4	5	9	2	2	2	9	4	4	5	6	9	8	5	3	6	5
1	3	1	1	9	9	4	4	2	2	3	3	7	1	9	2	7	4	1	*	*	3	9	4
1	4	2	1	9	9	4	4	3	6	2	3	2	4	6	6	3	7	5	6	5	2	8	4
1	2	3	1	9	9	4	4	4	2	8	5	9	*	*	*	*	*	1	1	5	2	9	4
1	2	3	2	8	9	4	4	4	2	5	4	7	*	*	*	*	*	1	2	5	4	9	4
1	6	5	1	9	9	4	4	4	8	3	3	2	4	8	5	7	2	6	5	5	3	6	4

Economic Indicators For Class IIIA And IIIB Counties

		Size of County		Real-Estate Values			Ages of Population				Incomes					
		Population	Land Area	Med House Val	Med Gross Rent	Av Farm Val./Acre	% Under 5	% 5–17	% 18 and Over	% 65 and Over	% Poverty	% Under $10,000	% $10–19,999	% $20–29,999	% $30–49,999	% Over $50,000
Wilkinson	IIIA	4	4	2	1	3	7	9	2	2	5	4	7	7	4	4
IDAHO																
Clark	IIIA	3	8	4	8	2	9	8	1	1	5	6	9	1	5	1
Lewis	IIIA	3	4	6	2	5	9	4	4	4	2	3	8	8	3	2
Shoshone	IIIB	5	9	5	5	6	8	8	2	2	2	1	5	9	8	4
ILLINOIS																
Alexander	IIIA	4	3	1	1	6	6	4	5	8	7	9	1	4	2	3
Brown	IIIA	3	3	3	3	8	3	3	7	9	5	6	8	2	3	6
Bureau	IIIA	7	5	8	9	9	3	5	6	6	1	1	4	9	9	8
Calhoun	IIIA	3	3	3	3	6	2	4	7	8	3	5	5	6	5	5
Cass	IIIA	4	3	5	7	9	4	4	6	6	2	2	2	9	8	6
Christian	IIIB	6	5	5	9	9	3	4	6	6	2	2	5	8	9	7
Clark	IIIA	4	4	4	5	9	3	2	8	8	3	4	6	6	5	8
Clay	IIIA	4	4	3	4	8	3	2	7	8	4	6	8	3	4	3
Coles	IIIB	8	4	7	9	9	2	1	9	3	2	2	4	7	8	8
Crawford	IIIA	5	4	5	7	9	3	1	8	7	1	2	5	8	8	8
De Witt	IIIA	4	3	8	9	9	5	3	6	5	2	1	3	9	9	8
Edgar	IIIA	5	4	4	6	9	4	2	7	7	3	4	4	6	7	6
Fayette	IIIA	5	5	5	6	8	4	2	7	7	3	4	7	5	5	6
Fulton	IIIA	7	5	7	9	9	5	3	6	6	2	2	4	9	9	5
Gallatin	IIIA	3	3	3	4	8	2	4	7	7	5	6	2	5	5	5
Hamilton	IIIA	4	4	3	5	7	2	1	9	9	4	7	6	3	3	5
Hancock	IIIA	5	5	5	7	9	4	3	7	7	2	2	7	8	7	5
Hardin	IIIA	3	3	2	1	4	2	3	8	7	7	8	5	2	2	2
Henderson	IIIA	4	3	5	8	9	5	5	5	4	2	2	5	9	7	6
Henry	IIIA	8	5	9	9	9	6	6	4	4	1	1	2	9	9	9
Jasper	IIIA	4	4	5	6	9	5	5	5	7	2	3	4	7	8	8
Jo Daviess	IIIA	5	4	8	7	8	4	7	4	4	1	1	6	9	9	6
Lawrence	IIIA	4	3	3	5	8	3	2	8	8	3	4	3	8	5	5
MaCoupin	IIIA	8	5	6	8	9	4	3	7	7	2	3	3	8	8	5
Marshall	IIIA	4	3	9	9	9	4	5	5	5	1	1	2	9	9	9
Massac	IIIB	4	3	3	6	5	3	2	8	7	4	5	3	6	7	4
Montgomery	IIIA	6	5	5	7	9	3	3	7	7	2	3	3	7	8	8
Morgan	IIIB	7	4	8	7	9	3	2	8	5	2	1	6	8	9	9
Moultrie	IIIA	4	3	7	8	9	5	2	7	7	1	1	4	9	9	9
Perry	IIIA	5	4	6	7	8	4	4	6	6	2	2	1	8	9	7
Piatt	IIIA	4	4	9	9	9	4	5	5	3	1	1	3	9	9	9
Pike	IIIA	5	5	3	4	8	3	2	8	8	4	5	7	4	4	5
Pulaski	IIIA	4	3	1	2	6	7	4	5	8	9	9	2	1	2	1

SOCIO-ECONOMIC STATUS					MINORITIES				RURAL-URBAN				ECONOMIC BASE					COUNTY CONDITIONS					
% Completed HS	% College or More	Families/Pop	% Married Couples	% W/O Husband	% Black	% Spanish	% Amer Indian	% Asian	% Urban	% Rural	% Farmers	% Out of County	Jobs/Pop	% Manufacturing	% Wholesale	% Retail	% Services	Physicians/Cap	Crimes/Cap	$ Police/Crimes	$ Educ/Enrollment	Carpool or Transit	Pop Density
1	2	2	1	9	9	4	4	2	5	2	2	8	1	4	3	7	5	4	*	*	3	9	4
8	9	4	6	4	3	5	5	2	2	5	8	1	*	*	*	*	*	1	7	5	8	3	3
8	7	6	7	3	3	4	4	9	2	5	6	3	8	5	9	1	3	4	7	5	9	3	4
7	5	5	6	4	3	5	5	3	4	1	1	1	*	*	*	*	*	6	8	5	5	4	4
3	3	3	1	9	9	4	4	3	8	2	2	7	9	4	6	5	5	6	9	5	7	7	5
7	4	7	6	4	3	4	4	3	2	9	9	5	7	2	9	2	3	1	2	5	6	3	4
8	6	6	7	3	3	5	4	7	6	7	5	6	7	4	6	5	5	8	3	5	5	4	5
4	2	5	8	2	3	4	4	5	2	9	9	8	*	*	*	*	*	3	2	5	4	8	4
8	4	5	6	4	3	4	4	2	8	5	4	4	6	5	7	4	4	6	5	5	4	4	5
8	4	6	6	4	3	4	4	4	8	5	4	6	7	4	8	2	5	6	3	5	4	8	5
8	4	8	7	3	3	4	4	3	7	7	7	5	6	4	6	6	3	4	3	5	5	4	5
6	2	8	8	2	3	4	4	3	7	7	7	4	6	4	8	4	2	4	4	5	8	3	5
5	9	1	4	6	3	4	4	8	9	3	2	2	9	5	3	7	5	8	5	5	3	4	7
9	5	8	8	3	3	4	4	4	7	5	4	2	*	*	*	*	*	5	4	5	4	3	5
8	5	7	7	3	3	4	4	4	8	5	4	6	9	4	7	4	3	4	8	5	3	5	5
8	6	8	6	4	3	4	4	3	8	6	5	3	6	5	6	6	3	6	9	5	5	5	5
6	3	5	7	3	3	4	4	4	5	7	7	3	*	*	*	*	*	4	3	5	5	4	5
8	4	7	7	4	3	4	4	6	8	4	4	7	5	4	3	6	6	7	6	5	9	5	5
4	1	6	6	4	3	4	4	3	2	6	5	4	4	3	9	2	2	5	4	5	5	3	4
5	3	9	7	3	3	4	4	6	6	9	8	6	2	3	6	8	2	4	1	6	6	4	4
8	7	7	7	3	3	4	4	5	5	8	7	7	4	3	9	1	7	5	5	5	6	3	4
3	2	8	5	5	3	4	4	2	2	3	4	3	*	*	*	*	*	5	6	5	6	3	4
8	3	7	8	2	3	4	4	3	2	8	8	9	2	2	9	1	3	2	2	5	4	5	4
8	6	6	7	3	3	4	4	5	8	5	4	7	7	4	5	6	3	5	4	5	4	4	6
5	3	7	8	2	3	4	4	2	6	9	9	4	5	4	9	1	2	2	4	5	4	3	4
8	5	4	7	3	3	4	4	3	5	7	6	7	5	4	3	3	9	4	4	5	5	4	5
8	4	7	6	5	3	4	4	3	6	5	4	4	*	*	*	*	*	5	9	5	6	4	5
8	4	7	7	4	3	4	4	5	7	5	4	8	5	3	7	5	3	4	3	5	5	6	6
9	5	6	8	2	3	4	4	5	4	7	5	9	5	4	9	4	2	4	4	5	7	7	5
6	4	9	4	6	4	4	4	5	8	3	4	5	4	5	2	8	4	3	6	5	7	6	6
7	4	7	7	3	3	4	4	3	8	6	5	4	7	4	4	7	3	5	3	5	5	7	5
7	9	3	5	6	4	4	4	6	9	4	3	3	9	4	3	6	6	9	9	5	3	6	6
7	5	7	8	2	3	4	4	3	6	6	5	8	4	5	9	3	2	4	3	5	3	6	5
6	4	7	5	4	3	4	4	5	8	4	4	5	5	6	5	6	4	4	5	5	3	5	5
8	9	8	8	2	3	4	4	8	6	5	4	9	*	*	*	*	*	5	3	5	9	4	5
8	4	8	7	3	3	4	4	5	5	8	8	4	*	*	*	*	*	5	4	5	6	3	4
3	3	4	1	9	9	4	4	3	2	5	4	8	1	3	4	8	3	2	3	5	9	6	5

Economic Indicators For Class IIIA And IIIB Counties

		SIZE OF COUNTY		REAL-ESTATE VALUES			AGES OF POPULATION				INCOMES					
		Population	Land Area	Med House Val	Med Gross Rent	Av Farm Val./Acre	% Under 5	% 5–17	% 18 and Over	% 65 and Over	% Poverty	% Under $10,000	% $10–19,999	% $20–29,999	% $30–49,999	% Over $50,000
Richland	IIIB	4	3	5	6	8	3	2	8	6	2	3	8	6	6	7
Saline	IIIA	6	3	4	4	7	2	1	9	9	4	6	1	5	7	6
Sangamon	IIIB	9	5	9	9	9	4	3	7	3	1	1	3	9	9	9
Schuyler	IIIA	3	4	6	7	8	3	3	8	8	3	4	5	7	6	6
Scott	IIIA	3	3	4	3	9	3	2	8	8	3	3	7	5	7	5
Shelby	IIIA	5	5	5	7	9	4	4	6	6	2	2	5	8	8	7
Stark	IIIA	3	3	7	9	9	4	5	6	6	2	1	5	9	8	9
Wabash	IIIA	4	3	6	7	9	6	2	7	5	2	2	2	9	8	8
Warren	IIIB	5	4	7	8	9	5	3	6	5	3	2	5	8	8	8
Wayne	IIIA	4	5	4	4	8	2	2	8	8	3	5	6	5	5	5
White	IIIA	4	4	4	6	8	2	1	9	9	2	4	5	5	7	8
INDIANA																
Adams	IIIB	6	3	8	7	9	9	8	1	2	2	1	4	9	9	7
Carroll	IIIA	5	3	7	8	9	4	5	5	3	1	1	8	9	9	7
Clay	IIIA	5	3	4	7	8	4	3	7	6	2	3	6	8	7	2
Clinton	IIIB	6	3	5	7	9	6	4	5	5	2	2	6	8	8	7
Daviess	IIIA	6	4	4	3	9	7	5	4	5	4	5	7	4	5	4
De Kalb	IIIB	6	3	7	8	8	7	7	2	2	1	1	5	9	9	6
Dubois	IIIB	6	4	9	8	7	6	7	3	2	1	1	5	9	9	9
Fayette	IIIB	6	3	6	8	9	7	7	3	2	2	1	9	8	6	4
Fountain	IIIA	5	3	4	6	9	4	5	5	4	1	2	6	8	8	4
Gibson	IIIB	6	4	6	8	9	4	3	7	5	2	2	2	9	9	8
Jackson	IIIB	6	4	6	8	7	6	5	4	3	2	2	5	9	7	4
Knox	IIIA	7	4	5	7	9	2	1	9	6	3	4	5	6	5	6
Orange	IIIB	5	3	4	4	7	6	4	6	5	4	5	9	3	3	3
Pike	IIIA	4	3	4	6	8	3	3	7	6	2	3	4	8	8	4
Pulaski	IIIA	4	4	6	9	9	7	6	3	5	2	2	7	7	8	8
Putnam	IIIB	6	4	8	7	9	1	3	8	3	2	1	3	9	9	5
Randolph	IIIB	6	4	5	6	9	5	6	4	3	2	1	8	9	6	3
Sullivan	IIIA	5	4	3	8	9	4	3	7	7	2	3	5	8	7	4
Union	IIIA	3	3	6	7	9	7	7	3	3	2	2	8	7	7	4
Vermillion	IIIA	4	3	3	7	9	3	4	7	6	2	4	5	7	6	3
Warren	IIIA	4	3	5	8	9	4	7	4	3	2	1	6	9	9	8
IOWA																
Adair	IIIA	4	4	4	4	7	5	1	8	9	5	5	7	3	5	5
Allamakee	IIIA	4	4	6	5	6	6	6	4	7	4	5	7	4	5	3
Appanoose	IIIA	4	4	2	5	5	5	2	7	8	5	7	4	5	2	2
Benton	IIIA	5	5	7	7	9	6	5	4	5	2	2	3	9	9	7
Bremer	IIIB	5	4	9	9	9	5	5	5	4	2	1	2	9	9	9

SOCIO-ECONOMIC STATUS					MINORITIES				RURAL-URBAN				ECONOMIC BASE					COUNTY CONDITIONS					
% Completed HS	% College or More	Families/Pop	% Married Couples	% W/O Husband	% Black	% Spanish	% Amer Indian	% Asian	% Urban	% Rural	% Farmers	% Out of County	Jobs/Pop	% Manufacturing	% Wholesale	% Retail	% Services	Physicians/Cap	Crunes/Cap	$ Police/Crimes	$ Educ/Enrollment	Carpool or Transit	Pop Density
7	6	7	7	4	3	4	4	6	8	6	5	2	8	5	3	7	4	9	6	5	9	6	5
6	3	7	5	6	4	4	4	3	9	3	3	3	6	3	5	7	3	8	5	5	7	4	6
8	9	4	2	8	4	4	4	9	9	2	2	1	9	3	4	2	9	9	9	5	4	9	9
8	4	8	8	2	3	4	4	3	7	9	8	6	*	*	*	*	*	4	2	5	4	3	4
8	3	7	8	2	3	4	4	4	2	9	7	8	*	*	*	*	*	3	3	5	8	4	4
8	3	7	8	2	3	4	4	6	5	8	7	9	3	3	7	6	2	4	3	5	4	9	5
9	5	5	8	2	3	4	4	4	2	8	7	8	4	3	9	1	2	3	3	5	8	5	4
8	4	6	5	5	3	4	5	4	9	3	3	2	7	5	5	6	3	5	8	5	3	4	6
7	8	4	6	5	3	4	4	9	8	7	6	4	8	4	6	6	3	6	9	5	4	5	5
5	2	9	8	3	3	4	4	5	6	8	8	4	*	*	*	*	*	3	2	5	5	3	4
7	4	8	6	4	3	4	4	5	7	5	4	5	8	3	9	1	1	9	4	5	7	3	5
7	3	3	7	3	3	5	4	5	7	8	5	3	7	8	5	7	2	5	4	5	3	4	7
9	4	7	8	2	3	4	4	2	3	8	6	8	5	5	9	1	4	5	2	5	3	4	5
8	4	7	7	4	3	4	4	3	6	4	3	9	4	4	4	7	4	4	9	5	4	7	6
8	5	6	7	4	3	5	4	5	8	5	3	5	6	6	5	7	3	4	2	5	5	4	6
7	3	5	6	5	3	4	4	4	7	8	5	4	6	4	6	6	3	5	3	5	3	4	6
8	4	5	7	3	3	4	4	6	8	6	4	5	6	7	7	4	4	5	2	5	3	4	7
5	5	2	7	3	3	4	4	3	8	4	4	2	9	7	7	3	5	8	3	5	5	4	7
6	3	6	4	6	3	4	4	6	9	3	2	2	5	9	2	8	5	5	7	5	4	5	8
8	4	7	7	3	3	4	4	5	7	6	5	7	7	6	5	8	2	4	*	5	7	6	5
7	5	7	6	4	3	4	4	7	8	4	3	5	*	*	*	*	*	3	4	5	4	5	6
7	3	7	6	4	3	4	4	7	8	4	3	4	8	5	5	6	5	6	8	5	3	5	6
7	5	4	5	6	3	4	4	5	9	4	3	2	9	3	7	3	6	9	4	5	7	6	7
6	3	6	5	5	3	4	4	3	4	4	4	4	5	5	3	1	9	6	*	5	6	7	5
7	2	8	8	3	3	4	4	7	5	4	4	8	2	3	4	9	2	2	9	5	5	6	5
8	3	5	7	3	3	4	4	6	2	9	7	6	5	4	9	1	1	6	2	5	5	4	5
8	7	2	8	3	3	4	4	5	6	5	4	5	4	5	4	6	4	4	*	5	3	4	6
8	3	7	7	3	3	4	4	5	6	7	5	5	4	9	5	6	3	4	2	5	8	3	6
8	4	8	7	3	3	4	4	2	5	5	4	7	*	*	*	*	*	4	*	6	3	7	5
7	4	7	7	3	3	4	4	7	2	8	6	9	*	*	*	*	*	3	2	5	5	3	5
8	4	7	6	4	3	4	4	5	6	3	3	9	*	*	*	*	*	4	1	5	3	6	6
8	4	7	8	2	3	4	4	4	2	9	8	9	2	3	9	1	2	3	*	6	4	5	4
9	5	8	9	1	3	4	4	4	2	9	9	3	8	3	7	6	2	2	3	5	6	3	4
7	5	3	7	3	3	4	4	3	5	9	9	2	8	4	7	4	4	4	4	5	8	3	4
8	5	7	5	5	3	4	4	4	8	7	7	2	6	4	3	7	5	4	9	5	6	4	5
9	4	5	8	2	3	4	4	5	6	9	8	7	6	3	9	2	3	4	5	5	7	5	5
8	8	4	9	1	3	4	4	5	6	8	7	6	7	4	7	4	5	5	5	5	7	7	6

Economic Indicators For Class IIIA And IIIB Counties		SIZE OF COUNTY		REAL-ESTATE VALUES			AGES OF POPULATION				INCOMES					
		Population	Land Area	Med House Val	Med Gross Rent	Av Farm Val./Acre	% Under 5	% 5–17	% 18 and Over	% 65 and Over	% Poverty	% Under $10,000	% $10–19,999	% $20–29,999	% $30–49,999	% Over $50,000
Buchanan	IIIB	5	4	7	8	9	9	8	2	3	3	2	3	9	8	8
Buena Vista	IIIB	5	4	8	8	9	4	1	8	7	1	1	5	8	9	9
Butler	IIIB	4	4	7	7	9	6	4	5	7	2	2	6	8	6	8
Cass	IIIA	4	4	5	5	8	3	2	8	8	2	2	8	7	5	7
Cedar	IIIA	5	4	9	9	9	5	4	5	5	2	1	3	9	9	9
Chickasaw	IIIA	4	4	8	6	9	6	8	3	5	3	2	6	8	8	5
Clay	IIIB	5	4	9	9	9	7	2	6	4	2	1	7	7	9	9
Clayton	IIIA	5	5	6	4	8	6	5	5	7	3	4	7	5	5	7
Davis	IIIA	4	4	4	6	6	5	4	6	7	7	6	4	4	4	8
Decatur	IIIA	4	4	2	3	5	2	1	9	8	6	7	6	3	2	1
Floyd	IIIB	5	4	7	6	9	5	5	5	6	2	2	7	7	8	8
Franklin	IIIA	4	4	7	8	9	4	2	8	8	2	2	7	7	7	7
Fremont	IIIA	4	4	3	7	8	5	2	7	8	5	3	8	6	5	7
Greene	IIIA	4	4	5	5	9	4	2	7	9	3	3	6	7	5	9
Guthrie	IIIA	4	4	4	5	8	3	2	8	9	4	4	6	6	6	4
Hancock	IIIB	4	4	7	8	9	7	4	5	6	2	1	8	9	7	8
Harrison	IIIA	4	4	4	5	8	4	5	5	8	4	4	5	6	7	5
Henry	IIIA	5	4	8	8	9	4	2	7	6	1	1	9	8	8	6
Howard	IIIA	4	4	5	5	9	4	4	6	9	3	4	5	5	6	9
Ida	IIIA	4	4	5	4	9	4	2	7	8	4	3	7	7	5	8
Jackson	IIIA	5	4	8	8	8	6	8	2	4	3	2	3	9	6	9
Jefferson	IIIA	4	4	6	6	9	2	1	9	6	3	3	8	4	7	5
Jones	IIIA	5	4	7	7	9	5	5	5	4	2	2	4	9	8	5
Lucas	IIIA	4	4	4	2	5	3	2	8	8	4	6	5	6	2	5
Madison	IIIA	4	4	7	5	8	5	5	5	7	3	3	3	7	8	5
Mahaska	IIIA	5	4	6	7	9	4	1	8	7	3	3	8	6	5	6
Monona	IIIA	4	4	3	5	8	3	2	8	9	4	4	9	3	5	7
Monroe	IIIA	4	4	4	5	4	3	2	8	8	2	4	8	6	4	3
Montgomery	IIIA	4	4	5	5	8	4	1	8	9	2	2	7	8	8	2
Muscatine	IIIB	7	4	9	9	9	7	6	4	3	2	1	2	9	9	9
Osceola	IIIA	3	3	5	6	9	5	4	6	8	3	2	8	6	9	7
Page	IIIA	5	4	5	4	8	4	1	8	9	2	3	8	5	6	4
Palo Alto	IIIA	4	4	6	6	9	4	4	6	7	2	3	7	5	8	8
Poweshiek	IIIB	5	4	8	8	9	2	2	8	5	2	2	7	8	7	6
Ringgold	IIIA	3	4	2	5	6	2	1	9	9	8	9	2	2	3	5
Sioux	IIIB	6	5	8	6	9	9	5	4	3	2	1	9	8	7	8
Taylor	IIIA	3	4	2	3	6	3	1	8	9	5	7	5	3	3	4
Union	IIIA	4	4	4	4	6	4	3	7	8	3	4	6	6	6	3
Van Buren	IIIA	4	4	1	3	6	5	3	6	8	5	7	5	3	3	2
Washington	IIIB	5	4	7	8	9	5	4	6	7	3	2	6	8	7	9
Wayne	IIIA	3	4	2	3	6	3	1	9	9	6	8	7	1	3	3

% Completed HS	% College or More	Families/Pop	% Married Couples	% W/O Husband	% Black	% Spanish	% Amer Indian	% Asian	% Urban	% Rural	% Farmers	% Out of County	Jobs/Pop	% Manufacturing	% Wholesale	% Retail	% Services	Physicians/Cap	Crimes/Cap	$ Police/Crimes	$ Educ/Enrollment	Carpool or Transit	Pop Density
8	4	2	7	3	3	4	4	6	5	9	7	6	5	3	9	3	3	8	6	5	4	8	5
9	9	5	9	2	3	4	4	8	8	8	7	2	9	3	7	5	4	7	8	5	5	3	5
8	3	7	9	1	3	4	4	6	2	9	9	7	5	3	9	1	2	2	2	5	7	4	5
9	6	7	8	2	3	4	4	7	8	8	8	2	9	3	7	5	3	6	4	5	9	3	4
9	6	6	8	3	3	4	4	8	4	9	8	8	7	3	8	4	3	3	3	5	8	3	5
8	4	3	7	3	3	4	4	3	5	9	8	4	8	4	9	1	3	4	3	5	6	8	5
9	8	6	8	3	3	4	4	9	9	7	7	1	9	3	9	1	4	7	8	5	7	3	5
8	4	5	8	2	3	4	4	7	2	9	9	3	5	4	8	3	4	5	3	5	8	8	4
8	3	7	9	1	3	4	4	3	6	9	9	4	4	3	7	5	4	9	3	5	5	4	4
6	8	2	7	3	3	4	4	3	5	8	8	3	5	3	9	2	2	5	2	5	3	3	4
9	7	5	8	3	3	4	4	6	8	8	7	3	*	*	*	*	*	6	6	5	7	4	5
9	6	8	8	2	3	4	4	9	7	9	9	4	7	4	9	2	3	2	4	5	5	3	4
9	7	8	8	3	3	4	4	5	2	9	8	7	4	2	9	1	5	4	5	5	8	3	4
9	7	7	8	3	3	4	4	8	7	9	9	2	7	4	8	3	4	6	6	5	8	3	4
9	3	7	8	2	3	4	4	5	2	9	9	5	6	3	9	3	3	4	3	5	9	5	4
9	5	6	8	2	3	4	4	3	5	9	9	3	6	3	9	1	3	3	3	5	8	3	4
9	4	6	7	3	3	4	4	2	4	9	8	5	6	2	8	4	3	3	5	5	7	4	4
9	8	4	7	3	3	4	4	8	7	7	6	3	9	4	5	1	9	8	4	5	8	4	5
8	4	4	8	2	3	4	4	3	7	9	9	2	7	3	9	2	3	3	3	5	9	3	4
9	7	7	9	1	3	4	4	3	2	9	9	2	7	3	8	2	4	1	4	5	8	3	4
7	4	3	7	3	3	4	4	6	5	9	7	6	7	3	7	4	4	5	5	5	6	7	5
9	9	2	7	3	3	4	5	9	9	7	7	2	7	5	6	5	3	4	7	5	3	3	5
8	5	3	7	3	3	4	4	3	8	9	8	4	6	4	9	3	2	4	3	5	6	5	5
9	4	7	7	4	3	4	4	8	8	8	8	2	7	3	5	7	3	2	8	5	6	3	4
9	4	7	8	2	3	4	4	4	6	9	9	7	6	2	5	6	5	3	3	5	8	4	4
8	7	7	8	3	3	4	4	9	8	8	7	4	9	3	7	5	3	5	9	5	4	4	5
9	4	8	7	3	3	4	4	3	5	9	9	3	9	2	8	1	6	4	5	5	8	3	4
9	3	6	7	3	3	4	4	6	8	9	9	4	*	*	*	*	*	3	8	5	7	3	4
9	7	8	7	3	3	4	4	5	8	8	7	2	9	4	7	4	4	5	6	5	7	3	5
7	7	4	6	5	3	6	4	8	9	4	3	2	9	6	2	3	9	6	9	5	6	4	7
7	4	6	9	2	3	4	4	5	7	9	9	3	*	*	*	*	*	4	2	6	5	3	4
9	7	6	7	3	3	4	4	6	9	7	7	2	9	4	7	5	3	7	7	5	6	5	5
8	7	3	8	2	3	4	4	9	7	9	9	3	7	3	7	7	2	4	5	5	8	3	4
8	9	3	7	3	3	4	4	9	8	8	7	2	9	4	6	6	3	6	5	5	4	4	5
9	5	9	8	2	3	4	4	7	2	9	9	2	6	3	9	3	2	4	3	5	9	4	4
4	6	1	9	1	3	4	4	3	8	8	8	2	7	4	8	4	2	5	2	5	3	3	5
9	3	9	8	2	3	4	4	4	2	9	9	4	5	3	9	1	1	2	3	5	8	3	4
9	5	6	6	4	3	4	4	9	9	7	7	1	9	3	6	6	4	6	8	5	9	4	5
9	4	7	8	2	3	4	4	4	2	9	9	6	3	3	9	2	1	2	5	5	8	3	4
9	7	5	7	3	3	4	4	6	6	8	8	4	9	4	7	5	3	6	4	5	7	4	5
9	4	9	8	2	3	4	4	6	2	9	9	2	6	4	9	2	2	4	5	5	7	3	4

Economic Indicators For Class IIIA And IIIB Counties

		SIZE OF COUNTY		REAL-ESTATE VALUES			AGES OF POPULATION				INCOMES					
		Population	Land Area	Med House Val	Med Gross Rent	Av Farm Val./Acre	% Under 5	% 5–17	% 18 and Over	% 65 and Over	% Poverty	% Under $10,000	% $10–19,999	% $20–29,999	% $30–49,999	% Over $50,000
Winnebago	IIIB	4	3	7	7	9	3	2	8	8	1	2	9	7	5	7
Worth	IIIA	4	3	6	4	9	4	1	8	8	1	1	9	7	8	6
KANSAS																
Allen	IIIA	4	4	3	5	3	6	2	7	8	2	4	8	4	5	4
Anderson	IIIA	4	4	3	3	3	4	3	7	9	3	5	8	3	5	5
Bourbon	IIIA	4	4	3	3	3	3	1	9	9	2	6	5	4	4	6
Brown	IIIA	4	4	2	3	6	5	1	8	9	3	5	8	3	4	6
Chase	IIIA	3	5	2	4	2	2	1	9	9	4	5	4	6	6	3
Chautauqua	IIIA	3	4	1	2	2	1	1	9	9	4	7	5	2	2	7
Cherokee	IIIA	5	4	2	2	4	3	4	7	8	4	6	5	4	3	4
Clay	IIIA	4	4	4	3	4	5	1	8	9	3	5	7	4	4	4
Comanche	IIIA	3	5	2	3	2	2	1	9	9	2	2	9	4	5	8
Cowley	IIIA	6	6	5	6	3	4	2	8	7	2	2	5	8	8	7
Crawford	IIIA	7	4	3	4	4	2	1	9	9	3	7	3	4	3	5
Dickinson	IIIA	5	5	4	4	3	3	2	8	9	3	4	7	6	6	5
Doniphan	IIIA	4	3	2	4	6	4	4	6	7	4	5	7	6	4	3
Elk	IIIA	3	4	1	1	2	2	1	9	9	4	8	2	3	2	3
Ellsworth	IIIA	3	5	2	3	2	3	1	9	9	3	5	8	5	3	3
Ford	IIIB	5	6	8	7	3	7	3	6	3	2	1	5	9	8	9
Franklin	IIIB	5	4	5	6	5	4	3	7	7	2	3	5	7	7	5
Greeley	IIIB	3	5	5	2	2	8	3	5	4	2	1	6	7	9	9
Greenwood	IIIA	4	6	1	4	2	2	1	9	9	3	6	5	4	4	6
Harper	IIIA	3	5	3	4	4	2	1	9	9	3	4	6	5	6	5
Kingman	IIIA	4	5	4	4	4	4	2	8	8	2	2	7	7	6	7
Kiowa	IIIA	3	5	3	3	3	6	1	9	8	2	4	6	6	6	6
Labette	IIIA	5	4	3	4	4	4	4	6	7	3	4	5	7	5	3
Lincoln	IIIA	3	5	1	1	3	2	1	9	9	2	6	9	3	2	2
Linn	IIIA	3	4	2	4	3	3	2	8	9	4	6	4	4	5	4
Lyon	IIIB	6	5	8	8	3	6	1	9	3	1	2	4	8	9	5
McPherson	IIIB	5	5	8	7	5	4	1	9	7	1	1	8	8	8	7
Marion	IIIA	4	5	3	3	4	1	1	9	9	2	4	8	5	5	4
Marshall	IIIA	4	5	2	2	4	2	1	9	9	4	5	6	4	5	7
Mitchell	IIIA	3	5	3	3	4	5	2	7	9	2	4	9	4	4	6
Montgomery	IIIA	7	4	3	5	4	5	2	7	8	2	4	6	7	5	6
Morris	IIIA	3	4	3	3	2	2	1	9	9	4	5	7	4	4	4
Neosho	IIIA	5	4	4	5	3	5	2	7	8	2	4	6	6	5	6
Ness	IIIA	3	6	3	2	2	4	1	9	9	2	4	6	6	6	8
Ottawa	IIIA	3	5	2	3	3	2	2	8	9	3	4	8	4	4	6
Pawnee	IIIA	3	5	5	4	4	2	1	9	7	2	2	9	7	8	4
Pratt	IIIA	4	5	5	7	4	4	1	9	8	2	2	6	8	7	7

SOCIO-ECONOMIC STATUS					MINORITIES				RURAL-URBAN				ECONOMIC BASE					COUNTY CONDITIONS					
% Completed HS	% College or More	Families/Pop	Married Couples	% W/O Husband	% Black	% Spanish	% Amer Indian	% Asian	% Urban	% Rural	% Farmers	% Out of County	Jobs/Pop	% Manufacturing	% Wholesale	% Retail	% Services	Physicians/Cap	Crimes/Cap	$ Police/Crimes	$ Educ/Enrollment	Carpool or Transit	Pop Density
9	6	5	8	2	3	4	4	5	6	8	8	2	*	*	*	*	*	2	3	5	9	5	5
9	4	7	7	3	3	4	4	7	2	9	9	8	5	3	9	3	2	2	6	5	6	5	4
8	8	6	6	4	3	4	5	3	8	5	6	3	9	4	8	3	3	6	6	5	8	3	5
8	5	7	8	2	3	4	5	3	7	9	9	5	5	3	7	4	3	5	2	5	7	4	4
8	7	7	7	4	3	4	4	7	9	6	6	2	8	3	7	3	4	9	9	4	6	5	4
9	6	6	7	3	3	5	8	4	6	8	8	2	6	4	9	1	3	4	3	5	7	3	4
9	8	8	8	2	3	4	4	4	2	9	9	7	*	*	*	*	*	3	4	5	8	4	3
9	4	9	7	3	3	4	6	7	2	8	8	3	3	2	9	4	2	7	3	5	5	4	4
7	4	8	6	5	3	4	6	6	9	4	5	8	3	4	4	8	3	3	7	5	3	4	5
9	7	8	8	2	3	4	4	3	8	8	8	2	8	5	7	5	3	8	4	5	6	3	4
9	9	9	9	1	3	4	4	2	2	8	9	1	6	2	7	2	8	7	2	5	9	4	3
9	7	6	6	4	4	5	5	4	9	4	3	2	7	4	2	8	5	7	8	5	5	4	5
7	9	4	5	5	3	4	5	8	9	3	3	2	8	4	5	4	6	7	9	4	3	3	6
9	7	7	8	3	3	5	4	7	8	7	6	3	8	3	9	2	3	4	3	5	8	3	4
7	4	5	6	3	3	4	5	3	3	8	7	8	*	*	*	*	*	4	3	5	9	4	4
9	4	9	8	2	3	4	5	8	2	8	9	4	2	2	4	5	7	3	2	5	8	3	4
9	8	8	8	2	3	5	4	5	2	7	8	2	*	*	*	*	*	5	4	5	9	3	4
8	9	3	7	4	3	6	5	4	9	3	3	1	9	3	6	4	5	9	9	4	8	4	4
8	7	6	7	3	3	5	5	5	8	5	5	4	7	4	3	8	4	6	7	5	5	6	5
9	6	8	9	1	3	7	4	2	2	8	9	1	*	*	*	*	*	5	5	5	9	3	3
9	6	9	7	3	3	4	5	3	7	7	8	3	5	2	3	4	8	3	4	5	7	4	4
9	8	9	8	2	3	4	4	3	6	7	8	2	8	3	7	3	4	7	3	5	8	3	4
9	6	7	8	2	3	4	4	3	7	9	9	5	5	3	8	6	2	5	3	5	7	3	4
9	9	8	8	2	3	4	4	3	2	7	8	2	*	*	*	*	*	4	6	5	9	3	3
8	6	5	5	5	4	5	5	5	8	5	5	2	6	6	5	4	6	9	8	5	6	5	5
9	7	9	7	2	3	4	4	7	2	9	9	3	6	2	9	5	1	3	2	5	9	4	4
9	4	8	8	2	3	4	5	4	2	9	9	5	2	3	7	7	1	2	4	5	8	4	4
7	9	1	6	4	3	6	5	9	9	3	3	2	9	5	2	6	8	9	9	4	2	4	5
8	9	5	8	2	3	4	4	6	9	6	6	2	8	4	6	4	4	5	4	5	6	3	4
8	8	7	9	2	3	4	4	4	4	9	9	4	5	3	7	5	3	4	2	5	7	3	4
9	6	9	7	2	3	4	4	3	6	9	9	2	8	3	8	3	4	4	2	5	9	3	4
9	9	4	8	2	3	4	4	8	9	7	7	1	9	3	7	3	6	5	5	5	8	3	4
8	6	7	5	5	4	4	5	7	9	3	3	2	8	6	3	8	4	7	9	5	6	4	6
9	7	9	8	2	3	4	5	3	2	9	9	4	*	*	*	*	*	4	3	5	5	4	4
9	6	6	7	3	3	5	4	8	9	5	5	3	9	5	4	8	3	6	6	5	6	3	5
9	8	8	9	1	3	4	4	4	2	9	9	1	*	*	*	*	*	7	2	5	9	4	3
9	6	8	8	2	3	4	4	4	2	8	9	5	4	2	9	3	2	6	2	5	8	5	4
9	9	6	7	4	3	5	5	9	9	6	7	2	8	3	5	7	3	9	5	5	9	5	4
9	9	8	8	2	3	4	5	9	9	5	5	2	9	3	4	7	4	9	9	5	9	3	4

Economic Indicators For Class IIIA And IIIB Counties

		SIZE OF COUNTY		REAL-ESTATE VALUES			AGES OF POPULATION				INCOMES					
		Population	Land Area	Med House Val	Med Gross Rent	Av Farm Val./Acre	% Under 5	% 5–17	% 18 and Over	% 65 and Over	% Poverty	% Under $10,000	% $10–19,999	% $20–29,999	% $30–49,999	% Over $50,000
Rawlins	IIIA	3	6	3	2	2	4	3	7	9	3	5	8	2	7	6
Reno	IIIB	9	6	7	8	5	5	2	7	4	2	1	8	8	8	7
Rice	IIIA	4	5	3	4	4	3	1	9	9	2	2	7	7	7	8
Russell	IIIA	4	5	4	4	2	2	1	9	9	2	3	5	6	5	9
Stafford	IIIA	3	5	3	4	4	2	1	9	9	3	4	8	6	2	6
Sumner	IIIA	5	6	5	6	5	6	2	7	7	1	1	4	9	9	5
Wabaunsee	IIIA	3	5	3	4	3	3	4	7	8	2	2	8	9	4	4
Washington	IIIA	4	5	1	1	4	3	2	8	9	5	7	8	2	3	5
Wilson	IIIA	4	4	2	2	3	5	2	7	9	4	6	7	5	2	2
Woodson	IIIA	3	4	2	5	2	2	1	9	9	2	7	4	3	2	3
KENTUCKY																
Ballard	IIIA	4	3	3	6	7	3	3	7	8	4	6	2	5	7	2
Bath	IIIA	4	3	2	1	4	5	6	5	4	9	9	2	2	3	1
Bourbon	IIIB	5	3	7	5	9	4	5	5	3	6	5	3	5	6	5
Boyd	IIIB	8	3	6	8	3	3	3	7	3	3	3	1	8	9	7
Bracken	IIIA	3	3	3	4	4	3	6	5	6	5	6	8	3	4	1
Caldwell	IIIA	4	3	3	3	5	1	2	8	8	2	6	2	5	7	3
Carlisle	IIIA	3	3	2	3	5	2	3	8	8	5	6	2	4	6	5
Carroll	IIIA	4	3	5	5	5	4	5	5	4	5	5	4	4	7	4
Crittenden	IIIA	4	3	2	2	4	2	3	8	7	4	6	2	7	4	2
Cumberland	IIIA	3	3	2	1	3	2	3	8	6	9	9	1	1	1	4
Fleming	IIIA	4	3	3	2	5	4	6	5	5	8	7	6	2	2	3
Graves	IIIB	6	4	4	4	7	2	2	8	8	4	4	5	6	6	3
Green	IIIA	4	3	3	1	5	2	3	7	6	8	8	6	1	1	3
Hancock	IIIA	3	3	6	8	5	8	9	1	2	4	2	1	9	7	2
Harrison	IIIA	4	3	8	4	6	4	4	6	6	6	6	3	5	5	3
Hart	IIIA	4	3	2	1	5	3	6	5	4	9	9	3	1	2	2
Hickman	IIIA	3	3	3	3	6	2	2	8	8	6	6	2	6	5	7
Logan	IIIA	5	4	4	4	7	4	4	6	5	5	6	6	4	4	3
McLean	IIIA	4	3	3	1	8	3	5	6	5	5	6	1	7	6	3
Marion	IIIB	4	3	5	2	4	8	9	1	2	8	7	7	3	2	4
Mason	IIIA	4	3	6	4	6	4	4	6	4	6	5	5	5	5	3
Monroe	IIIA	4	3	2	1	4	3	5	6	5	9	9	2	1	1	2
Nicholas	IIIA	3	3	4	2	4	4	4	6	5	7	7	6	2	4	3
Pendleton	IIIA	4	3	4	6	4	5	8	3	3	6	4	8	6	4	2
Robertson	IIIA	3	3	3	3	3	3	3	7	7	7	7	9	2	1	1
Spencer	IIIA	3	3	7	4	6	4	7	4	2	6	3	6	6	7	2
Todd	IIIA	4	3	3	2	8	4	5	5	6	6	8	3	3	3	6
Trigg	IIIA	4	4	6	6	6	2	4	7	6	6	5	7	4	3	7
Washington	IIIA	4	3	5	2	4	5	7	3	4	8	6	5	4	4	6

SOCIO-ECONOMIC STATUS					MINORITIES				RURAL-URBAN				ECONOMIC BASE					COUNTY CONDITIONS					
% Completed HS	% College or More	Families/Pop	% Married Couples	% W/O Husband	% Black	% Spanish	% Amer Indian	% Asian	% Urban	% Rural	% Farmers	% Out of County	Jobs/Pop	% Manufacturing	% Wholesale	% Retail	% Services	Physicians/Cap	Crunes/Cap	$ Police/Crimes	$ Educ/Enrollment	Carpool or Transit	Pop Density
9	8	7	8	2	3	4	4	2	2	9	9	1	5	2	9	1	4	4	1	5	9	3	3
9	8	6	7	4	3	5	5	5	9	3	3	1	9	4	6	4	5	8	9	5	7	3	5
9	9	7	8	2	3	5	5	5	7	6	6	3	7	3	8	2	6	4	4	5	7	3	4
9	7	9	7	3	3	4	4	6	9	4	6	2	9	3	6	4	6	5	8	5	9	3	4
9	9	9	8	2	3	4	4	7	2	8	8	3	4	2	8	5	2	7	5	5	9	3	4
9	5	8	8	3	3	5	5	7	7	6	6	7	4	4	3	9	2	5	5	5	6	5	4
9	6	8	9	1	3	4	4	7	2	9	9	9	*	*	*	*	*	4	4	5	6	7	4
8	4	7	8	1	3	4	4	3	2	9	9	3	7	2	9	3	1	4	2	5	9	5	4
8	6	8	8	3	3	4	4	4	9	6	6	3	3	7	6	4	4	6	3	5	6	3	4
9	5	8	7	2	3	4	5	7	2	9	9	4	3	3	7	5	3	2	6	5	5	4	4
6	4	8	7	4	4	4	4	6	2	7	7	8	*	*	*	*	*	3	2	5	7	5	5
1	2	6	6	4	4	4	4	3	2	9	8	9	*	*	*	*	*	4	2	5	3	8	5
5	5	7	3	7	5	4	4	4	7	7	5	7	4	5	6	4	5	5	4	5	3	6	6
7	6	7	5	6	3	4	4	5	9	2	1	4	9	6	6	3	6	9	9	5	2	8	9
3	2	6	6	5	3	4	4	4	2	9	9	7	*	*	*	*	*	3	2	5	7	6	5
5	4	8	4	6	4	4	4	2	9	5	6	5	7	4	2	7	6	5	6	5	3	4	5
7	1	9	7	4	3	4	4	2	2	9	8	8	*	*	*	*	*	1	2	5	4	7	4
3	3	5	2	8	4	4	4	2	8	6	5	2	7	7	9	1	3	5	7	5	3	8	6
4	2	8	7	3	3	5	4	3	7	5	6	6	3	6	4	7	3	3	2	5	4	8	4
1	3	8	2	8	4	4	4	2	2	9	9	2	*	*	*	*	*	2	2	5	5	9	4
2	2	6	6	4	3	5	4	2	5	9	9	4	3	5	7	6	2	4	2	5	4	5	5
5	4	9	7	4	4	4	4	3	6	6	5	5	6	6	9	1	4	6	4	5	2	5	6
2	1	9	8	3	4	4	4	2	2	9	9	6	2	5	8	5	2	6	2	5	3	9	5
5	2	5	8	2	3	4	4	2	2	6	7	5	1	9	2	6	2	2	2	5	3	7	5
3	3	7	5	6	3	4	4	8	7	8	8	4	6	6	6	4	5	6	2	5	3	6	5
1	2	7	5	5	5	4	4	3	2	9	9	7	4	4	9	1	4	5	4	4	2	5	5
6	4	8	5	6	5	4	4	2	2	8	8	8	2	7	9	1	2	4	3	5	9	7	4
3	2	7	4	6	5	4	4	5	6	7	7	3	4	8	8	4	2	4	3	5	4	5	5
4	2	8	7	4	3	4	4	4	2	7	7	9	2	4	8	4	3	4	4	5	7	9	5
2	2	2	2	8	5	4	4	4	7	8	7	6	2	4	4	8	3	4	7	5	2	9	5
3	5	6	3	7	5	4	4	5	8	6	5	2	8	6	8	4	3	9	3	5	3	8	6
1	2	8	5	5	4	4	4	3	7	7	9	3	2	8	7	4	3	3	2	5	3	8	5
2	2	7	5	4	3	4	4	4	2	8	8	6	*	*	*	*	*	4	2	5	3	8	5
3	2	5	6	5	3	4	4	2	2	7	9	9	2	6	8	2	5	3	2	5	2	9	5
2	3	8	5	4	3	4	4	7	2	9	9	9	*	*	*	*	*	1	2	5	4	9	4
2	2	7	6	4	3	4	4	2	2	9	9	9	*	*	*	*	*	3	3	5	3	9	5
2	2	7	5	5	6	4	4	4	2	9	7	6	2	6	8	4	2	4	3	5	2	6	5
4	5	8	6	4	6	4	4	5	2	7	6	5	3	6	3	8	4	3	3	5	6	7	4
2	4	4	6	4	5	4	4	3	6	9	9	7	2	5	8	3	2	3	6	5	2	8	5

Economic Indicators For Class IIIA And IIIB Counties

		SIZE OF COUNTY		REAL-ESTATE VALUES			AGES OF POPULATION				INCOMES					
		Population	Land Area	Med House Val	Med Gross Rent	Av Farm Val./Acre	% Under 5	% 5-17	% 18 and Over	% 65 and Over	% Poverty	% Under $10,000	% $10-19,999	% $20-29,999	% $30-49,999	% Over $50,000
LOUISIANA																
Acadia	IIIB	8	4	5	3	8	9	9	1	2	8	5	2	6	6	9
Avoyelles	IIIB	7	5	3	1	7	7	9	2	4	9	9	2	1	3	4
Bienville	IIIA	4	5	2	1	4	5	6	4	8	8	8	1	3	5	5
Catahoula	IIIA	4	5	2	2	6	9	7	2	3	9	9	1	1	4	8
Claiborne	IIIA	4	5	3	1	4	5	6	4	8	8	8	1	3	5	4
East Felicia	IIIA	5	4	5	2	6	7	7	3	3	7	4	3	7	7	6
Franklin	IIIA	5	4	3	1	6	8	8	2	6	9	9	1	2	3	5
Jackson	IIIB	4	4	3	1	6	6	6	4	7	8	7	1	6	2	4
Madison	IIIB	4	4	3	1	8	9	9	1	5	9	9	1	1	2	8
Pointe Coupe	IIIB	5	4	6	2	7	7	9	1	2	9	6	1	5	7	7
Richland	IIIA	5	4	3	1	7	8	8	2	6	9	9	1	2	4	7
Webster	IIIB	7	4	3	2	5	5	4	6	5	6	6	2	5	6	5
Winn	IIIA	4	5	2	2	5	8	6	3	5	9	9	1	3	4	2
MAINE																
Androscoggin	IIIB	9	4	8	7	6	4	5	5	3	3	3	9	6	4	3
Penobscot	IIIB	9	9	7	9	3	3	4	7	2	3	3	7	7	6	3
Piscataquis	IIIA	4	9	3	5	2	4	5	5	5	3	5	9	6	1	1
Somerset	IIIB	7	9	5	7	3	4	8	3	3	5	6	9	3	2	2
MARYLAND																
Dorchester	IIIB	6	4	6	7	9	1	2	8	6	3	4	6	6	6	6
Somerset	IIIA	5	3	4	4	9	2	2	8	6	3	5	7	3	5	3
Talbot	IIIB	5	3	9	9	9	1	1	9	8	2	1	6	7	9	9
MASSACHUSETTS																
Bristol	IIIB	9	4	8	7	9	2	4	7	4	2	2	4	8	8	5
Franklin	IIIB	9	4	7	9	6	2	2	8	4	2	2	6	8	7	5
MICHIGAN																
Alger	IIIA	4	5	4	6	3	4	6	4	4	3	4	7	7	4	2
Baraga	IIIA	4	5	4	4	2	5	7	3	6	4	6	2	6	4	1
Delta	IIIB	7	6	6	7	2	5	8	3	3	3	3	3	8	7	4
Dickinson	IIIA	5	5	6	9	3	3	2	8	7	1	4	4	7	6	3
Gogebic	IIIA	5	6	1	4	2	1	1	9	9	2	7	8	2	2	2
Houghton	IIIA	7	6	2	7	2	1	1	9	6	3	7	6	3	3	2
Huron	IIIB	6	5	5	8	8	5	6	4	6	3	3	7	7	5	4
Iron	IIIA	4	6	3	4	2	1	1	9	9	2	7	3	5	3	1
Mackinac	IIIB	4	6	4	7	2	4	6	5	6	3	5	8	6	2	1
Menominee	IIIA	5	6	5	7	2	6	6	4	5	2	3	8	6	5	2

SOCIO-ECONOMIC STATUS					MINORITIES				RURAL-URBAN				ECONOMIC BASE					COUNTY CONDITIONS					
% Completed HS	% College or More	Families/Pop	% Married Couples	% W/O Husband	% Black	% Spanish	% Amer Indian	% Asian	% Urban	% Rural	% Farmers	% Out of County	Jobs/Pop	% Manufacturing	% Wholesale	% Retail	% Services	Physicians/Cap	Crunes/Cap	$ Police/Crimes	$ Educ/Enrollment	Carpool or Transit	Pop Density
1	2	2	3	8	7	4	4	3	9	3	2	6	*	*	*	*	*	5	4	5	3	6	7
1	2	3	3	7	8	4	4	3	5	3	3	6	2	4	5	7	3	3	2	5	3	7	5
2	4	4	2	8	9	5	4	4	4	2	2	7	1	6	9	1	5	2	1	9	6	9	4
2	2	4	3	7	8	4	4	3	5	4	5	5	*	*	*	*	*	2	*	*	7	8	4
1	5	4	1	9	9	4	4	3	8	2	2	5	2	5	5	6	4	4	4	5	2	7	4
2	3	1	1	9	9	5	4	8	4	2	2	8	1	3	7	7	2	9	2	5	3	8	5
1	3	3	2	8	9	4	4	3	5	5	4	4	3	3	7	6	3	3	1	9	8	6	5
3	4	4	2	8	9	4	4	3	6	2	2	5	*	*	*	*	*	4	2	5	5	8	4
1	3	1	1	9	9	5	4	2	9	3	2	4	3	3	8	4	3	3	7	5	3	6	4
1	3	2	1	8	9	4	4	7	4	3	2	7	2	3	5	8	2	3	1	7	3	8	5
1	3	2	1	9	9	4	4	3	7	3	3	7	4	3	6	7	2	6	1	6	5	4	5
4	4	6	2	8	9	4	4	4	8	2	2	5	5	5	5	4	6	4	3	5	4	6	6
3	3	5	2	8	8	4	4	3	8	2	2	3	2	8	4	7	3	4	3	5	6	7	4
5	6	3	2	8	3	4	4	5	9	2	1	3	9	5	6	3	6	9	9	5	2	9	9
8	8	1	3	7	3	4	5	6	9	2	1	1	9	5	6	3	7	9	8	5	3	7	5
8	4	6	5	4	3	4	5	5	4	2	2	2	4	5	1	5	9	7	5	5	7	8	3
8	4	4	3	6	3	4	4	3	7	2	2	4	3	7	2	8	5	5	7	5	7	7	4
3	4	5	1	9	9	4	4	6	7	2	2	3	6	7	3	7	5	9	9	5	9	8	5
2	4	3	1	9	9	4	4	7	3	3	3	7	3	5	9	2	2	7	8	4	9	7	6
5	9	7	3	7	7	4	4	6	6	3	2	3	9	3	4	3	8	9	9	5	8	5	7
4	6	4	2	8	3	5	4	8	9	2	1	4	8	6	4	5	6	8	9	5	6	9	9
8	9	3	3	7	3	4	4	7	7	2	2	6	7	5	3	6	6	9	5	5	5	9	7
8	5	5	5	4	3	4	6	3	6	2	2	3	*	*	*	*	*	3	8	5	7	4	4
8	4	2	5	4	3	4	9	8	6	2	2	2	4	5	1	9	3	5	7	5	5	9	4
8	6	4	5	5	3	4	5	3	8	2	2	1	7	5	3	6	6	8	8	5	8	6	5
9	6	7	6	4	3	4	4	4	9	2	1	2	9	4	7	2	6	9	7	5	6	4	5
9	6	5	4	5	3	4	5	4	9	2	1	3	9	3	2	3	9	7	7	5	9	9	4
4	8	1	3	6	3	4	4	9	7	2	2	2	5	3	1	8	6	7	5	5	2	7	5
6	3	5	7	3	3	4	4	6	3	8	6	2	5	4	7	6	2	6	7	5	5	4	5
9	7	9	5	4	3	4	4	3	2	2	2	3	7	3	3	7	5	4	7	5	8	9	4
8	5	6	5	4	3	4	9	4	5	2	2	3	7	3	1	8	7	3	9	4	7	5	4
8	4	5	6	4	3	4	5	4	7	2	3	7	6	6	5	3	7	3	8	5	5	4	4

Economic Indicators For Class IIIA And IIIB Counties		SIZE OF COUNTY		REAL-ESTATE VALUES			AGES OF POPULATION				INCOMES					
		Population	Land Area	Med House Val	Med Gross Rent	Av Farm Val./Acre	% Under 5	% 5–17	% 18 and Over	% 65 and Over	% Poverty	% Under $10,000	% $10–19,999	% $20–29,999	% $30–49,999	% Over $50,000
Presque Isle	IIIB	4	4	6	7	2	4	6	5	6	5	6	2	6	4	6
Schoolcraft	IIIA	4	6	3	7	2	4	5	5	6	3	5	6	6	3	2
MINNESOTA																
Big Stone	IIIA	3	4	3	3	5	3	3	7	9	3	6	8	3	3	4
Carlton	IIIB	6	5	8	7	2	5	7	3	3	2	2	4	9	9	2
Chippewa	IIIB	4	4	6	6	7	7	2	6	8	3	4	7	5	5	4
Clearwater	IIIA	4	6	2	2	2	7	8	3	8	8	8	3	2	2	2
Cottonwood	IIIB	4	4	7	6	9	6	3	6	8	4	3	8	5	6	8
Fillmore	IIIA	5	5	6	4	7	4	4	6	8	4	5	5	6	4	6
Goodhue	IIIB	7	5	9	7	8	5	6	5	6	1	1	3	9	9	8
Grant	IIIA	3	4	4	6	6	3	2	8	9	4	6	8	2	3	7
Kittson	IIIA	3	6	2	4	3	4	2	7	9	3	4	5	6	5	4
Koochiching	IIIB	4	9	7	5	2	6	7	3	2	3	2	2	9	9	3
Lac Qui Parl	IIIA	4	5	4	3	5	4	2	7	9	5	5	7	5	5	4
Lake Of The	IIIB	3	7	4	6	2	3	5	6	7	5	5	8	6	1	2
Le Sueur	IIIB	5	4	9	7	9	7	8	3	5	2	2	4	8	8	8
Lincoln	IIIA	3	4	3	2	5	5	5	5	9	7	8	5	1	2	5
Lyon	IIIB	5	5	8	7	7	6	4	6	4	2	3	6	7	6	6
Mahnomen	IIIA	3	4	3	4	3	7	9	1	6	7	8	6	2	3	2
Marshall	IIIA	4	8	5	3	3	8	7	2	6	5	4	7	5	6	2
Martin	IIIB	5	5	8	6	9	4	3	7	7	2	2	8	7	8	8
Morrison	IIIB	6	6	6	4	3	8	9	1	5	7	6	7	4	3	5
Polk	IIIB	6	8	8	7	4	5	5	5	6	3	4	4	7	7	7
MINNESOTA																
Pope	IIIA	4	4	7	5	4	5	3	7	9	6	7	5	3	3	5
Red Lake	IIIA	3	4	3	1	4	7	9	2	6	7	7	5	3	4	2
Rice	IIIB	7	4	9	8	9	5	4	6	2	1	1	4	9	9	7
Roseau	IIIA	4	8	6	7	3	7	7	3	5	4	4	7	6	5	2
Swift	IIIA	4	5	5	2	6	6	5	5	8	6	6	7	2	3	6
Waseca	IIIB	5	4	9	7	9	8	3	5	4	2	2	6	8	8	8
MISSISSIPPI																
Amite	IIIA	4	5	2	2	3	8	9	2	5	9	9	1	2	3	2
Attala	IIIA	5	5	3	1	2	5	7	3	7	9	9	2	1	1	3
Benton	IIIA	3	3	3	2	2	8	9	1	5	7	8	6	2	2	2
Carroll	IIIA	4	4	3	3	3	7	8	2	5	9	9	2	2	2	2
Chickasaw	IIIA	4	4	3	2	3	8	8	2	4	7	7	7	3	2	2
Choctaw	IIIA	4	3	2	3	3	8	8	2	6	9	9	7	1	1	4
Copiah	IIIA	5	5	2	1	4	7	7	2	5	9	9	2	2	2	6

SOCIO-ECONOMIC STATUS					MINORITIES				RURAL-URBAN				ECONOMIC BASE					COUNTY CONDITIONS					
% Completed HS	% College or More	Families/Pop	% Married Couples	% W/O Husband	% Black	% Spanish	% Amer Indian	% Asian	% Urban	% Rural	% Farmers	% Out of County	Jobs/Pop	% Manufacturing	% Wholesale	% Retail	% Services	Physicians/Cap	Crimes/Cap	$ Police/Crimes	$ Educ/Enrollment	Carpool or Transit	Pop Density
6	3	6	7	3	3	4	5	8	5	2	3	5	3	3	2	9	3	2	5	5	5	4	4
7	5	6	6	4	3	4	8	7	8	2	2	2	6	3	2	7	7	7	9	5	8	5	4
8	5	4	9	1	3	4	4	7	6	9	8	2	8	3	6	7	2	5	2	6	9	3	4
8	6	3	6	4	3	4	7	5	7	3	3	5	4	6	1	9	3	6	6	5	8	4	5
8	6	6	8	2	3	4	4	6	8	9	8	3	9	3	9	1	6	5	2	5	8	7	4
4	4	3	5	3	3	4	9	3	2	7	9	3	3	3	2	9	3	5	7	5	8	4	4
8	6	6	8	2	3	4	4	4	6	9	9	2	8	4	7	5	2	3	2	5	8	4	4
8	5	5	8	2	3	4	4	7	3	9	9	3	7	3	9	3	2	4	1	6	7	3	4
8	7	4	8	2	3	4	5	7	8	7	6	4	8	5	4	6	5	7	6	5	7	4	5
8	5	8	8	2	3	4	4	7	2	9	9	2	8	2	9	1	2	3	5	5	9	3	4
8	6	6	7	2	3	4	4	2	2	9	9	2	7	3	8	5	2	4	5	5	9	3	4
8	5	4	6	3	3	4	6	4	8	2	2	1	*	*	*	*	*	7	9	5	8	5	3
7	5	6	8	1	3	4	4	7	2	9	9	2	*	*	*	*	*	5	2	5	9	3	4
7	7	7	8	2	3	4	4	2	2	5	8	3	*	*	*	*	*	8	8	5	8	4	3
7	7	4	8	2	3	4	4	6	4	7	6	8	8	4	9	1	2	5	3	5	4	6	5
6	4	4	8	1	3	4	4	5	2	9	9	2	5	2	8	5	3	5	3	5	8	3	4
6	7	1	8	2	3	4	4	9	8	7	5	1	*	*	*	*	*	7	5	5	5	3	5
3	3	1	4	3	3	4	9	2	2	9	9	3	5	2	5	7	3	2	9	5	9	3	4
6	4	3	8	1	3	4	4	2	2	9	9	3	5	2	9	2	2	2	3	5	9	3	4
8	5	6	8	3	3	4	4	9	8	8	7	1	9	4	7	5	3	7	5	5	7	3	5
4	3	1	7	3	3	4	4	7	5	9	8	3	4	4	4	7	4	5	7	5	7	4	4
6	7	2	6	4	3	5	5	4	8	6	6	4	9	3	7	3	4	6	7	5	7	5	4
8	5	6	8	1	3	4	4	4	4	9	9	2	5	3	8	3	3	5	6	5	6	4	4
5	2	2	6	2	3	4	4	3	2	9	9	4	*	*	*	*	*	1	1	6	9	3	4
5	9	1	7	3	3	4	4	9	9	5	4	3	8	4	5	6	5	5	7	5	3	4	7
5	4	4	7	2	3	4	5	5	2	9	9	1	*	*	*	*	*	4	6	5	8	3	4
7	4	4	7	2	3	4	4	7	6	9	9	2	8	3	8	3	4	4	4	5	9	3	4
8	6	3	7	2	3	4	4	9	8	7	6	2	7	8	8	3	3	5	7	5	6	4	5
2	3	2	2	8	9	4	4	4	2	4	5	8	1	9	6	4	5	2	1	7	2	8	4
2	4	4	2	9	9	4	4	3	7	2	3	3	4	6	5	4	6	4	6	5	3	8	4
1	2	3	4	6	9	4	4	2	2	4	4	9	*	*	*	*	*	2	1	6	3	9	4
1	3	4	2	8	9	5	4	2	2	4	5	9	1	3	2	9	1	2	2	5	1	9	4
2	3	3	2	8	9	4	4	2	7	3	3	4	3	9	5	3	6	5	3	5	4	9	5
2	2	4	2	8	8	4	4	2	2	3	4	7	1	9	1	8	5	4	1	5	4	9	4
2	3	1	1	9	9	4	4	3	7	2	3	7	2	7	4	8	3	4	2	5	4	7	5

Economic Indicators For Class IIIA And IIIB Counties

		SIZE OF COUNTY		REAL-ESTATE VALUES			AGES OF POPULATION				INCOMES					
		Population	Land Area	Med House Val	Med Gross Rent	Av Farm Val./Acre	% Under 5	% 5–17	% 18 and Over	% 65 and Over	% Poverty	% Under $10,000	% $10–19,999	% $20–29,999	% $30–49,999	% Over $50,000
Franklin	IIIA	3	4	2	1	3	6	6	4	6	9	9	1	4	2	1
Grenada	IIIB	5	4	5	2	3	7	8	2	3	7	6	4	4	4	6
Holmes	IIIA	5	5	1	1	5	9	9	1	5	9	9	1	1	1	2
Humphreys	IIIA	4	4	2	1	6	9	9	1	4	9	9	1	1	3	6
Issaquena	IIIA	3	3	2	4	7	8	9	1	2	9	9	1	1	2	9
Jasper	IIIA	4	4	2	1	3	8	8	2	4	9	8	7	1	2	2
Jefferson	IIIA	4	4	2	1	3	9	9	1	4	9	9	1	1	2	1
Jefferson Da	IIIA	4	3	3	2	3	8	9	1	4	9	8	1	3	3	4
Kemper	IIIA	4	5	2	1	2	7	9	1	6	9	9	2	1	1	2
Leake	IIIA	5	4	2	3	4	6	7	3	6	9	9	3	1	1	2
Leflore	IIIA	7	4	6	2	6	9	9	1	3	9	9	1	2	3	6
Monroe	IIIB	6	5	4	2	4	6	8	2	3	6	7	6	3	3	3
Montgomery	IIIA	4	3	2	2	3	5	7	3	7	9	9	4	1	2	2
Newton	IIIA	5	4	3	1	4	4	5	6	6	8	8	4	2	2	3
Noxubee	IIIA	4	4	2	1	5	9	9	1	4	9	9	2	1	1	4
Panola	IIIA	6	4	3	3	4	8	9	1	4	9	9	2	1	2	6
Perry	IIIA	4	4	2	3	5	8	9	1	2	9	8	4	3	3	4
Smith	IIIA	4	4	3	2	4	6	8	3	4	8	8	2	3	2	3
Sunflower	IIIA	6	5	3	2	7	9	9	1	3	9	9	1	2	3	5
Tate	IIIA	5	3	6	4	4	7	8	2	2	8	6	4	5	3	3
Walthall	IIIA	4	3	3	3	4	9	8	1	5	9	9	2	1	3	6
Webster	IIIA	4	4	3	1	3	4	4	6	8	6	7	7	3	1	3
Winston	IIIA	5	4	4	2	3	7	8	2	6	8	8	5	2	2	3
Yalobusha	IIIA	4	4	2	2	4	6	6	4	7	8	8	7	1	2	2
Yazoo	IIIA	5	5	3	2	4	9	9	1	5	9	9	1	2	2	8
MISSOURI																
Adair	IIIB	5	4	6	6	3	2	1	9	3	3	6	3	4	5	6
Audrain	IIIB	5	4	4	5	7	6	4	6	6	2	2	7	8	6	6
Barton	IIIA	4	4	2	3	5	4	1	8	9	3	6	9	2	2	3
Bates	IIIA	4	5	2	4	4	3	2	8	9	4	6	3	4	6	5
Buchanan	IIIA	9	3	4	6	7	4	2	7	6	2	3	5	7	6	6
Caldwell	IIIA	4	4	1	3	5	3	3	7	9	4	7	4	4	4	3
Carroll	IIIA	4	4	2	2	6	4	2	8	9	4	6	5	3	5	7
Chariton	IIIA	4	5	2	3	6	3	1	9	9	4	6	3	4	6	8
Clark	IIIA	4	4	2	3	5	6	5	5	7	4	5	7	4	4	6
Cooper	IIIA	4	4	4	4	5	3	4	6	7	3	4	8	5	5	5
Dade	IIIA	3	4	2	2	4	2	1	9	9	3	7	7	2	3	3
Daviess	IIIA	4	4	2	3	5	4	2	7	9	4	7	6	2	5	2
Gasconade	IIIB	4	4	3	4	3	2	1	9	9	3	5	7	5	5	3
Gentry	IIIA	3	4	2	3	4	2	1	9	9	5	8	6	1	3	3

% Completed HS	% College or More	Families/Pop	% Married Couples	% W/O Husband	% Black	% Spanish	% Amer Indian	% Asian	% Urban	% Rural	% Farmers	% Out of County	Jobs/Pop	% Manufacturing	% Wholesale	% Retail	% Services	Physicians/Cap	Crimes/Cap	$ Police/Crimes	$ Educ/Enrollment	Carpool or Transit	Pop Density
4	2	4	2	8	9	4	4	2	2	2	3	7	1	6	3	8	3	4	2	5	3	9	4
2	5	3	1	9	9	4	4	2	9	2	2	1	*	*	*	*	*	6	9	5	2	9	5
1	4	1	1	9	9	4	4	5	5	3	2	3	2	4	6	6	3	3	2	5	4	8	5
1	3	1	1	9	9	5	4	5	4	4	2	2	2	3	9	1	3	3	3	5	2	7	5
1	1	1	1	9	9	5	4	2	2	6	5	9	*	*	*	*	*	1	*	*	1	7	4
3	3	3	2	8	9	4	4	3	2	3	4	9	1	5	6	3	6	3	1	6	2	9	4
1	3	1	1	9	9	4	4	2	2	3	3	9	*	*	*	*	*	6	*	*	3	9	4
1	3	1	1	9	9	4	4	4	2	3	4	9	*	*	*	*	*	4	2	5	2	9	5
2	3	2	1	8	9	4	4	2	2	5	6	8	1	8	2	7	6	3	2	5	6	9	4
2	2	5	3	7	9	4	7	2	4	4	5	5	2	6	5	7	3	5	1	5	2	9	5
1	7	1	1	9	9	4	4	8	9	2	2	2	7	4	7	3	5	8	5	5	2	8	6
2	2	4	2	9	9	4	4	2	7	2	2	5	5	7	6	3	5	6	7	5	2	9	5
2	2	3	1	9	9	4	4	2	8	3	3	6	4	6	3	4	8	4	1	5	2	7	5
4	4	5	3	7	8	4	6	3	4	3	4	5	2	9	3	6	4	5	3	5	5	7	5
1	3	1	1	9	9	4	4	2	2	5	4	4	2	5	5	5	5	3	1	6	2	8	4
1	3	1	1	9	9	4	4	3	4	3	3	4	4	6	8	2	5	5	6	5	2	9	5
4	2	3	4	7	8	5	4	3	2	3	3	8	1	8	9	2	2	4	2	5	4	8	4
4	3	6	6	4	7	4	4	2	2	5	6	7	1	9	5	5	4	3	*	*	3	8	4
1	5	1	1	9	9	4	4	8	7	4	2	2	5	4	9	1	3	4	3	5	4	6	5
2	4	1	2	8	9	4	4	5	5	4	3	7	4	6	2	8	5	4	1	5	7	8	5
2	4	3	2	8	9	4	4	6	2	4	6	6	2	5	8	2	4	5	2	5	2	8	5
4	3	6	4	6	7	4	4	4	2	4	4	6	2	8	3	9	2	4	1	5	3	9	4
2	4	4	2	8	9	4	5	2	7	3	4	3	2	8	3	7	4	3	2	5	2	8	5
2	3	4	1	9	9	4	4	5	6	3	3	5	2	9	2	8	4	3	2	5	2	9	4
1	6	1	1	9	9	4	4	3	8	3	2	2	4	5	6	5	4	3	7	5	3	8	4
3	9	1	5	5	3	4	4	9	9	4	5	2	8	4	2	8	5	2	6	5	1	4	5
7	5	6	7	4	4	4	4	3	9	7	6	2	9	6	8	2	5	8	6	5	4	4	5
7	3	8	8	2	3	4	5	6	7	9	9	3	6	4	7	1	9	3	4	5	4	4	4
8	3	8	8	2	3	4	4	2	5	9	9	5	5	3	9	3	2	4	4	5	5	5	4
7	6	4	4	7	4	5	4	4	9	2	2	2	9	4	7	2	6	9	9	5	3	9	9
9	3	8	8	2	3	4	4	4	2	9	9	7	*	*	*	*	*	2	2	5	6	5	4
7	4	8	7	3	3	4	5	5	7	9	9	3	*	*	*	*	*	3	4	5	6	4	4
8	4	8	8	2	4	4	4	5	2	9	9	4	4	3	9	2	1	2	2	5	5	3	4
8	2	5	7	3	3	4	4	2	2	9	9	7	*	*	*	*	*	1	*	*	4	5	4
7	6	6	6	4	4	4	4	5	8	7	7	5	7	4	6	6	2	4	8	5	4	5	4
8	4	9	8	2	3	4	5	3	2	9	9	6	2	4	9	3	2	4	2	5	6	5	4
8	3	7	8	2	3	4	4	5	2	9	9	5	3	4	7	7	2	2	*	*	5	4	4
4	3	8	7	3	3	4	4	7	4	6	7	5	5	6	5	7	3	3	2	5	7	8	4
8	6	7	8	2	3	4	4	3	2	9	9	3	7	3	8	5	2	5	7	4	6	4	4

Economic Indicators For Class IIIA And IIIB Counties

		SIZE OF COUNTY		REAL-ESTATE VALUES			AGES OF POPULATION				INCOMES					
		Population	Land Area	Med House Val	Med Gross Rent	Av Farm Val./Acre	% Under 5	% 5–17	% 18 and Over	% 65 and Over	% Poverty	% Under $10,000	% $10–19,999	% $20–29,999	% $30–49,999	% Over $50,000
Grundy	IIIA	4	4	2	4	5	2	1	9	9	4	7	7	3	2	3
Harrison	IIIA	4	5	1	5	4	2	1	9	9	7	9	4	1	2	7
Henry	IIIA	5	5	3	5	5	3	2	8	9	3	7	2	4	6	4
Holt	IIIA	3	4	1	1	7	4	1	9	9	4	7	8	3	2	3
Jasper	IIIA	9	4	3	4	5	4	2	8	5	3	5	7	4	4	5
Knox	IIIA	3	4	1	1	5	2	3	8	9	7	7	6	2	2	8
Linn	IIIA	4	4	2	3	5	2	1	9	9	3	7	5	3	4	5
Livingston	IIIA	4	4	5	4	5	4	2	7	8	4	5	5	4	5	8
Macon	IIIA	4	5	3	3	4	3	2	8	9	3	5	6	4	4	5
Maries	IIIA	3	4	3	2	2	3	5	6	7	4	7	8	2	2	3
Marion	IIIA	6	4	4	4	5	5	3	7	7	2	4	5	7	5	4
Mercer	IIIA	3	4	1	2	4	1	1	9	9	6	9	4	1	2	4
Monroe	IIIA	4	4	3	3	6	5	2	7	8	5	5	9	5	2	4
Montgomery	IIIA	4	4	2	4	5	3	4	7	9	3	4	8	4	5	3
Osage	IIIA	4	4	4	3	2	6	8	3	6	3	3	6	7	5	4
Pemiscot	IIIA	5	4	1	2	8	8	8	2	6	9	9	2	1	2	2
Pettis	IIIB	6	4	4	7	5	4	2	7	7	2	4	6	5	5	7
Putnam	IIIA	3	4	1	3	3	1	3	8	9	7	9	3	1	1	5
Saline	IIIA	5	5	5	6	7	4	1	8	8	2	4	7	5	5	4
Schuyler	IIIA	3	3	1	2	4	2	3	8	9	6	8	5	2	2	6
Scotland	IIIA	3	4	1	2	5	3	3	7	9	6	9	2	1	3	7
Shannon	IIIA	3	6	1	3	3	3	6	5	5	9	9	3	1	1	1
Shelby	IIIA	3	4	1	2	6	3	1	8	9	4	8	6	2	3	2
Sullivan	IIIA	3	4	1	1	3	2	1	9	9	6	9	3	1	2	5
Vernon	IIIA	5	5	2	3	4	4	2	8	7	3	7	4	4	3	4
Worth	IIIA	3	3	1	3	5	3	1	9	9	6	9	3	1	2	4
MONTANA																
Big Horn	IIIB	4	9	7	4	1	9	9	1	1	7	4	6	4	7	5
Blaine	IIIA	3	9	5	3	1	9	9	1	3	7	6	4	5	4	7
Custer	IIIA	4	9	8	6	1	7	4	5	4	3	4	2	7	8	7
Fergus	IIIA	4	9	6	4	1	4	4	6	7	5	5	4	5	5	6
Golden Valle	IIIA	3	6	2	3	1	3	8	3	5	7	7	9	1	1	4
Judith Basin	IIIA	3	8	4	4	1	4	6	5	5	6	2	9	3	4	9
Madison	IIIA	3	9	8	3	2	4	2	7	7	3	5	4	8	3	2
Petroleum	IIIA	3	8	1	1	1	8	7	3	1	9	7	9	1	1	9
Phillips	IIIA	3	9	6	5	1	8	5	3	4	6	5	9	3	2	3
Powell	IIIB	3	9	6	4	2	3	3	7	2	2	2	9	6	6	6
Prairie	IIIA	3	8	2	3	1	4	5	6	8	9	9	4	1	1	4
Sweet Grass	IIIA	3	8	7	2	1	4	2	8	9	3	6	6	4	4	4
Teton	IIIA	3	9	7	4	2	8	4	4	5	4	3	8	5	6	9

SOCIO-ECONOMIC STATUS					MINORITIES				RURAL-URBAN				ECONOMIC BASE					COUNTY CONDITIONS					
% Completed HS	% College or More	Families/Pop	% Married Couples	% W/O Husband	% Black	% Spanish	% Amer Indian	% Asian	% Urban	% Rural	% Farmers	% Out of County	Jobs/Pop	% Manufacturing	% Wholesale	% Retail	% Services	Physicians/Cap	Crimes/Cap	$ Police/Crimes	$ Educ/Enrollment	Carpool or Transit	Pop Density
9	5	8	8	3	3	4	4	3	9	7	7	2	*	*	*	*	*	3	4	5	7	5	4
9	4	9	8	3	3	4	4	6	6	9	9	3	9	3	9	1	2	3	*	*	8	3	4
8	5	7	7	3	3	4	4	6	9	6	7	2	7	4	3	7	4	4	5	5	6	4	4
9	4	8	8	2	3	4	4	4	2	9	9	3	*	*	*	*	*	2	6	5	5	3	4
7	6	6	4	6	3	4	5	8	9	2	2	3	9	4	7	3	5	9	9	5	3	4	8
8	4	6	8	2	3	4	4	4	2	9	9	3	4	3	9	1	5	2	2	5	5	4	4
9	4	8	7	3	3	4	4	5	9	7	7	2	7	5	7	4	3	4	3	5	6	6	4
8	5	6	7	4	3	4	4	7	9	7	6	1	9	4	9	1	5	6	4	5	6	4	4
8	5	9	8	3	3	4	4	4	7	8	8	4	*	*	*	*	*	3	3	5	6	5	4
4	2	7	8	2	3	4	4	3	2	9	9	9	1	7	5	8	1	1	1	5	4	9	4
7	7	5	5	5	4	4	4	8	9	4	3	4	9	3	4	5	7	9	9	5	3	7	6
9	4	9	8	1	3	4	4	2	2	9	9	3	*	*	*	*	*	1	*	*	6	3	4
8	3	6	8	3	4	4	4	4	5	9	9	6	4	5	9	2	3	2	*	*	6	4	4
6	2	6	8	2	4	4	4	2	2	8	8	6	5	5	7	4	4	2	4	5	4	6	4
3	2	2	7	2	3	4	4	4	2	9	9	9	2	5	9	2	2	2	2	5	2	9	4
1	2	2	1	9	8	4	4	5	8	3	3	4	4	4	7	6	2	4	2	5	6	5	5
8	5	7	5	5	4	4	4	8	9	5	4	2	9	4	5	3	7	6	9	5	6	5	5
7	2	7	8	2	3	4	4	3	2	9	9	3	3	2	6	7	2	1	*	*	5	3	4
6	6	5	5	5	4	4	4	6	8	6	5	2	7	5	7	3	6	5	8	5	4	4	5
8	3	7	9	1	3	4	4	3	2	9	9	7	*	*	*	*	*	1	2	5	5	4	4
8	3	6	8	2	3	4	4	3	2	9	9	2	*	*	*	*	*	2	3	5	6	7	4
3	2	8	8	2	3	4	4	3	2	6	7	4	*	*	*	*	*	2	1	5	2	8	4
8	3	8	8	3	3	4	4	2	2	9	9	3	6	4	9	2	2	2	*	*	6	3	4
8	3	8	7	3	3	4	5	3	2	9	9	2	*	*	*	*	*	1	*	4	4	4	4
8	6	5	6	4	3	4	5	8	8	7	8	2	7	4	7	5	3	8	8	5	4	4	4
8	7	8	8	2	3	4	4	3	2	9	9	5	*	*	*	*	*	3	3	5	1	4	4
5	6	1	2	8	3	5	9	5	6	5	5	2	4	2	4	7	5	4	4	5	8	5	3
6	8	1	4	6	3	4	9	6	2	8	7	2	4	2	5	6	5	2	2	5	9	8	3
7	9	3	5	5	3	5	6	5	9	3	3	1	9	2	5	2	9	9	7	5	8	5	3
9	9	3	7	3	3	4	5	3	9	7	7	1	8	3	6	5	5	9	6	5	7	3	3
9	8	5	8	1	3	4	5	7	2	9	9	2	*	*	*	*	*	1	*	*	7	3	3
9	9	7	8	2	3	4	5	2	2	9	9	2	*	*	*	*	*	1	1	7	9	3	3
9	9	7	8	2	3	4	4	3	2	8	9	2	*	*	*	*	*	6	2	5	9	9	3
7	9	8	8	2	3	4	4	2	2	9	9	2	*	*	*	*	*	1	*	*	9	3	3
8	3	3	6	3	3	4	9	5	2	8	9	1	4	2	5	7	3	3	3	5	9	4	3
8	9	1	7	3	3	4	6	8	9	3	3	2	5	3	1	9	6	9	*	6	7	4	3
8	4	6	8	1	3	5	5	9	2	9	9	2	*	*	*	*	*	1	2	5	9	3	3
8	9	5	9	1	3	4	5	8	2	9	9	1	8	2	1	4	9	5	5	5	7	4	3
8	9	5	9	1	3	4	6	5	2	9	9	2	5	2	9	2	3	5	3	5	8	3	3

Economic Indicators For Class IIIA And IIIB Counties		SIZE OF COUNTY		REAL-ESTATE VALUES			AGES OF POPULATION				INCOMES					
		Population	Land Area	Med House Val	Med Gross Rent	Av Farm Val./Acre	% Under 5	% 5-17	% 18 and Over	% 65 and Over	% Poverty	% Under $10,000	% $10-19,999	% $20-29,999	% $30-49,999	% Over $50,000
Wibaux	IIIA	3	5	3	3	1	5	9	2	4	7	7	4	3	2	9
NEBRASKA																
Antelope	IIIA	4	5	3	2	4	7	4	5	8	8	8	3	2	2	5
Blaine	IIIA	3	5	1	6	1	3	8	3	7	9	8	9	1	2	2
Brown	IIIA	3	6	4	4	2	6	3	6	8	7	7	6	2	2	5
Buffalo	IIIB	6	5	9	8	6	6	1	8	3	2	2	7	7	7	8
Burt	IIIA	4	4	3	3	8	3	2	8	9	4	5	8	4	4	7
Butler	IIIA	4	4	2	5	8	5	3	6	9	3	4	6	5	5	8
Cherry	IIIA	3	9	4	7	1	6	2	6	5	3	2	9	3	7	9
Colfax	IIIA	4	3	4	5	7	5	3	6	9	4	5	5	5	5	8
Custer	IIIA	4	9	3	3	2	6	2	7	9	4	5	8	4	4	6
Dixon	IIIA	3	4	3	5	5	5	5	5	8	6	6	4	4	4	5
Dundy	IIIA	3	5	2	1	2	3	1	9	9	5	6	7	2	5	6
Fillmore	IIIA	3	4	4	5	8	3	2	7	9	2	2	9	5	6	7
Franklin	IIIA	3	4	1	2	5	2	1	9	9	5	6	8	2	2	6
Furnas	IIIA	3	5	2	2	3	2	1	9	9	5	7	6	3	2	1
Garden	IIIA	3	8	3	2	1	1	1	9	9	2	4	8	5	3	6
Garfield	IIIA	3	4	2	1	1	2	3	7	9	4	8	6	2	2	2
Gosper	IIIA	3	4	7	8	4	4	3	7	7	4	4	7	6	4	8
Hamilton	IIIA	4	4	7	7	9	6	6	4	4	2	1	9	8	7	8
Harlan	IIIA	3	4	2	2	3	2	2	9	9	6	6	6	2	4	6
Hitchcock	IIIA	3	5	2	5	2	8	2	7	8	4	5	9	4	3	4
Holt	IIIA	4	9	4	5	3	8	5	3	6	6	6	8	2	3	5
Hooker	IIIA	3	5	4	6	1	5	1	8	9	5	8	9	2	1	1
Jefferson	IIIA	4	4	2	3	7	2	1	9	9	4	5	8	5	3	5
Kearney	IIIA	3	4	7	7	8	4	3	7	7	2	1	9	7	7	8
Keith	IIIB	4	6	8	7	3	6	4	5	4	2	1	8	8	8	8
Keya Paha	IIIA	3	5	4	9	2	7	4	5	6	5	7	5	2	3	9
Knox	IIIA	4	6	3	2	2	5	4	6	9	6	8	4	2	2	6
Logan	IIIA	3	4	4	6	1	9	3	3	5	8	8	7	1	3	3
Loup	IIIA	3	4	1	8	1	3	4	7	7	4	6	7	5	1	8
Merrick	IIIA	4	4	5	6	7	7	6	4	6	3	2	7	9	5	5
Morrill	IIIA	3	7	4	2	2	7	3	6	7	7	7	6	3	3	3
Perkins	IIIA	3	5	6	6	4	8	2	6	8	4	5	5	5	7	5
Pierce	IIIA	4	4	5	5	5	7	4	5	7	3	4	9	5	3	6
Polk	IIIA	3	4	3	2	8	4	4	6	9	5	3	8	6	6	5
Red Willow	IIIA	4	5	7	5	3	6	2	7	6	2	2	5	7	9	7
Richardson	IIIA	4	4	2	3	5	2	1	9	9	4	6	7	2	5	2
Rock	IIIA	3	6	4	2	2	6	5	4	7	3	4	9	3	5	6
Saline	IIIA	4	4	5	6	6	2	1	9	9	2	3	4	8	7	6

SOCIO-ECONOMIC STATUS					MINORITIES				RURAL-URBAN				ECONOMIC BASE					COUNTY CONDITIONS					
% Completed HS	% College or More	Families/Pop	% Married Couples	% W/O Husband	% Black	% Spanish	% Amer Indian	% Asian	% Urban	% Rural	% Farmers	% Out of County	Jobs/Pop	% Manufacturing	% Wholesale	% Retail	% Services	Physicians/Cap	Crimes/Cap	$ Police/Crimes	$ Educ/Enrollment	Carpool or Transit	Pop Density
7	4	1	9	1	3	4	5	2	2	9	9	4	*	*	*	*	*	1	8	5	9	3	3
9	3	5	9	1	3	4	4	3	2	9	9	2	8	3	9	1	2	4	1	6	7	4	4
9	6	5	9	1	3	4	4	2	2	9	9	3	*	*	*	*	*	1	*	*	9	3	3
9	5	7	8	2	3	4	4	8	2	8	8	1	9	2	9	3	2	4	2	6	8	3	3
7	9	1	7	3	3	5	4	8	9	5	4	2	9	4	3	4	8	9	8	5	3	3	5
9	6	7	8	2	3	4	5	4	2	9	9	2	6	3	9	2	2	3	2	6	9	3	4
8	4	4	8	1	3	4	4	3	5	9	9	4	*	*	*	*	*	5	2	7	5	3	4
9	8	6	8	2	3	4	5	2	7	9	9	2	8	2	3	8	3	5	5	5	8	3	3
7	3	5	8	2	3	5	4	4	8	9	9	2	*	*	*	*	*	3	3	5	8	3	4
9	6	7	8	2	3	4	4	3	6	9	9	1	*	*	*	*	*	5	4	5	9	3	3
8	5	5	8	2	3	4	4	3	2	9	9	5	*	*	*	*	*	2	3	5	9	3	4
8	7	8	9	1	3	4	4	9	2	9	9	2	*	*	*	*	*	8	1	5	9	3	3
9	6	6	8	1	3	4	4	4	2	9	9	2	8	2	9	1	2	5	2	5	9	3	4
8	6	8	9	1	3	4	4	4	2	9	9	3	*	*	*	*	*	2	1	9	9	3	4
9	8	8	9	1	3	4	4	4	2	8	8	4	6	3	9	4	1	5	2	5	9	3	4
9	7	9	9	1	3	4	4	2	2	9	9	1	*	*	*	*	*	9	1	6	9	3	3
8	6	7	7	3	3	4	4	2	2	9	9	1	*	*	*	*	*	4	*	*	1	3	3
9	5	9	9	1	3	4	4	9	2	9	9	4	*	*	*	*	*	1	*	*	5	3	3
9	8	6	9	1	3	4	4	5	7	9	9	3	8	3	8	1	7	7	4	5	8	3	4
9	7	9	8	2	3	4	4	2	2	8	9	3	*	*	*	*	*	4	1	9	9	3	4
9	5	9	9	1	3	4	4	3	2	9	9	4	*	*	*	*	*	1	3	5	9	3	4
8	4	3	8	2	3	4	4	2	6	9	9	1	*	*	*	*	*	4	2	5	7	3	3
9	8	7	5	6	3	5	4	2	2	6	7	1	*	*	*	*	*	1	3	5	9	5	3
9	5	8	8	2	3	4	4	2	8	9	8	2	9	3	8	4	3	5	5	5	9	3	4
9	9	5	8	1	3	5	4	2	7	8	8	3	*	*	*	*	*	4	4	5	9	4	4
9	7	7	8	3	3	5	4	9	9	4	4	1	9	4	3	6	7	6	9	5	9	4	4
9	4	8	9	1	3	4	4	2	2	9	9	1	*	*	*	*	*	1	1	8	7	3	3
8	4	5	8	2	3	4	7	3	2	9	9	2	6	2	9	2	2	5	2	5	8	3	4
9	6	7	9	1	3	4	4	2	2	9	9	4	*	*	*	*	*	1	*	*	9	3	3
9	7	8	8	2	3	4	4	2	2	9	9	3	*	*	*	*	*	1	*	*	9	3	3
9	5	5	8	2	3	4	4	3	6	9	8	6	5	3	9	1	4	2	4	5	8	3	4
8	4	7	9	1	3	6	5	3	2	9	9	3	*	*	*	*	*	7	2	5	8	3	3
9	9	7	9	1	3	5	4	2	2	9	9	2	*	*	*	*	*	9	*	*	9	3	3
8	4	6	9	1	3	4	4	2	2	9	9	5	*	*	*	*	*	7	2	5	9	3	4
9	5	6	9	1	3	4	5	2	2	9	9	4	5	3	9	1	2	3	3	5	8	6	4
9	8	6	8	2	3	5	4	6	9	5	4	1	9	3	6	3	7	7	5	5	7	3	4
8	7	6	7	3	3	4	5	5	8	8	8	2	7	3	7	5	4	6	4	5	8	3	4
9	6	6	8	1	3	4	4	3	2	9	9	2	*	*	*	*	*	4	*	*	8	3	3
8	6	4	8	2	3	4	4	8	7	8	8	2	7	6	8	3	3	4	4	5	8	3	4

Economic Indicators For Class IIIA And IIIB Counties		SIZE OF COUNTY		REAL-ESTATE VALUES			AGES OF POPULATION				INCOMES					
		Population	Land Area	Med House Val	Med Gross Rent	Av Farm Val./Acre	% Under 5	% 5–17	% 18 and Over	% 65 and Over	% Poverty	% Under $10,000	% $10–19,999	% $20–29,999	% $30–49,999	% Over $50,000
Saunders	IIIA	5	5	6	7	8	5	5	5	6	2	2	7	8	8	7
Scotts Bluff	IIIB	7	5	8	7	6	7	5	4	4	2	2	8	6	7	6
Seward	IIIA	4	4	8	8	8	6	1	8	5	2	1	9	8	6	8
Sheridan	IIIA	3	9	4	4	1	7	3	6	7	4	5	1	5	8	9
Sioux	IIIA	3	9	2	8	2	4	3	7	4	3	2	8	7	3	9
Thayer	IIIA	3	4	2	3	7	2	2	9	9	2	4	8	5	5	4
Thomas	IIIA	3	5	2	7	1	8	4	4	3	4	2	9	7	2	9
Thurston	IIIA	3	3	3	2	6	9	9	1	4	8	5	8	3	4	7
Valley	IIIA	3	4	3	1	3	4	2	7	9	5	7	8	2	3	6
Wheeler	IIIA	3	4	2	4	2	9	8	2	3	7	5	9	1	2	3
York	IIIA	4	4	8	7	9	5	3	7	6	2	2	7	8	7	9
NEW HAMPSHIRE																
Coos	IIIA	6	8	5	6	3	3	4	7	5	2	3	9	6	4	3
NEW MEXICO																
De Baca	IIIA	3	9	2	2	1	2	2	9	9	5	9	3	1	2	5
Mora	IIIA	3	8	1	1	1	4	9	1	5	9	9	1	1	1	1
San Miguel	IIIA	5	9	3	3	1	7	7	3	2	9	9	2	1	2	2
Taos	IIIB	5	9	9	7	2	7	9	1	1	9	8	4	3	3	3
Union	IIIA	3	9	3	2	1	4	6	4	8	8	7	3	2	4	8
Cattaraugus	IIIB	9	7	4	7	3	4	6	4	3	3	3	7	7	5	3
Delaware	IIIB	7	7	5	8	4	2	3	7	5	3	3	9	5	5	3
Essex	IIIB	6	8	5	8	4	2	6	6	5	3	3	7	6	6	3
Franklin	IIIB	7	8	4	6	3	3	8	4	3	4	6	6	5	3	3
Fulton	IIIB	8	4	4	6	4	3	5	6	5	2	3	9	5	5	3
Hamilton	IIIB	3	8	6	6	9	1	4	8	7	3	5	9	2	3	2
Lewis	IIIA	5	7	3	7	3	7	9	1	2	3	2	9	6	4	4
Otsego	IIIB	8	6	5	9	3	1	1	9	5	3	4	8	5	4	5
Warren	IIIB	8	5	7	9	5	3	7	5	4	3	2	8	6	7	6
Wyoming	IIIB	7	4	6	8	4	5	7	4	2	2	1	9	9	7	4
Yates	IIIB	5	3	5	8	5	2	5	7	6	3	3	8	5	6	5
NORTH CAROLINA																
Anson	IIIA	5	4	3	3	5	6	8	3	4	5	6	8	3	3	2
Bertie	IIIA	5	4	2	2	6	5	8	3	3	9	9	4	1	1	3
Camden	IIIA	3	3	4	5	6	3	6	5	3	5	3	4	8	5	4
Caswell	IIIB	5	4	4	2	5	2	7	5	2	7	5	7	6	3	3
Duplin	IIIB	7	5	3	3	8	4	7	4	2	8	8	6	2	2	3
Edgecombe	IIIB	8	4	5	7	7	5	8	3	2	6	5	6	6	4	3
Gates	IIIA	4	3	3	2	7	2	5	6	4	7	5	6	6	3	2

% Completed HS	% College or More	Families/Pop	% Married Couples	% W/O Husband	% Black	% Spanish	% Amer Indian	% Asian	% Urban	% Rural	% Farmers	% Out of County	Jobs/Pop	% Manufacturing	% Wholesale	% Retail	% Services	Physicians/Cap	Crimes/Cap	$ Police/Crimes	$ Educ/Enrollment	Carpool or Transit	Pop Density
9	5	5	8	2	3	4	4	4	4	9	8	8	4	3	7	4	4	3	3	5	6	4	4
7	7	5	6	4	3	8	5	9	9	4	3	1	9	3	7	2	6	9	9	5	7	4	5
7	7	2	9	1	3	4	5	7	7	8	7	4	*	*	*	*	*	5	5	5	4	4	4
8	8	5	7	3	3	4	8	9	2	9	9	1	*	*	*	*	*	8	5	5	5	3	3
9	7	9	8	1	3	5	4	7	2	9	9	5	*	*	*	*	*	1	2	5	6	3	3
9	6	8	9	1	3	4	5	5	2	9	9	2	*	*	*	*	*	4	2	5	9	3	4
9	6	7	8	1	3	4	4	5	2	9	9	3	*	*	*	*	*	1	1	*	8	3	3
6	3	1	1	9	3	4	9	2	2	9	8	2	2	4	9	2	1	6	*	*	8	3	4
9	6	6	9	1	3	4	4	3	8	9	9	2	8	3	5	6	4	6	4	5	9	3	4
8	6	5	8	1	3	4	4	2	2	9	9	2	*	*	*	*	*	1	*	*	9	3	3
9	8	6	9	2	3	4	4	9	9	8	7	1	9	3	7	3	5	7	6	5	7	3	4
7	4	5	4	6	3	4	4	3	7	2	2	2	8	6	2	4	9	9	4	5	5	6	4
7	6	8	5	5	3	9	4	2	2	8	8	2	*	*	*	*	*	7	3	5	7	3	3
1	5	2	1	9	3	9	4	2	2	4	7	5	*	*	*	*	*	3	2	5	9	3	3
2	8	1	1	9	3	9	5	4	9	2	2	2	3	2	1	9	5	9	5	5	8	4	3
5	8	1	1	8	3	9	8	3	4	2	2	1	9	2	1	1	9	9	4	5	9	5	4
7	6	6	4	5	3	9	4	5	9	6	8	1	*	*	*	*	*	4	9	5	9	5	3
7	6	2	3	7	3	4	6	6	6	3	2	4	6	6	4	5	6	9	7	5	8	5	6
7	7	2	5	5	3	4	4	7	5	3	3	3	4	7	3	4	8	8	6	5	8	5	5
7	9	2	4	5	3	4	4	4	3	2	2	4	6	4	2	2	9	7	5	5	7	6	4
5	6	1	2	7	3	4	8	6	7	3	2	3	*	*	*	*	*	9	5	5	9	6	4
7	5	4	3	6	3	4	4	5	8	2	1	5	5	7	6	4	5	8	9	5	9	9	8
9	7	7	7	2	3	4	4	3	2	1	1	5	*	*	*	*	*	2	3	5	9	6	3
6	4	2	6	3	3	4	4	7	3	6	4	4	2	6	8	4	2	3	3	5	8	4	4
6	9	1	5	5	3	4	4	6	5	3	3	4	6	3	5	7	4	9	6	5	6	7	6
7	9	2	2	7	3	4	4	7	9	2	1	4	9	4	3	5	8	9	9	5	8	4	6
7	4	1	5	4	3	4	4	5	5	4	3	6	3	7	3	8	4	7	5	5	7	6	6
7	8	3	6	4	3	4	4	4	5	4	4	6	4	4	6	4	6	6	7	5	6	6	6
3	2	2	1	9	9	4	4	2	4	3	2	5	2	9	6	5	2	4	5	5	5	9	5
1	2	3	1	9	9	4	4	2	2	5	4	5	3	8	9	1	2	3	3	5	4	8	4
3	1	6	3	7	9	4	4	2	2	3	3	9	*	*	*	*	*	3	3	4	5	9	4
2	1	3	1	8	9	4	4	4	2	6	5	9	*	*	*	*	*	2	4	4	4	9	5
2	2	5	1	9	9	4	4	3	3	6	5	5	4	6	8	4	2	4	5	5	6	8	5
2	3	3	1	9	9	4	4	3	8	3	2	7	5	6	3	5	6	9	9	4	3	9	8
2	3	3	2	8	9	4	4	3	2	5	5	9	2	3	9	1	5	2	3	4	6	9	4

Economic Indicators For Class IIIA And IIIB Counties		SIZE OF COUNTY		REAL-ESTATE VALUES			AGES OF POPULATION				INCOMES					
		Population	Land Area	Med House Val	Med Gross Rent	Av Farm Val./Acre	% Under 5	% 5-17	% 18 and Over	% 65 and Over	% Poverty	% Under $10,000	% $10–19,999	% $20–29,999	% $30–49,999	% Over $50,000
Graham	IIIB	3	3	4	3	9	4	6	5	3	7	7	9	2	1	2
Granville	IIIB	6	4	6	2	6	1	6	6	2	5	4	7	5	5	4
Greene	IIIA	4	3	6	4	9	5	8	3	1	8	6	6	4	4	5
Halifax	IIIB	8	5	3	4	6	4	7	3	3	9	8	2	3	2	4
Hyde	IIIA	3	4	3	4	7	5	5	5	6	9	9	5	1	1	3
Jones	IIIB	4	4	3	3	8	5	7	4	2	7	7	8	2	2	2
Madison	IIIA	4	4	4	2	6	2	2	9	5	9	9	5	1	1	3
Martin	IIIB	5	4	5	5	8	4	7	4	2	8	7	7	3	3	3
Mitchell	IIIA	4	3	5	3	8	1	2	9	5	5	6	7	6	1	1
Northampton	IIIA	5	4	2	2	6	2	6	5	4	9	8	5	1	2	6
Pamlico	IIIB	4	3	3	5	6	2	5	6	4	7	7	5	4	4	3
Polk	IIIB	4	3	8	6	7	1	1	9	9	3	5	3	4	7	8
Tyrrell	IIIA	3	3	2	6	6	.6	4	5	6	8	8	9	1	2	1
Warren	IIIA	4	4	3	1	4	4	6	5	5	9	9	6	1	2	2
Washington	IIIB	4	3	5	4	8	6	8	2	2	7	4	2	8	7	5
Wilson	IIIB	8	3	8	7	9	3	6	5	2	6	4	6	6	6	5
NORTH DAKOTA																
Benson	IIIA	3	7	2	1	2	9	9	1	5	7	4	9	4	3	5
Billings	IIIA	3	6	4	6	1	6	9	1	1	6	1	1	7	9	9
Bottineau	IIIA	4	8	5	6	2	5	3	6	8	3	4	7	5	5	6
Bowman	IIIA	3	6	9	6	1	8	7	2	4	3	3	4	6	8	8
Cavalier	IIIA	3	7	6	5	3	4	6	5	7	4	3	6	6	6	7
Dickey	IIIA	3	6	6	4	2	6	4	6	7	5	6	5	4	4	5
Dunn	IIIA	3	8	4	4	1	8	7	2	2	7	4	6	4	7	9
McLean	IIIA	4	9	7	7	3	8	5	3	5	3	2	3	8	8	5
Oliver	IIIA	3	5	9	8	2	9	8	1	1	5	1	3	9	9	6
Pembina	IIIA	4	6	5	6	4	6	4	5	7	3	3	8	6	6	6
Pierce	IIIA	3	6	6	7	2	4	8	3	8	4	6	4	4	5	6
Ramsey	IIIA	4	6	7	7	3	5	5	5	6	2	2	5	8	8	5
Renville	IIIA	3	5	5	5	2	3	7	4	8	5	3	9	6	7	2
Richland	IIIA	5	7	6	8	5	5	1	9	5	2	2	8	7	8	6
Rolette	IIIB	4	5	5	1	2	9	9	1	1	9	7	3	4	3	4
Stutsman	IIIA	5	9	9	8	2	6	2	7	4	3	2	8	8	8	5
Traill	IIIA	4	5	7	6	6	4	1	8	9	2	2	7	7	8	8
OHIO																
Auglaize	IIIB	7	3	8	9	9	7	6	3	3	1	1	7	9	9	5
Belmont	IIIA	9	4	7	7	4	3	3	8	5	2	2	3	9	9	4
Champaign	IIIB	6	4	8	8	9	4	6	4	2	2	1	9	9	8	5
Clinton	IIIB	6	3	7	8	9	6	5	5	2	2	2	6	8	8	6

% Completed HS	% College or More	Families/Pop	% Married Couples	% W/O Husband	% Black	% Spanish	% Amer Indian	% Asian	% Urban	% Rural	% Farmers	% Out of County	Jobs/Pop	% Manufacturing	% Wholesale	% Retail	% Services	Physicians/Cap	Crimes/Cap	$ Police/Crimes	$ Educ/Enrollment	Carpool or Transit	Pop Density
2	2	8	6	5	3	4	8	2	2	3	3	2	*	*	*	*	*	7	2	7	1	9	4
2	3	1	1	9	9	4	4	8	7	4	4	5	2	7	6	5	3	9	7	5	4	8	6
2	2	3	1	9	9	4	4	2	2	6	4	9	1	5	8	3	3	2	4	5	5	8	6
2	3	2	1	9	9	4	6	8	7	2	2	3	7	5	4	7	5	5	7	5	6	6	6
2	4	4	1	9	9	4	4	3	2	5	4	3	*	*	*	*	*	2	3	5	5	7	4
2	2	4	1	9	9	4	4	2	2	7	4	9	*	*	*	*	*	6	2	5	4	9	4
1	5	6	5	5	3	4	4	4	2	6	9	7	1	4	1	9	4	4	2	7	2	9	5
2	4	3	1	9	9	4	4	3	5	4	3	4	6	5	8	2	4	4	2	5	6	6	6
3	4	9	6	4	3	4	4	7	2	3	3	5	5	6	2	8	6	7	1	9	9	9	6
1	2	1	1	9	9	4	4	3	2	3	3	8	2	7	9	1	3	4	4	5	4	8	5
3	4	7	3	7	9	4	5	4	2	2	2	8	*	*	*	*	*	4	3	5	7	9	5
5	9	9	5	5	5	4	4	4	2	2	2	8	3	5	1	8	8	9	4	6	4	6	6
1	2	5	1	8	9	4	4	2	2	3	4	6	2	5	8	4	3	1	5	5	7	9	4
1	2	2	1	9	9	4	7	7	2	5	4	9	1	6	3	7	6	3	2	9	5	9	5
2	4	3	1	9	9	4	4	6	6	3	3	5	*	*	*	*	*	4	7	5	4	7	5
2	6	3	1	9	9	4	4	4	9	2	2	2	9	5	5	1	9	9	9	5	5	7	9
4	4	1	2	6	4	4	9	2	2	9	9	2	*	*	*	*	*	4	2	5	5	5	3
6	5	3	9	1	3	4	5	2	2	9	9	5	*	*	*	*	*	1	4	5	4	3	3
6	7	4	7	2	3	4	5	6	6	9	9	2	*	*	*	*	*	4	4	5	7	4	3
7	6	2	8	2	3	4	4	3	2	9	9	1	9	2	6	5	4	6	6	5	9	3	3
7	7	4	7	1	3	4	4	2	2	9	9	2	*	*	*	*	*	3	4	5	9	4	3
6	6	3	8	1	3	4	4	8	2	9	9	1	8	3	9	1	4	5	3	5	5	3	4
6	3	3	8	1	3	4	9	2	2	9	9	3	*	*	*	*	*	1	2	5	6	3	3
6	7	4	8	1	3	4	8	3	2	9	9	3	*	*	*	*	*	4	4	5	7	5	4
5	2	4	9	1	3	4	6	3	2	9	9	6	*	*	*	*	*	1	3	5	5	6	3
7	7	5	7	3	3	4	4	8	2	7	8	2	*	*	*	*	*	5	3	5	8	3	4
4	4	3	7	2	3	4	4	9	9	9	9	1	7	3	6	8	2	9	2	5	6	5	4
7	8	2	6	4	3	4	6	5	9	6	7	2	*	*	*	*	*	9	9	5	9	3	4
8	6	5	8	1	3	4	4	3	2	9	9	3	*	*	*	*	*	5	2	5	9	3	3
6	5	1	7	2	3	4	5	4	8	8	8	3	7	3	8	3	3	6	6	5	3	3	4
1	3	1	1	9	3	4	9	2	2	6	6	1	*	*	*	*	*	7	3	5	6	3	4
6	8	2	6	4	3	4	5	9	9	6	6	1	9	3	6	3	7	9	9	5	5	4	4
7	9	3	7	2	3	4	4	4	2	8	8	2	*	*	*	*	*	5	3	5	7	3	4
8	4	5	7	3	3	4	4	5	8	5	4	6	7	7	4	5	6	5	4	5	3	3	8
8	3	7	4	6	3	4	4	6	8	2	2	7	4	4	3	8	4	7	8	5	3	7	9
8	4	6	6	4	4	4	4	5	6	5	4	8	5	6	4	7	3	6	7	5	4	4	6
7	6	5	6	4	3	4	4	4	8	4	4	5	6	6	5	6	3	7	3	5	5	5	7

Economic Indicators For Class IIIA And IIIB Counties		SIZE OF COUNTY		REAL-ESTATE VALUES			AGES OF POPULATION				INCOMES					
		Population	Land Area	Med House Val	Med Gross Rent	Av Farm Val./Acre	% Under 5	% 5–17	% 18 and Over	% 65 and Over	% Poverty	% Under $10,000	% $10–19,999	% $20–29,999	% $30–49,999	% Over $50,000
Columbiana	IIIB	9	4	7	8	7	5	5	5	3	2	1	4	9	9	5
Coshocton	IIIB	6	4	6	6	4	4	5	5	3	2	2	4	8	8	5
Fayette	IIIB	5	3	6	8	9	6	5	5	3	4	3	7	7	5	4
Hardin	IIIB	6	4	6	8	9	4	4	6	3	3	2	5	8	9	4
Harrison	IIIA	4	3	4	6	3	4	5	5	4	3	2	5	8	8	3
Knox	IIIB	7	4	8	7	8	3	3	7	3	2	2	8	7	6	5
Monroe	IIIA	4	4	6	5	3	4	7	4	4	3	3	1	9	7	3
Muskingum	IIIB	9	4	6	7	4	5	6	5	3	2	3	5	7	7	4
Noble	IIIA	4	3	4	6	3	7	5	4	5	3	3	5	8	6	2
Paulding	IIIA	5	3	6	8	9	8	9	1	1	1	1	3	9	9	3
Ross	IIIB	9	4	8	8	8	4	5	6	2	2	2	5	8	9	6
Scioto	IIIB	9	4	4	6	5	5	6	5	4	5	5	4	5	5	4
Tuscarawas	IIIB	9	4	8	8	6	4	4	6	3	2	2	7	9	7	4
Van Wert	IIIB	6	3	7	8	9	6	4	5	4	1	1	6	9	9	5
OKLAHOMA																
Alfalfa	IIIA	3	5	2	4	6	1	2	9	9	2	4	4	6	8	8
Beaver	IIIA	3	8	6	6	2	6	5	5	5	4	2	4	9	8	8
Caddo	IIIA	6	7	3	2	4	6	6	4	7	7	6	4	2	6	7
Coal	IIIA	3	4	1	1	2	5	4	6	9	8	9	2	1	2	3
Cotton	IIIA	3	4	2	2	4	4	2	7	9	5	8	4	3	3	2
Craig	IIIA	4	5	3	3	3	3	2	8	8	3	6	8	3	4	6
Dewey	IIIA	3	6	2	3	2	8	1	8	9	4	5	1	6	5	9
Ellis	IIIA	3	6	3	6	2	6	2	7	8	2	4	4	5	7	8
Grant	IIIA	3	6	2	5	5	3	1	9	9	3	3	8	4	8	8
Hughes	IIIA	4	5	1	1	2	2	2	8	9	7	9	2	1	2	2
Kay	IIIB	8	5	6	8	5	5	1	8	7	1	2	3	8	8	8
Kingfisher	IIIA	4	5	9	8	6	8	3	5	6	2	1	5	9	9	9
Kiowa	IIIA	4	6	2	1	4	3	1	8	9	8	9	1	3	2	5
Okfushkee	IIIA	4	4	1	1	2	2	7	5	9	8	9	1	2	2	2
Okmulgee	IIIA	7	4	2	4	4	3	3	7	7	6	8	2	3	3	3
Ottawa	IIIA	6	4	3	3	4	3	3	7	5	4	6	5	5	3	3
Pittsburg	IIIA	7	6	2	3	2	2	3	8	7	5	7	6	3	2	4
Roger Mills	IIIA	3	6	2	3	2	6	2	7	8	4	5	8	1	4	9
Seminole	IIIA	5	4	2	2	3	4	4	6	8	5	7	3	3	3	6
Tillman	IIIA	4	5	2	2	4	5	6	5	8	7	8	4	2	2	8
Baker	IIIA	4	9	7	7	2	4	3	6	6	3	4	6	5	7	3
Sherman	IIIA	3	5	4	8	2	7	4	5	3	4	2	8	7	7	3
PENNSYLVANIA																
Armstrong	IIIB	9	4	6	6	7	2	3	8	5	2	2	6	8	7	3

% Completed HS	% College or More	Families/Pop	% Married Couples	% W/O Husband	% Black	% Spanish	% Amer Indian	% Asian	% Urban	% Rural	% Farmers	% Out of County	Jobs/Pop	% Manufacturing	% Wholesale	% Retail	% Services	Physicians/Cap	Crimes/Cap	$ Police/Crimes	$ Educ/Enrollment	Carpool or Transit	Pop Density
8	4	6	5	5	3	4	4	5	8	2	2	7	5	5	3	7	5	6	5	5	3	4	9
8	4	6	6	4	3	4	4	8	7	3	3	2	5	7	3	6	5	4	4	5	5	5	6
6	3	7	5	5	3	4	4	7	8	4	3	5	8	5	3	8	4	5	9	4	3	4	6
7	5	2	7	4	3	4	4	5	8	6	4	5	4	6	6	6	2	6	7	5	3	4	6
8	2	6	6	4	3	4	4	4	5	3	3	7	3	5	7	3	5	4	9	4	4	4	5
8	6	4	7	4	3	4	4	5	6	4	3	4	5	4	2	6	7	7	5	5	3	4	7
8	2	6	7	3	3	4	4	3	4	4	6	5	*	*	*	*	*	2	*	*	9	8	5
7	4	4	4	6	4	4	4	4	6	2	2	3	7	5	5	5	6	9	8	5	5	5	8
8	2	5	7	4	3	4	4	3	2	5	6	7	*	*	*	*	*	3	*	*	4	6	4
7	1	4	8	3	3	5	4	3	3	5	4	9	2	6	6	6	4	3	2	5	4	5	5
6	4	3	4	6	4	4	4	7	7	2	2	3	7	5	3	7	5	7	9	4	5	4	7
5	3	4	3	7	4	4	4	5	8	2	2	3	6	3	3	7	5	8	9	4	4	5	8
8	3	6	6	4	3	4	4	5	8	2	2	3	8	5	3	6	6	6	5	5	6	4	9
9	3	6	8	3	3	4	4	7	8	5	4	5	6	7	6	4	4	5	7	5	5	3	6
8	9	8	9	1	3	4	5	2	2	9	9	2	4	2	9	4	2	3	4	5	8	4	4
8	9	9	9	2	3	4	5	3	2	9	9	4	*	*	*	*	*	3	5	5	9	5	3
4	5	5	5	6	4	5	9	3	4	5	5	3	*	*	*	*	*	3	4	5	6	3	4
2	3	6	5	6	3	4	9	3	2	7	9	6	*	*	*	*	*	3	2	5	5	6	4
7	4	8	6	4	3	5	9	2	7	7	7	4	*	*	*	*	*	2	5	5	3	4	4
7	4	5	6	4	4	4	9	5	8	7	8	3	5	3	4	8	3	9	6	5	4	4	4
8	7	8	7	2	3	4	7	5	2	8	9	3	4	2	9	4	2	2	5	5	9	3	4
8	8	8	8	2	3	4	5	3	2	9	9	3	*	*	*	*	*	9	3	5	7	4	3
9	9	9	8	2	3	4	5	3	2	9	9	3	5	2	9	1	2	2	4	5	8	3	4
4	4	8	5	5	4	4	9	3	7	5	6	4	*	*	*	*	*	7	6	5	3	5	4
8	9	8	7	4	3	5	8	7	9	3	2	1	9	4	4	6	5	8	9	5	3	4	6
7	7	7	8	2	4	4	6	2	6	8	7	3	8	2	6	3	6	3	4	5	8	3	4
6	5	8	6	4	4	6	7	4	7	5	5	3	5	3	8	4	3	6	3	5	7	3	4
3	3	5	4	6	6	4	9	5	6	5	7	7	1	4	3	8	3	3	2	5	5	5	4
5	4	5	3	8	6	4	9	5	9	2	3	4	4	3	3	7	6	6	8	5	2	5	6
6	4	6	5	6	3	4	9	5	8	3	3	2	7	6	3	3	9	4	7	5	3	6	
6	5	7	5	6	4	4	9	8	8	3	3	2	5	3	3	5	7	8	6	5	3	4	5
6	6	9	8	2	3	4	8	5	2	9	9	5	*	*	*	*	*	2	4	5	2	4	3
5	5	6	3	7	5	4	9	6	8	3	4	4	4	5	4	6	5	4	8	4	5	4	5
4	7	5	5	6	5	8	6	9	8	5	4	2	6	4	6	1	9	3	7	5	4	3	4
9	8	7	7	3	3	4	5	9	9	4	5	1	*	*	*	*	*	7	9	5	7	4	3
9	9	8	9	1	3	5	5	9	2	9	9	3	*	*	*	*	*	1	6	5	9	4	3
8	3	7	6	4	3	4	4	3	4	2	2	8	4	5	2	8	4	5	3	5	7	6	8

Economic Indicators For Class IIIA And IIIB Counties

		SIZE OF COUNTY		REAL-ESTATE VALUES			AGES OF POPULATION				INCOMES					
		Population	Land Area	Med House Val	Med Gross Rent	Av Farm Val./Acre	% Under 5	% 5-17	% 18 and Over	% 65 and Over	% Poverty	% Under $10,000	% $10–19,999	% $20–29,999	% $30–49,999	% Over $50,000
Bedford	IIIB	7	6	6	6	6	4	6	5	3	4	4	9	5	3	3
Blair	IIIB	9	4	4	7	9	3	3	7	5	2	3	7	8	5	4
Bradford	IIIB	8	6	5	8	4	5	8	3	3	3	3	9	7	5	3
Cambria	IIIB	9	4	5	7	5	2	3	8	4	2	2	4	9	8	6
Carbon	IIIA	8	3	4	6	9	1	2	9	6	1	2	8	8	7	3
Clinton	IIIB	7	5	6	7	7	2	2	8	3	2	2	9	8	4	3
Fayette	IIIA	9	5	4	5	6	2	4	7	5	4	4	3	7	7	4
Forest	IIIA	3	4	4	5	5	1	4	8	7	2	4	9	5	3	2
Huntington	IIIB	7	5	4	5	5	2	4	7	3	3	4	8	6	3	2
Jefferson	IIIA	7	4	6	6	5	4	4	6	5	2	2	7	8	6	6
Lebanon	IIIB	9	3	8	8	9	3	3	7	3	1	1	6	9	9	6
Luzerne	IIIA	9	5	5	7	8	1	1	9	7	2	3	8	7	5	4
Lycoming	IIIB	9	6	8	8	7	3	3	7	3	2	2	8	8	7	4
Mifflin	IIIB	7	3	4	6	6	2	6	6	4	3	3	6	7	5	2
Northumberla	IIIA	9	4	3	5	8	1	2	8	7	2	5	8	6	3	2
Potter	IIIA	4	6	4	6	3	4	8	3	4	4	5	8	6	2	2
Schuylkill	IIIA	9	5	2	4	7	1	2	9	7	2	4	9	5	3	3
Somerset	IIIB	9	6	6	7	5	4	3	7	4	2	2	7	8	6	5
Sullivan	IIIA	3	4	5	6	5	1	5	7	7	3	4	9	3	3	2
Susquehanna	IIIA	7	5	6	7	5	4	6	4	4	3	3	8	7	5	3
Venango	IIIB	9	4	5	8	5	4	4	6	3	2	1	5	9	8	6
Washington	IIIB	9	5	8	8	8	2	2	8	4	2	1	2	9	9	8
SOUTH CAROLINA																
Abbeville	IIIA	5	4	4	2	4	3	5	5	3	4	3	9	7	4	2
Allendale	IIIA	4	3	2	2	3	8	9	1	3	9	9	1	3	1	6
Chester	IIIA	6	4	3	3	3	4	7	3	3	4	4	3	8	5	2
Clarendon	IIIA	5	4	4	1	6	7	9	1	2	9	8	5	3	2	3
Dillon	IIIB	6	3	3	3	7	9	9	1	1	9	8	6	2	2	5
Fairfield	IIIA	5	4	3	3	3	5	9	2	3	8	5	5	5	5	2
Laurens	IIIB	8	5	4	4	4	2	5	6	2	2	2	7	8	6	3
Lee	IIIA	5	3	3	2	5	9	9	1	1	9	6	8	3	3	3
McCormick	IIIA	3	3	3	1	4	6	9	2	2	8	7	4	6	2	2
Newberry	IIIA	6	4	4	3	5	2	3	7	5	3	3	5	8	5	5
Saluda	IIIA	4	4	5	2	4	5	7	4	3	7	5	8	6	2	2
Union	IIIB	6	4	2	3	3	3	5	6	3	2	3	8	7	4	1
SOUTH DAKOTA																
Bennett	IIIA	3	6	4	1	1	9	9	1	2	9	9	3	1	3	2
Brookings	IIIB	5	5	9	7	4	3	1	9	2	3	4	7	5	6	3
Butte	IIIA	3	9	7	4	1	7	5	4	5	4	5	8	4	3	7

SOCIO-ECONOMIC STATUS					MINORITIES				RURAL-URBAN				ECONOMIC BASE					COUNTY CONDITIONS					
% Completed HS	% College or More	Families/Pop	% Married Couples	% W/O Husband	% Black	% Spanish	% Amer Indian	% Asian	% Urban	% Rural	% Farmers	% Out of County	Jobs/Pop	% Manufacturing	% Wholesale	% Retail	% Services	Physicians/Cap	Crimes/Cap	$ Police/Crimes	$ Educ/Enrollment	Carpool or Transit	Pop Density
7	2	6	6	4	3	4	4	3	2	3	3	5	7	3	2	6	7	4	4	4	6	5	5
9	4	5	3	8	3	4	4	5	9	2	1	1	9	4	4	4	8	9	5	5	5	8	9
8	4	4	5	5	3	4	4	6	5	3	3	4	4	6	4	6	4	9	5	4	7	6	6
7	4	4	3	6	3	4	4	4	9	2	1	2	8	4	2	7	6	9	4	5	5	9	9
8	3	7	4	6	3	4	4	7	9	2	1	8	3	8	1	8	6	7	4	5	6	8	8
7	5	4	4	6	3	4	4	5	5	2	2	4	6	7	2	8	6	7	6	4	6	6	5
7	3	5	2	8	4	4	4	5	6	2	2	7	7	4	4	7	4	6	5	5	4	8	9
8	2	6	6	3	3	4	4	4	2	2	2	6	3	7	1	9	4	4	9	4	8	5	4
7	4	2	4	6	3	4	4	5	5	2	2	5	4	5	4	6	5	7	5	4	4	8	5
8	4	6	5	5	3	4	4	4	6	2	2	5	6	7	7	3	4	6	4	5	5	5	6
7	5	5	5	5	3	4	4	9	7	2	2	5	8	6	3	7	5	8	7	5	5	5	9
8	6	5	1	9	3	4	4	6	9	2	1	2	8	5	4	4	6	9	5	5	5	9	9
8	6	4	4	6	3	4	4	8	9	2	2	2	8	6	7	3	5	9	8	5	7	9	7
7	3	6	5	5	3	4	4	4	4	3	2	3	6	6	4	6	4	8	6	5	9	6	8
8	3	7	3	7	3	4	4	3	8	2	2	6	5	7	3	7	5	5	4	5	5	6	9
7	4	4	5	4	3	4	4	7	4	3	3	5	3	5	1	6	9	8	5	4	5	8	4
8	2	7	2	7	3	4	4	6	8	2	1	4	5	7	4	5	5	7	4	5	4	7	9
7	3	6	6	5	3	4	4	4	4	2	2	5	6	4	5	1	9	6	4	5	5	6	6
7	4	2	6	3	3	4	4	2	2	3	4	7	*	*	*	*	*	2	7	4	8	8	4
8	4	5	5	4	3	4	4	6	2	3	3	8	2	5	2	7	7	5	3	4	8	7	5
8	5	5	5	5	3	4	4	8	8	2	2	2	6	7	3	6	5	9	6	5	7	5	7
8	7	6	4	6	4	4	4	5	9	2	2	7	7	5	3	5	7	8	5	5	5	9	9
1	4	4	1	9	9	4	4	3	5	2	2	6	2	9	1	8	3	4	6	5	1	8	5
1	5	1	1	9	9	5	4	7	7	2	2	7	4	5	3	3	9	3	7	5	2	9	4
1	4	3	1	9	9	4	4	2	6	2	2	4	5	9	8	1	5	6	9	5	2	9	5
1	3	1	1	9	9	5	4	6	4	3	3	6	5	4	3	3	9	3	8	5	2	9	5
1	3	1	1	9	9	4	5	8	5	3	2	4	5	5	6	3	7	4	8	5	2	8	6
1	4	1	1	9	9	4	4	2	3	2	2	8	2	8	1	9	3	3	7	5	3	9	4
1	4	2	1	9	9	4	4	3	7	2	2	4	3	9	2	7	5	6	5	5	1	7	6
1	3	1	1	9	9	4	4	2	4	3	2	8	2	5	7	4	4	3	4	5	2	9	5
1	4	1	1	9	9	5	4	2	2	2	2	8	1	9	2	7	6	2	3	5	3	9	4
2	7	4	2	8	9	4	4	4	6	2	2	5	4	8	2	8	4	7	7	5	2	8	5
2	3	3	2	8	9	4	4	2	4	4	4	9	2	8	6	5	3	2	4	5	1	9	5
2	4	6	1	9	9	4	4	4	6	2	2	3	3	9	1	9	3	4	8	5	3	9	6
5	4	1	2	7	3	4	9	2	2	9	9	2	*	*	*	*	*	3	3	5	6	3	3
3	9	1	8	2	3	4	4	9	9	6	6	2	9	3	7	5	4	6	5	5	1	3	5
7	7	5	6	4	3	5	5	3	9	6	7	2	8	3	7	5	3	3	5	5	6	9	3

Economic Indicators For Class IIIA And IIIB Counties		SIZE OF COUNTY		REAL-ESTATE VALUES			AGES OF POPULATION				INCOMES					
		Population	Land Area	Med House Val	Med Gross Rent	Av Farm Val./Acre	% Under 5	% 5-17	% 18 and Over	% 65 and Over	% Poverty	% Under $10,000	% $10-19,999	% $20-29,999	% $30-49,999	% Over $50,000
Charles Mix	IIIA	4	6	2	3	2	9	8	1	6	9	8	5	2	2	2
Codington	IIIB	5	4	7	6	2	8	3	5	4	2	4	7	5	5	7
Corson	IIIA	3	9	1	1	1	9	9	1	1	9	9	1	1	5	3
Davison	IIIB	4	4	5	5	2	7	2	7	6	3	5	6	7	2	3
Day	IIIA	3	6	2	3	2	5	4	6	9	6	8	7	2	2	2
Deuel	IIIA	3	4	1	3	3	4	6	5	8	8	9	4	2	2	2
Dewey	IIIA	3	9	1	1	1	9	9	1	1	9	7	3	3	3	4
Grant	IIIA	4	4	6	5	2	7	7	3	6	3	5	9	4	3	2
Hamlin	IIIA	3	4	1	4	3	6	4	5	9	7	9	4	2	1	2
Lawrence	IIIA	5	5	8	7	2	6	2	7	4	3	4	7	5	6	2
Perkins	IIIA	3	9	3	3	1	5	3	6	6	6	6	3	4	5	7
Roberts	IIIA	4	6	2	1	2	7	8	2	8	8	8	3	2	3	2
Ziebach	IIIA	3	8	1	1	1	9	9	1	1	9	9	4	1	2	2
TENNESSEE																
Carroll	IIIB	6	4	3	4	4	3	3	7	6	5	7	6	4	2	3
Crockett	IIIA	4	3	3	3	8	3	5	6	7	7	7	7	3	2	4
Gibson	IIIB	8	4	4	4	7	2	4	7	7	5	6	6	4	3	4
Giles	IIIA	5	4	4	4	4	3	4	7	6	5	5	8	4	5	4
Hancock	IIIA	3	3	2	1	4	5	5	5	4	9	9	1	1	1	1
Hardeman	IIIB	5	4	3	2	4	7	7	3	5	9	8	6	3	1	3
Haywood	IIIA	5	4	4	2	6	8	8	2	5	9	9	3	1	2	4
Lake	IIIA	3	3	3	1	8	5	6	5	6	9	9	3	1	2	6
Lincoln	IIIA	5	4	4	4	5	2	4	7	4	5	5	8	4	4	3
Obion	IIIB	6	4	4	5	7	4	4	6	5	4	5	4	6	5	5
TEXAS																
Armstrong	IIIA	3	5	3	6	1	3	1	9	9	2	3	2	8	9	8
Baylor	IIIA	3	5	2	1	2	1	1	9	9	3	7	3	5	4	3
Borden	IIIA	3	5	1	1	1	7	7	3	2	5	3	4	3	8	9
Carson	IIIA	3	5	3	8	2	5	6	4	4	2	1	4	9	9	9
Childress	IIIA	3	5	2	4	2	4	1	8	9	3	8	2	3	3	4
Coke	IIIA	3	5	2	1	2	1	1	9	9	2	5	1	6	5	9
Coleman	IIIA	4	7	1	1	2	3	1	9	9	4	8	5	2	2	3
Collingswort	IIIA	3	5	1	3	2	3	4	6	9	8	8	1	1	7	4
Colorado	IIIA	5	5	4	4	5	4	2	7	8	6	6	1	5	6	9
Comanche	IIIA	4	5	2	1	3	1	1	9	9	4	8	1	2	4	9
Concho	IIIA	3	6	1	1	2	4	3	7	9	5	7	4	1	3	9
Cottle	IIIA	3	5	1	1	2	4	2	8	9	6	7	3	1	6	9
Dallam	IIIA	3	7	1	6	2	9	7	2	3	6	6	9	1	3	3
Delta	IIIA	3	3	1	1	3	1	2	9	9	5	9	2	1	2	3

SOCIO-ECONOMIC STATUS					MINORITIES				RURAL-URBAN				ECONOMIC BASE					COUNTY CONDITIONS					
% Completed HS	% College or More	Families/Pop	% Married Couples	% W/O Husband	% Black	% Spanish	% Amer Indian	% Asian	% Urban	% Rural	% Farmers	% Out of County	Jobs/Pop	% Manufacturing	% Wholesale	% Retail	% Services	Physicians/Cap	Crimes/Cap	$ Police/Crimes	$ Educ/Enrollment	Carpool or Transit	Pop Density
5	5	1	3	6	3	4	9	4	2	9	9	1	*	*	*	*	*	5	3	5	7	3	4
8	7	3	6	4	3	4	4	7	9	5	4	1	9	3	7	2	6	9	7	5	4	3	4
2	2	1	1	9	3	4	9	7	2	9	9	3	*	*	*	*	*	2	1	9	6	3	3
7	8	2	6	5	3	4	6	6	9	4	3	1	9	3	5	5	5	9	8	5	4	3	5
7	6	5	6	2	3	4	8	2	2	9	9	1	5	3	9	2	4	3	1	6	7	4	4
6	4	5	8	1	3	4	4	4	2	9	9	2	*	*	*	*	*	4	1	5	5	3	4
2	3	1	1	9	3	4	9	2	2	9	7	1	*	*	*	*	*	2	*	*	4	3	3
7	5	3	8	2	3	4	4	4	8	9	9	2	6	4	4	7	4	3	2	5	9	3	4
7	3	5	8	2	3	4	4	3	2	9	9	3	*	*	*	*	*	1	*	*	7	3	4
8	9	2	5	5	3	4	5	9	9	2	2	2	9	3	2	4	9	8	8	5	3	4	4
8	6	7	8	2	3	4	5	3	2	9	9	1	*	*	*	*	*	4	*	*	8	3	3
5	4	1	3	5	3	4	9	5	5	9	9	2	*	*	*	*	*	4	*	*	7	5	4
2	2	1	1	8	3	4	9	3	2	9	8	4	*	*	*	*	*	1	*	*	1	3	3
2	3	9	5	6	5	4	4	6	6	4	4	6	3	7	5	7	3	5	4	5	3	8	5
3	2	7	3	7	7	4	4	2	4	6	4	8	2	9	9	2	2	3	3	5	2	3	6
4	3	8	3	8	7	4	4	4	8	4	3	3	4	8	4	6	5	5	5	5	2	6	7
4	3	8	3	7	6	4	4	7	6	6	7	3	5	7	6	4	5	5	4	5	2	7	5
1	1	8	4	6	3	4	4	3	2	9	9	9	*	*	*	*	*	3	1	5	4	9	5
1	2	1	1	9	9	5	4	7	5	2	3	3	2	5	5	8	2	7	4	5	2	7	5
1	3	2	1	9	9	4	4	3	8	4	3	5	3	5	5	7	3	5	6	5	2	7	5
1	2	4	1	9	7	4	4	2	2	3	2	5	*	*	*	*	*	3	4	5	3	8	5
3	3	8	4	6	5	4	4	8	6	7	7	5	4	7	8	2	5	6	4	5	3	8	5
5	3	8	4	6	5	4	4	5	7	4	3	3	*	*	*	*	*	7	4	5	3	5	6
8	9	9	9	1	3	5	4	2	2	8	9	8	*	*	*	*	*	1	4	5	4	4	3
6	5	9	8	2	4	6	5	2	9	3	5	1	8	2	5	5	5	5	5	5	4	3	3
3	6	9	9	1	3	8	4	2	2	9	9	5	*	*	*	*	*	1	1	6	9	9	3
7	8	7	9	1	3	5	5	7	2	5	4	6	*	*	*	*	*	1	2	5	7	3	4
4	4	8	6	4	4	8	4	3	9	3	3	1	*	*	*	*	*	8	6	5	2	3	4
6	7	9	8	2	3	8	5	9	2	5	6	5	*	*	*	*	*	3	7	5	8	3	3
4	4	9	6	5	4	7	4	6	9	5	6	3	5	4	4	2	9	7	3	5	5	4	4
4	9	7	6	4	4	8	5	5	9	7	5	2	*	*	*	*	*	6	5	5	4	3	3
2	4	5	4	5	7	9	4	3	7	4	5	4	9	3	6	5	4	8	4	5	4	4	4
3	5	9	7	3	3	8	4	4	6	8	8	3	7	3	9	3	2	3	3	5	6	3	4
3	8	7	8	2	3	9	4	7	2	8	9	6	*	*	*	*	*	1	3	5	5	5	3
2	4	8	8	3	4	9	4	2	2	6	5	1	*	*	*	*	*	6	3	6	5	3	3
6	3	5	6	3	3	9	4	2	9	7	4	3	*	*	*	*	*	5	6	5	6	3	3
3	4	8	5	5	5	4	5	5	2	5	7	8	*	*	*	*	*	2	4	5	4	7	4

Economic Indicators For Class IIIA And IIIB Counties

		SIZE OF COUNTY		REAL-ESTATE VALUES			AGES OF POPULATION				INCOMES					
		Population	Land Area	Med House Val	Med Gross Rent	Av Farm Val./Acre	% Under 5	% 5–17	% 18 and Over	% 65 and Over	% Poverty	% Under $10,000	% $10–19,999	% $20–29,999	% $30–49,999	% Over $50,000
De Witt	IIIA	5	5	2	2	4	3	2	8	9	7	8	1	3	4	6
Dickens	IIIA	3	5	1	1	1	5	2	7	9	8	9	1	1	3	1
Donley	IIIA	3	5	2	2	1	1	1	9	9	6	7	1	5	3	7
Eastland	IIIA	5	5	1	3	2	2	1	9	9	4	8	3	3	2	5
Edwards	IIIA	3	9	1	2	1	8	9	1	5	9	8	3	1	3	6
Falls	IIIA	4	5	1	1	3	2	2	8	9	8	9	1	2	3	2
Fannin	IIIA	5	5	1	2	3	1	1	9	9	4	6	4	4	5	4
Fayette	IIIA	5	5	5	3	6	2	1	9	9	5	7	1	5	5	6
Fisher	IIIA	3	5	1	1	2	3	3	7	9	4	3	4	7	5	9
Foard	IIIA	3	4	1	1	2	2	1	9	9	5	8	3	1	4	9
Garza	IIIB	3	5	1	3	1	9	7	2	4	5	4	5	4	7	9
Goliad	IIIA	3	5	3	5	3	3	7	4	6	6	5	1	7	4	8
Gonzales	IIIA	4	6	2	2	3	6	5	5	8	7	8	2	2	5	5
Grayson	IIIB	9	5	4	8	5	3	2	8	6	2	2	4	8	8	7
Hall	IIIA	3	5	2	1	2	5	2	7	9	9	8	2	2	3	8
Hardeman	IIIA	3	4	1	4	2	4	2	7	9	4	5	1	7	5	9
Haskell	IIIA	3	5	1	2	2	3	2	8	9	5	6	2	3	5	9
Hill	IIIA	5	5	2	3	4	2	1	9	9	4	8	3	3	4	6
Jack	IIIA	3	5	2	5	2	4	1	8	9	3	4	6	4	6	7
Jackson	IIIB	4	5	4	7	4	6	5	4	4	4	3	2	8	7	6
Jeff Davis	IIIA	3	9	1	2	1	6	3	6	5	8	7	7	2	2	6
Jim Hogg	IIIB	3	6	1	3	1	9	9	1	3	9	7	1	5	3	9
Jones	IIIA	4	5	1	2	2	4	4	6	9	4	6	2	4	5	9
Karnes	IIIA	4	5	2	3	3	7	7	3	6	7	7	1	4	7	7
Kimble	IIIB	3	6	3	1	2	1	3	8	9	4	6	5	5	2	4
King	IIIA	3	5	1	1	1	8	7	3	1	4	4	8	9	1	6
Kinney	IIIA	3	7	1	2	2	4	9	2	5	9	9	5	1	2	2
Knox	IIIA	3	5	1	1	2	2	3	8	9	7	7	1	3	7	9
Lamb	IIIB	5	6	2	7	4	9	8	2	5	6	4	7	3	6	7
La Salle	IIIA	3	7	1	1	2	9	9	1	3	9	9	1	1	3	4
Lavaca	IIIA	5	5	3	2	4	3	1	8	9	4	7	2	5	5	4
Leon	IIIA	4	6	2	4	4	2	1	9	9	8	9	1	2	5	5
Lipscomb	IIIA	3	5	4	8	2	9	4	4	4	3	2	4	7	8	9
McCulloch	IIIA	4	6	2	5	2	2	2	8	9	7	9	2	1	4	7
Martin	IIIA	3	5	3	4	2	6	9	1	3	4	3	1	8	8	9
Mason	IIIA	3	5	3	1	3	2	1	9	9	4	7	4	1	6	3
Mills	IIIA	3	5	2	1	2	1	1	9	9	5	8	7	2	1	2
Mitchell	IIIA	4	5	1	4	1	5	5	5	9	7	6	3	2	7	9
Nolan	IIIA	4	5	2	5	2	6	4	5	7	4	4	4	5	6	8
Presidio	IIIA	3	9	1	1	1	5	9	1	5	9	9	1	1	1	3
Robertson	IIIA	4	5	1	2	4	5	5	5	9	8	8	1	3	3	7

SOCIO-ECONOMIC STATUS					MINORITIES				RURAL-URBAN				ECONOMIC BASE					COUNTY CONDITIONS					
% Completed HS	% College or More	Families/Pop	% Married Couples	% W/O Husband	% Black	% Spanish	% Amer Indian	% Asian	% Urban	% Rural	% Farmers	% Out of County	Jobs/Pop	% Manufacturing	% Wholesale	% Retail	% Services	Physicians/Cap	Crimes/Cap	$ Police/Crimes	$ Educ/Enrollment	Carpool or Transit	Pop Density
2	3	5	4	6	5	9	4	3	8	4	6	4	6	4	5	6	4	4	3	5	7	4	4
2	2	8	8	2	4	9	4	4	2	8	8	2	*	*	*	*	*	3	5	5	7	4	3
5	7	9	8	2	4	5	4	2	2	6	6	3	6	2	1	9	5	3	6	5	6	3	3
5	5	7	6	4	3	6	4	7	9	4	4	2	6	3	8	3	4	5	4	5	8	3	4
2	6	3	6	4	3	9	4	4	2	5	8	2	*	*	*	*	*	4	2	5	9	6	3
2	5	4	2	8	8	7	4	3	7	5	5	5	4	3	2	7	6	8	3	5	3	5	4
4	6	7	6	4	5	4	4	5	6	4	5	5	3	4	3	9	2	4	3	5	3	5	4
2	4	8	7	3	5	6	4	7	4	7	9	3	9	3	7	6	2	6	2	5	3	3	4
4	5	7	9	2	4	9	4	4	2	8	8	4	*	*	*	*	*	8	3	5	6	3	4
4	7	8	6	4	4	8	4	2	2	6	7	2	*	*	*	*	*	4	2	5	4	3	3
2	5	5	6	4	4	9	6	5	9	5	4	2	*	*	*	*	*	5	5	5	9	3	4
2	4	5	7	3	5	9	4	3	2	5	8	7	*	*	*	*	*	2	2	5	7	8	4
2	3	3	3	7	5	9	4	3	8	6	7	2	7	4	9	2	4	3	5	5	4	3	4
6	8	7	5	6	4	4	5	6	9	2	2	2	8	5	3	6	6	9	9	4	3	3	7
5	3	7	8	2	5	9	4	3	9	5	4	2	6	2	7	3	5	5	3	5	8	3	4
3	7	7	7	3	5	7	4	2	9	5	4	2	*	*	*	*	*	4	4	5	4	3	4
2	7	8	8	2	4	9	4	8	8	6	6	2	5	2	5	7	3	5	4	5	5	3	4
4	4	7	6	5	5	6	4	7	6	4	5	5	*	*	*	*	*	7	5	5	4	5	4
5	3	9	8	2	3	5	4	4	9	3	5	4	4	3	7	5	4	5	3	5	4	4	4
2	4	5	5	5	5	9	4	2	8	4	4	7	*	*	*	*	*	3	3	5	8	6	4
2	9	6	8	3	3	9	4	4	2	4	4	2	*	*	*	*	*	5	1	6	6	3	3
1	4	2	2	8	3	9	4	2	9	2	2	5	*	*	*	*	*	2	2	5	7	4	3
3	6	7	7	3	4	9	4	9	9	5	4	7	*	*	*	*	*	5	3	5	5	4	4
1	4	3	4	6	3	9	4	2	9	5	5	3	7	3	7	5	3	3	2	5	3	4	4
6	4	8	6	4	3	9	4	2	9	4	8	2	*	*	*	*	*	6	2	5	4	9	3
8	3	8	9	1	4	7	4	2	2	9	8	3	2	2	1	9	1	1	2	5	9	9	3
1	3	3	5	4	4	9	5	9	2	5	3	2	7	2	1	1	9	1	1	*	4	6	3
3	6	8	7	3	4	9	4	4	2	6	5	3	*	*	*	*	*	3	4	5	9	3	4
2	5	5	8	3	4	9	4	3	7	6	4	3	5	4	8	3	5	4	6	5	5	3	4
1	3	1	2	7	3	9	4	2	9	2	3	5	*	*	*	*	*	2	2	5	9	7	3
2	4	7	6	4	5	7	4	3	7	7	8	5	5	5	4	7	4	5	3	5	2	4	4
3	5	8	5	5	7	5	4	3	2	5	7	4	*	*	*	*	*	5	2	5	6	5	4
6	9	8	9	1	3	7	5	3	2	6	6	4	5	2	9	1	2	3	2	5	9	3	3
2	7	7	7	4	3	9	4	2	9	4	4	1	8	3	4	7	4	6	6	5	3	3	4
3	2	5	8	1	3	9	4	3	2	8	7	4	*	*	*	*	*	2	4	5	7	5	3
4	9	9	8	2	3	9	4	3	2	8	9	2	8	2	9	2	4	1	2	5	8	4	3
3	8	9	8	2	3	7	4	9	2	9	9	3	*	*	*	*	*	6	2	5	6	5	4
3	4	5	6	4	4	9	4	4	9	5	4	2	6	3	5	8	2	4	6	5	6	5	4
4	3	7	6	5	4	9	4	4	9	2	2	1	9	4	6	4	6	5	9	5	5	3	4
1	7	1	2	7	3	9	4	3	2	2	2	2	*	*	*	*	*	7	2	5	4	4	3
2	3	2	1	9	9	7	4	2	7	4	5	5	3	3	6	7	3	4	8	4	4	6	4

Economic Indicators For Class IIIA And IIB Counties		SIZE OF COUNTY		REAL-ESTATE VALUES			AGES OF POPULATION				INCOMES					
		Population	Land Area	Med House Val	Med Gross Rent	Av Farm Val./Acre	% Under 5	% 5-17	% 18 and Over	% 65 and Over	% Poverty	% Under $10,000	% $10–19,999	% $20–29,999	% $30–49,999	% Over $50,000
Runnels	IIIA	4	6	1	2	2	4	3	7	9	5	6	6	3	4	8
Stonewall	IIIA	3	5	2	3	1	4	1	9	9	4	6	5	5	5	2
Throckmorton	IIIA	3	5	1	1	1	1	1	9	9	6	8	2	2	3	9
Wharton	IIIB	7	6	6	7	5	7	6	4	4	5	3	1	8	9	8
Wheeler	IIIA	3	5	2	7	2	6	2	7	9	4	5	1	5	7	9
Wilbarger	IIIA	4	5	2	4	1	4	2	8	9	5	6	1	4	5	9
Zavala	IIIB	4	7	1	1	2	9	9	1	1	9	9	2	1	2	2
VERMONT																
Franklin	IIIB	6	4	8	9	4	7	8	2	2	4	3	8	6	6	5
Rutland	IIIB	8	5	8	9	3	2	3	7	4	2	2	9	7	6	4
Washington	IIIB	8	4	8	8	5	3	4	7	3	2	2	9	6	6	4
Windham	IIIB	6	5	8	9	6	3	3	7	4	3	3	8	5	5	6
VIRGINIA																
Accomack	IIIA	6	4	4	4	8	2	3	8	7	6	8	3	2	4	6
Brunswick	IIIA	4	4	4	2	4	2	6	6	3	8	8	5	3	2	3
Charlotte	IIIA	4	4	4	1	4	2	7	5	4	8	7	5	3	2	2
Grayson	IIIA	4	4	3	2	5	1	3	8	5	4	7	9	1	2	3
Halifax	IIIA	6	5	4	2	3	3	6	6	3	6	5	8	5	2	3
King and Queen	IIIA	3	3	6	8	5	4	2	7	4	4	6	5	4	5	7
Lancaster	IIIB	4	3	8	9	7	1	1	9	9	4	5	2	5	6	9
Lunenburg	IIIA	4	4	3	4	4	2	5	6	4	5	7	6	3	4	3
Mathews	IIIA	3	2	9	7	9	1	1	9	9	1	3	4	7	7	8
Macklenburg	IIIA	6	4	4	3	4	3	4	7	4	7	6	7	4	3	5
Nelson	IIIA	4	4	4	4	4	1	4	7	5	5	6	3	5	4	6
Northampton	IIIA	4	3	3	3	8	3	2	8	7	8	9	3	1	2	2
Northumberland	IIIA	4	3	8	7	8	1	1	9	9	2	3	7	5	5	9
Nottoway	IIIB	4	3	3	7	6	2	3	8	7	4	5	6	6	4	4
Richmond	IIIA	3	3	7	9	7	2	2	8	6	4	4	5	6	6	7
Rockbrige	IIIA	4	4	6	6	5	1	4	7	2	4	4	8	5	5	3
Scott	IIIB	5	4	4	4	4	2	4	7	4	8	8	4	4	2	1
Smyth	IIIB	6	4	5	5	5	2	4	7	3	3	5	9	3	2	4
Southampton	IIIA	5	4	7	2	7	2	4	7	2	8	5	3	7	6	3
Surry	IIIA	3	3	4	7	6	3	7	4	4	6	5	8	4	4	5
WASHINGTON																
Lincoln	IIIA	4	9	5	6	2	3	3	7	7	2	1	9	8	7	9
Pacific	IIIB	4	5	7	7	9	3	1	9	8	2	4	3	6	7	9
Wahkiakum	IIIA	3	3	9	7	9	5	7	4	4	3	2	1	9	9	9

	SOCIO-ECONOMIC STATUS					MINORITIES				RURAL-URBAN				ECONOMIC BASE					COUNTY CONDITIONS					
	% Completed HS	% College or More	% Families/Pop	% Married Couples	% W/O Husband	% Black	% Spanish	% Amer Indian	% Asian	% Urban	% Rural	% Farmers	% Out of County	Jobs/Pop	% Manufacturing	% Wholesale	% Retail	% Services	Physicians/Cap	Crimes/Cap	$ Police/Crimes	$ Educ/Enrollment	Carpool or Transit	Pop Density
	2	5	7	7	3	3	9	4	7	9	6	7	2	6	4	8	3	2	5	2	5	4	4	4
	5	4	9	8	2	3	7	4	2	2	8	8	2	2	2	7	3	5	7	2	5	7	3	3
	5	8	9	8	2	3	6	4	9	2	8	8	2	1	2	3	8	5	4	2	5	7	3	3
	2	6	3	4	6	7	9	4	2	8	3	3	4	8	3	6	3	6	8	8	5	7	6	5
	5	7	9	7	3	3	6	5	9	7	5	5	2	*	*	*	*	*	5	4	5	9	3	4
	4	7	5	6	5	5	7	5	8	9	3	3	1	7	3	4	5	6	7	6	5	7	6	4
	1	2	1	2	8	3	9	4	3	9	2	2	3	*	*	*	*	*	3	3	5	6	7	4
	6	4	2	3	7	3	4	5	3	6	4	3	4	4	5	3	8	4	7	*	*	4	7	5
	8	9	2	3	7	3	4	4	5	6	2	2	2	9	4	2	1	9	9	1	9	4	6	6
	7	9	1	3	7	3	5	4	7	6	2	2	2	9	3	3	4	9	9	*	*	4	7	6
	8	9	2	2	7	3	4	4	6	7	2	2	2	9	4	2	1	9	9	9	5	6	6	5
	2	4	5	1	9	9	5	4	4	2	2	2	3	*	*	*	*	*	5	4	5	3	7	6
	1	3	2	1	9	9	4	4	2	2	5	4	6	2	7	3	5	7	3	4	5	4	9	4
	1	2	4	2	7	9	4	4	3	2	6	6	8	1	9	3	5	6	3	5	5	3	8	4
	2	2	9	5	5	4	4	4	4	2	4	6	9	1	9	1	4	8	9	2	5	2	9	5
	1	2	6	2	8	9	4	4	4	2	7	6	9	*	*	*	*	*	8	3	5	4	9	5
	2	3	6	2	6	9	4	5	2	2	4	4	9	1	5	4	7	4	2	2	5	4	9	4
	4	9	9	3	7	9	4	4	9	2	2	2	3	9	4	9	1	7	9	4	5	4	8	6
	2	3	5	2	8	9	4	4	6	2	6	5	5	*	*	*	*	*	2	3	5	3	8	4
	6	7	8	5	6	7	4	4	5	2	2	2	8	2	3	3	6	7	6	2	5	3	9	7
	2	4	5	2	8	9	4	4	3	5	4	4	3	7	7	3	7	4	6	7	5	4	9	5
	1	6	5	2	7	8	4	4	2	2	3	4	9	*	*	*	*	*	6	3	5	6	9	4
	1	4	3	1	9	9	5	4	7	2	3	2	3	6	5	8	2	5	9	7	5	5	9	6
	4	7	9	5	5	9	5	4	2	2	3	3	7	2	7	5	3	7	7	4	5	4	7	5
	1	5	3	2	8	9	4	4	2	5	3	3	4	7	5	4	5	6	9	7	5	3	8	5
	2	5	5	2	7	9	4	4	2	2	4	3	8	7	5	9	2	2	2	2	5	4	9	5
	2	8	7	5	4	4	4	4	4	2	3	4	9	*	*	*	*	*	7	6	5	4	9	4
	2	2	8	5	5	3	4	4	2	4	4	6	9	*	*	*	*	*	3	3	5	5	9	5
	1	3	7	4	7	3	4	4	5	4	2	3	3	5	7	3	6	7	9	4	5	3	9	4
	1	4	2	2	8	9	4	4	3	2	5	3	9	*	*	*	*	*	8	3	5	3	7	5
	1	3	2	2	8	9	6	4	2	2	7	4	9	*	*	*	*	*	4	3	5	7	9	4
	9	9	8	9	1	3	4	5	4	2	8	8	2	*	*	*	*	*	6	3	5	9	3	3
	9	6	8	7	3	3	4	6	9	4	2	2	3	5	5	2	8	6	5	9	5	8	6	4
	8	4	7	8	1	3	5	5	6	2	4	5	5	*	*	*	*	*	5	8	5	2	8	4

Economic Indicators For Class IIIA And IIIB Counties

County	Class	Population	Land Area	Med House Val	Med Gross Rent	Av Farm Val./Acre	% Under 5	% 5-17	% 18 and Over	% 65 and Over	% Poverty	% Under $10,000	% $10-19,999	% $20-29,999	% $30-49,999	% Over $50,000
WEST VIRGINIA																
Braxton	IIIA	4	4	5	3	3	3	5	6	6	8	8	3	3	2	2
Gilner	IIIA	3	3	6	3	2	4	2	7	5	7	9	3	2	1	3
Harrison	IIIB	9	3	7	6	3	3	3	7	5	4	4	5	6	6	6
Lewis	IIIA	5	3	7	3	3	4	3	7	7	5	6	5	5	2	4
McDowell	IIIA	8	4	1	2	9	8	9	1	2	8	6	3	6	4	3
Marion	IIIB	9	3	7	7	3	2	2	8	5	3	3	5	7	7	4
Marshall	IIIB	7	3	8	7	3	3	5	6	2	2	2	2	9	9	3
Mason	IIIB	5	4	7	6	3	6	5	5	2	3	3	4	7	8	5
Wetzel	IIIA	5	3	9	7	4	4	8	4	3	3	3	1	9	9	4
WISCONSIN																
Ashland	IIIA	4	6	4	4	2	4	4	6	8	3	6	8	3	3	2
Buffalo	IIIA	4	4	6	6	4	5	6	5	7	3	4	7	5	5	7
Chippewa	IIIB	8	6	7	8	4	6	8	2	3	2	2	7	8	7	6
Clark	IIIA	6	6	5	6	4	7	8	2	6	4	5	7	4	4	5
Columbia	IIIB	7	5	9	8	7	4	5	5	5	1	1	6	9	8	5
Crawford	IIIA	4	4	6	5	4	6	8	3	6	4	5	7	4	3	7
Dodge	IIIB	9	5	9	9	8	5	5	5	4	1	1	4	9	9	8
Douglas	IIIA	7	7	5	8	2	4	2	7	5	2	3	4	8	7	3
Grant	IIIB	8	6	8	8	6	6	5	5	4	2	2	6	7	8	7
Green Lake	IIIB	5	3	8	7	7	3	4	7	8	2	2	8	6	7	7
Iowa	IIIA	5	5	7	7	6	6	7	3	4	2	3	8	7	5	7
Iron	IIIA	3	5	3	4	2	2	1	9	9	3	9	8	1	1	1
Jackson	IIIA	4	6	5	6	4	6	4	5	7	3	5	6	7	2	5
Lafayette	IIIA	4	4	6	7	8	7	7	3	4	2	2	8	7	7	7
Langlade	IIIA	5	5	5	5	3	4	6	4	7	3	5	8	3	5	3
Marinette	IIIB	7	7	6	8	4	5	4	5	7	2	4	6	8	4	3
Monroe	IIIB	6	5	7	7	5	5	6	4	4	2	2	7	7	6	7
Pepin	IIIB	3	3	7	7	4	6	7	3	7	2	3	8	6	5	5
Price	IIIA	4	6	6	5	2	5	6	5	8	3	6	5	5	2	3
Richland	IIIA	4	4	6	6	4	5	4	6	6	2	4	8	5	4	7
Rusk	IIIA	4	5	5	5	3	5	7	4	6	4	6	8	3	2	2
Sauk	IIIB	7	5	8	8	6	4	5	5	6	2	2	8	8	6	7
Shawano	IIIB	6	5	7	7	6	4	7	4	6	2	3	7	6	6	6
Taylor	IIIB	5	5	7	7	3	8	8	2	4	3	3	6	7	5	8
Vernon	IIIA	5	5	7	5	5	4	4	6	8	3	5	5	5	5	5
WYOMING																
Goshen	IIIB	4	9	9	5	1	6	3	6	5	2	4	4	5	7	8
Niobrara	IIIA	3	9	7	4	1	4	2	8	8	5	5	4	4	6	7

SOCIO-ECONOMIC STATUS					MINORITIES				RURAL-URBAN				ECONOMIC BASE					COUNTY CONDITIONS					
% Completed HS	% College or More	Families/Pop	% Married Couples	% W/O Husband	% Black	% Spanish	% Amer Indian	% Asian	% Urban	% Rural	% Farmers	% Out of County	Jobs/Pop	% Manufacturing	% Wholesale	% Retail	% Services	Physicians/Cap	Crimes/Cap	$ Police/Crimes	$ Educ/Enrollment	Carpool or Transit	Pop Density
3	4	6	2	7	3	4	4	5	2	2	3	5	2	3	7	6	2	2	2	5	5	8	4
1	6	2	4	6	3	4	4	5	2	2	3	3	*	*	*	*	*	2	2	5	4	7	4
7	7	6	3	7	3	4	4	6	8	2	2	2	9	3	7	1	8	9	4	5	3	9	9
5	3	4	2	8	3	4	4	3	6	2	2	3	*	*	*	*	*	6	2	5	4	5	5
1	1	3	2	8	6	4	4	7	2	1	1	2	2	3	3	9	3	5	2	5	7	6	7
7	7	6	3	7	4	4	4	5	7	2	1	2	8	4	2	8	6	8	6	5	2	8	9
8	3	5	5	5	3	4	4	8	8	2	2	7	3	7	1	9	4	5	6	5	5	7	8
5	3	7	6	4	3	4	4	8	4	2	3	7	2	6	2	8	5	6	3	5	5	9	6
6	5	5	5	5	3	4	4	7	8	2	2	7	4	5	1	9	3	6	4	5	7	9	6
7	7	2	3	6	3	4	8	7	9	2	3	2	6	5	1	9	5	9	9	5	7	4	4
7	4	5	7	3	3	4	4	3	4	9	9	5	4	3	6	8	2	3	4	5	7	4	4
7	4	2	7	3	3	4	4	6	7	6	5	4	5	5	6	4	5	6	5	5	6	6	5
6	3	2	8	2	3	4	4	4	3	9	9	3	4	4	9	2	3	5	4	5	7	4	4
9	7	5	7	3	3	4	4	5	6	6	5	6	8	4	4	5	7	6	8	5	9	5	6
7	5	2	6	3	3	4	4	3	7	9	8	3	6	4	3	7	4	4	7	5	5	5	4
7	5	3	8	2	3	4	4	8	8	6	4	5	5	7	4	6	4	6	6	5	2	4	7
8	7	2	2	8	3	4	5	5	9	2	2	3	9	3	5	6	5	5	9	5	5	9	5
6	8	1	8	3	3	4	4	5	6	8	6	4	6	3	5	7	3	5	4	5	6	4	5
8	6	6	7	3	3	4	4	2	6	5	5	4	8	6	2	6	7	5	4	5	7	5	5
8	6	2	7	2	3	4	4	4	4	9	8	4	5	3	7	5	3	4	4	5	6	3	4
9	5	7	4	5	3	4	4	6	2	2	2	8	*	*	*	*	*	3	3	5	8	9	4
8	4	4	6	3	3	4	6	5	4	7	7	3	7	3	3	8	4	3	8	5	9	4	4
8	4	3	7	2	3	4	4	3	2	9	9	5	3	3	9	1	4	3	1	7	8	3	4
7	4	4	6	4	3	4	5	4	8	4	4	2	8	4	7	3	6	5	8	5	7	4	4
8	4	5	6	4	3	4	4	4	7	3	3	3	7	7	3	8	4	6	9	5	7	4	4
8	4	2	6	3	3	4	5	7	7	7	7	2	7	4	5	6	5	4	6	5	5	4	5
6	4	3	7	2	3	4	4	4	2	9	8	4	9	3	9	1	1	6	2	5	9	3	5
8	4	4	6	3	3	4	4	3	4	4	6	2	8	4	9	1	2	4	4	5	6	5	4
7	6	5	7	3	3	4	4	8	6	9	9	3	5	4	7	4	4	6	5	5	3	4	4
6	5	3	6	4	3	4	4	4	5	7	7	2	3	6	4	8	3	4	3	5	8	7	4
8	7	4	6	4	3	4	5	6	7	6	5	2	9	4	4	4	7	7	8	5	7	4	5
6	3	4	7	2	3	4	7	3	4	7	7	5	6	4	5	6	3	5	6	5	6	4	5
4	3	2	8	2	3	4	4	4	4	9	8	2	5	5	9	1	2	5	4	5	7	3	4
7	6	5	7	3	3	4	4	4	3	9	9	3	4	3	7	5	3	4	3	5	7	3	5
8	8	6	8	2	3	7	4	3	8	8	7	2	9	3	7	2	6	7	8	5	9	4	3
9	7	8	7	3	3	4	4	2	2	8	9	1	*	*	*	*	*	1	3	5	9	3	3

Seventeen

Successful investing in the turbulent years ahead

IN the 1940s, invincible competition from the Thrifty Drug chain in Los Angeles had closed two of my father's stores, depleted his capital, punctured his self-confidence, and made him a Thrifty employee. Until he retired, my father filled their prescriptions, sold their toys and nylon stockings, and gave thanks for the medical insurance that came with the job. No longer did he scour the classified ads for great real-estate buys. Instead, he spent hours with his old crony, Shomstein, reminiscing about bygone adventures in real estate—their past triumphs and near-misses. When he drove through Hollywood in his 1937 Chevy he would occasionally slow down near the corner of Gower and Sunset Boulevard: "See that drug store? It's the main hang-out of Western bit players in Gower Gulch. Could have bought it for $7,500 down. Today . . ." He would lift his shoulders in a gesture acknowledging the end of a golden age. It was the same with an old mansion near the intersection of Wilshire and Western. A thousand dollars down would have captured that prize. "Those days are gone forever."

Yes, those days *are* gone forever, but the era of rising prices lasted far longer than my father could have imagined. He died in 1952. Had he lived into the 1960s and 1970s he would have been amazed at the heights to which prices climbed in Los Angeles.

In the 1980s, we are once again undergoing radical change. In another economic context, a new region of opportunity is developing, as burgeoning with promise as Los Angeles was in the 1940s.

To help the investor capitalize on that opportunity and to prevent potential pitfalls, I offer some final words of caution and advice.

Do not count on inflation to provide capital gains in real estate. In the late 1970s, inflation was tangible, predictable, and bankable. From 1975 to 1980 the general price level flew up anywhere from 5.8 to 13.5 percent a year. Real estate was never far behind and often ahead.

Inflation was the explosive force wired into every recommended investment strategy. Mavens urged, "Get your money into real estate as quickly as possible." Leaving money in the bank was to see it wither away. And, of course, the faster people spent their money on real estate—and everything else that caught their fancy—the more rapidly inflation progressed. By 1979 it was not unusual to overhear any neighbor at the next table in any restaurant along Wilshire Boulevard saying something like: "It was a steal at $98,500. By the time I finish putting a coat of paint on it, you'll see, I'll sell it for $125,000. Over $20,000 profit on an equity of only $20,000."

But as we made a transition to the economy of the Caring Conserver, conditions changed. (See Chapter Eight.) The inflationary spiral created by the preceding economy of consumption spending had at last become intolerable. The American public was ready for strong action. In the mid-1980s the least we can expect is strong defenses by the Federal Reserve Board. Up to the time of publication, the Fed has put the fight against inflation above every other policy objective. However, brief episodes of inflation may still intrude in the future.

Reject the proposition that metropolitan areas will continue to dominate national expansion. Don't base real-estate investments on metropolitan growth. Seeing adjoining metropolitan areas grow and almost touch, we visualize continuing growth filling the corridors between them, creating massive urban consolidations. But because metropolitan growth will be increasingly arrested by migrations to the fifth region of opportunity, stress on metropolitan areas should be decisively rejected as a factor in investment. (See Chapters Six–Eleven.)

Coordinate investment and career decisions. Investments, like careers, should develop and grow profitable over many years. Ideally, investment decisions should be made *at the same time* as career decisions.

Say you are offered two positions. One is in Boise, Idaho, and the other in Oakland, California. In Boise you are within commuting distance of Ada, Canyon, Boise, Elmore, and Gem counties. In Oakland, you are within commuting distance of Contra Costa, San Francisco, Solano, and San Mateo counties. If the two career positions are approximately equal in intrinsic advantages, you should give serious consideration to the factor of investment advantages. In the long run, counties near Boise are likely to have a higher potential for investment than those in the vicinity of Oakland.

Determine the reasons for a county's growth in the 1970s. The major reason should be an abundance of resources attractive to the emerging economy. Be wary of a county whose growth depends upon a very few large companies or government agencies.

Although comparative population growth provides the basis for initial screening, it is essential to broaden your inquiry. Make first-hand explorations. When you come to an area to interview for a job or to start a business, take time to talk to recent migrants. Find out what drew them to this area rather than to any other. Do those original attractions still hold? Does the county still seem beautiful, peaceful, friendly, unpolluted, safe? How does this area compare with others in which they have lived? To what extent are the migrants pleased to have made the move? Has the new area improved or deteriorated in its ability to meet their needs?

Diligent probing will reveal that growth, even impressive growth, may occur for the wrong reasons—"wrong," that is, from an investor's point of view. Consider Thurston County, Washington, home of Olympia, the state capital. Its comparative growth designates this county as Class V. Close examination will show that rapid growth during the 1970s was motivated by the steep rise in expenditures by the state government. This was prior to the era of deep cuts—a trend portended by California's Proposition 13.

In the 1980s, it is no secret that state governments are seldom growing at their former headlong pace. Reacting to the excesses of the 1970s, voters all over the country have been decisively voting for cutbacks in government spending. In the state of Washington, as elsewhere, we *expect* programs to be curtailed or abandoned, jobs eliminated, retired individuals not replaced. It is evident that real-estate values in Thurston County are erroneously based on the expectation of continued rapid growth in both the number of government employees and general population. Under these circumstances an investment in this county should be considered with caution.

Plans to construct a military base provide another illustration of a "wrong" reason to invest. Say the army announces that it is going to locate a new base for satellite research in County X. Immediately—like prospectors thronging into the gold fields on news of a strike—investors rush to buy. The lucky ones buy cheaply and realize some short-term gains, but they must beat the "insiders," those who were first to get wind of the plan. They must also contend with long-time resident-owners now convinced of an unrealistically bountiful future.

Another factor adds to the risk: what the army gives, it can also take away. The billion-dollar program funding the base in "Xanadu County" is part of one president's strategy for the defense of the country, but an opponent in the next election may vow to dismantle the program. If the opponent is elected, and if the base is in fact dismantled, property values will fall as quickly as they rose.

Invest only in counties where anticipated increases in population are the result of the fifth migration.

Start your investigations with the county unit. After you isolate a favorable county, divide it into smaller areas. Counties are never uniform throughout their domain. If a county is classified as "obsolete," that condition is likely to prevail in much of it. But there may also be portions that can be classified as "deaccelerating," "risky," or even "maximum potential."

Once you have narrowed your search to a few counties, you are ready to consider individual census tracts. Their potential (compared with that of the county as a whole) can be initially estimated by rates of growth during 1960 to 1980. Promising tracts—those that turn upward after 1970—should be examined further by interviews with local real-estate agents, businessmen and residents. Based on the analyses in Chapters Eleven–Fifteen, make tentative classifications. Does a tract show the characteristics of a Class I, II, or VII county?

Select counties for investment that are actively committed to comprehensive planning. In the May 1983 meetings of the Urban Land Institute in Seattle, real-estate developers and location specialists discussed industry's changing requirements—especially from the point of view of high-tech firms. One conclusion stood out above all others: high-tech industrialists increasingly insist on comprehensive community planning.

At the center of this emphasis on planning is the compelling need to accommodate what is coming to be the scarcest factor of production—labor. Not the blue-collar sort—the riveters, mechanics, and arc welders—but programmers, system analysts, mathematicians, and scientists on whose coveted brains rest the success or failure of an entire enterprise. Many of these cerebral types are young and of a generation increasingly rejecting the "strident commercialism" of the past. Their "other end of the rainbow" is a different world view. The old expectation that happiness can be retailed by leading department stores is replaced by recognition that the good life bubbles up from within. (See Chapter Eight.) They seek quality, not quantity. They will agree to live and work only in "quality" neighborhoods, at "quality" jobs and in counties providing a "quality" environment. Planned communities in the thinly settled rural counties will not only attract such individuals, but will keep them so content that they cannot be stolen by competing firms.

The new penturbs must never look like overgrown suburbs. "Quality" means keeping small towns small. It means preserving the fragile balance between rural charm and urban growth. To please people of the new age, counties must coordinate and regulate their growth; they must demonstrate conscious choices in their integration of the residential, industrial, and commercial landscape. Unless steps are taken at the proper time only the first migrants will find what they are looking for, and only for a limited time. As people spill into the rural areas by the millions they will inevitably trample the environment that once attracted them.

A community's willingness to enforce a comprehensive plan becomes a major criterion for investment. To confirm a county's suitability for investment, inquire into the record of past and present planning programs. Talk to analysts of the county's planning department and, if possible, to planning commissioners. Request copies of the latest master plan, building and zoning codes. Examine minutes covering recent meetings of the planning commission. Find articles in the local newspapers dealing with current land-use issues.

From this initial research the single question to be raised is this: does this county demonstrate a willingness to support a high level of planning activity? Without that support, a county's "prime" classification may be seriously compromised.

Take care not to confuse comprehensive planning of the penturbs with efforts to rehabilitate old cities like Youngstown, Fort Wayne, or Detroit. Restoration of those old industrial cities cannot be guaranteed by efforts to attract new industries. The clutch of the past is too insistent, too binding. It cannot be dismissed at the will of the local Chamber of Commerce. (See Chapter Ten.) Theory dictates that many decades are likely to intervene before an obsolete or obsolescing area will prove useful to an emerging economy.

Above all, avoid states and counties where planning locks in the past. Consider Oregon. In 1973 this verdant state enacted Senate Bill 100 to protect its forests and farm land from urban encroachment—the helter-skelter and capricious growth reminiscent of Los Angeles and other large metropolitan areas. "Keep the barbarian developers at bay," argued the bill's proponents. "We want both cities and countryside. But we don't want a chaotic mongrelization of the two. Let them be equal but separate."

Motivated by rising sentiment against unplanned growth, Oregon legislators created a kind of fortress wall around its cities. Urban migrants to Oregon were enjoined to locate on land *inside* the wall. Those aspiring to locate *outside* the wall had better be prepared to farm, mine, or grow forests.

Good planning, however, does not imitate the past but accelerates and guides change in the service of the new order. Senate Bill 100 fails to do this. By imprisoning every city in an iron corset, it resurrects an obsolete, defunct, and often inappropriate urban pattern. The compact city best suited the nineteenth century, when the entire nation strained toward maximum expansion of heavy industry. Compact cities were useful then. They provided greater efficiencies. By settling masses of desperately poor people cheek by jowl, these cities made savings in transportation costs that helped capitalize further industrial expansions. Today we need to develop a very different type of city—one that balances conservation with larger residential spaces and high-quality environments.

Such a city cannot be achieved by remodeling boom towns of the Little King circa 1960, like Portland, Eugene, or Salem. Oregon must compete with the rest of the nation, where other locations will often be cheaper and more easily adapted to meet the new demands. History demonstrates that every new economy develops its own region of opportunity. So long as better alternatives are available elsewhere, the attempt to force new growth into mature cities of the Little King will be ill-starred.

Choose "improved" real estate that earns a current income. Improvements such as stores, houses, and industrial parks bring income that can offset current costs and also offer a degree of tax shelter. A strategic purchase made near the end of a recession (see Chapter Two) needs to be buttressed by current income. Improved real estate bought during a depressed period should return an income commensurate with its depression price. Even that reduced amount helps ensure against foreclosure because of the involuntary loss of a job or business. The game plan is to weather all storms until the next boom.

Do not neglect the finer points of real-estate investment. You will find a wealth of valuable books on every aspect of real-estate investment—financing, choice of brokers, time of the year to buy or sell, bargaining, and investment calculations. Here is a recommended list:

Allen, Robert G. *Nothing Down*. New York: Simon and Schuster, 1984.

Beaton, William R., and Terry Robertson. *Real Estate Investment*. 2d ed. Englewood Cliffs, NJ: Prentice Hall, 1977.

Bockl, George. *How Real Estate Fortunes Are Made*. Englewood Cliffs, NJ: Prentice Hall, 1972.

Bruss, Robert. *The Smart Investor's Guide to Real Estate: Big Profits from Small Investments*. 4th ed. New York: Crown Publishers, 1985.

Hatfield, Weston P. *The Weekend Real Estate Investor*. New York: McGraw-Hill, 1978.

Henry, Rene A., Jr. *How to Profitably Buy and Sell Land*. New York: John Wiley & Sons, 1977.

Lowry, Albert J. *How You Can Become Financially Independent by Investing in Real Estate*. New York: Simon and Schuster, 1982.

Young, Jean, and Jim Young. *Buying Right in Country Real Estate*. New York: New American Library, 1979.

Wiley, Robert J. *Real Estate Investment: Analysis and Strategy*. New York: Ronald Press, 1977.

Above all, rely on the fundamentals of long-term not short-term change. Investors willing to plan for a period of years rather than months will enjoy surer success in the decades ahead. Since short-term price movements are erratic and unpredictable, pursuit of short-term gains invites expensive and time-wasting failures, especially in the unstable economic climate ahead. By comparison, the long-term appreciation of real-estate values *in the region of opportunity* can be anticipated with far greater certainty. We can count on two long-term forces propelling values upward: the rise of a new economy (with its attendant population pressures) and the rise from bust to boom.

Expect the building of penturbia to bring down the average price of real estate everywhere else in the nation. Individual owners will be temporarily disgruntled, but the economy will gain as a whole.

Reader: You're so sure?

Author: Let me put it this way. Suppose a mountain of pure molybdenum and other precious metals used in manufacturing steel came crashing out of the heavens into the great eastern desert of California. For only the cost of digging it up, we are suddenly enriched by a hoard worth hundreds of billions at present prices. But prices depend on supply and demand. Now, supply has suddenly increased. Therefore, prices must fall, first of the precious metals, then of the capital equipment incorporating them, and then of the goods and services produced by that equipment. Because cheaper goods and services stimulate demand, wages remain high and buy more than ever. Purchasing power grows. The additional purchasing power measures the value of our heavenly gift.

Reader: But a region of opportunity is no mountain of molybdenum falling from the sky.

Author: True, penturbia has been with us since the beginning of time. Call it a sleeping treasure. It sleeps in the minds of men and women until it is awakened or "discovered" by a turbulent economy in search of equilibrium. But the effect is the same. A vast supply becomes available at almost no cost and a sluggish economy is quickened by it. Such an event is precipitated by the emergence of every new region of opportunity.

Prices will rise in penturbia. They must, to reflect growing populations. And the percentage rise will be rapid at first, because it starts off from a very low base. But, paradoxically, that rise reduces the average price of all urban land. Those millions of newly developed acres that you and other investors add to the urban land supply will compete with land in the metropolitan areas. In newly developing counties, land values will rise, in metropolitan counties they will fall. Gradually, the two will become more equal in value.

Reader: . . . And society is the winner.

Author: Yes, society is the winner, because penturbia will boost the inventory of places in which to live and work. The average standard of living will rise. Each exuberant investor with an eye for figures will help to fashion raw farm land worth $688 an acre in 1980 into the coveted real estate of the future. When developed, the new land—abundant, desirable, and affordable—substitutes for scarce suburban land now selling for $200,000 an acre and more. Here is land for high-tech and other dynamic industries that are spearheading change. They won't pay as little as $688 an acre (plus the cost of water, electric, sewers, roads, etc.) for the land they need. Neither will they pay anything approaching $200,000. Nor will families have to pay today's outrageous prices to keep a roof over their heads. That's only the beginning. Think of the immense contribution to the economy made by the "gift" of millions of penturban acres.

Reader: Ah, the millennium.

Author: Hardly. We should expect an era of turbulent adjustment ahead as migrants, by increasing numbers, leave the metropolitan areas to create a new kind of life and a new kind of city in the fifth region of opportunity. But we should also expect regeneration as we press forward to solve our economic problems in new ways.

Reader: Can you compress your book into one final message you would like the real-estate investor to remember?

Author: Remember this: to succeed in today's real-estate market, put yourself in the vanguard of society's effort to solve its most pressing economic problems. Let that honorable objective be your guide. Let it determine when, where, and how you invest. That is the surest way to minimize your risk. Why? Because the outcome that is best for the economy and the country is the one most likely to prevail.

For over two centuries we have been taught to tend our own self-interests, to let Adam Smith's invisible hand translate private incentives into public well-being. That attitude is obsolete and must be reversed. Contemplate the public interest. Tend the public interest. In the coming decades, cultivate your private and public gardens with equal vigor. Make the invisible hand visible by your conscious efforts to improve the lot of your community, your nation, your economy, your world.

Notes

Introduction: Forecasting opportunities in real estate

1. Unless otherwise indicated, the U.S. Bureau of the Census is the source for all population data, 1790–1980; data on 1790–1960 were assembled from historical tables in the 1900 and 1930 census volumes as well as from *Population Abstract of the United States,* ed. John L. Androit (McLean, VA: Androit Associates, 1980). Data for 1970, 1977, and 1980 were obtained from a computer tape of the *County and City Data Book, 1983.* The latter was also the source for the special compilations of Chapter Sixteen. Unless otherwise noted, U.S. data through 1970 on all items other than population and other than the tables appearing in Chapter Fifteen were compiled from U.S. Bureau of the Census, *Historical Statistics of the United States: Colonial Times to 1970,* Bicentennial Edition, Parts 1 and 2 (Washington, DC, 1975). Continuations of this series to 1980 or later were obtained from U.S. Bureau of the Census, *Statistical Abstract of the United States: 1982–83,* 103rd ed. (Washington, DC, 1982).

2. For a given decade, the comparative population growth of a county (or group of counties) is the standard score of a county's percentage change in population during the decade—where the mean and standard deviation are determined from the percentage changes of all counties in the United States, weighted by population. The graph of comparative growth for a sequence of decades is obtained by adding standard scores. A county that grows by one standard score every decade would be shown as a straight line rising by one unit every decade; it goes from 1 to 2 to 3, and so on. A county that grows at the national average rate would neither rise nor fall; it would remain at 0.

To find the index of comparative growth of County X during decade Y:

1. Find P_2 (population in County X at end of decade Y).

2. Find P_1 (population in County X at beginning of decade Y).

3. The ratio between P_1 and P_2 is P_2/P_1. Call it R_x.

4. Look up the mean ratio and standard deviation of United States counties during decade Y in the table below. (The mean ratio is P_2 of all counties counted together divided by P_1 of all counties. The standard deviation is the weighted dispersion of all P_2/P_1 ratios around the mean.)

Period	Mean Ratio	Standard Deviation
1790–1800	1.16191354	0.61962000
1800–1810	1.21523363	0.37620528
1810–1820	1.21419513	0.39319323
1820–1830	1.21704102	0.35865448
1830–1840	1.21365029	0.54575174
1840–1850	1.27025290	0.71617372
1850–1860	1.28905532	0.61776068
1860–1870	1.20836107	0.46188956
1870–1890	1.26159643	0.70763985
1890–1900	1.19217559	0.23883655
1900–1910	1.19077992	0.32592865
1910–1920	1.13415637	0.25361517
1920–1930	1.15994335	0.29964296
1930–1940	1.07261012	0.13469702
1940–1950	1.14250709	0.22520144
1950–1960	1.18182347	0.31409541
1960–1970	1.12973349	0.25027983
1970–1980	1.11444038	0.19734477

5. I_y = the index of comparative growth for County X during decade Y. I_y = (Rx − Mean Ratio Y)/Standard Deviation Y.

6. The index of comparative growth (for County X during decade Y) is represented on a graph as the number of (standard score) units by which the index of County X is higher or lower at the end of decade Y than it was at the beginning of decade Y.

3. Homer Hoyt, *One Hundred Years of Land Values in Chicago* (Chicago: University of Chicago Press, 1933), Appendix III, Table LXXX ("Aggregate Value of all the Square Miles of Land in the 1933 Corporate Limits of Chicago"). Estimate for 1951 from Homer Hoyt, "The Capital Value of Chicago," *Savings and Homeownership,* First Federal Savings and Loan Association, December 1951, p. 1.

One: Opportunity, obsolescence, and instability

1. John Steinbeck, *The Red Pony.* (New York: The Viking Press, 1945), p. 130.

2. Larger countries may receive more than one migration, at times belonging to two successives regions of opportunity. Where a county joins in a general acceleration of growth, but does not show a subsequent decline because new growth outweighs decline, it is excluded from the current region of opportunity.

3. James A. Stone, "Disposition of the Public Domain in Wayne County" (M.A. thesis, University of Nebraska, 1952), Table XXIII ("Yearly Average Price of Land Sold by State, Railroads, and Large Land Holders").

Two: The first region of opportunity, 1760–1789

1. Since the keeping of uniform statistics for counties did not begin until 1790, the analysis of the first region of opportunity is necessarily based on populations of entire colonies. These units are far too large to allow discrimination between locations of growth and decline. (At times even counties are too large.) The use of smaller units would have shown that the regions of obsolescence and opportunity are present, at times, within the same colony. Colonies where this condition was judged to be particularly likely were excluded from the roster of either region—of obsolescence or of opportunity.

2. Thomas J. Wertenberg, cited in George R. Taylor, "American Economic Growth Before 1840," reprinted in *Essays in Colonial History,* ed. Paul Goodman (New York: Holt, Rinehart & Winston, 1967), p. 387.

3. "It appears probable that in spite of the higher nominal prices paid for tobacco there was a period of almost continuous depression from about

1760 or 1761 until about the beginning of the eighth decade, followed in turn by several years of good prices." L. C. Gray, "The Market Surplus Problem of Colonial Tobacco," in *Essays in Colonial History,* (cited in note 2, this chapter), p. 320.

4. Taylor, p. 388.

Three: The second region of opportunity, 1817–1846

1. Howard R. Smith, *Economic History of the United States* (New York: Ronald Press, 1955).

2. Henry Clay, Speech on American Industry in the House of Representatives, March 30 and 31 in *State Papers and Speeches on the Tariff,* ed. Frank W. Taussig (Cambridge, Harvard University Press, 1893) p. 254.

3. Douglass C. North, *The Economic Growth of the United States, 1790–1860* (New York: W. W. Norton, 1966), p. 190.

4. A county was included in the second region of opportunity if its comparative growth was greater than average for any two successive decades during 1790–1850 and if its comparative growth during the period 1860–1890 was less than average.

5. Homer Hoyt, *One Hundred Years of Land Values in Chicago* (Chicago: University of Chicago Press, 1933), p. 109. The difference between Old and New Chicago was not merely in location. The old city was a typical small river city of the Mississippi Valley. Hoyt cites a contemporary description written in 1867: "In all Chicago there is not one tenement house. Thrifty workmen own the houses they live in, and the rest can still hire a whole house. Consequently, seven-tenths of Chicago consists of small wooden houses in streets with wooden sidewalks and roads of prairie black" (pp. 87–88).

6. Edwin M. Chapman, "Land Speculation in Tate County, 1836–1861" (M.A. thesis, University of Mississippi, 1942). Chapman found that during the twenty-five-year period preceding the Civil War, there were thirty-five owners of 2,000 or more acres in Tate County who appeared to be "speculators" in land. Frequently the same individuals operated for themselves, in partnerships, and in land companies. Thus, two individuals could constitute three "speculators" (A, B, and A-B). At one time these thirty-five entities owned a total of 313,513.64 acres in the county. Typically, each entity bought and sold a number of properties and experienced varying rates of return.

The rate of return measures the rate (compounded annually) at which the purchase price grows into the sale price. If the purchase price is $100 and the sale price at the end of one year is $110, the rate of return is 10 percent. Obviously, the calculation requires four facts about each individual transaction: dates of purchase and sale and prices of purchase and sale.

Unfortunately, Chapman's unit of analysis was not the individual transaction but the individual speculator. He grouped all purchases made by a particular speculator and dated them by the earliest purchase and the last sale. Consequently, the duration of most transactions will be overstated—sometimes grossly overstated—and the calculated return will be understated.

But Chapman's understatement is moderated by the fact that I have not subtracted taxes and other costs from speculative gains. These costs depend on duration of the investment. Hence they are apt to be less important for properties sold in the 1840s than in the 1850s. Those sold in the 1840s were held an average of 4.3 years, in the 1850s, 20 years. If costs had been subtracted, the 1850s returns would have been even lower as compared with the 1840s. My conclusion—that rates of return are highly correlated with the index of comparative growth—holds with even greater force.

Of Chapman's thirty-five groups of transactions (the thirty-five "speculators"), sixteen were unsuitable for analysis because the original document did not specify prices. Another group of transactions was unsuitable because Chapman failed to provide dates of purchase and sale. Yet another group was rejected because the prices given were far out of line with comparable transactions in Chapman's study: Benjamin A. White reportedly bought land in 1840 at $5.07 an acre when prices paid by all other speculators varied between $1.30 and $2.80. Furthermore, the sale price was a relatively low $1.67, when all other sale prices from 1840 to 1861 varied between $2.50 and $4.89. It seems likely that the purchase price was unduly high because it included a building that was excluded from the subsequent sale. (Chapman points out that prices rarely reflected improvements and therefore he did not take them into account.) Chapman's data were not a sample. He studied every one of the largest speculators in Tate

County from 1836 to 1861. Because I rejected speculators only on the grounds indicated above, the remaining seventeen speculators should approximate an unbiased sample.

In the text, for simplicity, the word *transaction* refers to each speculator's group of transactions.

Four: The third region of opportunity, 1873–1900

1. Gray Emerson Cardiff, *The Coming Real Estate Crash* (New Rochelle, NY: Arlington House, 1979), pp. 13–18.

2. Homer Hoyt, *One Hundred Years of Land Values in Chicago* (Chicago: University of Chicago Press, 1933), Table LXXX, p. 470. The value of land within the 1933 corporate limits of Chicago rose from $168,800 in 1833 to $2,000,000,000 in 1933. Because the land was not completely settled in 1833, the comparison is overstated. But it is understated, too. In 1926 the total value of land in Chicago was $5,000,000,000. Furthermore, the rise of land in the city center—the kind traded in the 1830s—was much steeper than that of other parts of the city.

Five: The fourth region of opportunity, 1929–1958

1. *U.S. News and World Report,* March 12, 1984.

2. *Fortune,* December 15, 1980.

3. *Ladies' Home Journal,* February 1978.

4. *U.S. News,* April 8, 1974.

5. *New York Times Magazine,* March 15, 1980.

6. Ibid., p. 17.

Seven: Predicting regions of opportunity

1. Billions lost by the Washington Public Power Supply System in defunct nuclear power plants can be traced to the practice of extrapolating steady increases in demand for electricity at a time when demand peaked and fell.

2. John Tipple, "The Robber Baron in the Gilded Age," in *The Gilded Age: A Reappraisal*, ed. A. W. Morgan (1963), p. 16.

3. Ibid., p. 17.

4. John K. Winkler, *Morgan the Magnificent* (1932), p. 311.

5. Homer Hoyt, *One Hundred Years of Land Values in Chicago* (Chicago: University of Chicago Press, 1933), Table LXXX, p. 470.

6. Ibid., pp. 345, 346.

7. Historical Statistics of the United States: Colonial Times to 1970, Series OH329, Miles of Railroad Built: 1830 to 1925.

8. Christian Science Monitor, April 4, 1978, p. 6.

9. Peter L. Bernstein, "Capital Shortage: Cyclical or Secular?" *Challenge,* November–December 1975, p. 8; *Statistical Abstract of the United States: 1983.*

10. Leon M. Lederman (director of Fermi National Accelerator Laboratory), "The Erosion of U.S. Technological Strength," *Christian Science Monitor,* September 17, 1980, p. 16.

11. Seattle Times, July 28, 1983, p. A3.

12. Steven Hofman and Matthew Cook, "Crumbling America: Put It in the Budget," *Wall Street Journal,* October 7, 1982, p. 13.

Eight: Predicting penturbia—the fifth region of opportunity

1. Wallace F. Smith, *Urban Development, The Process and Problems* (Berkeley, CA: University of California Press, 1975), p. 1.

2. Calvin L. Beale, *The Revival of Population Growth in Non-metropolitan America* (Economic Development Division, Economic Research Service, U.S. Department of Agriculture, June 1975, ERS-605).

3. C. Jack Tucker, "Changing Patterns of Migration between Metropolitan and Nonmetropolitan Areas in the United States: Recent Evidence," *Demography,* November 1976; Peter A. Morrison, "Rural Renaissance in America? The Revival of Population Growth in Remote

Areas," *Population Bulletin* (Washington, DC: Population Reference Bureau, 1976); Peter A. Morrison, *Current Demographic Change in Regions of the United States* (Rand Paper Series, November 1977); George Sternlieb and James W. Hughes, "New Regional and Metropolitan Realities of America," *Journal of the American Institute of Planners,* July 1977, pp. 227–41; Curtis C. Roseman, *Changing Migration Patterns within the United States* (Washington, DC: Association of American Geographers, 1977); John M. Wardell, "Equilibrium and Change in Nonmetropolitan Growth," *Rural Sociology,* Summer 1977, pp. 156–79.

4. Newsweek, July 6, 1981, p. 26.

5. Reported in the *Wall Street Journal,* May 14, 1976.

6. Ibid.

7. Daniel Yankelovich, "New Rules in American Life: Searching for Self-fulfillment in a World Turned Upside Down," *Psychology Today,* April 1981.

8. Cited in "Openers," *American Demographics,* February 1981, p. 13.

9. James D. Williams and Andrew J. Sofranko, "Why People Move," *American Demographics,* July–August 1981, pp. 30–31.

10. Cited in "Openers," *American Demographics,* February 1981, pp. 12–13.

11. Williams and Sofranko, p. 31.

12. Ibid.

13. Ibid.

Ten: Land can and does depreciate

1. Saul Bellow, *The Dean's December* (New York: Pocket Books, 1982), p. 212.

2. Edgar M. Hoover and Ray Vernon, *Anatomy of a Metropolis* (Cambridge: Harvard University Press, 1959), p. 272.

Eleven: Decelerating and obsolescing counties: Classes IV and V

1. Quoted in Scott Donaldson, *The Suburban Myth* (New York: Columbia University Press, 1969), p. 70.

2. The description of Levitt's operations based on William Manchester, *The Glory and the Dream* (New York: Little, Brown, 1973), p. 528.

3. Ibid.

4. Inc., September 1982.

Twelve: Risky counties: Classes IV and V

1. Class V counties were defined by standard scores greater than zero during both 1950–1970 and 1970–1980.

2. Class IV counties were defined by standard scores less than zero during 1950–1970 and less than 1950–1970 during 1970–1980.

3. The reader may wonder, Is population alone a sufficient basis for determining classes? Land values sometimes rise even though population falls—an apparent contradiction to the general rule. This occurs when a county with a small land area (like San Francisco County, California, or the Borough of Manhattan, New York) expands its urban services to commuters from surrounding counties. Population falls and land values are driven up as scarce land is commandeered by high-paying urban facilities such as office buildings, factories, shopping centers, etc. At the same time, the decline of the night-time population is compensated for by the rise of the daytime population—commuters who work, shop, or pursue other urban activities. ("Population" is synonymous here with "night-time population.")

When we see population falling and land values rising we think there is a contradiction. There is none. We are simply looking at the wrong populations. It is not the population of the commuting county itself that is relevant. Nor is the daytime population more than a secondary factor. What is pertinent is the night-time population *of the surrounding counties.* That population is the ultimate reservoir controlling the number of potential commuters. If that reservoir shrinks, we can expect a decline in the number of commuters as well as a decline in land values.

Thirteen: Counties of maximum potential: Class I

1. The comparative growth rate of Class I counties from 1970 to 1980 must be one standard score or better. If growth is normally distributed, Class I includes the fastest growing 15.88 percent of the national population.

2. Seattle Times, July 3, 1983.

3. Ibid.

4. This reduction is subject to modification in the 1985–1986 tax-reform legislation.

Fourteen: Comparison of counties in classes I, II, and III

1. Unless otherwise indicated, averages and standard deviations are weighted by county populations. The comparative growth rate of Class II counties from 1970 to 1980 is measured by a standard score greater than zero and less than one.

2. The comparative growth rate of class III counties from 1970 to 1980 is less than zero, but it is greater than its own standard score for 1950 to 1970.

Sixteen: An opportunity atlas

1. The nine classes were defined by the following standard deviations from the mean.

9	over +1.22 standard deviation units
8	+.76 to +1.22
7	+.43 to +.76
6	+.14 to +.43

5   −.14 to +.14
4   −.14 to −.43
3   −.43 to −.76
2   −.76 to −1.22
1   less than −1.22

The distributions of several traits among the counties were heavily skewed. A few counties showed very large percentages and most others very little. In these cases the standard deviation was correspondingly large; and no counties were given indexes of 1, 2, or 3. This occurred in the following traits: Population; Land Area; Population Density; Percent Urban; $ Police/Crimes; Carpooling or Public Transit; Percent Blacks; Percent Spanish; Percent American Indian; and Percent Asians.

Appendix A

1980 population (in thousands) and class of all U.S. counties (except those in Alaska and Hawaii). See Chapters 11 to 14.

ALABAMA	(POP. CLASS)				
		Greene	11.0 IIIA	Washington	16.8 IIIB
		Hale	15.6 IIIA	Wilcox	14.7 IV
Autauga	32.2 V	Henry	15.3 IIA	Winston	21.9 IB
Baldwin	78.5 V	Houston	74.6 IB		
Barbour	24.7 IIIA	Jackson	51.4 IB		
Bibb	15.7 IIA	Jefferson	671.3 VII	**ARIZONA**	
Blount	36.4 IB	Lamar	16.4 IIA	Apache	52.1 V
Bullock	10.5 IV	Lauderdale	80.5 V	Cochise	85.6 V
Butler	21.6 IIIA	Lawrence	30.1 IIIB	Coconino	75.0 V
Calhoun	119.7 V	Lee	76.2 V	Gila	37.0 IB
Chambers	39.1 IIIA	Limestone	46.0 IIIB	Graham	22.8 V
Cherokee	18.7 IIA	Lowndes	13.2 IIIA	Greenlee	11.4 VII
Chilton	30.6 IB	Macon	26.8 IIIB	Maricopa	1509.0 VI
Choctaw	16.8 IIIA	Madison	196.9 VII	Mohave	55.8 V
Clarke	27.7 IIIA	Marengo	25.0 IIIA	Navajo	67.6 V
Clay	13.7 IIIA	Marion	30.0 IB	Pima	531.4 V
Cleburne	12.5 IIA	Marshall	65.6 IIB	Pinal	90.9 V
Coffee	38.5 IIIB	Mobile	364.9 V	Santa Cruz	20.4 V
Colbert	54.5 VII	Monroe	22.6 IIIA	Yavapai	68.1 V
Conecuh	15.8 IIIA	Montgomery	197.0 V	Yuma	90.5 V
Coosa	11.3 IIIA	Morgan	90.2 V		
Covington	36.8 IIIA	Perry	15.0 IIIA		
Crenshaw	14.1 IIIA	Pickens	21.4 IIIA	**ARKANSAS**	
Cullman	61.6 IIB	Pike	28.0 IIA	Arkansas	24.1 IIIB
Dale	47.8 VII	Randolph	20.0 IIIA	Ashley	26.5 IIIB
Dallas	53.9 IV	Russell	47.3 VII	Baxter	27.4 IB
De Kalb	53.6 IB	St. Clair	41.2 IB	Benton	78.1 IB
Elmore	43.3 IB	Shelby	66.2 IB	Boone	26.0 IB
Escambia	38.4 IIIB	Sumter	16.9 IIIA	Bradley	13.8 IIIA
Etowah	103.0 VII	Talladega	73.8 V	Calhoun	6.0 IIIA
Fayette	18.8 IIA	Tallapoosa	38.6 IIB	Carroll	16.2 IA
Franklin	28.3 IIB	Tuscaloosa	137.5 V	Chicot	17.7 IIIA
Geneva	24.2 IIIA	Walker	68.6 IB		

Clark	23.3 IIIA	Pulaski	340.6 V	Plumas	17.3 V
Clay	20.6 IIIA	Randolph	16.8 IA	Riverside	663.1 VI
Cleburne	16.9 IA	St. Francis	30.8 IIIB	Sacramento	783.3 VI
Cleveland	7.8 IIA	Saline	53.1 V	San Benito	25.0 V
Columbia	26.6 IIIB	Scott	9.6 IIA	San Ber-	
Conway	19.5 IIA	Searcy	8.8 IIA	nardino	895.0 VI
Craighead	63.2 IB	Sebastian	95.1 IIB	San Diego	1861.8 VI
Crawford	36.8 IB	Sevier	14.0 IA	San Francisco	678.9 IV
Crittenden	49.4 IIIB	Sharp	14.6 IA	San Joaquin	347.3 V
Cross	20.4 IIIA	Stone	9.0 IA	San Luis	
Dallas	10.5 IIIA	Union	48.5 IIIA	Obispo	155.4 V
Desha	19.7 IIIA	Van Buren	13.3 IA	San Mateo	587.3 VII
Drew	17.9 IIA	Washington	100.4 V	Santa Barbara	298.6 VI
Faulkner	46.1 IB	White	50.8 IB	Santa Clara	1295.0 VI
Franklin	14.7 IA	Woodruff	11.2 IIIA	Santa Cruz	188.1 V
Fulton	9.9 IA	Yell	17.0 IIA	Shasta	115.7 V
Garland	70.5 V			Sierra	3.0 IA
Grant	13.0 IA			Siskiyou	39.7 IIB
Greene	30.7 IB	**CALIFORNIA**		Solano	235.2 V
Hempstead	23.6 IA			Sonoma	299.6 V
Hot Spring	26.8 IB	Alameda	1105.3 VII	Stanislaus	265.9 V
Howard	13.4 IIA	Alpine	1.0 V	Sutter	52.2 V
Independence	30.1 IB	Amador	19.3 IB	Tehama	38.8 V
Izard	10.7 IA	Butte	143.8 V	Trinity	11.8 V
Jackson	21.6 IIIA	Calaveras	20.7 V	Tulare	245.7 V
Jefferson	90.7 IIIB	Colusa	12.7 IV	Tuolumne	33.9 V
Johnson	17.4 IA	Contra Costa	656.3 VI	Ventura	529.1 VI
Lafayette	10.2 IIIA	Del Norte	18.2 V	Yolo	113.3 VI
Lawrence	18.4 IIA	El Dorado	85.8 V	Yuba	49.7 V
Lee	15.5 IV	Fresno	514.6 V		
Lincoln	13.3 IIIA	Glenn	21.3 V		
Little River	13.9 IA	Humboldt	108.5 VII	**COLORADO**	
Logan	20.1 IIA	Imperial	92.1 IB		
Lonoke	34.5 IA	Inyo	17.8 V	Adams	245.9 VI
Madison	11.3 IIA	Kern	403.0 V	Alamosa	11.7 IV
Marion	11.3 IA	Kings	73.7 VII	Arapahoe	293.6 V
Miller	37.7 IIB	Lake	36.3 V	Archuleta	3.6 IA
Mississippi	59.5 IIIA	Lassen	21.6 V	Baca	5.4 IIIA
Monroe	14.0 IV	Los Angeles	7477.5 VII	Bent	5.9 IV
Montgomery	7.7 IA	Madera	63.1 V	Boulder	189.6 VI
Nevada	11.0 IIIA	Marin	222.5 VII	Chaffee	13.2 V
Newton	7.7 IA	Mariposa	11.1 V	Cheyenne	2.1 IIIA
Ouachita	30.5 IIIB	Mendocino	66.7 V	Clear Creek	7.3 V
Perry	7.2 IA	Merced	134.5 V	Conejos	7.7 IIIA
Phillips	34.7 IV	Modoc	8.6 IIB	Costilla	3.0 IIIA
Pike	10.3 IIA	Mono	8.5 V	Crowley	2.9 IIIA
Poinsett	27.0 VII	Monterey	290.4 VI	Custer	1.5 IA
Polk	17.0 IA	Napa	99.1 V	Delta	21.2 IB
Pope	39.0 IB	Nevada	51.6 V	Denver	492.3 VII
Prairie	10.1 IIIA	Orange	1932.7 VI	Dolores	1.6 VII
		Placer	117.2 V	Douglas	25.1 V

Eagle	13.3 V	Litchfield	156.7 VII	Indian River	59.8 V
Elbert	6.8 IA	Middlesex	129.0 VI	Jackson	39.1 IIB
El Paso	309.4 VI	New Haven	761.3 VII	Jefferson	10.7 IA
Fremont	28.6 IB	New London	238.4 VII	Lafayette	4.0 IA
Garfield	22.5 IB	Tolland	114.8 VII	Lake	104.8 V
Gilpin	2.4 V	Windham	92.3 VII	Lee	205.2 VI
Grand	7.4 V			Leon	148.6 V
Gunnison	10.6 IB			Levy	19.8 IB
Hinsdale	.4 IA	**DELAWARE**		Liberty	4.2 IA
Huerfano	6.4 IIIA	Kent	98.2 VI	Madison	14.8 IIIA
Jackson	1.8 VII	New Castle	398.1 VII	Manatee	148.4 V
Jefferson	371.7 VI	Sussex	98.0 V	Marion	122.4 V
Kiowa	1.9 IIIA			Martin	64.0 V
Kit Carson	7.5 IIIA			Monroe	63.1 VI
Lake	8.8 VII	**DISTRICT OF COLUMBIA**		Nassau	32.8 V
La Plata	27.4 IA	Washington	638.3 VII	Okaloosa	109.9 VI
Larimer	149.1 V			Okeechobee	20.2 V
Las Animas	14.8 IIIA			Orange	471.0 VI
Lincoln	4.6 IIIA	**FLORIDA**		Osceola	49.2 V
Logan	19.8 IIIB			Palm Beach	576.8 V
Mesa	81.5 V	Alachua	151.3 V	Pasco	193.6 V
Mineral	.8 IIA	Baker	15.2 V	Pinellas	728.5 VI
Moffat	13.1 V	Bay	97.7 V	Polk	321.6 V
Montezuma	16.5 V	Bradford	20.0 V	Putnam	50.5 V
Montrose	24.3 V	Brevard	272.9 VI	St. Johns	51.3 V
Morgan	22.5 IIB	Broward	1018.2 VI	St. Lucie	87.1 V
Otero	22.5 IV	Calhoun	9.2 IIA	Santa Rosa	55.9 V
Ouray	1.9 IA	Charlotte	58.4 VI	Sarasota	202.2 VI
Park	5.3 IA	Citrus	54.7 V	Seminole	179.7 V
Phillips	4.5 IIIA	Clay	67.0 V	Sumter	24.2 IB
Pitkin	10.3 VI	Collier	85.9 VI	Suwannee	22.2 IA
Prowers	13.0 IIIA	Columbia	35.3 V	Taylor	16.5 IB
Pueblo	125.9 VII	Dade	1625.7 VII	Union	10.1 IB
Rio Blanco	6.2 V	De Soto	19.0 V	Volusia	258.7 V
Rio Grande	10.5 VII	Dixie	7.7 V	Wakulla	10.8 IB
Routt	13.4 IA	Duval	571.0 VII	Walton	21.3 IB
Saguache	3.9 IIIA	Escambia	233.7 VI	Washington	14.5 IA
San Juan	.8 IIIA	Flagler	10.9 V		
San Miguel	3.1 IA	Franklin	7.6 IIIB	**GEORGIA**	
Sedgwick	3.2 IIIA	Gadsden	41.5 IIIB		
Summit	8.8 V	Gilchrist	5.7 IA	Appling	15.5 IB
Teller	8.0 IA	Glades	5.9 V	Atkinson	6.1 IIIA
Washington	5.3 IIIA	Gulf	10.6 VII	Bacon	9.3 V
Weld	123.4 IB	Hamilton	8.7 IIA	Baker	3.8 IIIA
Yuma	9.6 IIA	Hardee	19.3 V	Baldwin	34.6 VII
		Hendry	18.5 V	Banks	8.7 IA
		Hernando	44.4 V	Barrow	21.3 IB
CONNECTICUT		Highlands	47.5 V	Bartow	40.7 IB
Fairfield	807.1 VII	Hillsborough	646.9 V	Ben Hill	16.0 IA
Hartford	807.7 VII	Holmes	14.7 IA	Berrien	13.5 IIA

Bibb	150.2 VII	Fulton	589.9 VII	Paulding	26.1 V
Bleckley	10.7 IIIB	Gilmer	11.1 V	Peach	19.1 V
Brantley	8.7 IA	Glascock	2.3 IIIA	Pickens	11.6 IIB
Brooks	15.2 IIIA	Glynn	54.9 VII	Pierce	11.8 IA
Bryan	10.1 IB	Gordon	30.0 IB	Pike	8.9 IA
Bulloch	35.7 IIB	Grady	19.8 IIIA	Polk	32.3 VII
Burke	19.3 IIIA	Greene	11.3 IIIA	Pulaski	8.9 IIIA
Butts	13.6 IA	Gwinnett	166.9 V	Putnam	10.2 IA
Calhoun	5.7 IV	Habersham	25.0 V	Quitman	2.3 IIIA
Camden	13.3 V	Hall	75.6 V	Rabun	10.4 IB
Candler	7.5 IIA	Hancock	9.4 IIIA	Randolph	9.5 IIIA
Carroll	56.3 IB	Haralson	18.4 IIB	Richmond	181.6 VI
Catoosa	36.9 V	Harris	15.4 IA	Rockdale	36.7 V
Charlton	7.3 IB	Hart	18.5 IIA	Schley	3.4 IIA
Chatham	202.2 VII	Heard	6.5 IA	Screven	14.0 IIA
Chatta-		Henry	36.3 V	Seminole	9.0 IB
hoochee	21.7 VII	Houston	77.6 VI	Spalding	47.8 V
Chattooga	21.8 VII	Irwin	8.9 IIIA	Stephens	21.7 VII
Cherokee	51.6 V	Jackson	25.3 IIA	Stewart	5.8 IV
Clarke	74.4 VI	Jasper	7.5 IA	Sumter	29.3 IIIA
Clay	3.5 IIIA	Jeff Davis	11.4 IB	Talbot	6.5 IIIA
Clayton	150.3 VI	Jefferson	18.4 IIIA	Taliaferro	2.0 IV
Clinch	6.6 IIIA	Jenkins	8.8 IIIA	Tattnall	18.1 IIIA
Cobb	297.7 VI	Johnson	8.6 IIA	Taylor	7.9 IIIA
Coffee	26.8 IIB	Jones	16.5 V	Telfair	11.4 IIIA
Colquitt	35.3 IIIB	Lamar	12.2 IIB	Terrell	12.0 IIIA
Columbia	40.1 V	Lanier	5.6 IIB	Thomas	38.0 IIIB
Cook	13.4 IIIB	Laurens	36.9 IIA	Tift	32.8 V
Coweta	39.2 IB	Lee	11.6 IA	Toombs	22.5 IIB
Crawford	7.6 IA	Liberty	37.5 V	Towns	5.6 IB
Crisp	19.4 IIIB	Lincoln	6.7 IIA	Treutlen	6.0 IIIA
Dade	12.3 V	Long	4.5 IA	Troup	50.0 V
Dawson	4.7 IA	Lowndes	67.9 V	Turner	9.5 IIIA
Decatur	25.4 IIA	Lumpkin	10.7 V	Twiggs	9.3 IIA
De Kalb	483.0 VI	McDuffie	18.5 V	Union	9.3 IA
Dodge	16.9 IIIA	McIntosh	8.0 IIIB	Upson	25.9 VII
Dooly	10.8 IIIA	Macon	14.0 IIIA	Walker	56.4 V
Dougherty	100.7 VI	Madison	17.7 IA	Walton	31.2 IB
Douglas	54.5 V	Marion	5.2 IIIA	Ware	37.1 IIIB
Early	13.1 IIIA	Meriwether	21.2 IIA	Warren	6.5 IIIA
Echols	2.2 IIA	Miller	7.0 IIIA	Washington	18.8 IIIA
Effingham	18.3 V	Mitchell	21.1 IIA	Wayne	20.7 V
Elbert	18.7 IIIA	Monroe	14.6 IA	Webster	2.3 IIIA
Emanuel	20.7 IIA	Montgomery	7.0 IIA	Wheeler	5.1 IIA
Evans	8.4 IIB	Morgan	11.5 IIA	White	10.1 IB
Fannin	14.7 IIIB	Murray	19.6 IA	Whitfield	65.7 V
Fayette	29.0 V	Muscogee	170.1 VII	Wilcox	7.6 IIIA
Floyd	79.8 VII	Newton	34.4 IB	Wilkes	10.9 IIIA
Forsyth	27.9 V	Oconee	12.4 IA	Wilkinson	10.3 IIIA
Franklin	15.1 IIA	Oglethorpe	8.9 IIA	Worth	18.0 IA

IDAHO

Ada	173.0 V
Adams	3.3 IIB
Bannock	65.4 V
Bear Lake	6.9 IIA
Benewah	8.2 IA
Bingham	36.4 V
Blaine	9.8 V
Boise	2.9 IA
Bonner	24.1 IB
Bonneville	65.9 V
Boundary	7.2 V
Butte	3.3 V
Camas	.8 IIA
Canyon	83.7 V
Caribou	8.6 V
Cassia	19.4 IIB
Clark	.7 IIIA
Clearwater	10.3 VII
Custer	3.3 IIA
Elmore	21.5 VI
Franklin	8.8 IIA
Fremont	10.8 IA
Gem	11.9 IB
Gooding	11.8 V
Idaho	14.7 IIB
Jefferson	15.3 IB
Jerome	14.8 V
Kootenai	59.7 V
Latah	28.7 IIB
Lemhi	7.4 V
Lewis	4.1 IIIA
Lincoln	3.4 V
Madison	19.4 V
Minidoka	19.7 V
Nez Perce	33.2 VII
Oneida	3.2 IIA
Owyhee	8.2 V
Payette	15.7 V
Power	6.8 IB
Shoshone	19.2 IIIB
Teton	2.8 IA
Twin Falls	52.9 V
Valley	5.6 IB
Washington	8.8 IIA

ILLINOIS

Adams	71.6 IV
Alexander	12.2 IIIA
Bond	16.2 IIA
Boone	28.6 VI
Brown	5.4 IIIA
Bureau	39.1 IIIA
Calhoun	5.8 IIIA
Carroll	18.7 IV
Cass	15.0 IIIA
Champaign	168.3 VII
Christian	36.4 IIIB
Clark	16.9 IIIA
Clay	15.2 IIIA
Clinton	32.6 IIB
Coles	52.2 IIIB
Cook	5253.6 IV
Crawford	20.8 IIIA
Cumberland	11.0 IIA
De Kalb	74.6 VII
De Witt	18.1 IIIA
Douglas	19.7 IV
Du Page	658.8 VI
Edgar	21.7 IIIA
Edwards	7.9 IIA
Effingham	30.9 IB
Fayette	22.1 IIIA
Ford	15.2 IV
Franklin	43.2 IIA
Fulton	43.6 IIIA
Gallatin	7.5 IIIA
Greene	16.6 IV
Grundy	30.5 V
Hamilton	9.1 IIIA
Hancock	23.8 IIIA
Hardin	5.3 IIIA
Henderson	9.1 IIIA
Henry	57.9 IIIB
Iroquois	32.9 IV
Jackson	61.5 VI
Jasper	11.3 IIIA
Jefferson	36.5 IIB
Jersey	20.5 IIB
Jo Daviess	23.5 IIIA
Johnson	9.6 IA
Kane	278.4 VII
Kankakee	102.9 VII
Kendall	37.2 V
Knox	61.6 IV
Lake	440.3 VI
La Salle	112.0 IV
Lawrence	17.8 IIIA
Lee	36.3 IV
Livingston	41.3 IV
Logan	31.8 IV
McDonough	37.4 IV
McHenry	147.8 VI
McLean	119.1 V
Macon	131.3 VII
Macoupin	49.3 IIIA
Madison	247.6 VII
Marion	43.5 IIB
Marshall	14.4 IIIA
Mason	19.4 IIB
Massac	14.9 IIIB
Menard	11.7 IA
Mercer	19.2 IIA
Monroe	20.1 VII
Montgomery	31.6 IIIA
Morgan	37.5 IIIB
Moultrie	14.5 IIIA
Ogle	46.3 IV
Peoria	200.4 VII
Perry	21.7 IIIA
Piatt	16.5 IIIA
Pike	18.8 IIIA
Pope	4.4 IIA
Pulaski	8.8 IIIA
Putnam	6.0 IIA
Randolph	35.6 IIB
Richland	17.5 IIIB
Rock Island	165.9 VII
St. Clair	267.5 VII
Saline	28.4 IIIA
Sangamon	176.0 IIIB
Schuyler	8.3 IIIA
Scott	6.1 IIIA
Shelby	23.9 IIIA
Stark	7.3 IIIA
Stephenson	49.5 IV
Tazewell	132.0 VII
Union	17.7 IV
Vermilion	95.2 IV
Wabash	13.7 IIIA
Warren	21.9 IIIB
Washington	15.4 IIA
Wayne	18.0 IIIA
White	17.8 IIIA
Whiteside	65.9 VII
Will	324.4 V
Williamson	56.5 IIA
Winnebago	250.8 VII
Woodford	33.3 IIB

INDIANA

Adams	29.6 IIIB
Allen	294.3 VII
Bartholomew	65.0 VI
Benton	10.2 IV
Blackford	15.5 IV
Boone	36.4 IIB
Brown	12.3 V
Carroll	19.7 IIIA
Cass	40.9 IV
Clark	88.8 VI
Clay	24.8 IIIA
Clinton	31.5 IIIB
Crawford	9.8 IA
Daviess	27.8 IIIA
Dearborn	34.2 IIB
Decatur	23.8 IV
De Kalb	33.6 IIIB
Delaware	128.5 VII
Dubois	34.2 IIIB
Elkhart	137.3 VII
Fayette	28.2 IIIB
Floyd	61.1 VII
Fountain	19.0 IIIA
Franklin	19.6 IIA
Fulton	19.3 IIB
Gibson	33.1 IIIB
Grant	80.9 VII
Greene	30.4 IIA
Hamilton	82.0 V
Hancock	43.9 V
Harrison	27.2 IB
Hendricks	69.8 VI
Henry	53.3 VII
Howard	86.8 VII
Huntington	35.5 IV
Jackson	36.5 IIIB
Jasper	26.1 V
Jay	23.2 IV
Jefferson	30.4 IIB
Jennings	22.8 V
Johnson	77.2 VI
Knox	41.8 IIIA
Kosciusko	59.5 V
Lagrange	25.5 V
Lake	522.9 VII
La Porte	108.6 VII
Lawrence	42.4 IIB
Madison	139.3 VII
Marion	765.2 VII

Marshall	39.1 IIB
Martin	11.0 IV
Miami	39.8 VII
Monroe	98.7 VI
Montgomery	35.5 IV
Morgan	51.9 VI
Newton	14.8 IB
Noble	35.4 IIB
Ohio	5.1 IA
Orange	18.6 IIIB
Owen	15.8 IA
Parke	16.3 IIA
Perry	19.3 IV
Pike	13.4 IIIA
Porter	119.8 V
Posey	26.4 IB
Pulaski	13.2 IIIA
Putnam	29.1 IIIB
Randolph	29.9 IIIB
Ripley	24.3 IIB
Rush	19.6 IV
St. Joseph	241.6 VII
Scott	20.4 V
Shelby	39.8 VII
Spencer	19.3 IIA
Starke	21.9 V
Steuben	24.6 V
Sullivan	21.1 IIIA
Switzerland	7.1 IIA
Tippecanoe	121.7 VII
Tipton	16.8 IV
Union	6.8 IIIA
Vanderburgh	167.5 VII
Vermillion	18.2 IIIA
Vigo	112.3 IV
Wabash	36.6 IV
Warren	8.9 IIIA
Warrick	41.4 IB
Washington	21.9 IIB
Wayne	76.0 VII
Wells	25.4 IV
White	23.8 IIB
Whitley	26.2 IIB

IOWA

Adair	9.5 IIIA
Adams	5.7 IV
Allamakee	15.1 IIIA
Appanoose	15.5 IIIA

Audubon	8.5 IV
Benton	23.6 IIIA
Black Hawk	137.9 VII
Boone	26.1 IV
Bremer	24.8 IIIB
Buchanan	22.9 IIIB
Buena Vista	20.7 IIIB
Butler	17.6 IIIB
Calhoun	13.5 IV
Carroll	22.9 IV
Cass	16.9 IIIA
Cedar	18.6 IIIA
Cerro Gordo	48.4 IV
Cherokee	16.2 IV
Chickasaw	15.4 IIIA
Clarke	8.6 IIA
Clay	19.5 IIIB
Clayton	21.0 IIIA
Clinton	57.1 IV
Crawford	18.9 IV
Dallas	29.5 IIB
Davis	9.1 IIIA
Decatur	9.7 IIIA
Delaware	18.9 IV
Des Moines	46.2 IV
Dickinson	15.6 IB
Dubuque	93.7 IV
Emmet	13.3 IV
Fayette	25.4 IV
Floyd	19.5 IIIB
Franklin	13.0 IIIA
Fremont	9.4 IIIA
Greene	12.1 IIIA
Grundy	14.3 IV
Guthrie	11.9 IIIA
Hamilton	17.8 IV
Hancock	13.8 IIIB
Hardin	21.7 IV
Harrison	16.3 IIIA
Henry	18.8 IIIA
Howard	11.1 IIIA
Humboldt	12.2 IV
Ida	8.9 IIIA
Iowa	15.4 IV
Jackson	22.5 IIIA
Jasper	36.4 IV
Jefferson	16.3 IIIA
Johnson	81.7 VI
Jones	20.4 IIIA
Keokuk	12.9 IV

County	Value		County	Value		County	Value
Kossuth	21.8 IV		Atchison	18.3 IV		Lincoln	4.1 IIIA
Lee	43.1 IV		Barber	6.5 IV		Linn	8.2 IIIA
Linn	169.7 VII		Barton	31.3 VII		Logan	3.4 IV
Louisa	12.0 IIA		Bourbon	15.9 IIIA		Lyon	35.1 IIIB
Lucas	10.3 IIIA		Brown	11.9 IIIA		McPherson	26.8 IIIB
Lyon	12.8 IV		Butler	44.7 IIA		Marion	13.5 IIIA
Madison	12.5 IIIA		Chase	3.3 IIIA		Marshall	12.7 IIIA
Mahaska	22.8 IIIA		Chautauqua	5.0 IIIA		Meade	4.7 IV
Marion	29.6 IIB		Cherokee	22.3 IIIA		Miami	21.6 IIA
Marshall	41.6 IV		Cheyenne	3.6 IV		Mitchell	8.1 IIIA
Mills	13.4 IIA		Clark	2.5 IV		Montgomery	42.2 IIIA
Mitchell	12.3 IV		Clay	9.8 IIIA		Morris	6.4 IIIA
Monona	11.6 IIIA		Cloud	12.4 IV		Morton	3.4 VII
Monroe	9.2 IIIA		Coffey	9.3 IA		Nemaha	11.2 IV
Montgomery	13.4 IIIA		Comanche	2.5 IIIA		Neosho	18.9 IIIA
Muscatine	40.4 IIIB		Cowley	36.8 IIIA		Ness	4.4 IIIA
O'Brien	16.9 IV		Crawford	37.9 IIIA		Norton	6.6 IV
Osceola	8.3 IIIA		Decatur	4.5 IV		Osage	15.3 IIA
Page	19.0 IIIA		Dickinson	20.1 IIIA		Osborne	5.9 IV
Palo Alto	12.7 IIIA		Doniphan	9.2 IIIA		Ottawa	5.9 IIIA
Plymouth	24.7 IV		Douglas	67.6 VI		Pawnee	8.0 IIIA
Pocahontas	11.3 IV		Edwards	4.2 IV		Phillips	7.4 IV
Polk	303.1 VII		Elk	3.9 IIIA		Pottawatomie	14.7 IA
Pottawattamie	86.5 IV		Ellis	26.0 IV		Pratt	10.2 IIIA
Poweshiek	19.3 IIIB		Ellsworth	6.6 IIIA		Rawlins	4.1 IIIA
Ringgold	6.1 IIIA		Finney	23.8 V		Reno	64.9 IIIB
Sac	14.1 IV		Ford	24.3 IIIB		Republic	7.5 IV
Scott	160.0 VI		Franklin	22.0 IIIB		Rice	11.9 IIIA
Shelby	15.0 IV		Geary	29.8 VII		Riley	63.5 VI
Sioux	30.8 IIIB		Gove	3.7 IV		Rooks	7.0 IV
Story	72.3 V		Graham	3.9 IV		Rush	4.5 IV
Tama	19.5 IV		Grant	6.9 V		Russell	8.8 IIIA
Taylor	8.3 IIIA		Gray	5.1 IIA		Saline	48.9 VII
Union	13.8 IIIA		Greeley	1.8 IIIB		Scott	5.7 VII
Van Buren	8.6 IIIA		Greenwood	8.7 IIIA		Sedgwick	366.5 VII
Wapello	40.2 IV		Hamilton	2.5 IV		Seward	17.0 VII
Warren	34.8 V		Harper	7.7 IIIA		Shawnee	154.9 VII
Washington	20.1 IIIB		Harvey	30.5 IIB		Sheridan	3.5 IV
Wayne	8.1 IIIA		Haskell	3.8 VII		Sherman	7.7 IV
Webster	45.9 IV		Hodgeman	2.2 IV		Smith	5.9 IV
Winnebago	13.0 IIIB		Jackson	11.6 IIA		Stafford	5.6 IIIA
Winneshiek	21.8 IV		Jefferson	15.2 IA		Stanton	2.3 VII
Woodbury	100.8 IV		Jewell	5.2 IV		Stevens	4.7 V
Worth	9.0 IIIA		Johnson	270.2 VI		Sumner	24.9 IIIA
Wright	16.3 IV		Kearny	3.4 IIB		Thomas	8.4 IIB
			Kingman	8.9 IIIA		Trego	4.1 IV
KANSAS			Kiowa	4.0 IIIA		Wabaunsee	6.8 IIIA
			Labette	25.6 IIIA		Wallace	2.0 IV
Allen	15.6 IIIA		Lane	2.4 IV		Washington	8.5 IIIA
Anderson	8.7 IIIA		Leavenworth	54.8 IV		Wichita	3.0 IV

Wilson	12.1 IIIA	Greenup	39.1 IIB	Owsley	5.7 IIA
Woodson	4.6 IIIA	Hancock	7.7 IIIA	Pendleton	10.9 IIIA
Wyandotte	172.3 IV	Hardin	88.9 VI	Perry	33.7 IA
		Harlan	41.8 IIA	Pike	81.1 V
KENTUCKY		Harrison	15.1 IIIA	Powell	11.1 IB
		Hart	15.4 IIIA	Pulaski	45.8 IB
Adair	15.2 IIA	Henderson	40.8 IIB	Robertson	2.2 IIIA
Allen	14.1 IIA	Henry	12.7 IIA	Rockcastle	13.9 IIA
Anderson	12.5 IA	Hickman	6.0 IIIA	Rowan	19.0 V
Ballard	8.7 IIIA	Hopkins	46.1 IIB	Russell	13.7 IA
Barren	34.0 IIB	Jackson	11.9 V	Scott	21.8 IB
Bath	10.0 IIIA	Jefferson	685.0 VII	Shelby	23.3 IA
Bell	34.3 VII	Jessamine	26.1 V	Simpson	14.6 IIB
Boone	45.8 VI	Johnson	24.4 IA	Spencer	5.9 IIIA
Bourbon	19.4 IIIB	Kenton	137.0 IV	Taylor	21.1 IB
Boyd	55.5 IIIB	Knott	17.9 V	Todd	11.8 IIIA
Boyle	25.0 V	Knox	30.2 IA	Trigg	9.3 IIIA
Bracken	7.7 IIIA	Larue	11.9 IIB	Trimble	6.2 IIA
Breathitt	17.0 IIA	Laurel	38.9 IB	Union	17.8 IIA
Breckinridge	16.8 IIA	Lawrence	14.1 IA	Warren	71.8 V
Bullitt	43.3 V	Lee	7.7 IIA	Washington	10.7 IIIA
Butler	11.0 IIA	Leslie	14.8 V	Wayne	17.0 IIA
Caldwell	13.4 IIIA	Letcher	30.6 IA	Webster	14.8 IIA
Calloway	30.0 VII	Lewis	14.5 IIA	Whitley	33.3 IA
Campbell	83.3 IV	Lincoln	19.0 IIB	Wolfe	6.6 IIA
Carlisle	5.4 IIIA	Livingston	9.2 IA	Woodford	17.7 IB
Carroll	9.2 IIIA	Logan	24.1 IIIA		
Carter	25.0 IA	Lyon	6.4 IIA	**LOUISIANA**	
Casey	14.8 IIA	McCracken	61.3 IV		
Christian	66.8 V	McCreary	15.6 IA	Acadia	56.4 IIIB
Clark	28.3 IIB	McLean	10.0 IIIA	Allen	21.3 VII
Clay	22.7 V	Madison	53.3 V	Ascension	50.0 V
Clinton	9.3 IIA	Magoffin	13.5 IA	Assumption	22.0 IIA
Crittenden	9.2 IIIA	Marion	17.9 IIIB	Avoyelles	41.3 IIIB
Cumberland	7.2 IIIA	Marshall	25.6 V	Beauregard	29.6 IB
Daviess	85.9 VII	Martin	13.9 V	Bienville	16.3 IIIA
Edmonson	9.9 IIA	Mason	17.7 IIIA	Bossier	80.7 V
Elliott	6.9 IIA	Meade	22.8 VI	Caddo	252.3 VII
Estill	14.4 IIA	Menifee	5.1 IA	Calcasieu	167.2 VI
Fayette	204.1 VI	Mercer	19.0 IIA	Caldwell	10.7 IIA
Fleming	12.3 IIIA	Metcalfe	9.4 IIA	Cameron	9.3 IIB
Floyd	48.7 V	Monroe	12.3 IIIA	Catahoula	12.2 IIIA
Franklin	41.8 V	Montgomery	20.0 IB	Claiborne	17.0 IIIA
Fulton	8.9 IV	Morgan	12.1 IIA	Concordia	22.9 VII
Gallatin	4.8 IIA	Muhlenberg	32.2 IIA	De Soto	25.7 IIA
Garrard	10.8 IIA	Nelson	27.5 IIB	East Baton	
Grant	13.3 IA	Nicholas	7.1 IIIA	Rouge	366.1 V
Graves	34.0 IIIB	Ohio	21.7 IIA	East Carroll	11.7 IV
Grayson	20.8 IA	Oldham	27.7 V	East Feliciana	19.0 IIIA
Green	11.0 IIIA	Owen	8.9 IIA	Evangeline	33.3 VII

Franklin	24.1 IIIA
Grant	16.7 IA
Iberia	63.7 VII
Iberville	32.1 IV
Jackson	17.3 IIIB
Jefferson	454.5 VI
Jefferson	
Davis	32.1 VII
Lafayette	150.0 V
Lafourche	82.4 VI
La Salle	17.0 IB
Lincoln	39.7 IIB
Livingston	58.8 V
Madison	15.9 IIIB
Morehouse	34.8 VII
Natchitoches	39.8 IIB
Orleans	557.5 VII
Ouachita	139.2 V
Plaquemines	26.0 VII
Pointe Coupee	24.0 IIIA
Rapides	135.2 V
Red River	10.4 IIA
Richland	22.1 IIIA
Sabine	25.2 IA
St. Bernard	64.0 VI
St. Charles	37.2 VI
St. Helena	9.8 IV
St. James	21.4 IV
St. John the	
Baptist	31.9 V
St. Landry	84.1 VII
St. Martin	40.2 IB
St. Mary	64.2 VII
St. Tammany	110.8 V
Tangipahoa	80.6 IB
Tensas	8.5 IV
Terrebonne	94.3 V
Union	21.1 IIA
Vermilion	48.4 IIB
Vernon	53.4 VII
Washington	44.2 VII
Webster	43.6 IIIB
West Baton	
Rouge	19.0 VI
West Carroll	12.9 VII
West Feliciana	12.1 IIA
Winn	17.2 IIIA

MAINE

Androscoggin	99.6 IIIB
Aroostook	91.3 IV
Cumberland	215.7 V
Franklin	27.0 IIB
Hancock	41.7 IIA
Kennebec	109.8 IIB
Knox	32.9 IIA
Lincoln	25.6 IA
Oxford	48.9 IIB
Penobscot	137.0 IIIB
Piscataquis	17.6 IIIA
Sagadahoc	28.7 V
Somerset	45.0 IIIB
Waldo	28.4 IA
Washington	34.9 IIA
York	139.6 V

MARYLAND

Allegany	80.5 IV
Anne Arundel	370.7 VI
Baltimore	655.6 VII
Calvert	34.6 V
Caroline	23.1 IIB
Carroll	96.3 V
Cecil	60.4 VI
Charles	72.7 V
Dorchester	30.6 IIIB
Frederick	114.7 V
Garrett	26.4 IB
Harford	145.9 VI
Howard	118.5 V
Kent	16.6 IV
Montgomery	579.0 VII
Prince	
Georges	665.0 VII
Queen Annes	25.5 IB
St. Marys	59.8 V
Somerset	19.1 IIIA
Talbot	25.6 IIIB
Washington	113.0 IV
Wicomico	64.5 V
Worcester	30.8 IB
Baltimore City	786.7 IV

MASSACHUSETTS

Barnstable	147.9 V

Berkshire	145.1 IV
Bristol	474.6 IIIB
Dukes	8.9 IB
Essex	633.6 IV
Franklin	64.3 IIIB
Hampden	443.0 IV
Hampshire	138.8 VI
Middlesex	1367.0 IV
Nantucket	5.0 IA
Norfolk	606.5 VII
Plymouth	405.4 VI
Suffolk	650.1 IV
Worcester	646.3 IV

MICHIGAN

Alcona	9.7 IB
Alger	9.2 IIIA
Allegan	81.5 V
Alpena	32.3 VII
Antrim	16.1 IA
Arenac	14.7 IB
Baraga	8.4 IIIA
Barry	45.7 V
Bay	119.8 VII
Benzie	11.2 V
Berrien	171.2 VII
Branch	40.1 VII
Calhoun	141.5 VII
Cass	49.4 VI
Charlevoix	19.9 IIA
Cheboygan	20.6 IB
Chippewa	29.0 IV
Clare	23.8 V
Clinton	55.8 VI
Crawford	9.4 V
Delta	38.9 IIIB
Dickinson	25.3 IIIA
Eaton	88.3 V
Emmet	22.9 IB
Genesee	450.4 VII
Gladwin	19.9 V
Gogebic	19.6 IIIA
Grand	
Traverse	54.8 V
Gratiot	40.4 IV
Hillsdale	42.0 IIB
Houghton	37.8 IIIA
Huron	36.4 IIIB
Ingham	275.5 VII

Ionia	51.8 IIB	**MINNESOTA**		Mille Lacs	18.4 IIB
Iosco	28.3 VI			Morrison	29.3 IIIB
Iron	13.6 IIIA	Aitkin	13.4 IIA	Mower	40.3 VII
Isabella	54.1 V	Anoka	195.9 VI	Murray	11.5 IV
Jackson	151.4 VII	Becker	29.3 IIB	Nicollet	26.9 VII
Kalamazoo	212.3 VII	Beltrami	30.9 IIB	Nobles	21.8 IV
Kalkaska	10.9 IA	Benton	25.1 IIB	Norman	9.3 IV
Kent	444.5 VII	Big Stone	7.7 IIIA	Olmsted	92.0 VII
Keweenaw	1.9 IV	Blue Earth	52.3 VII	Otter Tail	51.9 IIA
Lake	7.7 V	Brown	28.6 IV	Pennington	15.2 V
Lapeer	70.0 V	Carlton	29.9 IIIB	Pine	19.8 IIA
Leelanau	14.0 IB	Carver	37.0 V	Pipestone	11.6 IV
Lenawee	89.9 VII	Cass	21.0 V	Polk	34.8 IIIB
Livingston	100.2 V	Chippewa	14.9 IIIB	Pope	11.6 IIIA
Luce	6.6 VII	Chisago	25.7 V	Ramsey	459.7 VII
Mackinac	10.1 IIIB	Clay	49.3 VII	Red Lake	5.4 IIIA
Macomb	694.6 VII	Clearwater	8.7 IIIA	Redwood	19.3 IV
Manistee	23.0 IIA	Cook	4.0 IIB	Renville	20.4 IV
Marquette	74.1 V	Cottonwood	14.8 IIIB	Rice	46.0 IIIB
Mason	26.3 IIB	Crow Wing	41.7 IIB	Rock	10.7 IV
Mecosta	36.9 V	Dakota	194.2 VI	Roseau	12.5 IIIA
Menominee	26.2 IIIA	Dodge	14.7 IIB	St. Louis	222.2 IV
Midland	73.5 VI	Douglas	27.8 IB	Scott	43.7 V
Missaukee	10.0 IA	Faribault	19.7 IV	Sherburne	29.9 V
Monroe	134.6 VI	Fillmore	21.9 IIIA	Sibley	15.4 IV
Montcalm	47.5 IIB	Freeborn	36.3 IV	Stearns	108.1 V
Montmorency	7.4 V	Goodhue	38.7 IIIB	Steele	30.3 IIB
Muskegon	157.5 V	Grant	7.1 IIIA	Stevens	11.3 IV
Newaygo	34.9 V	Hennepin	941.4 VII	Swift	12.9 IIIA
Oakland	1011.7 VI	Houston	18.3 IV	Todd	24.9 IIA
Oceana	22.0 IB	Hubbard	14.0 IB	Traverse	5.5 IV
Ogemaw	16.4 V	Isanti	23.6 V	Wabasha	19.3 IIB
Ontonagon	9.8 IV	Itasca	43.0 IIB	Wadena	14.1 IIB
Osceola	18.9 IA	Jackson	13.6 IV	Waseca	18.4 IIIB
Oscoda	6.8 V	Kanabec	12.1 IB	Washington	113.5 VI
Otsego	14.9 V	Kandiyohi	36.7 IIB	Watonwan	12.3 IV
Ottawa	157.1 VI	Kittson	6.6 IIIA	Wilkin	8.4 IV
Presque Isle	14.2 IIIB	Koochiching	17.5 IIIB	Winona	46.2 IV
Roscommon	16.3 V	Lac Qui Parle	10.5 IIIA	Wright	58.6 V
Saginaw	228.0 VII	Lake	13.0 VII	Yellow	
St. Clair	138.8 V	Lake of the		Medicine	13.6 IV
St. Joseph	56.0 V	Woods	3.7 IIIB		
Sanilac	40.7 IIB	Le Sueur	23.4 IIIB	**MISSISSIPPI**	
Schoolcraft	8.5 IIIA	Lincoln	8.2 IIIA		
Shiawassee	71.1 V	Lyon	25.2 IIIB	Adams	38.0 VII
Tuscola	56.9 IIB	McLeod	29.6 IV	Alcorn	33.0 IB
Van Buren	66.8 V	Mahnomen	5.5 IIIA	Amite	13.3 IIIA
Washtenaw	264.7 VI	Marshall	13.0 IIIA	Attala	19.8 IIIA
Wayne	2337.8 VII	Martin	24.6 IIIB	Benton	8.1 IIIA
Wexford	25.1 IB	Meeker	20.5 IIB	Bolivar	45.9 IV

County	Value	County	Value	County	Value
Calhoun	15.6 VII	Pike	36.1 IIA	Christian	22.4 IA
Carroll	9.7 IIIA	Pontotoc	20.9 IIA	Clark	8.4 IIIA
Chickasaw	17.8 IIIA	Prentiss	24.0 IIB	Clay	136.4 VII
Choctaw	8.9 IIIA	Quitman	12.6 IV	Clinton	15.9 IA
Claiborne	12.2 IA	Rankin	69.4 V	Cole	56.6 IB
Clarke	16.9 IIA	Scott	24.5 IIB	Cooper	14.6 IIIA
Clay	21.0 IIB	Sharkey	7.9 IV	Crawford	18.3 IB
Coahoma	36.9 IV	Simpson	23.4 IIB	Dade	7.3 IIIA
Copiah	26.5 IIIA	Smith	15.0 IIIA	Dallas	12.0 IIA
Covington	15.9 IIA	Stone	9.7 IIB	Daviess	8.9 IIIA
De Soto	53.9 V	Sunflower	34.8 IIIA	De Kalb	8.2 IIA
Forrest	66.0 V	Tallahatchie	17.1 IV	Dent	14.5 IA
Franklin	8.2 IIIA	Tate	20.1 IIIA	Douglas	11.5 IA
George	15.2 V	Tippah	18.7 IIA	Dunklin	36.3 VII
Greene	9.8 IIA	Tishomingo	18.4 IA	Franklin	71.2 V
Grenada	21.0 IIIB	Tunica	9.6 IV	Gasconade	13.1 IIIB
Hancock	24.5 V	Union	21.7 IIA	Gentry	7.8 IIIA
Harrison	157.6 VI	Walthall	13.7 IIIA	Greene	185.3 V
Hinds	250.9 V	Warren	51.6 IIB	Grundy	11.9 IIIA
Holmes	22.9 IIIA	Washington	72.3 VII	Harrison	9.8 IIIA
Humphreys	13.9 IIIA	Wayne	19.1 IIB	Henry	19.6 IIIA
Issaquena	2.5 IIIA	Webster	10.3 IIIA	Hickory	6.3 IA
Itawamba	20.5 IB	Wilkinson	10.0 IV	Holt	6.8 IIIA
Jackson	118.0 VI	Winston	19.4 IIIA	Howard	10.0 IV
Jasper	17.2 IIIA	Yalobusha	13.1 IIIA	Howell	28.8 IB
Jefferson	9.1 IIIA	Yazoo	27.3 IIIA	Iron	11.0 IIB
Jefferson Davis	13.8 IIIA			Jackson	629.2 IV
Jones	61.9 VII	**MISSOURI**		Jasper	86.9 IIIA
Kemper	10.1 IIIA			Jefferson	146.1 VI
Lafayette	31.0 IB	Adair	24.8 IIIB	Johnson	39.0 VI
Lamar	23.8 IB	Andrew	13.9 IIA	Knox	5.5 IIIA
Lauderdale	77.2 IIB	Atchison	8.6 IV	Laclede	24.3 IB
Lawrence	12.5 IIA	Audrain	26.4 IIIB	Lafayette	29.9 IIA
Leake	18.7 IIIA	Barry	24.4 IA	Lawrence	28.9 IIA
Lee	57.0 IB	Barton	11.2 IIIA	Lewis	10.9 IV
Leflore	41.5 IIIA	Bates	15.8 IIIA	Lincoln	22.1 V
Lincoln	30.1 IIB	Benton	12.1 IA	Linn	15.4 IIIA
Lowndes	57.3 V	Bollinger	10.3 IIA	Livingston	15.7 IIIA
Madison	41.6 IA	Boone	100.3 V	McDonald	14.9 IIA
Marion	25.7 IIB	Buchanan	87.8 IIIA	Macon	16.3 IIIA
Marshall	29.2 IA	Butler	37.6 V	Madison	10.7 IA
Monroe	36.4 IIIB	Caldwell	8.6 IIIA	Maries	7.5 IIIA
Montgomery	13.3 IIIA	Callaway	32.2 IB	Marion	28.6 IIIA
Neshoba	23.7 IIA	Camden	20.0 V	Mercer	4.6 IIIA
Newton	19.9 IIIA	Cape Girardeau	58.8 IIB	Miller	18.5 IA
Noxubee	13.2 IIIA	Carroll	12.1 IIIA	Mississippi	15.7 VII
Oktibbeha	36.0 V	Carter	5.4 IA	Moniteau	12.0 IIA
Panola	28.1 IIIA	Cass	51.0 VI	Monroe	9.7 IIIA
Pearl River	33.7 V	Cedar	11.8 IA	Montgomery	11.5 IIIA
Perry	9.8 IIIA	Chariton	10.4 IIIA	Morgan	13.8 IA
				New Madrid	22.9 VII

Newton	40.5 IB	Carbon	8.0 IIA	Wibaux	1.4 IIIA
Nodaway	21.9 IV	Carter	1.7 IV	Yellowstone	108.0 V
Oregon	10.2 IIA	Cascade	80.6 VII	Yellowstone	
Osage	12.0 IIIA	Chouteau	6.0 IV	National Park	.2 IB
Ozark	7.9 IA	Custer	13.1 IIIA		
Pemiscot	24.9 IIIA	Daniels	2.8 IV		
Perry	16.7 IIB	Dawson	11.8 VII	**NEBRASKA**	
Pettis	36.3 IIIB	Deer Lodge	12.5 VII		
Phelps	33.6 V	Fallon	3.7 IV	Adams	30.6 IV
Pike	17.5 VII	Fergus	13.0 IIIA	Antelope	8.6 IIIA
Platte	46.3 V	Flathead	51.9 V	Arthur	.5 IV
Polk	18.8 IA	Gallatin	42.8 V	Banner	.9 IV
Pulaski	42.0 VII	Garfield	1.6 IV	Blaine	.8 IIIA
Putnam	6.0 IIIA	Glacier	10.6 VII	Boone	7.3 IV
Ralls	8.9 IIA	Golden Valley	1.0 IIIA	Box Butte	13.6 IA
Randolph	25.4 IIA	Granite	2.7 IV	Boyd	3.3 IV
Ray	21.3 IA	Hill	17.9 VII	Brown	4.3 IIIA
Reynolds	7.2 IIA	Jefferson	7.0 IA	Buffalo	34.7 IIIB
Ripley	12.4 IA	Judith Basin	2.6 IIIA	Burt	8.8 IIIA
St. Charles	144.1 VI	Lake	19.0 V	Butler	9.3 IIIA
St. Clair	8.6 IIA	Lewis and		Cass	20.2 IIA
St. Francois	42.6 IIB	Clark	43.0 V	Cedar	11.3 IV
St. Louis	973.8 VII	Liberty	2.3 IV	Chase	4.7 IIA
St. Louis City	453.0 IV	Lincoln	17.7 VII	Cherry	6.7 IIIA
Ste.		McCone	2.7 IV	Cheyenne	10.0 VII
Genevieve	15.1 IIB	Madison	5.4 IIIA	Clay	8.1 IV
Saline	24.9 IIIA	Meagher	2.1 IV	Colfax	9.8 IIIA
Schuyler	4.9 IIIA	Mineral	3.6 V	Cuming	11.6 IV
Scotland	5.4 IIIA	Missoula	76.0 V	Custer	13.8 IIIA
Scott	39.6 V	Musselshell	4.4 IIA	Dakota	16.5 IB
Shannon	7.8 IIIA	Park	12.6 IIB	Dawes	9.6 IV
Shelby	7.8 IIIA	Petroleum	.6 IIIA	Dawson	22.3 IIB
Stoddard	29.0 IIA	Phillips	5.3 IIIA	Deuel	2.4 IV
Stone	15.5 IA	Pondera	6.7 IV	Dixon	7.1 IIIA
Sullivan	7.4 IIIA	Powder River	2.5 IV	Dodge	35.8 VII
Taney	20.4 IB	Powell	6.9 IIIB	Douglas	397.0 VII
Texas	21.0 IIA	Prairie	1.8 IIIA	Dundy	2.8 IIIA
Vernon	19.8 IIIA	Ravalli	22.4 V	Fillmore	7.9 IIIA
Warren	14.9 IA	Richland	12.2 IB	Franklin	4.3 IIIA
Washington	17.9 IIB	Roosevelt	10.4 IV	Frontier	3.6 IV
Wayne	11.2 IA	Rosebud	9.8 IA	Furnas	6.4 IIIA
Webster	20.4 IA	Sanders	8.6 IB	Gage	24.4 IV
Worth	3.0 IIIA	Sheridan	5.4 IV	Garden	2.8 IIIA
Wright	16.1 IIA	Silver Bow	38.0 IV	Garfield	2.3 IIIA
		Stillwater	5.5 IIA	Gosper	2.1 IIIA
		Sweet Grass	3.2 IIIA	Grant	.8 IV
MONTANA		Teton	6.4 IIIA	Greeley	3.4 IV
		Toole	5.5 IV	Hall	47.6 IV
Beaverhead	8.1 IV	Treasure	.9 IV	Hamilton	9.3 IIIA
Big Horn	11.0 IIIB	Valley	10.2 IV	Harlan	4.2 IIIA
Blaine	6.9 IIIA	Wheatland	2.3 IV	Hayes	1.3 IV
Broadwater	3.2 IA				

Hitchcock	4.0 IIIA	**NEVADA**		Passaic	447.5 VII
Holt	13.5 IIIA	Churchill	13.9 V	Salem	64.6 VII
Hooker	.9 IIIA	Clark	463.0 VI	Somerset	203.1 VII
Howard	6.7 IV	Douglas	19.4 V	Sussex	116.1 V
Jefferson	9.8 IIIA	Elko	17.2 IB	Union	504.0 VII
Johnson	5.2 IV	Esmeralda	.7 IIA	Warren	84.4 V
Kearney	7.0 IIIA	Eureka	1.1 IA		
Keith	9.3 IIIB	Humboldt	9.4 V	**NEW MEXICO**	
Keya Paha	1.3 IIIA	Lander	4.0 V		
Kimball	4.8 VII	Lincoln	3.7 IA	Bernalillo	419.7 VI
Knox	11.4 IIIA	Lyon	13.5 V	Catron	2.7 IA
Lancaster	192.8 V	Mineral	6.2 VII	Chaves	51.1 V
Lincoln	36.4 IB	Nye	9.0 V	Colfax	13.6 IIA
Logan	.9 IIIA	Pershing	3.4 IB	Curry	42.0 VII
Loup	.8 IIIA	Storey	1.5 IA	De Baca	2.4 IIIA
McPherson	.5 IV	Washoe	193.6 V	Dona Ana	96.3 V
Madison	31.3 IIB	White Pine	8.1 IV	Eddy	47.8 V
Merrick	8.9 IIIA	Carson City	32.0 V	Grant	26.2 IIB
Morrill	6.0 IIIA			Guadalupe	4.4 IV
Nance	4.7 IV			Harding	1.0 IV
Nemaha	8.3 IV	**NEW HAMPSHIRE**		Hidalgo	6.0 IB
Nuckolls	6.7 IV			Lea	55.9 VI
Otoe	15.1 IV	Belknap	42.8 IB	Lincoln	10.9 IB
Pawnee	3.9 IV	Carroll	27.9 IA	Los Alamos	17.5 V
Perkins	3.6 IIIA	Cheshire	62.1 V	Luna	15.5 V
Phelps	9.7 IV	Coos	35.1 IIIA	McKinley	56.4 V
Pierce	8.4 IIIA	Grafton	65.8 IIB	Mora	4.2 IIIA
Platte	28.8 IV	Hillsborough	276.6 V	Otero	44.6 VII
Polk	6.3 IIIA	Merrimack	98.3 IB	Quay	10.5 VII
Red Willow	12.6 IIIA	Rockingham	190.3 V	Rio Arriba	29.2 IIB
Richardson	11.3 IIIA	Strafford	85.4 V	Roosevelt	15.6 VII
Rock	2.3 IIIA	Sullivan	36.0 IIB	Sandoval	34.7 V
Saline	13.1 IIIA			San Juan	81.4 V
Sarpy	86.0 VI	**NEW JERSEY**		San Miguel	22.7 IIIA
Saunders	18.7 IIIA			Santa Fe	75.3 V
Scotts Bluff	38.3 IIIB	Atlantic	194.1 IV	Sierra	8.4 V
Seward	15.7 IIIA	Bergen	845.3 VII	Socorro	12.5 IA
Sheridan	7.5 IIIA	Burlington	362.5 VI	Taos	19.4 IIIB
Sherman	4.2 IV	Camden	471.6 VII	Torrance	7.4 IA
Sioux	1.8 IIIA	Cape May	82.2 V	Union	4.7 IIIA
Stanton	6.5 IIA	Cumberland	132.8 VII	Valencia	61.1 V
Thayer	7.5 IIIA	Essex	851.1 IV		
Thomas	.9 IIIA	Gloucester	199.9 VI	**NEW YORK**	
Thurston	7.1 IIIA	Hudson	556.9 IV		
Valley	5.6 IIIA	Hunterdon	87.3 V	Albany	285.9 IV
Washington	15.5 IIB	Mercer	307.8 VII	Allegany	51.7 IIB
Wayne	9.8 IV	Middlesex	595.8 VII	Bronx	1168.9 IV
Webster	4.8 IV	Monmouth	503.1 VII	Broome	213.6 VII
Wheeler	1.0 IIIA	Morris	407.6 VII	Cattaraugus	85.6 IIIB
York	14.7 IIIA	Ocean	346.0 VI	Cayuga	79.8 IV

Chautauqua	146.9 IV	Warren	54.8 IIIB	Halifax	55.2 IIIB
Chemung	97.6 IV	Washington	54.7 IV	Harnett	59.5 V
Chenango	49.3 IV	Wayne	84.5 VII	Haywood	46.4 VII
Clinton	80.7 VII	Westchester	866.5 VII	Henderson	58.5 V
Columbia	59.4 IIB	Wyoming	39.8 IIIB	Hertford	23.3 IV
Cortland	48.8 IV	Yates	21.4 IIIB	Hoke	20.3 IB
Delaware	46.8 IIIB			Hyde	5.8 IIIA
Dutchess	245.0 VII			Iredell	82.5 IIB
Erie	1015.4 IV	**NORTH CAROLINA**		Jackson	25.8 IIB
Essex	36.1 IIIB	Alamance	99.3 VII	Johnston	70.5 IIB
Franklin	44.9 IIIB	Alexander	24.9 V	Jones	9.7 IIIB
Fulton	55.1 IIIB	Alleghany	9.5 IIB	Lee	36.7 V
Genesee	59.4 IV	Anson	25.6 IIIA	Lenoir	59.8 VII
Greene	40.8 IB	Ashe	22.3 IIB	Lincoln	42.3 IB
Hamilton	5.0 IIIB	Avery	14.4 IIB	McDowell	35.1 V
Herkimer	66.7 IV	Beaufort	40.3 IIB	Macon	20.1 IB
Jefferson	88.1 IV	Bertie	21.0 IIIA	Madison	16.8 IIIA
Kings	2230.9 IV	Bladen	30.4 V	Martin	25.9 IIIB
Lewis	25.0 IIIA	Brunswick	35.7 IB	Mecklenburg	404.2 VI
Livingston	57.0 VII	Buncombe	160.9 VII	Mitchell	14.4 IIIA
Madison	65.1 VII	Burke	72.5 V	Montgomery	22.4 IIB
Monroe	702.2 VII	Cabarrus	85.8 V	Moore	50.5 IB
Montgomery	53.4 IV	Caldwell	67.7 V	Nash	67.1 IIB
Nassau	1321.5 VII	Camden	5.8 IIIA	New Hanover	103.4 V
New York	1428.2 IV	Carteret	41.0 V	Northampton	22.5 IIIA
Niagara	227.3 VII	Caswell	20.7 IIIB	Onslow	112.7 VII
Oneida	253.4 IV	Catawba	105.2 V	Orange	77.0 V
Onondaga	463.9 VII	Chatham	33.4 IIB	Pamlico	10.3 IIIB
Ontario	88.9 IIA	Cherokee	18.9 IIB	Pasquotank	28.4 VII
Orange	259.6 V	Chowan	12.5 IIB	Pender	22.2 IB
Orleans	38.4 IV	Clay	6.6 IB	Perquimans	9.4 IIA
Oswego	113.9 IIB	Cleveland	83.4 V	Person	29.1 IIB
Otsego	59.0 IIIB	Columbus	51.0 VII	Pitt	90.1 VI
Putnam	77.1 VI	Craven	71.0 V	Polk	12.9 IIIB
Queens	1891.3 VII	Cumberland	247.1 VI	Randolph	91.7 V
Rensselaer	151.9 IV	Currituck	11.0 IA	Richmond	45.4 IIB
Richmond	352.1 V	Dare	13.3 IB	Robeson	101.6 V
Rockland	259.5 VI	Davidson	113.1 V	Rockingham	83.4 V
St. Lawrence	114.2 IV	Davie	24.5 IB	Rowan	99.1 VII
Saratoga	153.7 V	Duplin	40.9 IIIB	Rutherford	53.7 IIB
Schenectady	149.9 IV	Durham	152.7 V	Sampson	49.6 VII
Schoharie	29.7 IIA	Edgecombe	55.9 IIIB	Scotland	32.2 V
Schuyler	17.6 IV	Forsyth	243.6 VI	Stanly	48.5 V
Seneca	33.7 IV	Franklin	30.0 IIB	Stokes	33.0 IB
Steuben	99.2 IV	Gaston	162.5 VII	Surry	59.4 IIB
Suffolk	1284.2 VI	Gates	8.8 IIIA	Swain	10.2 IIA
Sullivan	65.1 IB	Graham	7.2 IIIB	Transylvania	23.4 V
Tioga	49.8 VII	Granville	34.0 IIIB	Tyrrell	3.9 IIIA
Tompkins	87.0 V	Greene	16.1 IIIA	Union	70.3 IB
Ulster	158.1 VI	Guilford	317.1 VII	Vance	36.7 IIB

Wake	301.3 V	Richland	19.2 IIIA	Hardin	32.7 IIIB
Warren	16.2 IIIA	Rolette	12.1 IIIB	Harrison	18.1 IIIA
Washington	14.8 IIIB	Sargent	5.5 IV	Henry	28.3 IV
Watauga	31.6 IB	Sheridan	2.8 IV	Highland	33.4 IIB
Wayne	97.0 V	Sioux	3.6 IV	Hocking	24.3 IIA
Wilkes	58.6 V	Slope	1.1 IV	Holmes	29.4 IB
Wilson	63.1 IIIB	Stark	23.6 IIB	Huron	54.6 VII
Yadkin	28.4 V	Steele	3.1 IV	Jackson	30.5 IIA
Yancey	14.9 IIA	Stutsman	24.1 IIIA	Jefferson	91.5 IV
		Towner	4.0 IV	Knox	46.3 IIIB
NORTH DAKOTA		Traill	9.6 IIIA	Lake	212.8 VII
		Walsh	15.3 IV	Lawrence	63.8 IIB
Adams	3.5 IV	Ward	58.3 VII	Licking	120.9 VI
Barnes	13.9 IV	Wells	6.9 IV	Logan	39.1 IIB
Benson	7.9 IIIA	Williams	22.2 IIB	Lorain	274.9 VII
Billings	1.1 IIIA			Lucas	471.7 IV
Bottineau	9.2 IIIA	**OHIO**		Madison	33.0 IIB
Bowman	4.2 IIIA			Mahoning	289.4 IV
Burke	3.8 IV	Adams	24.3 IA	Marion	67.9 IV
Burleigh	54.8 V	Allen	112.2 VII	Medina	113.1 V
Cass	88.2 IIB	Ashland	46.1 VII	Meigs	23.6 IIA
Cavalier	7.6 IIIA	Ashtabula	104.2 VII	Mercer	38.3 IV
Dickey	7.2 IIIA	Athens	56.3 IV	Miami	90.3 VII
Divide	3.4 IV	Auglaize	42.5 IIIB	Monroe	17.3 IIIA
Dunn	4.6 IIIA	Belmont	82.5 IIIA	Montgomery	571.6 VII
Eddy	3.5 IV	Brown	31.9 IIA	Morgan	14.2 IIA
Emmons	5.8 IV	Butler	258.7 VI	Morrow	26.4 IB
Foster	4.6 IV	Carroll	25.5 IIB	Muskingum	83.3 IIIB
Golden Valley	2.3 IV	Champaign	33.6 IIIB	Noble	11.3 IIIA
Grand Forks	66.1 VII	Clark	150.2 VII	Ottawa	40.0 VII
Grant	4.2 IV	Clermont	128.4 VI	Paulding	21.3 IIIA
Griggs	3.7 IV	Clinton	34.6 IIIB	Perry	31.0 IIA
Hettinger	4.2 IV	Columbiana	113.5 IIIB	Pickaway	43.6 VII
Kidder	3.8 IV	Coshocton	36.0 IIIB	Pike	22.8 IIB
La Moure	6.4 IV	Crawford	50.0 IV	Portage	135.8 VII
Logan	3.4 IV	Cuyahoga	1498.4 VII	Preble	38.2 VII
McHenry	7.8 IV	Darke	55.0 IIB	Putnam	32.9 IV
McIntosh	4.8 IV	Defiance	39.9 VII	Richland	131.2 VII
McKenzie	7.1 IIA	Delaware	53.8 V	Ross	65.0 IIIB
McLean	12.3 IIIA	Erie	79.6 VII	Sandusky	63.2 VII
Mercer	9.4 IA	Fairfield	93.6 V	Scioto	84.5 IIIB
Morton	25.1 IA	Fayette	27.4 IIIB	Seneca	61.9 IV
Mountrail	7.6 IV	Franklin	869.1 VII	Shelby	43.0 IIB
Nelson	5.2 IV	Fulton	37.7 IIB	Stark	378.8 VII
Oliver	2.4 IIIA	Gallia	30.0 IIA	Summit	524.4 VII
Pembina	10.3 IIIA	Geauga	74.4 VI	Trumbull	241.8 VII
Pierce	6.1 IIIA	Greene	129.7 VII	Tuscarawas	84.6 IIIB
Ramsey	13.0 IIIA	Guernsey	42.0 IIA	Union	29.5 IB
Ransom	6.6 IV	Hamilton	873.2 VII	Van Wert	30.4 IIIB
Renville	3.6 IIIA	Hancock	64.5 VII	Vinton	11.5 IA

Warren	99.2 VI	Logan	26.8 IA	Grant	8.2 V
Washington	64.2 IIB	Love	7.4 IA	Harney	8.3 IIB
Wayne	97.4 VI	McClain	20.2 IA	Hood River	15.8 V
Williams	36.3 IV	McCurtain	36.1 IA	Jackson	132.4 V
Wood	107.3 V	McIntosh	15.5 IA	Jefferson	11.5 V
Wyandot	22.6 IV	Major	8.7 IIA	Josephine	58.8 V
		Marshall	10.5 IA	Klamath	59.1 V
		Mayes	32.2 IB	Lake	7.5 V
OKLAHOMA		Murray	12.1 IIA	Lane	275.2 V
		Muskogee	66.9 IIA	Lincoln	35.2 V
Adair	18.5 IB	Noble	11.5 IIA	Linn	89.4 V
Alfalfa	7.0 IIIA	Nowata	11.4 IIA	Malheur	26.8 V
Atoka	12.7 IIA	Okfuskee	11.1 IIIA	Marion	204.6 V
Beaver	6.8 IIIA	Oklahoma	568.9 VII	Morrow	7.5 IA
Beckham	19.2 IA	Okmulgee	39.1 IIIA	Multnomah	562.6 VII
Blaine	13.4 IIA	Osage	39.3 IA	Polk	45.2 V
Bryan	30.5 IIA	Ottawa	32.8 IIIA	Sherman	2.1 IIIA
Caddo	30.9 IIIA	Pawnee	15.3 IA	Tillamook	21.1 V
Canadian	56.4 IB	Payne	62.4 V	Umatilla	58.8 V
Carter	43.6 IIA	Pittsburg	40.5 IIIA	Union	23.9 IB
Cherokee	30.6 IB	Pontotoc	32.5 IIA	Wallowa	7.2 IIA
Choctaw	17.2 IIA	Pottawatomie	55.2 IA	Wasco	21.7 VII
Cimarron	3.6 IV	Pushmataha	11.7 IA	Washington	245.8 V
Cleveland	133.1 V	Roger Mills	4.7 IIIA	Wheeler	1.5 IV
Coal	6.0 IIIA	Rogers	46.4 V	Yamhill	55.3 V
Comanche	112.4 VII	Seminole	27.4 IIIA		
Cotton	7.3 IIIA	Sequoyah	30.7 IA		
Craig	15.0 IIIA	Stephens	43.4 IIB	**PENNSYLVANIA**	
Creek	59.0 IA	Texas	17.7 VII	Adams	68.2 IIB
Custer	25.9 IIA	Tillman	12.3 IIIA	Allegheny	1450.0 IV
Delaware	23.9 IB	Tulsa	470.5 VI	Armstrong	77.7 IIIB
Dewey	5.9 IIIA	Wagoner	41.8 IB	Beaver	204.4 IV
Ellis	5.5 IIIA	Washington	48.1 V	Bedford	46.7 IIIB
Garfield	62.8 IIB	Washita	13.7 IIA	Berks	312.5 IV
Garvin	27.8 IIA	Woods	10.9 IV	Blair	136.6 IIIB
Grady	39.4 IA	Woodward	21.1 IB	Bradford	62.9 IIIB
Grant	6.5 IIIA			Bucks	479.2 VI
Greer	7.0 IV			Butler	147.9 IIIB
Harmon	4.5 IV	**OREGON**		Cambria	183.2 IIIB
Harper	4.7 IV			Cameron	6.6 VII
Haskell	11.0 IIA	Baker	16.1 IIIA	Carbon	53.2 IIIA
Hughes	14.3 IIIA	Benton	68.2 V	Centre	112.7 VI
Jackson	30.3 VII	Clackamas	241.9 V	Chester	316.6 VI
Jefferson	8.1 IIA	Clatsop	32.4 V	Clarion	43.3 IIB
Johnston	10.3 IA	Columbia	35.6 IB	Clearfield	83.5 IIA
Kay	49.8 IIIB	Coos	64.0 V	Clinton	38.9 IIIB
Kingfisher	14.1 IIIA	Crook	13.0 V	Columbia	61.9 IIB
Kiowa	12.7 IIIA	Curry	16.9 VI	Crawford	88.8 VII
Latimer	9.8 IIA	Deschutes	62.1 V	Cumberland	178.5 VI
Le Flore	40.6 IA	Douglas	93.7 V	Dauphin	232.3 IV
Lincoln	26.6 IA	Gilliam	2.0 IV		

Delaware	555.0 VII	Newport	81.3 VII	Williamsburg	38.2 V
Elk	38.3 IV	Providence	571.3 IV	York	106.7 V
Erie	279.7 VII	Washington	93.3 VII		
Fayette	159.4 IIIA				
Forest	5.0 IIIA			**SOUTH DAKOTA**	
Franklin	113.6 IIB			Aurora	3.6 IV
Fulton	12.8 IIB	**SOUTH CAROLINA**		Beadle	19.1 IV
Greene	40.4 IIA			Bennett	3.0 IIIA
Huntingdon	42.2 IIIB	Abbeville	22.6 IIIA	Bon Homme	8.0 IV
Indiana	92.2 IIB	Aiken	105.6 VI	Brookings	24.3 IIIB
Jefferson	48.3 IIIA	Allendale	10.7 IIIA	Brown	36.9 IV
Juniata	19.1 IIB	Anderson	133.2 IB	Brule	5.2 IV
Lackawanna	227.9 IV	Bamberg	18.1 IIA	Buffalo	1.7 IV
Lancaster	362.3 V	Barnwell	19.8 IIA	Butte	8.3 IIIA
Lawrence	107.1 IV	Beaufort	65.3 V	Campbell	2.2 IV
Lebanon	108.5 IIIB	Berkeley	94.7 V	Charles Mix	9.6 IIIA
Lehigh	272.3 IV	Calhoun	12.2 IIA	Clark	4.8 IV
Luzerne	343.0 IIIA	Charleston	276.9 VI	Clay	13.6 IV
Lycoming	118.4 IIIB	Cherokee	40.9 IIB	Codington	20.8 IIIB
McKean	50.6 IV	Chester	30.1 IIIA	Corson	5.1 IIIA
Mercer	128.2 IV	Chesterfield	38.1 IIB	Custer	6.0 IA
Mifflin	46.9 IIIB	Clarendon	27.4 IIIA	Davison	17.8 IIIB
Monroe	69.4 V	Colleton	31.7 IIA	Day	8.1 IIIA
Montgomery	643.6 VII	Darlington	62.7 IIB	Deuel	5.2 IIIA
Montour	16.6 IV	Dillon	31.0 IIIB	Dewey	5.3 IIIA
Northampton	225.4 IV	Dorchester	58.7 V	Douglas	4.1 IV
North-		Edgefield	17.5 IIA	Edmunds	5.1 IV
umberland	100.3 IIIA	Fairfield	20.7 IIIA	Fall River	8.4 IIA
Perry	35.7 IB	Florence	110.1 V	Faulk	3.3 IV
Philadelphia	1688.2 IV	Georgetown	42.4 V	Grant	9.0 IIIA
Pike	18.2 V	Greenville	287.9 V	Gregory	6.0 IV
Potter	17.7 IIIA	Greenwood	57.8 IIB	Haakon	2.7 IV
Schuylkill	160.6 IIIA	Hampton	18.1 IIA	Hamlin	5.2 IIIA
Snyder	33.5 IIB	Horry	101.4 V	Hand	4.9 IV
Somerset	81.2 IIIB	Jasper	14.5 IB	Hanson	3.4 IV
Sullivan	6.3 IIIA	Kershaw	39.0 IIB	Harding	1.7 IV
Susquehanna	37.8 IIIA	Lancaster	53.3 V	Hughes	14.2 V
Tioga	40.9 IV	Laurens	52.2 IIIB	Hutchinson	9.3 IV
Union	32.8 V	Lee	18.9 IIIA	Hyde	2.0 IV
Venango	64.4 IIIB	Lexington	140.3 V	Jackson	3.4 VI
Warren	47.4 IV	McCormick	7.7 IIIA	Jerauld	2.9 IV
Washington	217.0 IIIB	Marion	34.1 IIA	Jones	1.4 IV
Wayne	35.2 IIA	Marlboro	31.6 IIA	Kingsbury	6.6 IV
Westmoreland	392.2 IV	Newberry	31.2 IIIA	Lake	10.7 IV
Wyoming	26.4 IB	Oconee	48.6 IIB	Lawrence	18.3 IIIA
York	312.9 V	Orangeburg	82.2 IIB	Lincoln	13.9 IIA
		Pickens	79.2 V	Lyman	3.8 IV
		Richland	269.7 VI	McCook	6.4 IV
RHODE ISLAND		Saluda	16.1 IIIA	McPherson	4.0 IV
		Spartanburg	201.8 V	Marshall	5.4 IV
Bristol	46.9 VII	Sumter	88.2 VII	Meade	20.7 V
Kent	154.1 VII	Union	30.7 IIIB		

Mellette	2.2 IV	Grainger	16.7 IIA	Smith	14.9 IIA
Miner	3.7 IV	Greene	54.4 IIB	Stewart	8.6 IIA
Minnehaha	109.4 V	Grundy	13.7 V	Sullivan	143.9 V
Moody	6.6 IV	Hamblen	49.3 V	Sumner	85.7 V
Pennington	70.3 VI	Hamilton	287.7 V	Tipton	32.9 IIB
Perkins	4.7 IIIA	Hancock	6.8 IIIA	Trousdale	6.1 IIA
Potter	3.6 IV	Hardeman	23.8 IIIB	Unicoi	16.3 VII
Roberts	10.9 IIIA	Hardin	22.2 IB	Union	11.7 IA
Sanborn	3.2 IV	Hawkins	43.7 V	Van Buren	4.7 IB
Shannon	11.3 V	Haywood	20.3 IIIA	Warren	32.6 IIB
Spink	9.2 IV	Henderson	21.3 IB	Washington	88.7 V
Stanley	2.5 VII	Henry	28.6 IIA	Wayne	13.9 IIB
Sully	1.9 IV	Hickman	15.1 IA	Weakley	32.8 IIA
Todd	7.3 VII	Houston	6.8 IIA	White	19.5 IIB
Tripp	7.2 IV	Humphreys	15.9 IIB	Williamson	58.1 V
Turner	9.2 IV	Jackson	9.3 IIA	Wilson	56.0 V
Union	10.9 IIA	Jefferson	31.2 IB		
Walworth	7.0 IV	Johnson	13.7 IIA		
Yankton	18.9 IV	Knox	319.6 V	**TEXAS**	
Ziebach	2.3 IIIA	Lake	7.4 IIIA	Anderson	38.3 IA
		Lauderdale	24.5 IA	Andrews	13.3 VI
		Lawrence	34.1 IIA	Angelina	64.1 V
TENNESSEE		Lewis	9.7 IB	Aransas	14.2 V
		Lincoln	26.4 IIIA	Archer	7.2 IA
Anderson	67.3 V	Loudon	28.5 V	Armstrong	1.9 IIIA
Bedford	27.9 IIA	McMinn	41.8 IIB	Atascosa	25.0 V
Benton	14.9 IB	McNairy	22.5 IB	Austin	17.7 IA
Bledsoe	9.4 IB	Macon	15.7 IA	Bailey	8.1 VII
Blount	77.7 V	Madison	74.5 IIB	Bandera	7.0 IA
Bradley	67.5 V	Marion	24.4 IIB	Bastrop	24.7 IA
Campbell	34.9 V	Marshall	19.6 IIA	Baylor	4.9 IIIA
Cannon	10.2 IA	Maury	51.0 IIB	Bee	26.0 V
Carroll	28.2 IIIB	Meigs	7.4 IA	Bell	157.8 V
Carter	50.2 V	Monroe	28.7 IB	Bexar	988.8 VI
Cheatham	21.6 V	Montgomery	83.3 V	Blanco	4.6 IA
Chester	12.7 IB	Moore	4.5 IA	Borden	.8 IIIA
Claiborne	24.5 IA	Morgan	16.6 IB	Bosque	13.4 IA
Clay	7.6 IIA	Obion	32.7 IIIB	Bowie	75.3 VII
Cocke	28.7 IIB	Overton	17.5 IIA	Brazoria	169.5 V
Coffee	38.3 V	Perry	6.1 IIA	Brazos	93.5 V
Crockett	14.9 IIIA	Pickett	4.3 IIA	Brewster	7.5 IV
Cumberland	28.6 V	Polk	13.6 IIA	Briscoe	2.5 IV
Davidson	477.8 VII	Putnam	47.6 V	Brooks	8.4 VII
Decatur	10.8 IIA	Rhea	24.2 IB	Brown	33.0 IB
De Kalb	13.5 IA	Roane	48.4 V	Burleson	12.3 IA
Dickson	30.0 IB	Robertson	37.0 IB	Burnet	17.8 IB
Dyer	34.6 IIB	Rutherford	84.0 V	Caldwell	23.6 IIA
Fayette	25.3 IIA	Scott	19.2 V	Calhoun	19.5 VII
Fentress	14.8 V	Sequatchie	8.6 V	Callahan	10.9 IA
Franklin	31.9 IIB	Sevier	41.4 IB	Cameron	209.7 V
Gibson	49.4 IIIB	Shelby	777.1 VII	Camp	9.2 IIA
Giles	24.6 IIIA				

Carson	6.6 IIIA	Gaines	13.1 V	Kerr	28.7 V
Cass	29.4 IA	Galveston	195.9 VI	Kimble	4.0 IIIB
Castro	10.5 VII	Garza	5.3 IIIB	King	.4 IIIA
Chambers	18.5 V	Gillespie	13.5 IB	Kinney	2.2 IIIA
Cherokee	38.1 IIA	Glasscock	1.3 IIA	Kleberg	33.3 VII
Childress	6.9 IIIA	Goliad	5.1 IIIA	Knox	5.3 IIIA
Clay	9.5 IIA	Gonzales	16.8 IIIA	Lamar	42.1 IIA
Cochran	4.8 VII	Gray	26.3 IV	Lamb	18.6 IIIB
Coke	3.1 IIIA	Grayson	89.7 IIIB	Lampasas	12.0 IB
Coleman	10.4 IIIA	Gregg	99.4 V	La Salle	5.5 IIIA
Collin	144.5 V	Grimes	13.5 IIA	Lavaca	19.0 IIIA
Collingsworth	4.6 IIIA	Guadalupe	46.7 IB	Lee	10.9 IA
Colorado	18.8 IIIA	Hale	37.5 VII	Leon	9.5 IIIA
Comal	36.4 V	Hall	5.5 IIIA	Liberty	47.0 V
Comanche	12.6 IIIA	Hamilton	8.2 IIA	Limestone	20.2 IIA
Concho	2.9 IIIA	Hansford	6.2 VII	Lipscomb	3.7 IIIA
Cooke	27.6 IIA	Hardeman	6.3 IIIA	Live Oak	9.6 IA
Coryell	56.7 V	Hardin	40.7 V	Llano	10.1 IB
Cottle	2.9 IIIA	Harris	2409.5 V	Loving	.0 IV
Crane	4.6 V	Harrison	52.2 IIB	Lubbock	211.6 VI
Crockett	4.6 V	Hartley	3.9 V	Lynn	8.6 IV
Crosby	8.8 IV	Haskell	7.7 IIIA	McCulloch	8.7 IIIA
Culberson	3.3 VII	Hays	40.5 V	McLennan	170.7 V
Dallam	6.5 IIIA	Hemphill	5.3 IA	McMullen	.7 IV
Dallas	1556.3 VI	Henderson	42.6 IA	Madison	10.6 IA
Dawson	16.1 VII	Hidalgo	283.2 V	Marion	10.3 IIA
Deaf Smith	21.1 VI	Hill	25.0 IIIA	Martin	4.6 IIIA
Delta	4.8 IIIA	Hockley	23.2 V	Mason	3.6 IIIA
Denton	143.1 V	Hood	17.7 IA	Matagorda	37.8 IB
De Witt	18.9 IIIA	Hopkins	25.2 IA	Maverick	31.3 V
Dickens	3.5 IIIA	Houston	22.2 IA	Medina	23.1 IIB
Dimmit	11.3 IB	Howard	33.1 VII	Menard	2.3 IV
Donley	4.0 IIIA	Hudspeth	2.7 IIA	Midland	82.6 VI
Duval	12.5 VII	Hunt	55.2 IIB	Milam	22.7 IIA
Eastland	19.4 IIIA	Hutchinson	26.3 VII	Mills	4.4 IIIA
Ector	115.3 VI	Irion	1.3 IA	Mitchell	9.0 IIIA
Edwards	2.0 IIIA	Jack	7.4 IIIA	Montague	17.4 IIA
Ellis	59.7 IA	Jackson	13.3 IIIB	Montgomery	128.4 V
El Paso	479.8 V	Jasper	30.7 IB	Moore	16.5 V
Erath	22.5 IA	Jeff Davis	1.6 IIIA	Morris	14.6 IIB
Falls	17.9 IIIA	Jefferson	250.9 VII	Motley	1.9 VII
Fannin	24.2 IIIA	Jim Hogg	5.1 IIIB	Nacogdoches	46.7 IB
Fayette	18.8 IIIA	Jim Wells	36.4 VII	Navarro	35.3 IIA
Fisher	5.8 IIIA	Johnson	67.6 V	Newton	13.2 IIB
Floyd	9.8 IV	Jones	17.2 IIIA	Nolan	17.3 IIIA
Foard	2.1 IIIA	Karnes	13.5 IIIA	Nueces	268.2 VI
Fort Bend	130.8 V	Kaufman	39.0 IIA	Ochiltree	9.5 VII
Franklin	6.8 IA	Kendall	10.6 IB	Oldham	2.2 VII
Freestone	14.8 IA	Kenedy	.5 IV	Orange	83.8 VI
Frio	13.7 IB	Kent	1.1 IV	Palo Pinto	24.0 VII

Panola	20.7 IA	Val Verde	35.9 V	Wasatch	8.5 IA
Parker	44.6 V	Van Zandt	31.4 IA	Washington	26.0 V
Parmer	11.0 VII	Victoria	68.8 V	Wayne	1.9 IA
Pecos	14.6 VII	Walker	41.7 V	Weber	144.6 VI
Polk	24.4 IA	Waller	19.7 IB		
Potter	98.6 VII	Ward	13.9 VII	**VERMONT**	
Presidio	5.1 IIIA	Washington	21.9 IIA		
Rains	4.8 IA	Webb	99.2 V	Addison	29.4 IB
Randall	75.0 VI	Wharton	40.2 IIIB	Bennington	33.3 IIB
Reagan	4.1 V	Wheeler	7.1 IIIA	Caledonia	25.8 IIA
Real	2.4 IIB	Wichita	121.0 VII	Chittenden	115.5 VI
Red River	16.1 IIA	Wilbarger	15.9 IIIA	Essex	6.3 IIA
Reeves	15.8 VII	Willacy	17.4 V	Franklin	34.7 IIIB
Refugio	9.2 VII	Williamson	76.5 IA	Grand Isle	4.6 IA
Roberts	1.1 IA	Wilson	16.7 IA	Lamoille	16.7 IB
Robertson	14.6 IIIA	Winkler	9.9 VII	Orange	22.7 IA
Rockwall	14.5 IA	Wise	26.5 IA	Orleans	23.4 IIA
Runnels	11.8 IIIA	Wood	24.6 IA	Rutland	58.3 IIIB
Rusk	41.3 V	Yoakum	8.2 VI	Washington	52.3 IIIB
Sabine	8.7 IA	Young	19.0 IA	Windham	36.9 IIIB
San Augustine	8.7 IIA	Zapata	6.6 V	Windsor	51.0 IIB
San Jacinto	11.4 IA	Zavala	11.6 IIIB		
San Patricio	58.0 V				
San Saba	6.2 IIA			**VIRGINIA**	
Schleicher	2.8 IA	**UTAH**		Accomack	31.2 IIIA
Scurry	18.1 V	Beaver	4.3 IIA	Albemarle	55.7 V
Shackelford	3.9 IIA	Box Elder	33.2 V	Alleghany	14.3 IIA
Shelby	23.0 IIA	Cache	57.1 IB	Amelia	8.4 IA
Sherman	3.1 VII	Carbon	22.1 V	Amherst	29.1 IIB
Smith	128.3 V	Daggett	.7 VI	Appomattox	11.9 IB
Somervell	4.1 IA	Davis	146.5 VI	Arlington	152.5 VII
Starr	27.2 IB	Duchesne	12.5 IA	Augusta	53.7 IB
Stephens	9.9 IIA	Emery	11.4 IA	Bath	5.8 IIA
Sterling	1.2 IIA	Garfield	3.6 IIA	Bedford	34.9 IA
Stonewall	2.4 IIIA	Grand	8.2 VI	Bland	6.3 IIA
Sutton	5.1 V	Iron	17.3 V	Botetourt	23.2 IB
Swisher	9.7 VII	Juab	5.5 IA	Brunswick	15.6 IIIA
Tarrant	860.8 VI	Kane	4.0 IA	Buchanan	37.9 V
Taylor	110.9 VI	Millard	8.9 IA	Buckingham	11.7 IIA
Terrell	1.5 IV	Morgan	4.9 V	Campbell	45.4 VII
Terry	14.5 VII	Piute	1.3 IIA	Caroline	17.9 IA
Throckmorton	2.0 IIIA	Rich	2.1 IA	Carroll	27.2 IIB
Titus	21.4 IB	Salt Lake	619.0 V	Charles City	6.6 IV
Tom Green	84.7 V	San Juan	12.2 V	Charlotte	12.2 IIIA
Travis	419.5 V	Sanpete	14.6 IA	Chesterfield	141.3 V
Trinity	9.4 IA	Sevier	14.7 IA	Clarke	9.9 IB
Tyler	16.2 IB	Summit	10.1 IA	Craig	3.9 IIA
Upshur	28.5 IB	Tooele	26.0 V	Culpeper	22.6 V
Upton	4.6 VII	Uintah	20.5 IB	Cumberland	7.8 IA
Uvalde	22.4 V	Utah	218.1 V	Dickenson	19.8 V

Dinwiddie	22.6 IV	Rappahannock	6.0 IIA	Martinsville	18.1 VII
Essex	8.8 IA	Richmond	6.9 IIIA	Newport News	144.9 VII
Fairfax	596.9 VI	Roanoke	72.9 VII	Norfolk	266.9 VII
Fauquier	35.8 IB	Rockbridge	17.9 IIIA	Norton	4.7 IIB
Floyd	11.5 IIA	Rockingham	57.0 V	Petersburg	41.0 V
Fluvanna	10.2 IA	Russell	31.7 IB	Poquoson	8.7 IB
Franklin	35.7 IB	Scott	25.0 IIIB	Portsmouth	104.5 VII
Frederick	34.1 VI	Shenandoah	27.5 IIB	Radford	13.2 V
Giles	17.8 VII	Smyth	33.3 IIIB	Richmond	219.2 VII
Gloucester	20.1 V	Southampton	18.7 IIIA	Roanoke	100.2 VII
Goochland	11.7 IIB	Spotsylvania	34.4 V	Salem	23.9 VII
Grayson	16.5 IIIA	Stafford	40.4 V	South Boston	7.0 IV
Greene	7.6 IA	Surry	6.0 IIIA	Staunton	21.8 VII
Greensville	10.9 IIA	Sussex	10.8 IV	Suffolk	47.6 VII
Halifax	30.5 IIIA	Tazewell	50.5 V	Virginia Beach	262.1 VI
Hanover	50.3 V	Warren	21.2 V	Waynesboro	15.3 VII
Henrico	180.7 V	Washington	46.4 IIB	Williamsburg	9.8 IV
Henry	57.6 VI	Westmoreland	14.0 IIB	Winchester	20.2 V
Highland	2.9 IIA	Wise	43.8 IA		
Isle of Wight	21.6 IIB	Wythe	25.5 IIB	**WASHINGTON**	
James City	22.7 VI	York	35.4 VI		
King and				Adams	13.2 VII
Queen	5.9 IIIA	**Independent Cities**		Asotin	16.8 V
King George	10.5 V	**of Virginia**		Benton	109.4 V
King William	9.3 IA			Chelan	45.0 VII
Lancaster	10.1 IIIB	Alexandria	103.2 VII	Clallam	51.6 V
Lee	25.9 IA	Bedford	5.9 IV	Clark	192.2 V
Loudoun	57.4 V	Bristol	19.0 V	Columbia	4.0 IV
Louisa	17.8 IA	Buena Vista	6.7 IV	Cowlitz	79.5 V
Lunenburg	12.1 IIIA	Charlottesville	39.9 VII	Douglas	22.1 V
Madison	10.2 IIA	Chesapeake	114.4 IB	Ferry	5.8 IA
Mathews	7.9 IIIA	Clifton Forge	5.0 IV	Franklin	35.0 V
Mecklenburg	29.4 IIIA	Colonial		Garfield	2.4 IV
Middlesex	7.7 IA	Heights	16.5 VII	Grant	48.5 VI
Montgomery	63.5 V	Covington	9.0 VII	Grays Harbor	66.3 IIB
Nelson	12.2 IIIA	Danville	45.6 VII	Island	44.0 V
New Kent	8.7 V	Emporia	4.8 IV	Jefferson	15.9 V
Northampton	14.6 IIIA	Fairfax	19.3 VII	King	1269.7 VII
North-		Falls Church	9.5 VII	Kitsap	147.1 V
umberland	9.8 IIIA	Franklin	7.3 IV	Kittitas	24.8 IV
Nottoway	14.6 IIIB	Fredericksburg	15.3 VII	Klickitat	15.8 IB
Orange	18.0 IB	Galax	6.5 IV	Lewis	56.0 IB
Page	19.4 IIB	Hampton	122.6 VII	Lincoln	9.6 IIIA
Patrick	17.6 IIA	Harrisonburg	19.6 V	Mason	31.1 V
Pittsylvania	66.1 IIB	Hopewell	23.3 VII	Okanogan	30.6 V
Powhatan	13.0 V	Lexington	7.2 IV	Pacific	17.2 IIIB
Prince Edward	16.4 IIB	Lynchburg	66.7 IB	Pend Oreille	8.5 IA
Prince George	25.7 VII	Manassas	15.4 IB	Pierce	485.6 V
Prince William	144.7 VI	Manassas		San Juan	7.8 IB
Pulaski	35.2 V	Park	6.5 IV	Skagit	64.1 V

Skamania 7.9 V	Pocahontas 9.9 IIA	Juneau 21.0 IIA
Snohomish 337.7 VI	Preston 30.4 IIA	Kenosha 123.1 VII
Spokane 341.8 V	Putnam 38.1 V	Kewaunee 19.5 IV
Stevens 28.9 IA	Raleigh 86.8 V	La Crosse 91.0 V
Thurston 124.2 V	Randolph 28.7 IIB	Lafayette 17.4 IIIA
Wahkiakum 3.8 IIIA	Ritchie 11.4 IIA	Langlade 19.9 IIIA
Walla Walla 47.4 V	Roane 15.9 IIA	Lincoln 26.5 IIB
Whatcom 106.7 IB	Summers 15.8 IIA	Manitowoc 82.9 IV
Whitman 40.1 IV	Taylor 16.5 IIA	Marathon 111.2 IIB
Yakima 172.5 V	Tucker 8.6 IIA	Marinette 39.3 IIIB
	Tyler 11.3 IIA	Marquette 11.6 IA
WEST VIRGINIA	Upshur 23.4 IB	Menominee 3.3 IB
	Wayne 46.0 V	Milwaukee 964.9 VII
Barbour 16.6 IIA	Webster 12.2 V	Monroe 35.0 IIIB
Berkeley 46.7 IB	Wetzel 21.8 IIIA	Oconto 28.9 IIB
Boone 30.4 V	Wirt 4.9 IIA	Oneida 31.2 V
Braxton 13.8 IIIA	Wood 93.6 IV	Outagamie 128.7 VII
Brooke 31.1 IV	Wyoming 35.9 V	Ozaukee 66.9 V
Cabell 106.8 IV		Pepin 7.4 IIIB
Calhoun 8.2 IIA		Pierce 31.1 IIB
Clay 11.2 IIA	**WISCONSIN**	Polk 32.3 IB
Doddridge 7.4 IIA		Portage 57.4 V
Fayette 57.8 IIA	Adams 13.4 IB	Price 15.7 IIIA
Gilmer 8.3 IIIA	Ashland 16.7 IIIA	Racine 173.1 VII
Grant 10.2 IIB	Barron 38.7 IIB	Richland 17.4 IIIA
Greenbrier 37.6 IIA	Bayfield 13.8 IIA	Rock 139.4 VII
Hampshire 14.8 IA	Brown 175.2 VII	Rusk 15.5 IIIA
Hancock 40.4 IV	Buffalo 14.3 IIIA	St. Croix 43.2 IB
Hardy 10.0 IIA	Burnett 12.3 IA	Sauk 43.4 IIIB
Harrison 77.7 IIIB	Calumet 30.8 VI	Sawyer 12.8 IB
Jackson 25.7 V	Chippewa 52.1 IIIB	Shawano 35.9 IIIB
Jefferson 30.3 IB	Clark 32.9 IIIA	Sheboygan 100.9 IV
Kanawha 231.4 VII	Columbia 43.2 IIIB	Taylor 18.8 IIIB
Lewis 18.8 IIIA	Crawford 16.5 IIIA	Trempealeau 26.1 IIB
Lincoln 23.6 IB	Dane 323.5 VI	Vernon 25.6 IIIA
Logan 50.6 VII	Dodge 75.0 IIIB	Vilas 16.5 V
McDowell 49.8 IIIA	Door 25.0 IB	Walworth 71.5 VI
Marion 65.7 IIIB	Douglas 44.4 IIIA	Washburn 13.1 IB
Marshall 41.6 IIIB	Dunn 34.3 IIB	Washington 84.8 V
Mason 27.0 IIIB	Eau Claire 78.8 V	Waukesha 280.3 VI
Mercer 73.9 IIB	Florence 4.1 IA	Waupaca 42.8 IIB
Mineral 27.2 IIB	Fond Du Lac 88.9 IV	Waushara 18.5 IA
Mingo 37.3 V	Forest 9.0 IIA	Winnebago 131.7 VII
Monongalia 75.0 IIB	Grant 51.7 IIIB	Wood 72.7 VII
Monroe 12.8 IIA	Green 30.0 IIB	
Morgan 10.7 IB	Green Lake 18.3 IIIB	
Nicholas 28.1 V	Iowa 19.8 IIIA	**WYOMING**
Ohio 61.3 IV	Iron 6.7 IIIA	
Pendleton 7.9 IIA	Jackson 16.8 IIIA	Albany 29.0 VII
Pleasants 8.2 IIA	Jefferson 66.1 VII	Big Horn 11.8 IIA

Campbell	24.3 V	Johnson	6.7 IB	Sheridan	25.0 IB
Carbon	21.8 V	Laramie	68.6 V	Sublette	4.5 V
Converse	14.0 IA	Lincoln	12.1 IA	Sweetwater	41.7 IB
Crook	5.3 IIA	Natrona	71.8 V	Teton	9.3 V
Fremont	38.9 V	Niobrara	2.9 IIIA	Uinta	13.0 IA
Goshen	12.0 IIIB	Park	21.6 V	Washakie	9.4 V
Hot Springs	5.7 V	Platte	11.9 IA	Weston	7.1 V

Appendix B

Because necessary data before 1960 are not available, Alaska and Hawaii cannot be included in Appendix A. This appendix provides a partial substitute. Index numbers vary from 1 to 9 (1 = lowest, 5 = average; 9 highest; see Chapter Sixteen for further explanation of index numbers). Column 1 indexes population growth for 1970–1977; column 2 indexes population growth for 1977–1980; column 3 indexes population growth for 1970–1980. An asterisk indicates that the needed data are not available.

INDEXES OF POPULATION GROWTH, AS COMPARED WITH TOTAL U.S. GROWTH, FOR COUNTIES IN ALASKA AND HAWAII.

ALASKA	(1)	(2)	(3)
Aleutian Islands	5	1	3
Anchorage	9	2	9
Bethel	*	*	7
Bristol Bay	3	1	2
Dillingham	5	9	7
Fairbanks North Star	8	2	6
Haines	8	1	6
Juneau	9	4	9
Kenai Peninsula	9	9	9
Ketchikan Gateway	6	3	5
Kobuk	7	4	7
Kodiak Island	2	8	4
Matanuska-Susitna	9	9	9
Nome	7	2	5
North Slope			
Prince of Wales-	5	9	7
Outer Ke	6	1	3
Sitka	9	6	8
Skagway-Yakutat-Angoon	7	8	7
Southeast Fairbanks	8	9	8
Valdex-Cordova	9	1	9
Wade Hampton	7	3	6
Wrangell-Petersburg	9	2	7
Yukon-Koyukum	*	*	5
HAWAII			
Hawaii	9	9	9
Honolulu	7	5	7
Kalawao	*	*	3
Kauai	8	9	8
Maui	9	9	9

Subject Index

A and B counties of penturbia, 129,
   135
Ada County, Idaho, 252
Allen, Robert G., 257
Aristocrats, 58, 59
Austin, Texas, 116–117
"Automobility," 76

Bantam Capitalist (1789–1900), 59,
   94
   excesses of, 60–61
   and migration to the Mississippi
      Valley, 60
Beale, Calvin L., 79, 89–90
Beaton, William R., 256
Bellow, Saul, 99
Benner, Susan, 115–117
Bockl, George, 256
Boise, Idaho, 252
Boston, Mass., 58
   obsolescence in 1860–1890,
      101
Bowles, Glady K., 89, 90
Bronx, N.Y., 99
Bruss, Robert, 256

Canyon County, Idaho, 252
Capital shortage, 71, 83; *see also*
   overconsumption
Caring Conserver (1958–   ), 73–77
   and environmental movement,
      111
   evidence, 92
   "higher reasons" (imperatives
      of the group), 91
   increased priority of future,
      75–76
   inevitable excesses in twenty-
      first century, 93–94
   opposition to the Little King, 75
   transformed role of the poor, 74
   trickle now, flood later, 93
   and volunteering, 90
Carnegie, Andrew, 62–63
Chapman, Edwin M., 30
Chewelah, Washington, 128
Chicago (Cook County)
   archetype and hub of third
      region of opportunity, 36–39
   burdened by obsolescence after
      1900, 103
   declining years, 66

Index of Figures